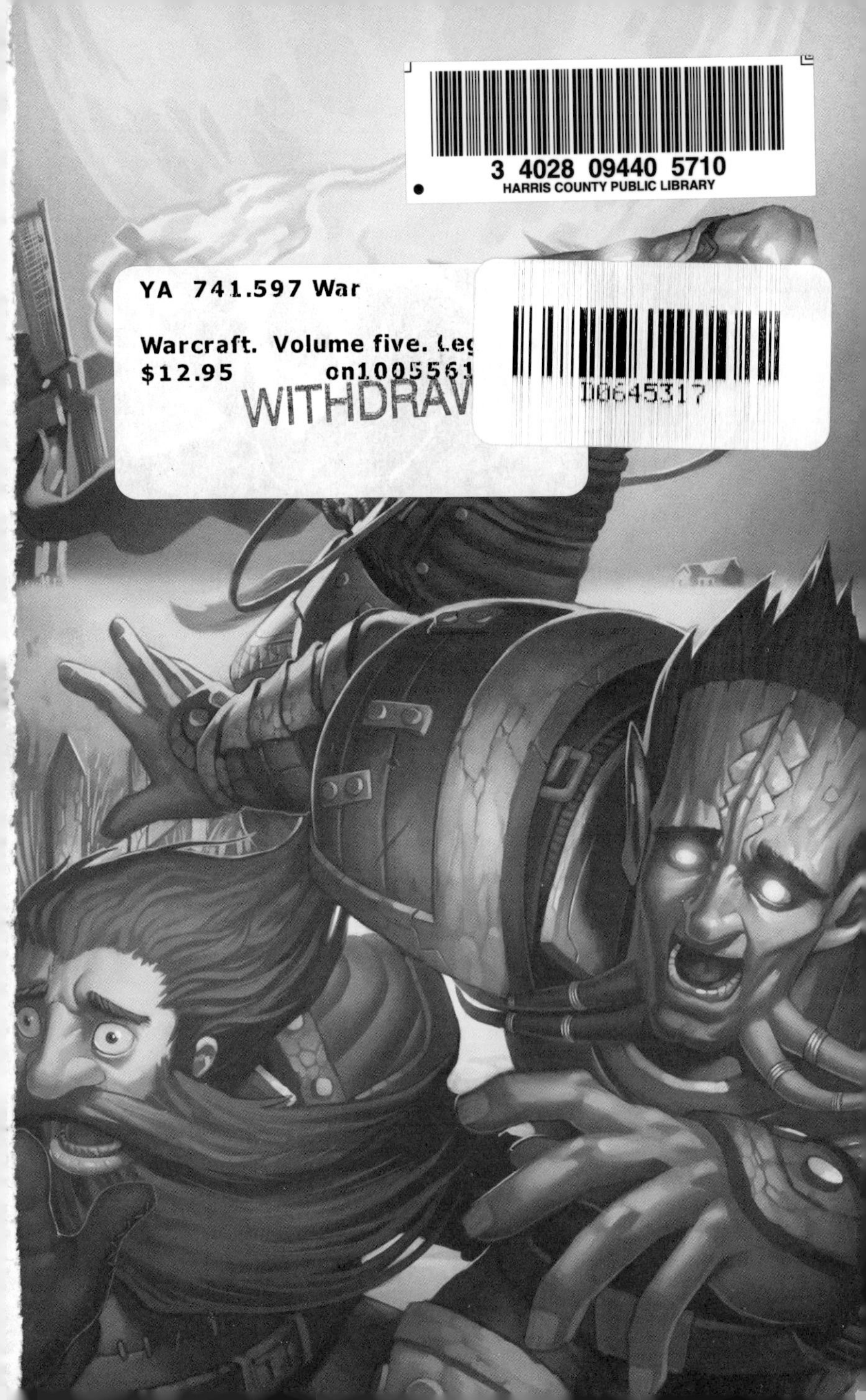

Warcraft: Legends Vol. 5

Layout and Lettering - Michael Paolilli
Creative Consultant - Michael Paolilli
Graphic Designer - Louis Csontos
Cover Artist - UDON with Saejin Oh

BLIZZARD ENTERTAINMENT

Senior Vice President,
Story and Franchise Development - Lydia Bottegoni
Director, Creative Development - Ralph Sanchez
Lead Editor, Publishing - Robert Simpson
Senior Editor - Cate Gary
Associate Copy Editor - Allison Monahan
Producer - Brianne M Loftis
Story Consultation and Development - James Waugh
Art Director - Glenn Rane
Vice President, Global Consumer Products - Matt Beecher
Senior Manager, Global Licensing - Byron Parnell
Additional Development - Cameron Dayton, Samwise Didier,
Evelyn Fredericksen, Tommy Newcomer
Special Thanks - Sean Copeland, Phillip Hillenbrand,
Christi Kugler, Alix Nicholaeff, and Justin Parker

This book contains material originally published by TOKYOPOP Inc.

First Blizzard Entertainment printing: March 2018

ISBN: 978-1-9456-8313-8

10 9 8 7 6 5 4 3 2 1

Printed in China

WarCraft®

LEGENDS™

VOLUME FIVE

BLIZZARD
ENTERTAINMENT

WARCRAFT

LEGENDS

VOLUME FIVE

A WARRIOR MADE--PART 2   06
BY CHRISTIE GOLDEN & IN-BAE KIM

WARRIOR: UNITED   28
BY GRACE RANDOLPH & ERICA AWANO

THE FIRST GUARDIAN   76
BY LOUISE SIMONSON & SEUNG-HUI KYE

A CLEANSING FIRE   118
BY EVELYN FREDERICKSEN & RYO KAWAKAMI

NIGHTMARES   160
BY RICHARD A. KNAAK & ROB TEN PAS

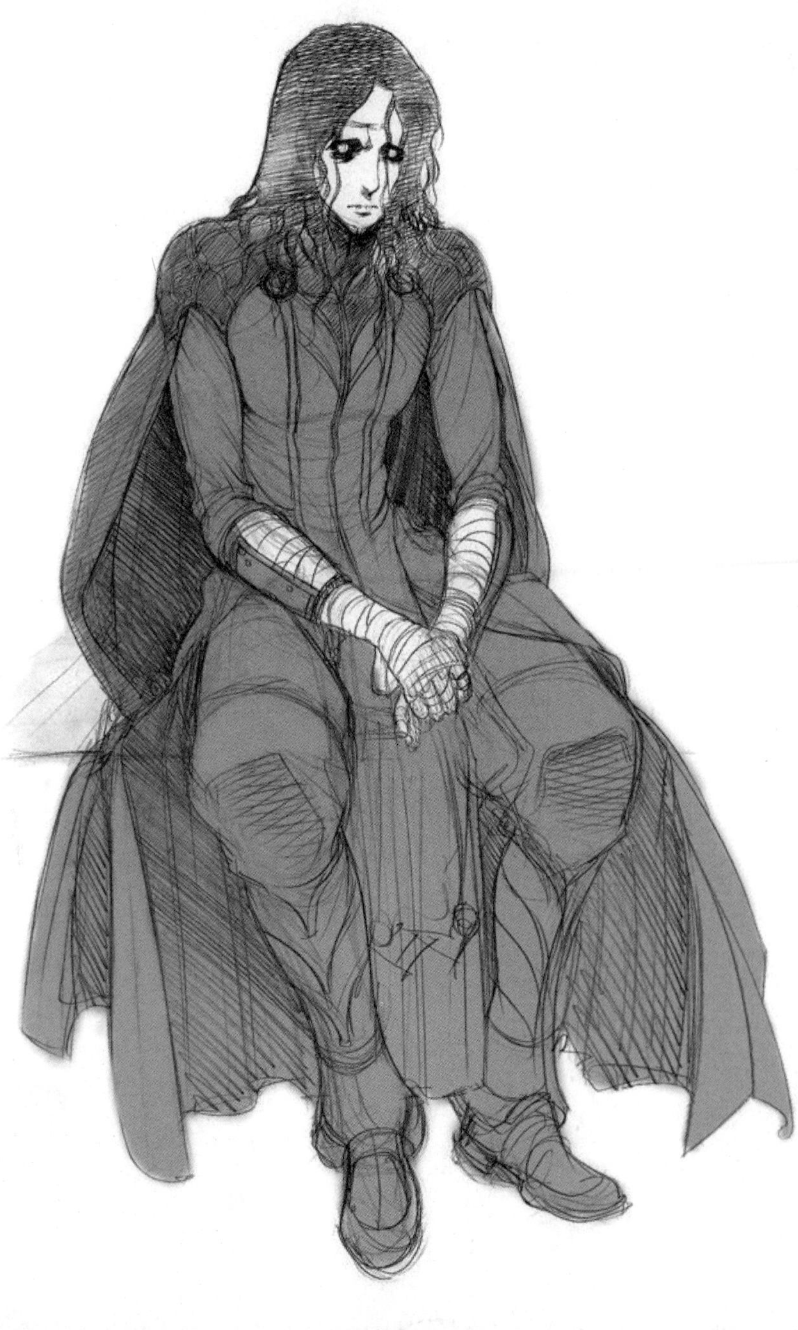

WARCRAFT®
LEGENDS™
VOLUME FIVE

A WARRIOR MADE--PART 2

WRITTEN BY CHRISTIE GOLDEN

PENCILS BY IN-BAE KIM
INKS BY IN-BAE KIM & MI-JIN BAE
TONES BY MARA AUM

EDITORIAL TRANSLATION: JANICE KWON
LETTERER: MICHAEL PAOLILLI

STORY SO FAR

Draka was a Frostwolf clan orc born with a frail and weak body.
Though loved unconditionally by her parents, the same can't be
said for her fellow clan members, who viewed Draka's condition
as an embarrassment--so much so that they banished Draka and
her parents to the outskirts of the village.

Years later, when Draka was a young woman, she decided to
take her destiny into her own hands and restore her family's
honor. To do this she sought the council of Mother Kashur, the
kind, elderly village shaman. Draka begged Mother Kashur to
create a potion or spell to make her stronger and rid her of her
shameful, sickly body.

Mother Kashur agreed to help, and requested Draka make an
arduous journey to find the three ingredients she would need
for the spell: for speed and grace she would need the feather
of a windroc, for support of her clan the horn of a talbuk, and
finally, for strength and determination, the fur of a clefthoof.
With renewed hope for redemption, Draka set out on her
dangerous journey.

At first it was difficult even finding shelter and hunting food
for herself, but through perseverance Draka gradually
developed enough skills and confidence to not only survive,
but to face her first challenge--the windroc. Tracking the bird
to its nest in Terokkar forest proved difficult as the terrain was
harsh, but Draka managed to overcome her fears and confront
the bird. Through skills she developed while hunting game for
food, Draka was able to spear and kill the bird--and obtain the
first ingredient of the spell!

And now, with two more ingredients left, her path to honor
has only just begun as the hardest challenges have yet to be
conquered...

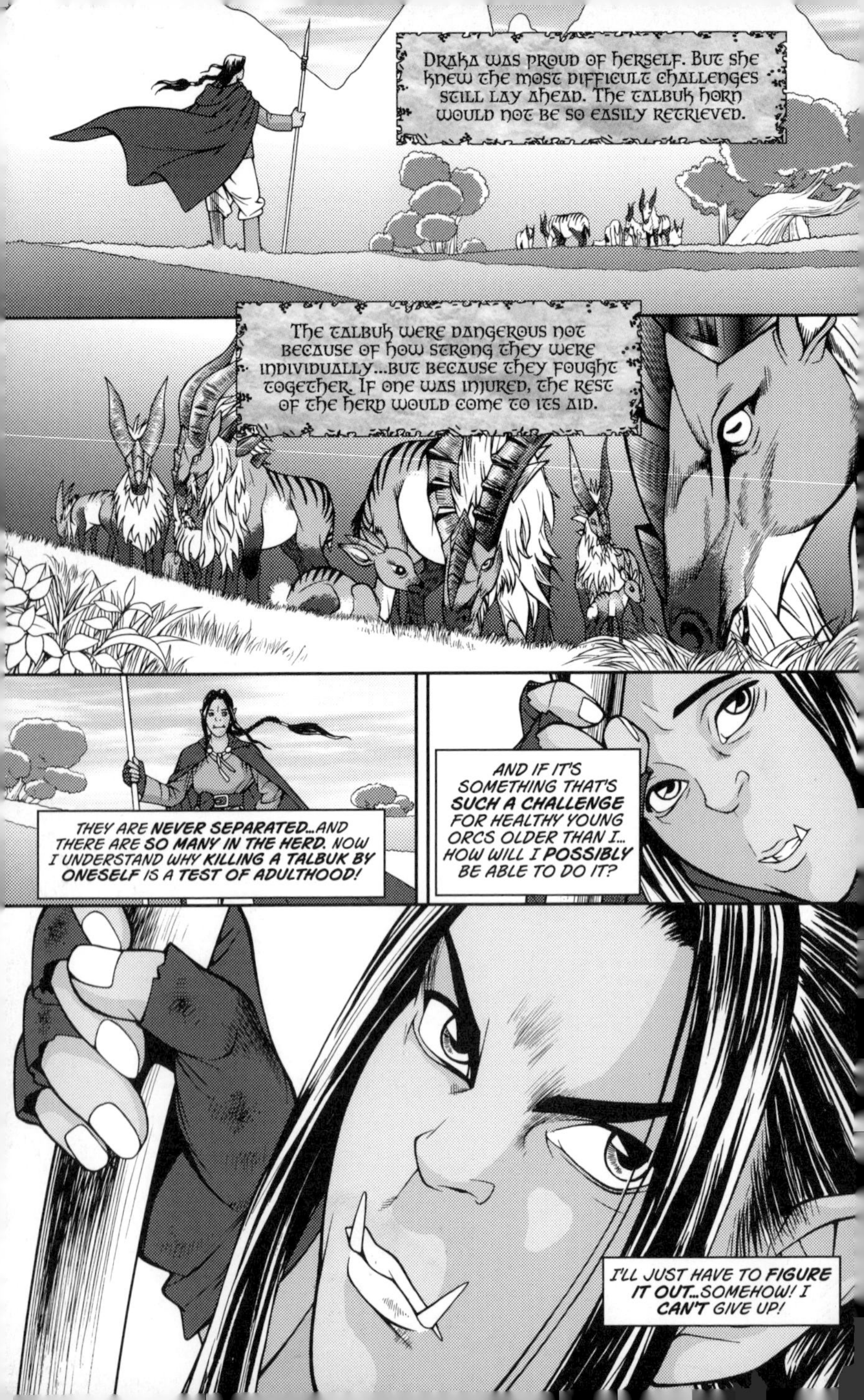

Draka was proud of herself. But she knew the most difficult challenges still lay ahead. The talbuk horn would not be so easily retrieved.
The talbuk were dangerous not because of how strong they were individually...but because they fought together. If one was injured, the rest of the herd would come to its aid.
THEY ARE NEVER SEPARATED...AND THERE ARE SO MANY IN THE HERD. NOW I UNDERSTAND WHY KILLING A TALBUK BY ONESELF IS A TEST OF ADULTHOOD!
AND IF IT'S SOMETHING THAT'S SUCH A CHALLENGE FOR HEALTHY YOUNG ORCS OLDER THAN I... HOW WILL I POSSIBLY BE ABLE TO DO IT?
I'LL JUST HAVE TO FIGURE IT OUT...SOMEHOW! I CAN'T GIVE UP!

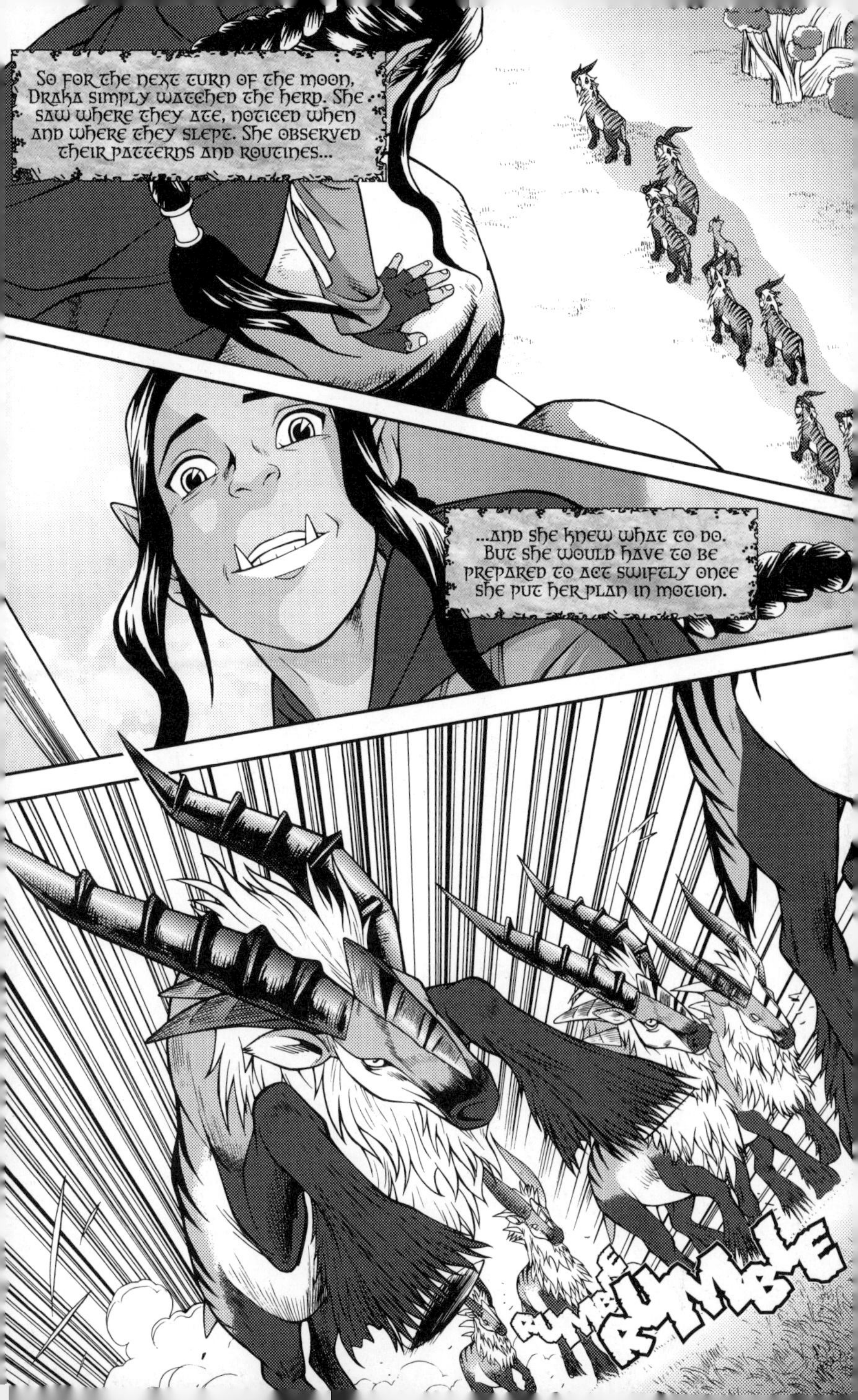
So for the next turn of the moon, Draka simply watched the herd. She saw where they ate, noticed when and where they slept. She observed their patterns and routines...
...and she knew what to do. But she would have to be prepared to act swiftly once she put her plan in motion.
RUMBLE RUMBLE

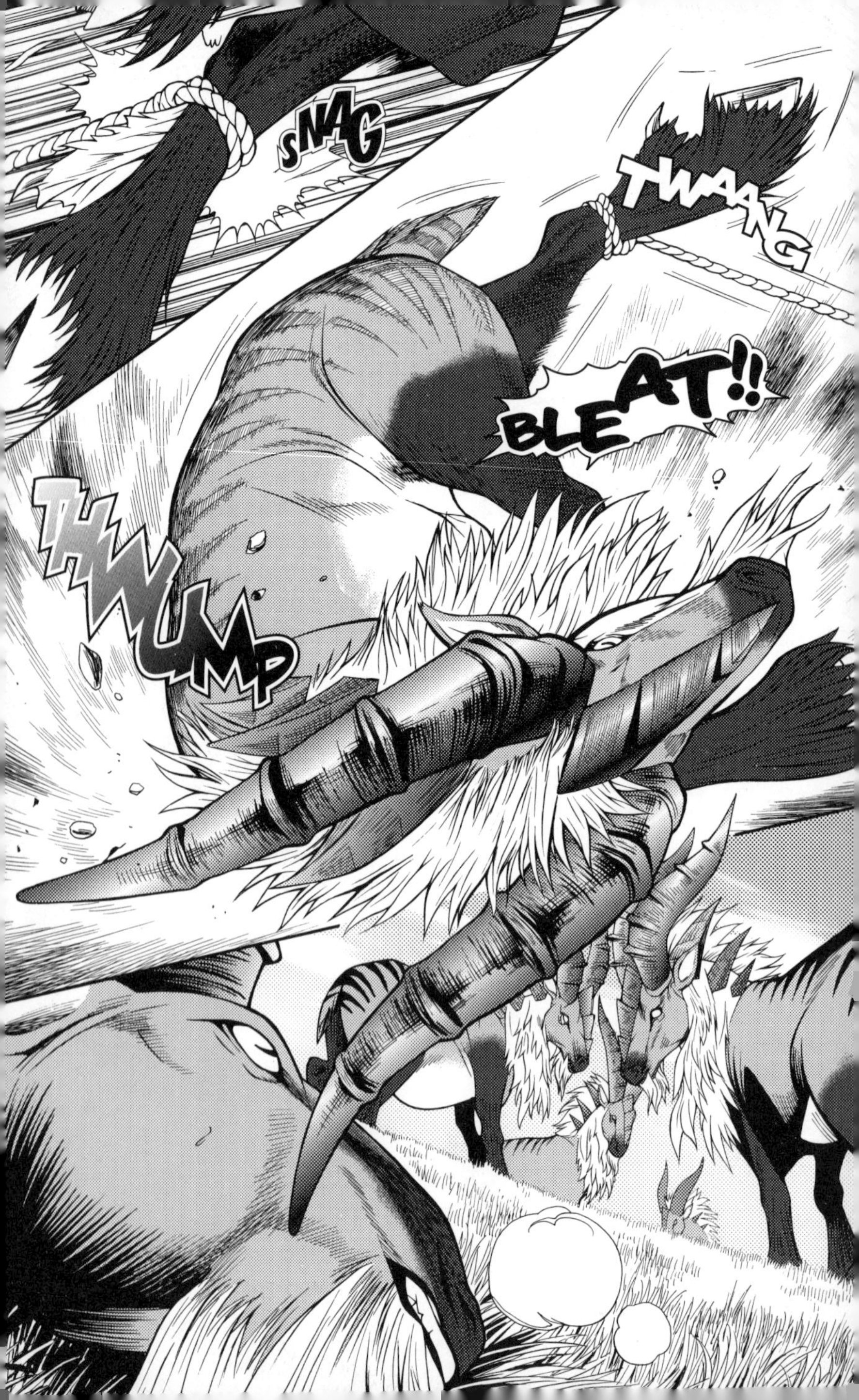
TWAANG
SNAG
BLEAT!!
THWUMP

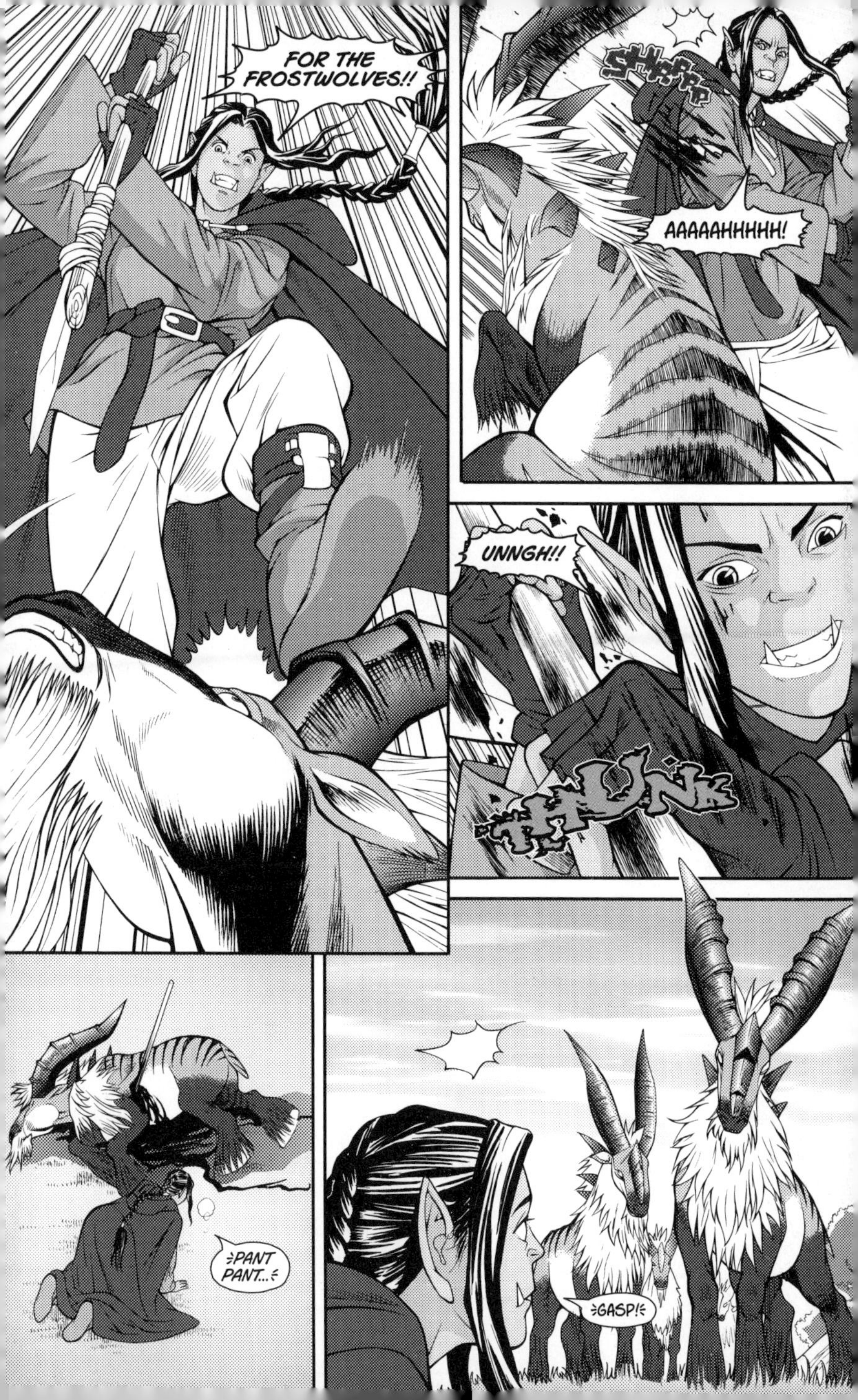
FOR THE FROSTWOLVES!!
AAAAAHHHHH!
UNNGH!!
THUNK
PANT PANT...
GASP!

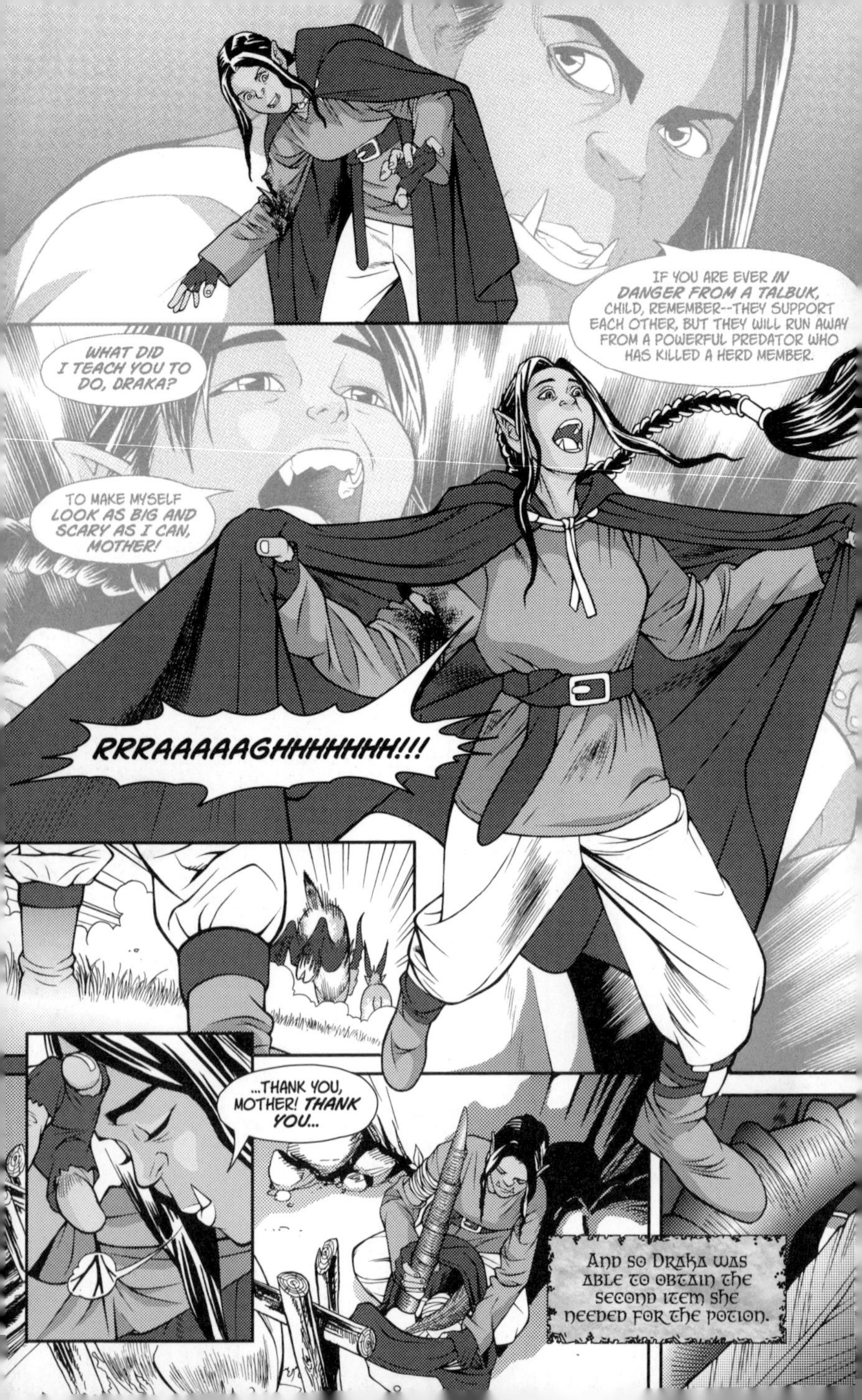
IF YOU ARE EVER IN DANGER FROM A TALBUK, CHILD, REMEMBER--THEY SUPPORT EACH OTHER, BUT THEY WILL RUN AWAY FROM A POWERFUL PREDATOR WHO HAS KILLED A HERD MEMBER.
WHAT DID I TEACH YOU TO DO, DRAKA?
TO MAKE MYSELF LOOK AS BIG AND SCARY AS I CAN, MOTHER!
RRRAAAAAAGHHHHHHHH!!!
...THANK YOU, MOTHER! THANK YOU...
And so Draka was able to obtain the second item she needed for the potion.

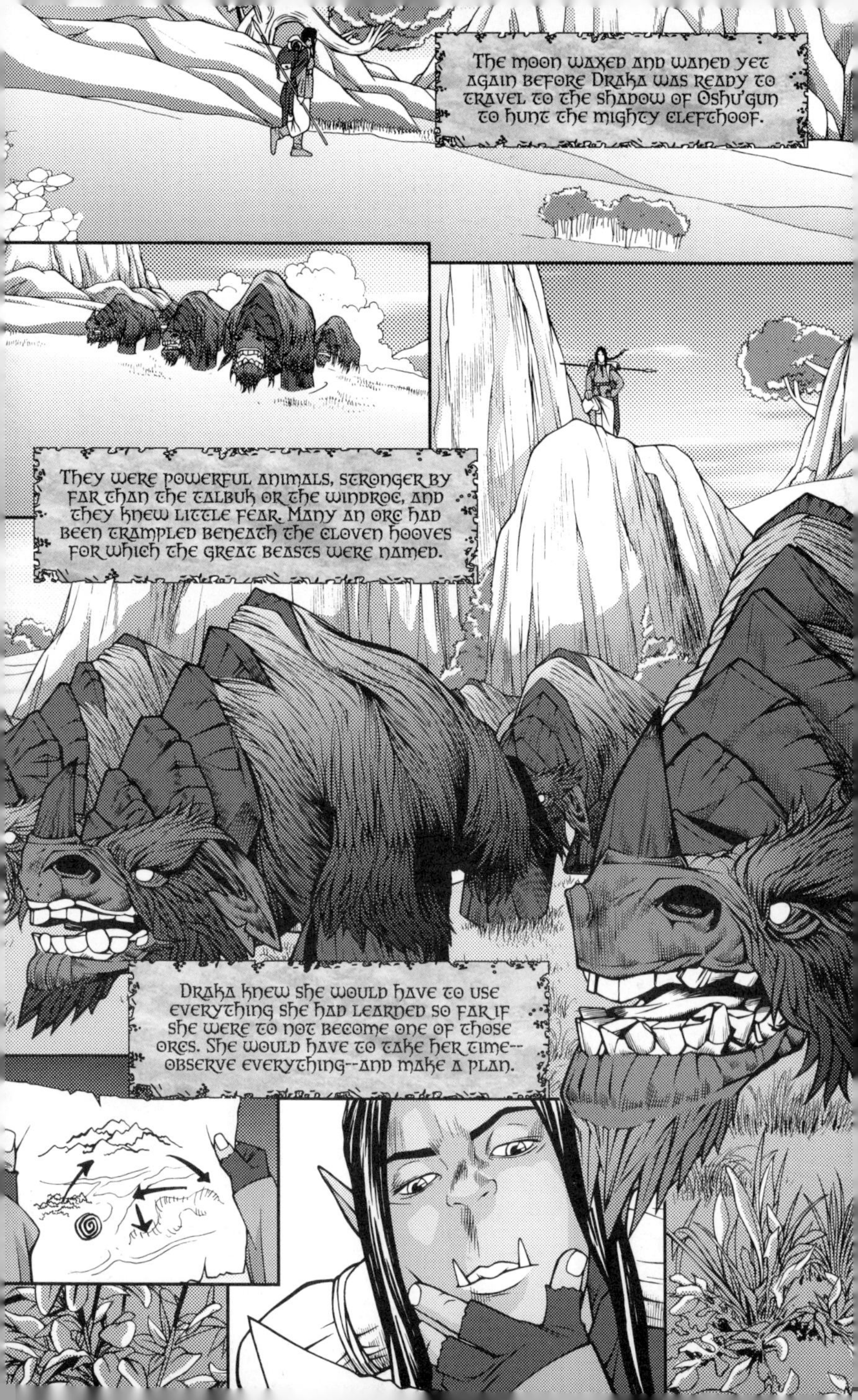
The moon waxed and waned yet again before Draka was ready to travel to the shadow of Oshu'gun to hunt the mighty clefthoof.
They were powerful animals, stronger by far than the talbuk or the windroc, and they knew little fear. Many an orc had been trampled beneath the cloven hooves for which the great beasts were named.
Draka knew she would have to use everything she had learned so far if she were to not become one of those orcs. She would have to take her time--observe everything--and make a plan.

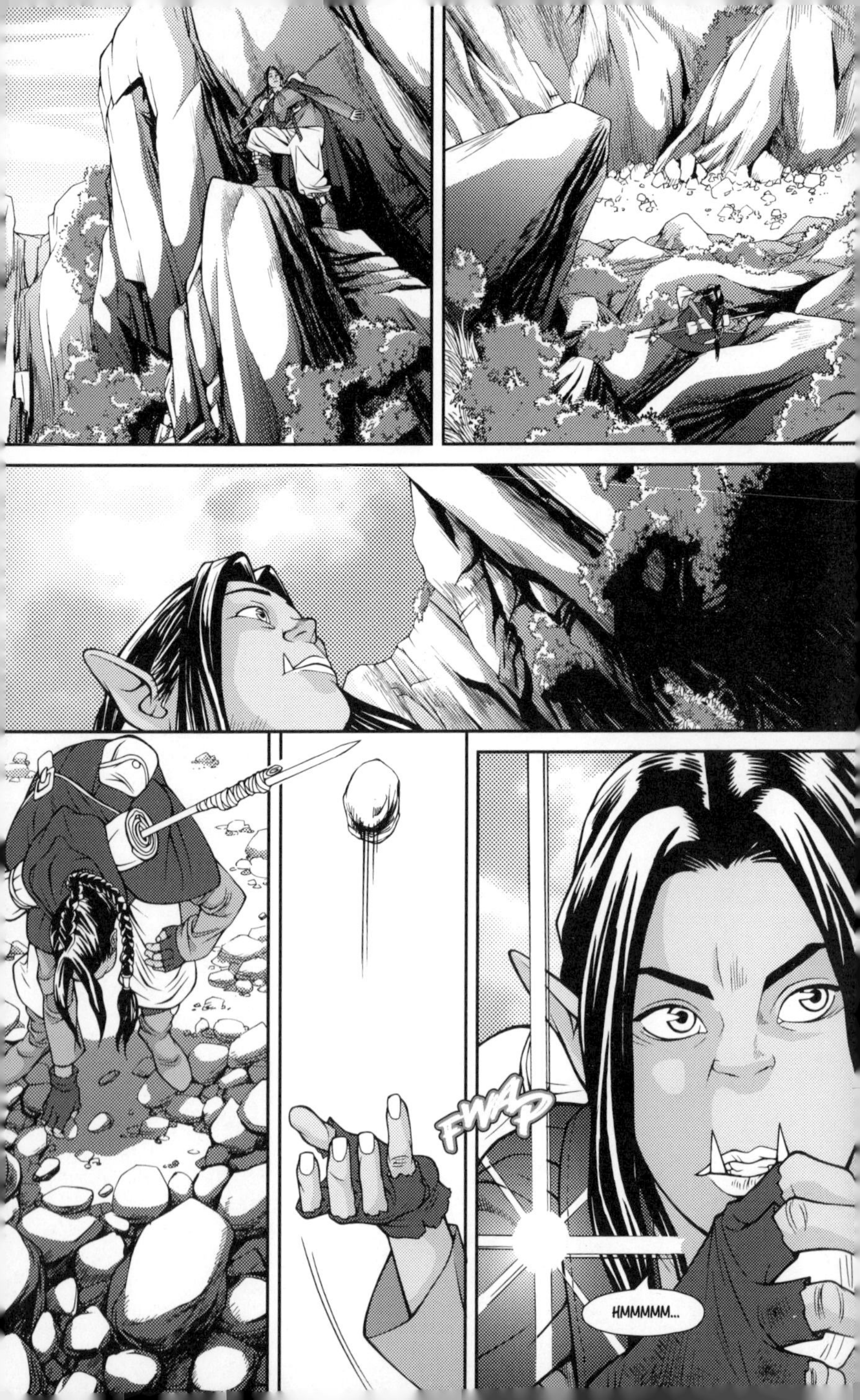
FWAP
HMMMMM...

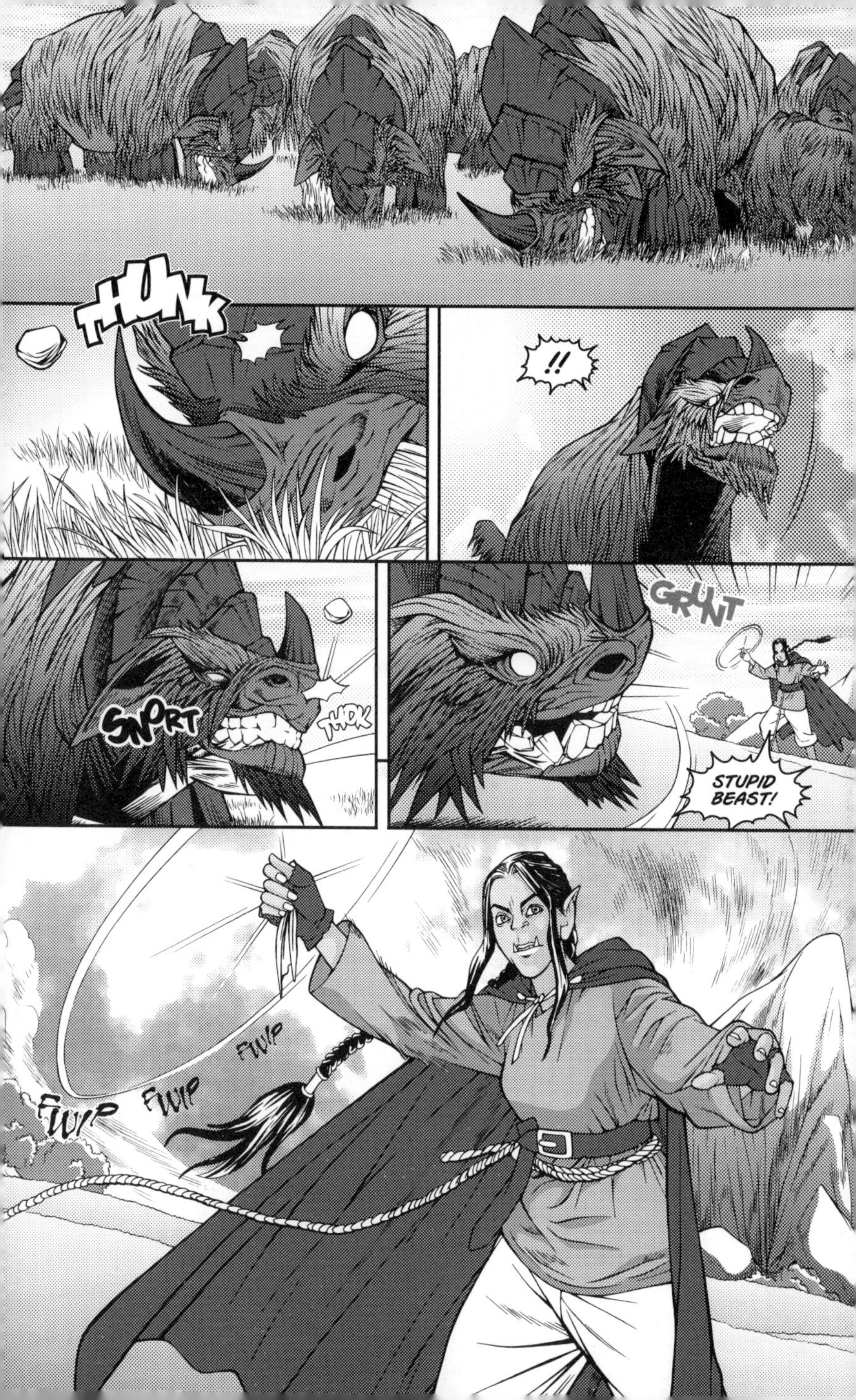
THUNK
!!
SNORT
THDK
GRUNT
STUPID BEAST!
FWIP
FWIP
FWIP

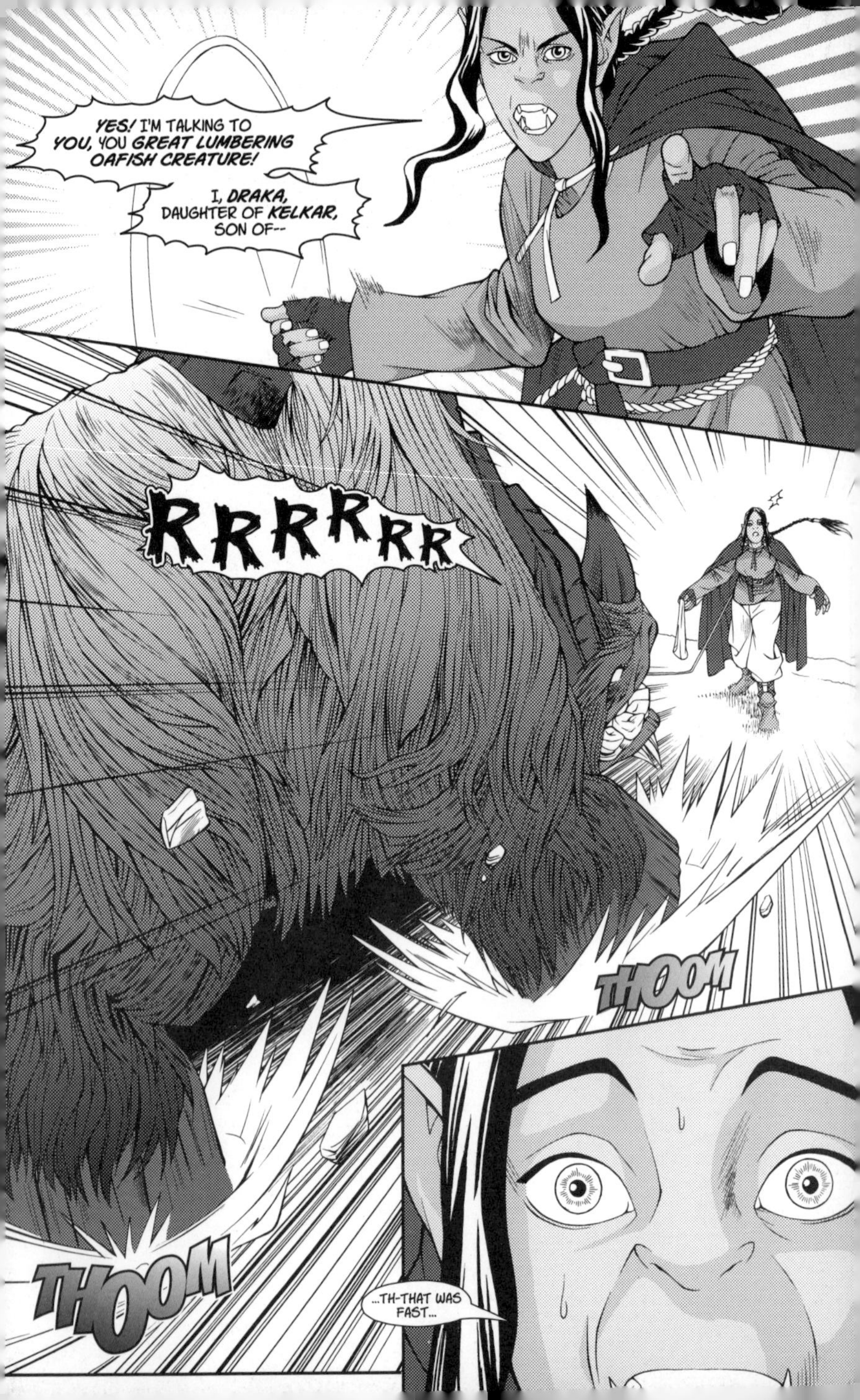
YES! I'M TALKING TO YOU, YOU GREAT LUMBERING OAFISH CREATURE!
I, DRAKA, DAUGHTER OF KELKAR, SON OF--
RRRRRR
THOOM
THOOM
...TH-THAT WAS FAST...

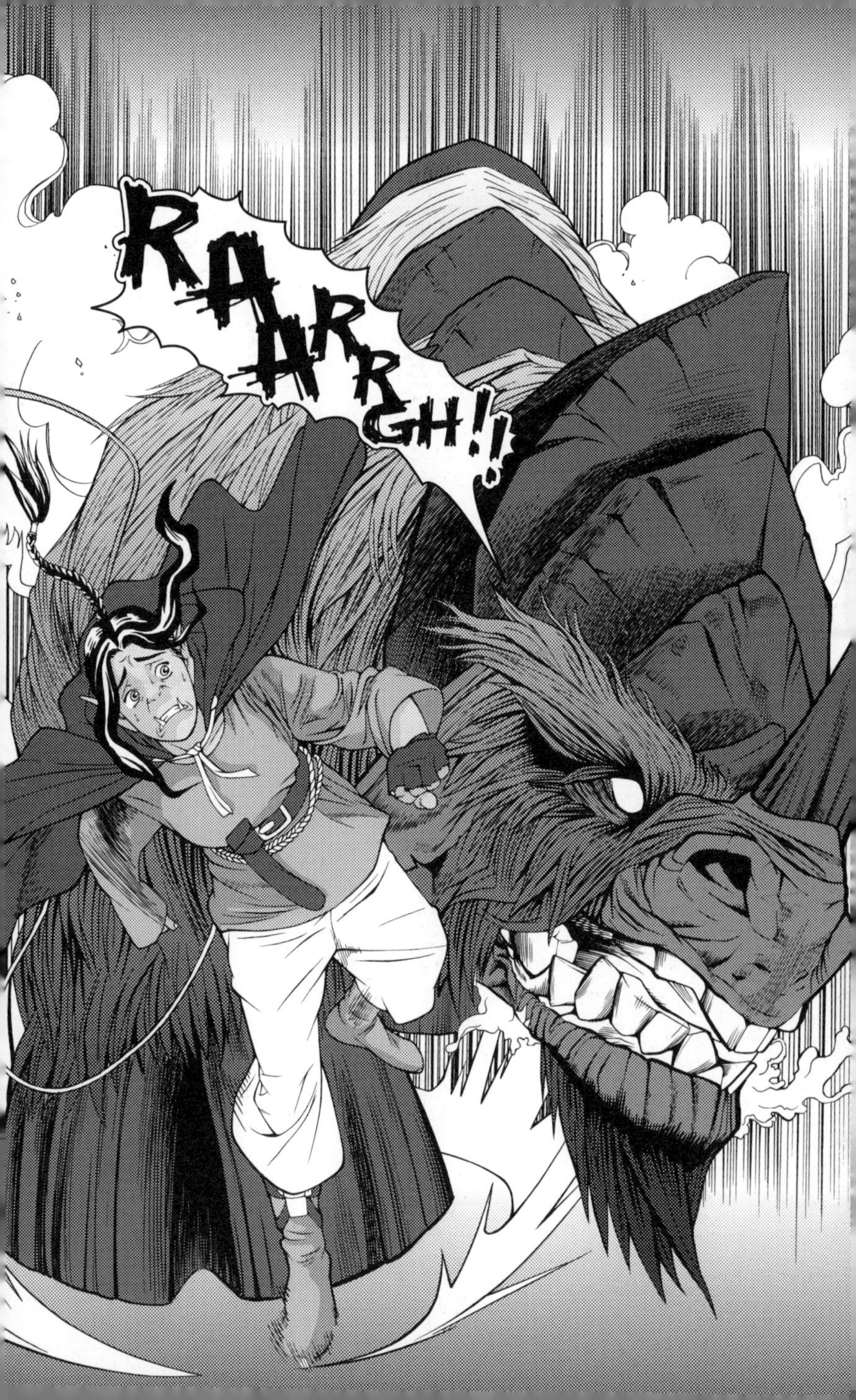
RAARRRGH!!

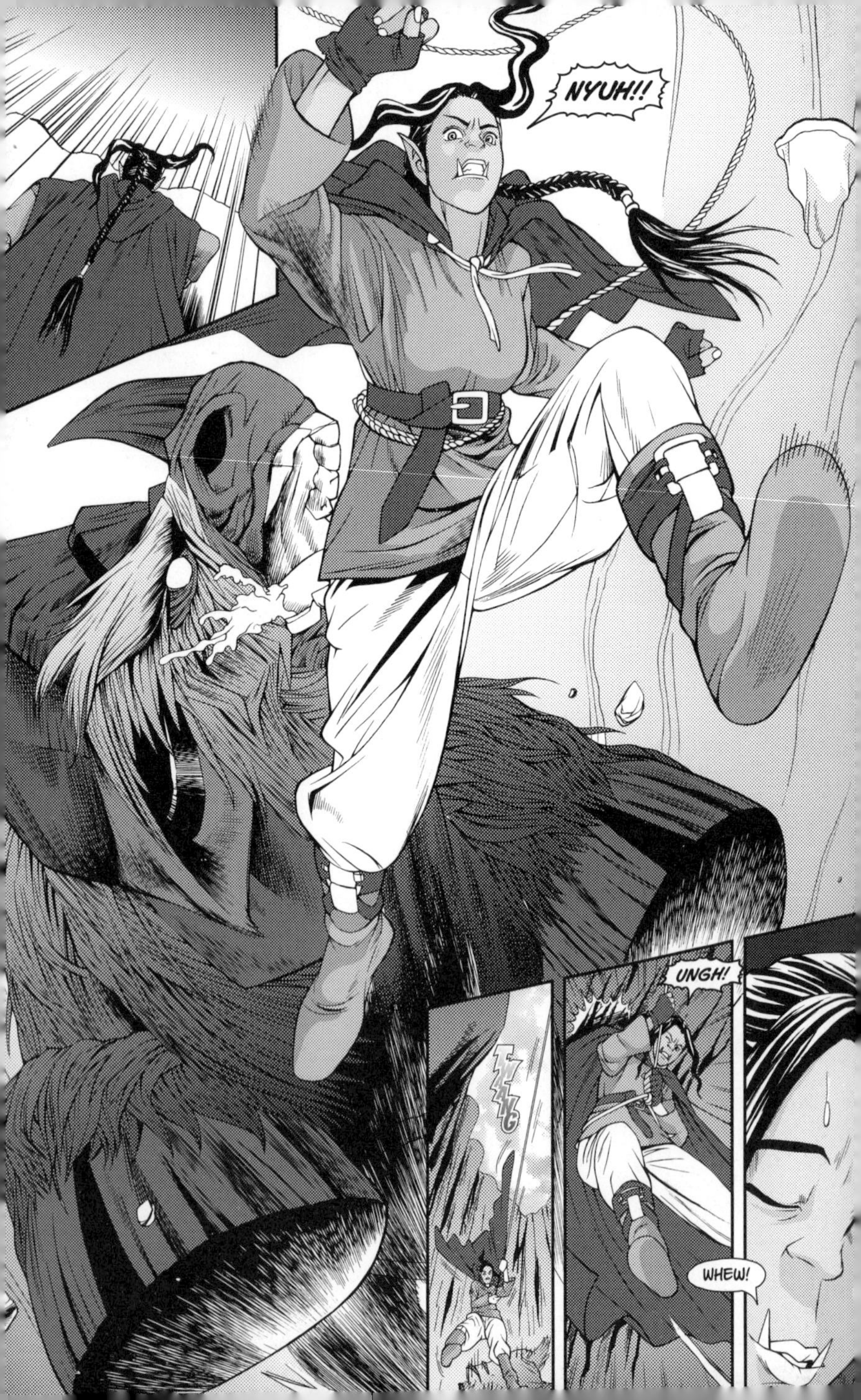
NYUH!!
UNGH!
TWANG
WHEW!

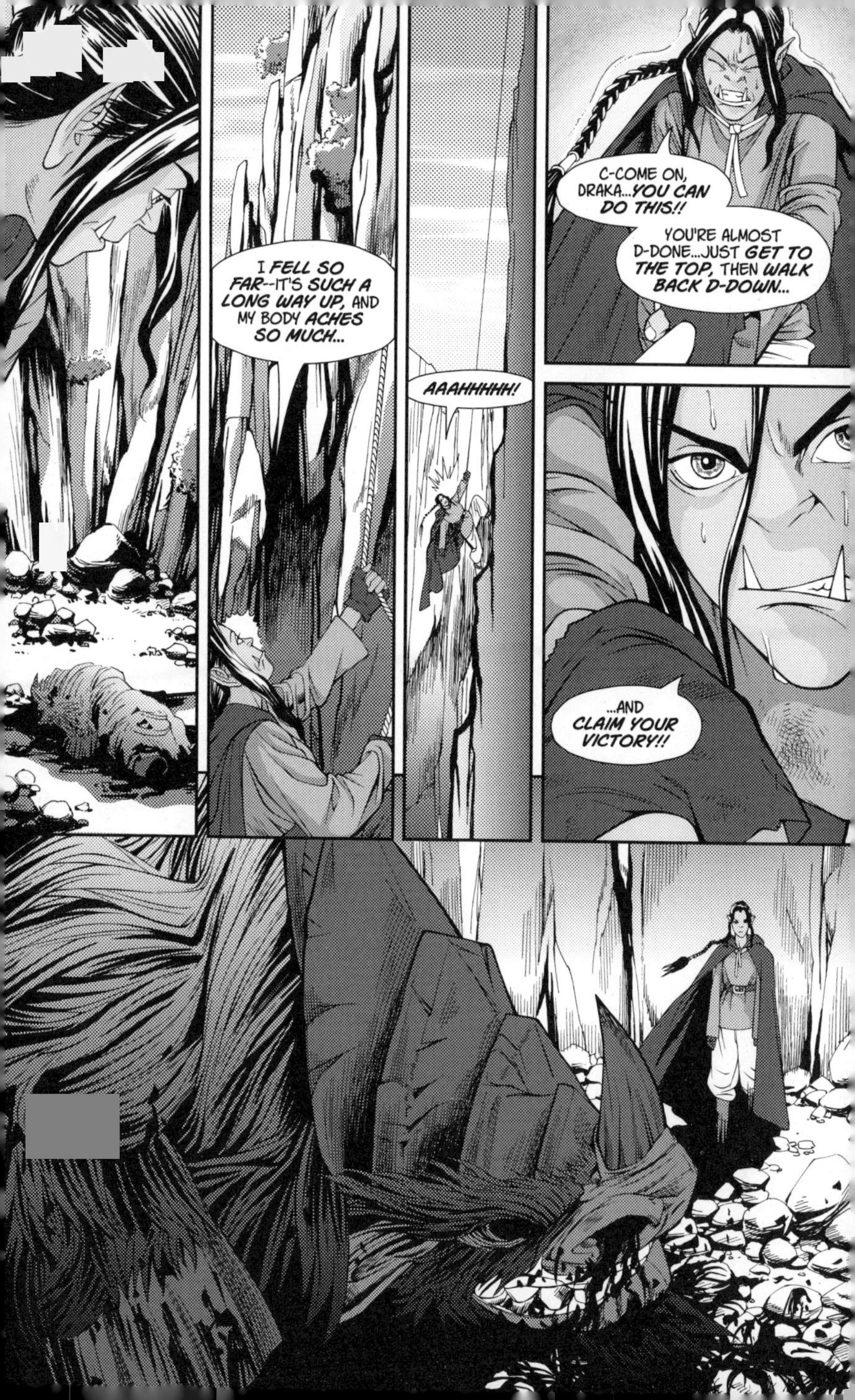
I FELL SO FAR--IT'S SUCH A LONG WAY UP, AND MY BODY ACHES SO MUCH...
AAAHHHHH!
C-COME ON, DRAKA...YOU CAN DO THIS!!
YOU'RE ALMOST D-DONE...JUST GET TO THE TOP, THEN WALK BACK D-DOWN...
...AND CLAIM YOUR VICTORY!!

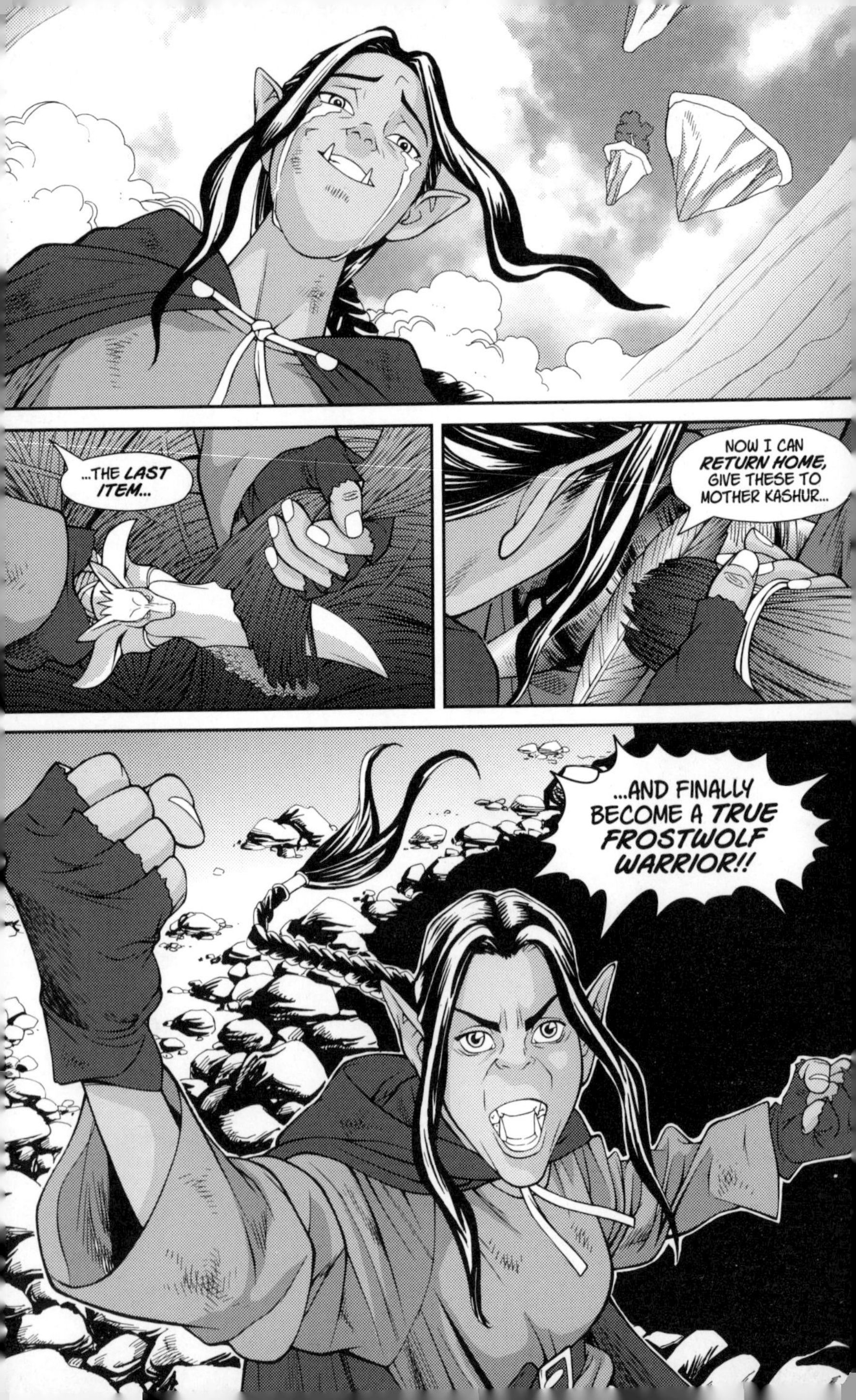
...THE LAST ITEM...
NOW I CAN RETURN HOME, GIVE THESE TO MOTHER KASHUR...
...AND FINALLY BECOME A TRUE FROSTWOLF WARRIOR!!

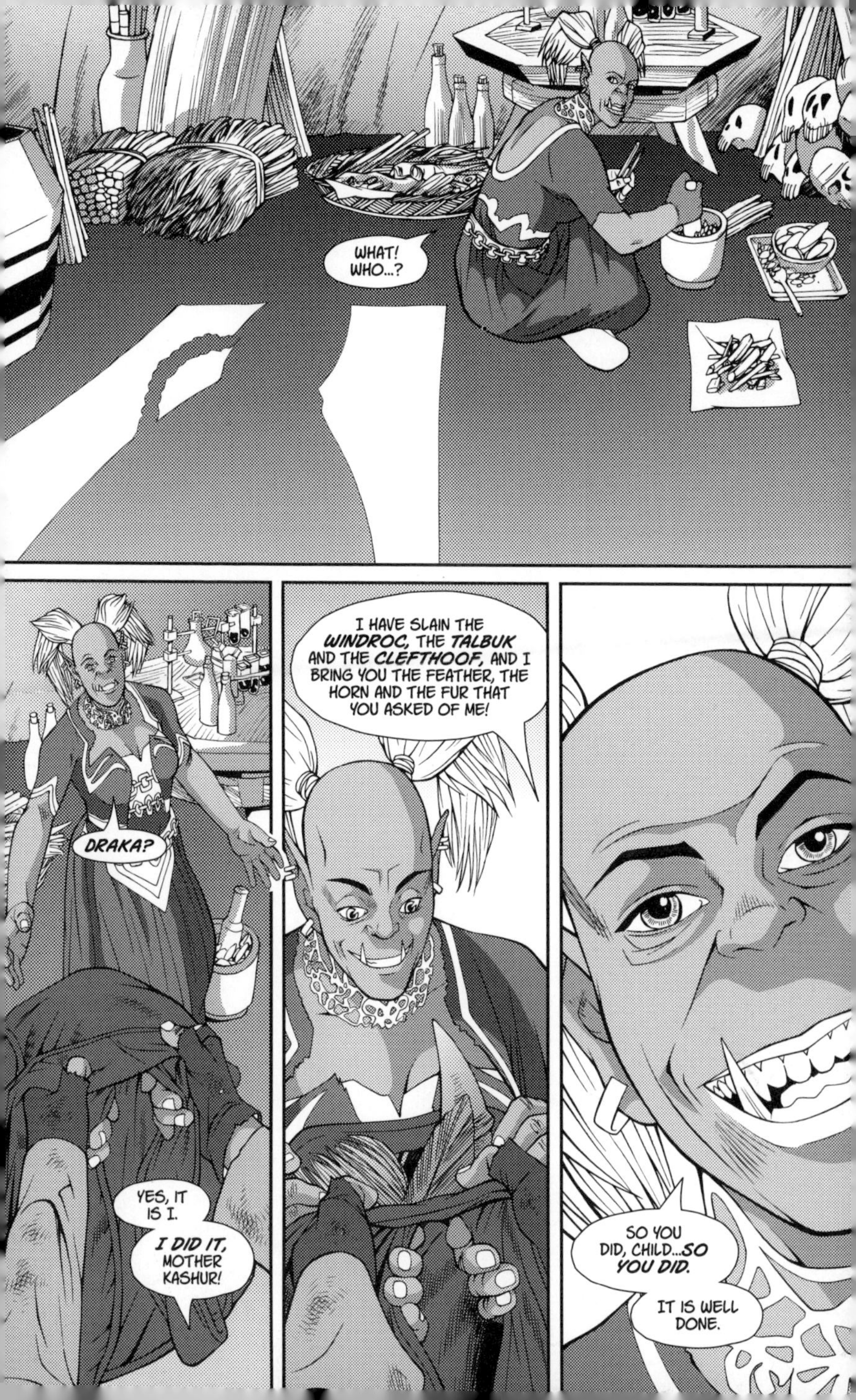
WHAT! WHO...?
DRAKA?
YES, IT IS I.
I DID IT, MOTHER KASHUR!
I HAVE SLAIN THE ***WINDROC,*** THE ***TALBUK*** AND THE ***CLEFTHOOF,*** AND I BRING YOU THE FEATHER, THE HORN AND THE FUR THAT YOU ASKED OF ME!
SO YOU DID, CHILD...***SO YOU DID.***
IT IS WELL DONE.

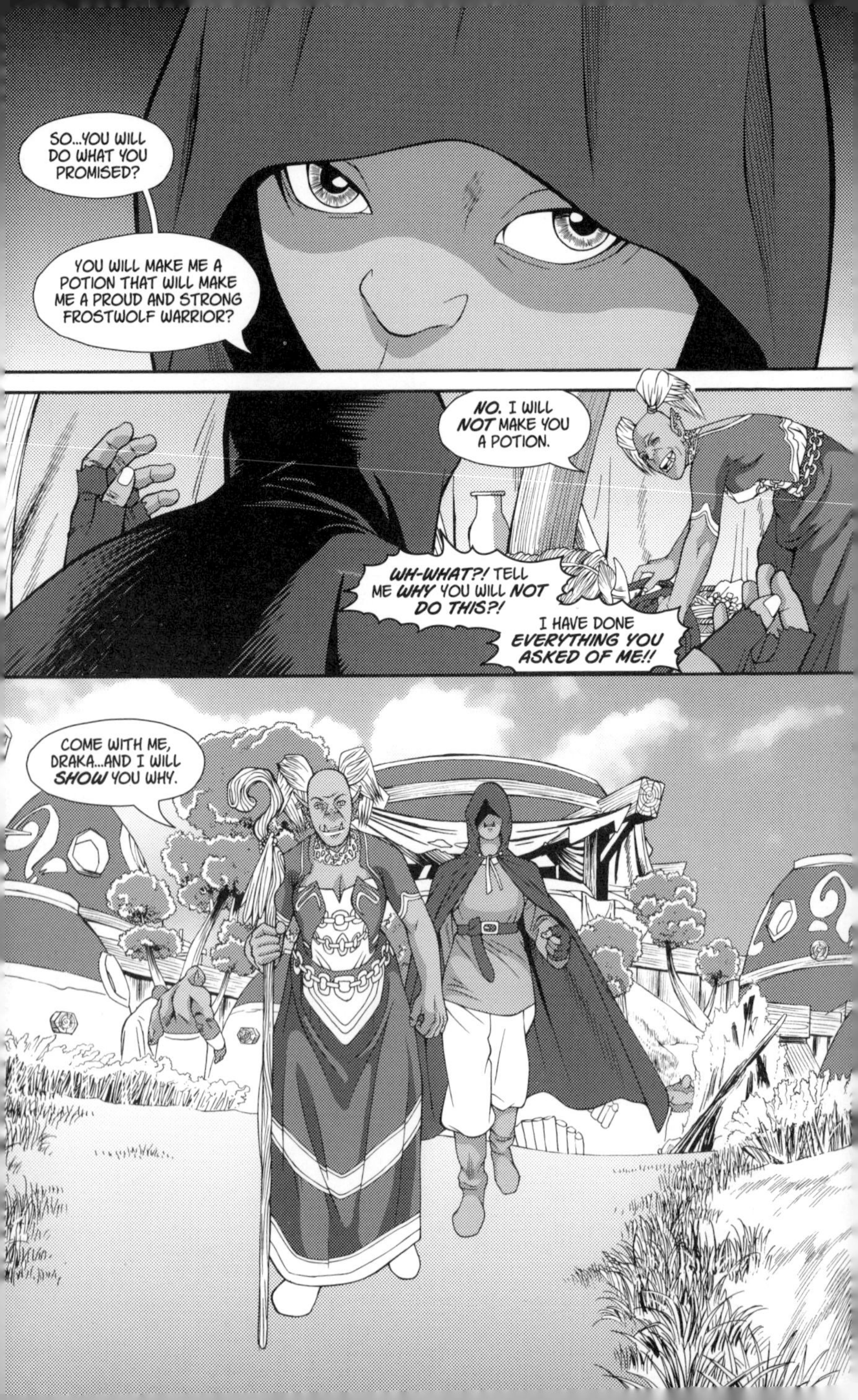
SO...YOU WILL DO WHAT YOU PROMISED?
YOU WILL MAKE ME A POTION THAT WILL MAKE ME A PROUD AND STRONG FROSTWOLF WARRIOR?
NO. I WILL NOT MAKE YOU A POTION.
WH-WHAT?! TELL ME WHY YOU WILL NOT DO THIS?!
I HAVE DONE EVERYTHING YOU ASKED OF ME!!
COME WITH ME, DRAKA...AND I WILL SHOW YOU WHY.

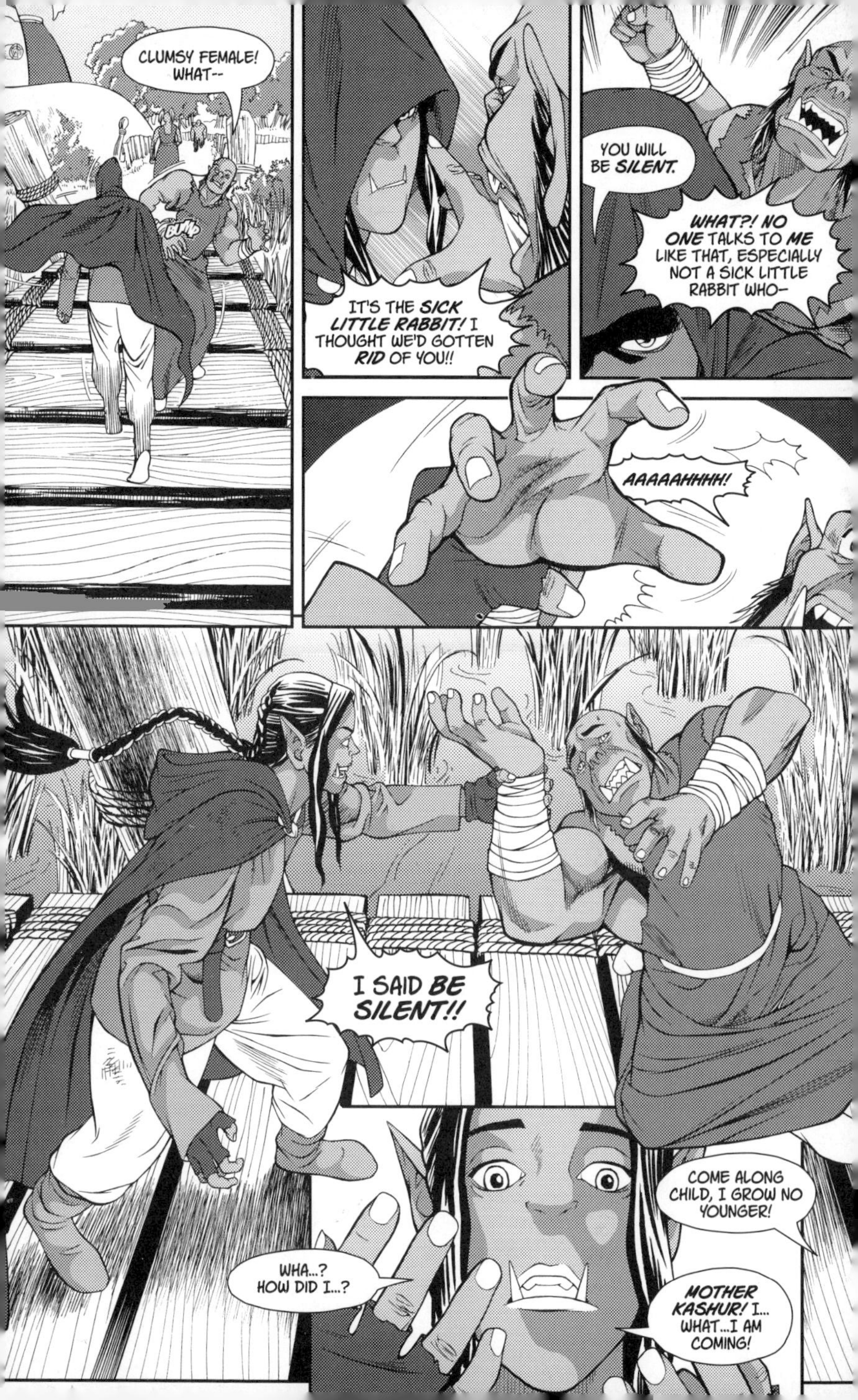
CLUMSY FEMALE! WHAT--
BUMP
IT'S THE SICK LITTLE RABBIT! I THOUGHT WE'D GOTTEN RID OF YOU!!
YOU WILL BE SILENT.
WHAT?! NO ONE TALKS TO ME LIKE THAT, ESPECIALLY NOT A SICK LITTLE RABBIT WHO-
AAAAAHHHH!
I SAID BE SILENT!!
WHA...? HOW DID I...?
COME ALONG CHILD, I GROW NO YOUNGER!
MOTHER KASHUR! I... WHAT...I AM COMING!

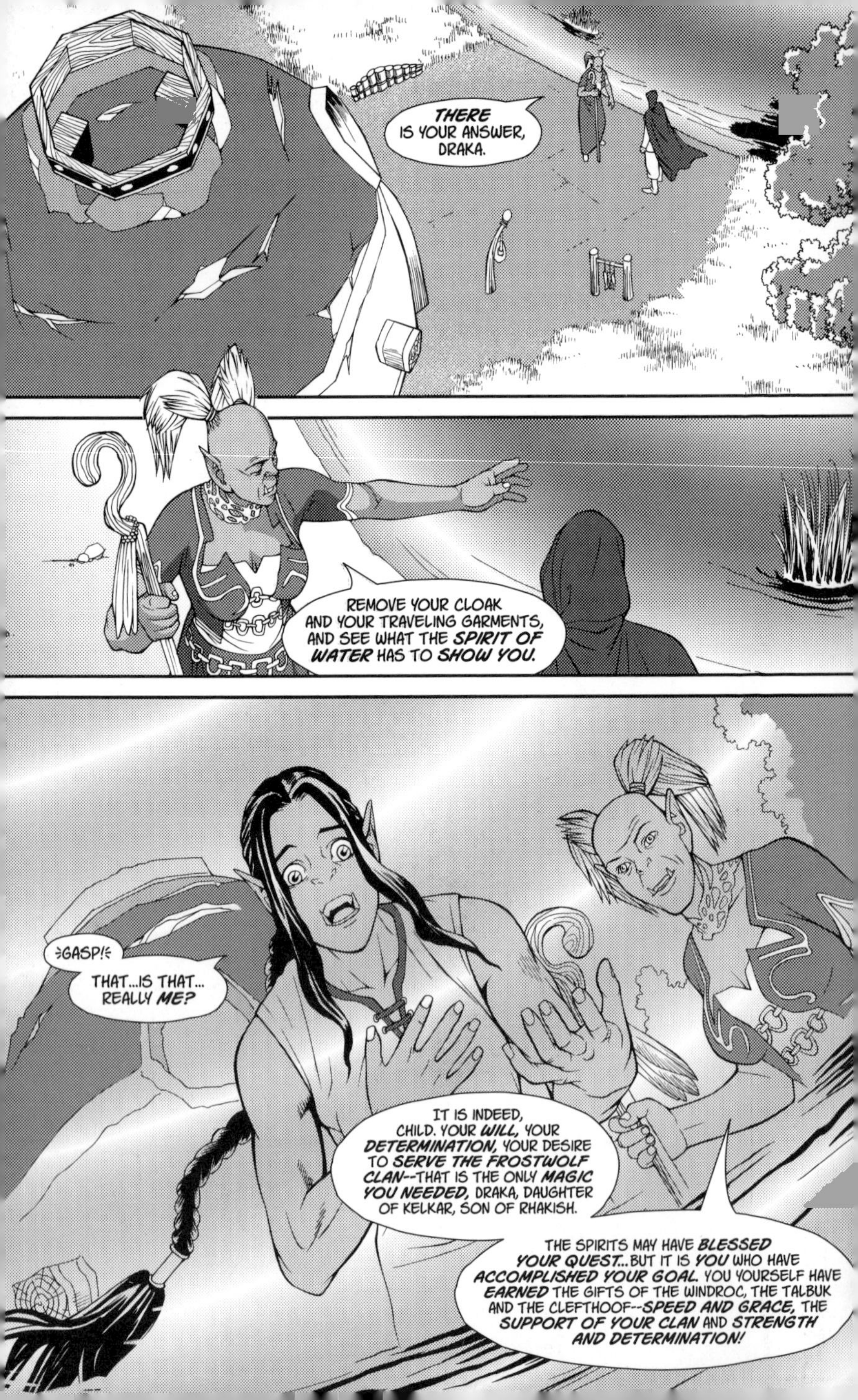
THERE IS YOUR ANSWER, DRAKA.
REMOVE YOUR CLOAK AND YOUR TRAVELING GARMENTS, AND SEE WHAT THE SPIRIT OF WATER HAS TO SHOW YOU.
GASP!
THAT...IS THAT... REALLY ME?
IT IS INDEED, CHILD. YOUR WILL, YOUR DETERMINATION, YOUR DESIRE TO SERVE THE FROSTWOLF CLAN--THAT IS THE ONLY MAGIC YOU NEEDED, DRAKA, DAUGHTER OF KELKAR, SON OF RHAKISH.
THE SPIRITS MAY HAVE BLESSED YOUR QUEST...BUT IT IS YOU WHO HAVE ACCOMPLISHED YOUR GOAL. YOU YOURSELF HAVE EARNED THE GIFTS OF THE WINDROC, THE TALBUK AND THE CLEFTHOOF--SPEED AND GRACE, THE SUPPORT OF YOUR CLAN AND STRENGTH AND DETERMINATION!

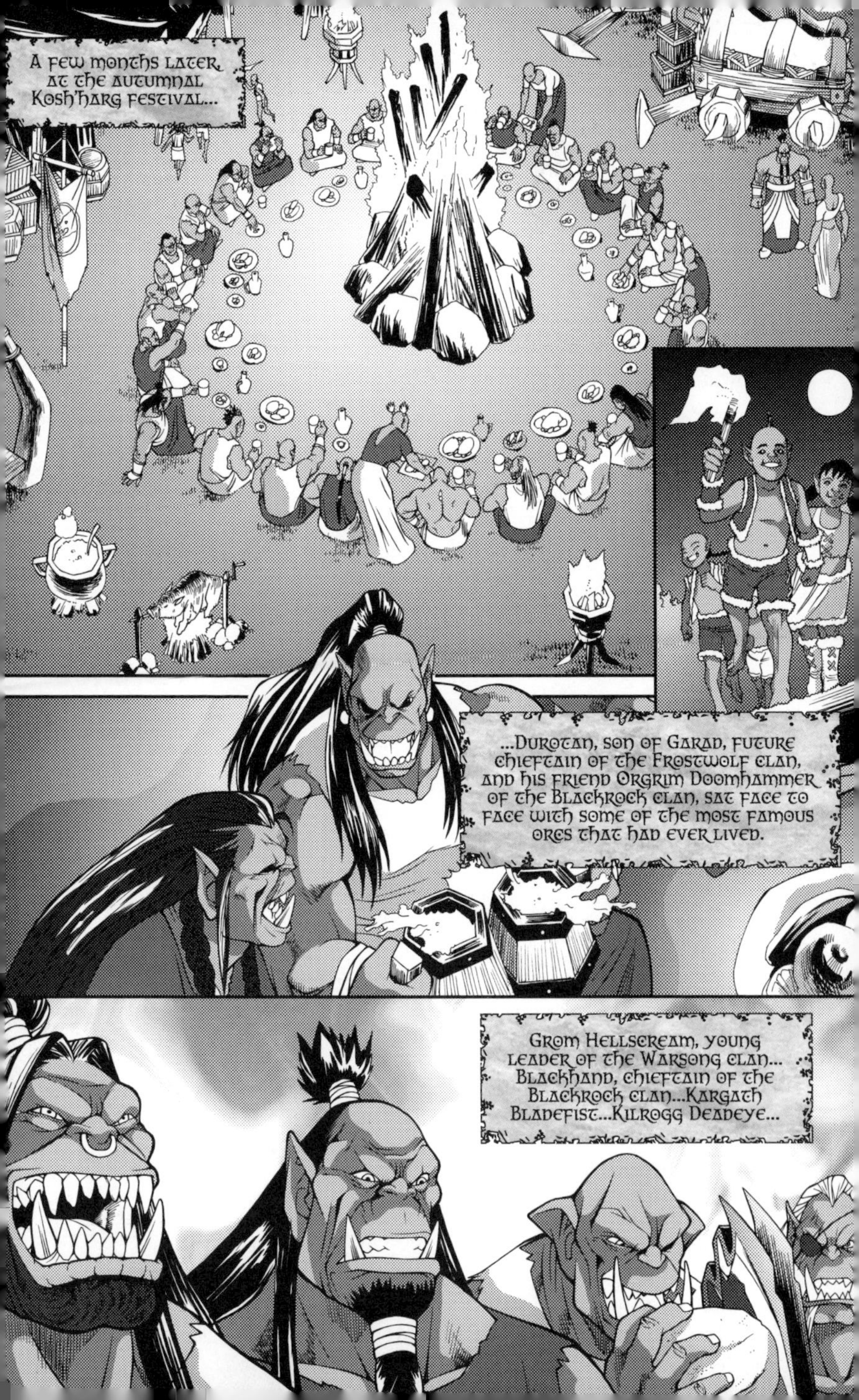
A few months later, at the autumnal Kosh'harg festival...
...Durotan, son of Garad, future chieftain of the Frostwolf clan, and his friend Orgrim Doomhammer of the Blackrock clan, sat face to face with some of the most famous orcs that had ever lived.
Grom Hellscream, young leader of the Warsong clan... Blackhand, chieftain of the Blackrock clan...Kargath Bladefist...Kilrogg Deadeye...

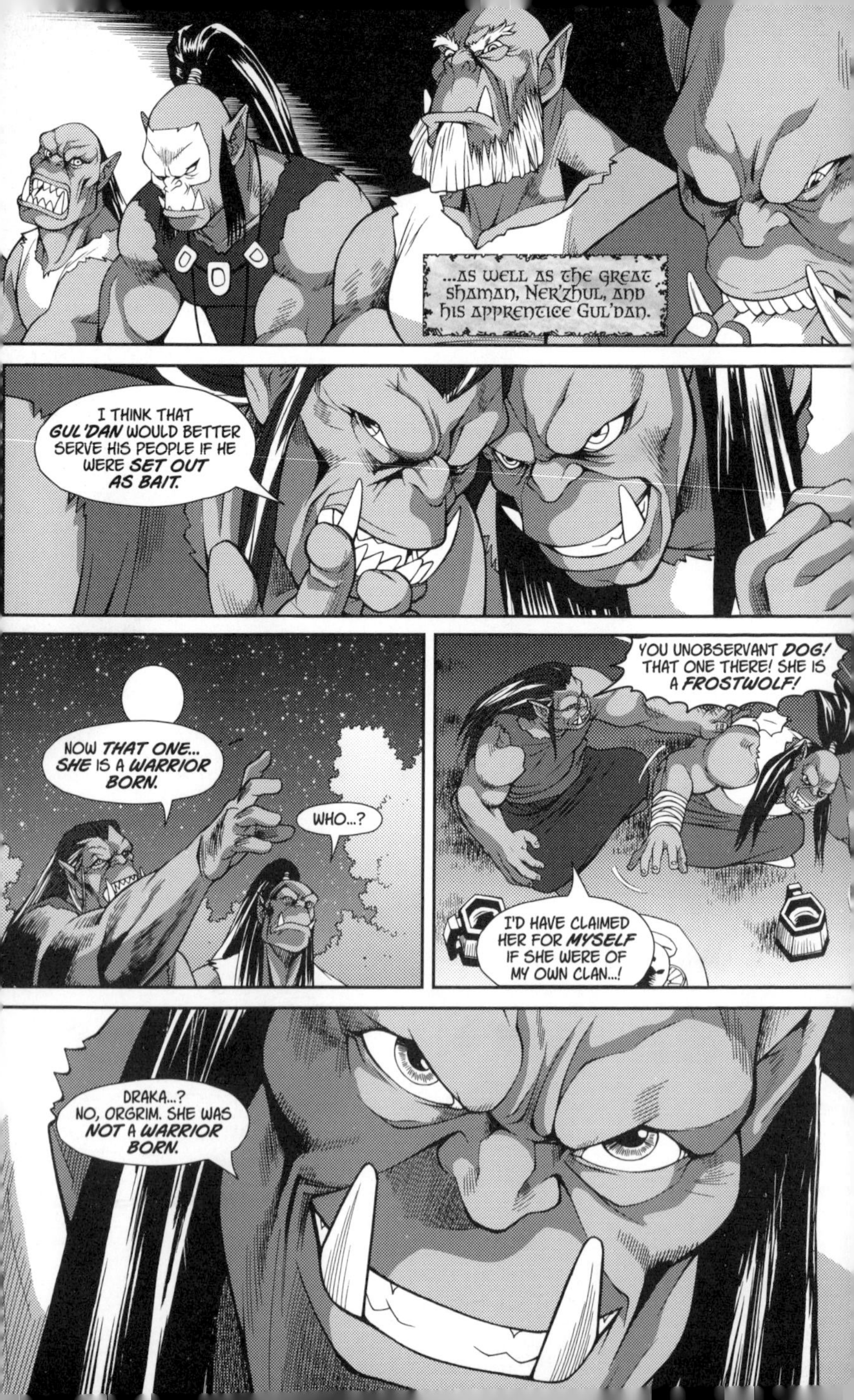
...AS WELL AS THE GREAT SHAMAN, NER'ZHUL, AND HIS APPRENTICE GUL'DAN.
I THINK THAT GUL'DAN WOULD BETTER SERVE HIS PEOPLE IF HE WERE SET OUT AS BAIT.
NOW THAT ONE... SHE IS A WARRIOR BORN.
WHO...?
YOU UNOBSERVANT DOG! THAT ONE THERE! SHE IS A FROSTWOLF!
I'D HAVE CLAIMED HER FOR MYSELF IF SHE WERE OF MY OWN CLAN...!
DRAKA...? NO, ORGRIM. SHE WAS NOT A WARRIOR BORN.

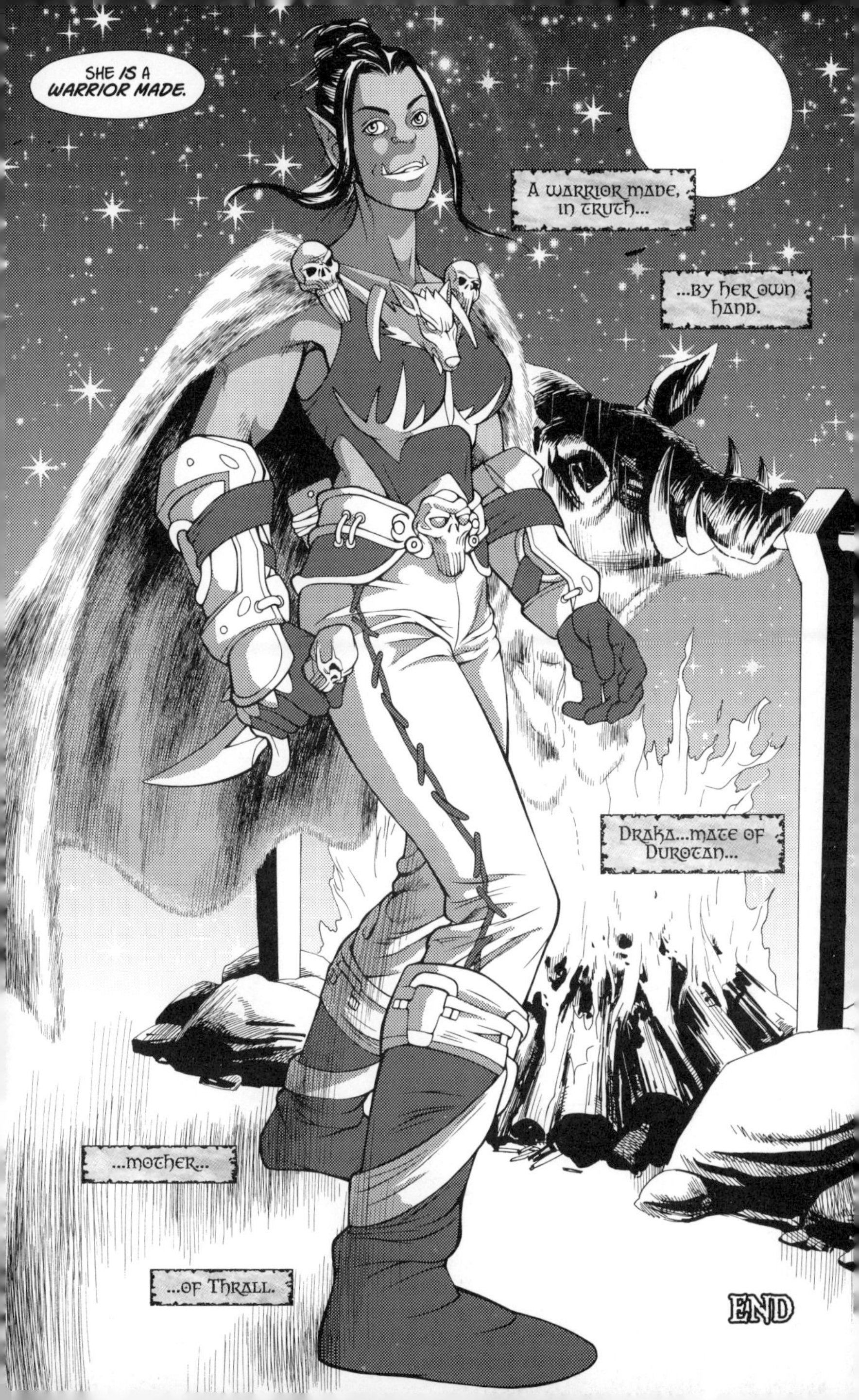
SHE IS A WARRIOR MADE.
A WARRIOR MADE, IN TRUTH...
...BY HER OWN HAND.
DRAKA...MATE OF DUROTAN...
...MOTHER...
...OF THRALL.
END

WARCRAFT

LEGENDS

VOLUME FIVE

WARRIOR: UNITED

WRITTEN BY GRACE RANDOLPH

PENCILS BY ERICA AWANO
INKS BY TOMAS AIRA & LEANDRO RIZZO
TONES BY GONZALO DUARTE

RETOUCH ARTIST & LETTERER: MICHAEL PAOLILLI

STORY SO FAR

The Wildhammer dwarves are a close-knit clan, yet one of their own, a dwarf named Kardan, was raising a human girl named Lieren. Kardan kept the details surrounding Lieren's past a secret, even to Lieren herself. And though he raised her as any loving father would, Lieren still felt like an outsider, which lead to an obsession with uncovering her past.

One night Lieren secretly followed Kardan to the high elf retreat Quel'Danil, where she made a shocking discovery... she had a twin sister named Loania. Raised by a high elf named Voldana, Loania--just like Lieren--had no knowledge of her past, or that she had a twin sister.

With their ruse revealed, it was with guilty hearts that Kardan and Voldana told the girls how they accompanied their birth father, a human paladin named Dougan, on his mission to rescue villagers from the cursed tower of Karazhan. Unfortunately, brave hearts and noble intentions were not enough to defeat the evil within and they were forced to retreat...but not before Dougan was killed in the process. Kardan and Voldana sadly delivered the news to Dougan's wife but, so immense was her grief her mind snapped, rendering her unfit to raise their twin baby girls. And so Kardan and Voldana decided to honor their fallen colleague by raising the twin daughters as their own.

While Lieren and Loania shared little in common besides their appearance, they both insisted on going to see their mother. However, upon arrival at their old home, the twins learned that their mother had died, only to be reborn as one of the undead. The girls set upon the grisly task of finding and freeing their mother from her rotting prison of flesh...by beheading her.

It was then, with their mother's soul finally laid her to rest, Lieren and Loania swore an oath at her grave...

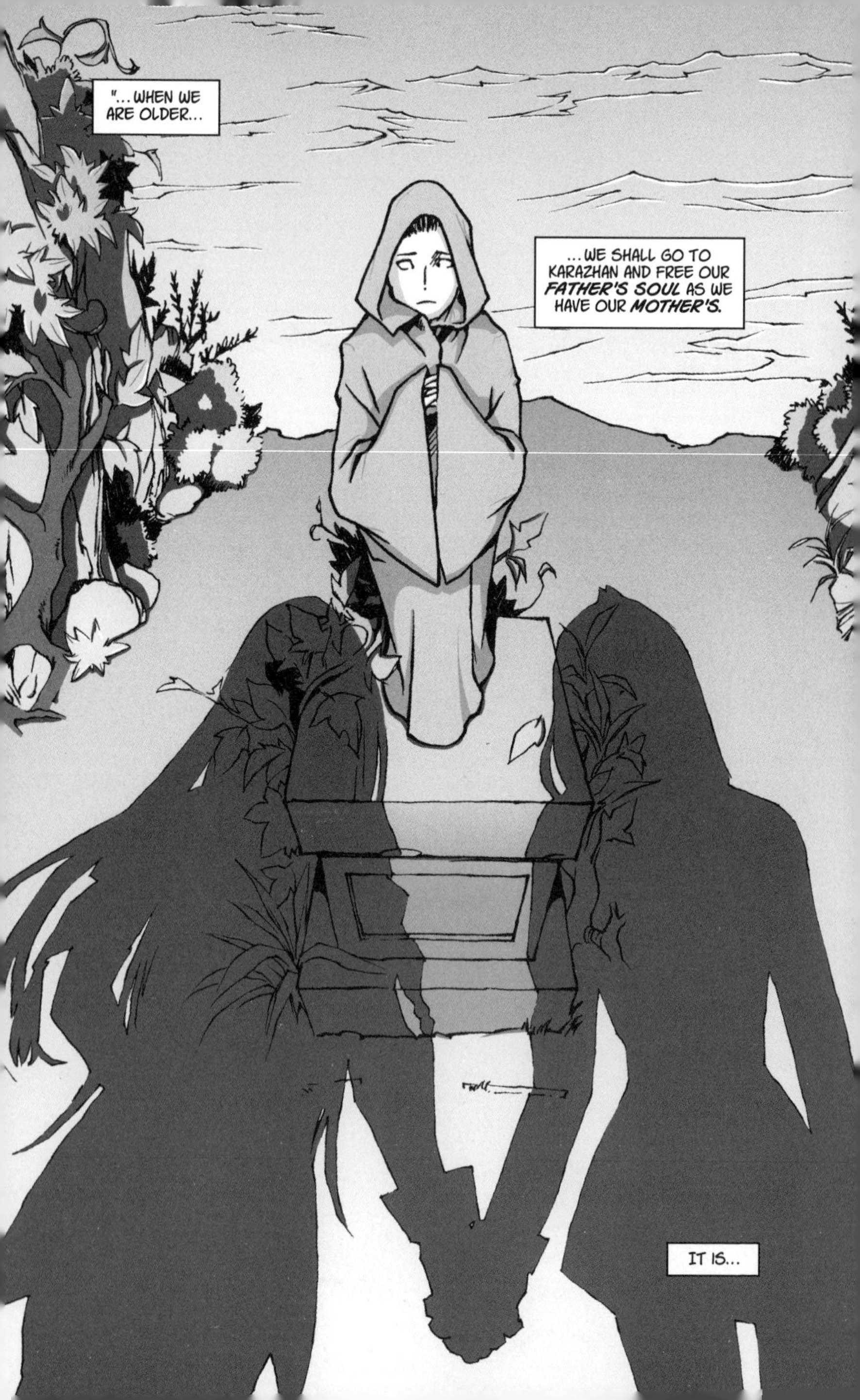
"...WHEN WE ARE OLDER...
...WE SHALL GO TO KARAZHAN AND FREE OUR ***FATHER'S SOUL*** AS WE HAVE OUR ***MOTHER'S.***
IT IS...

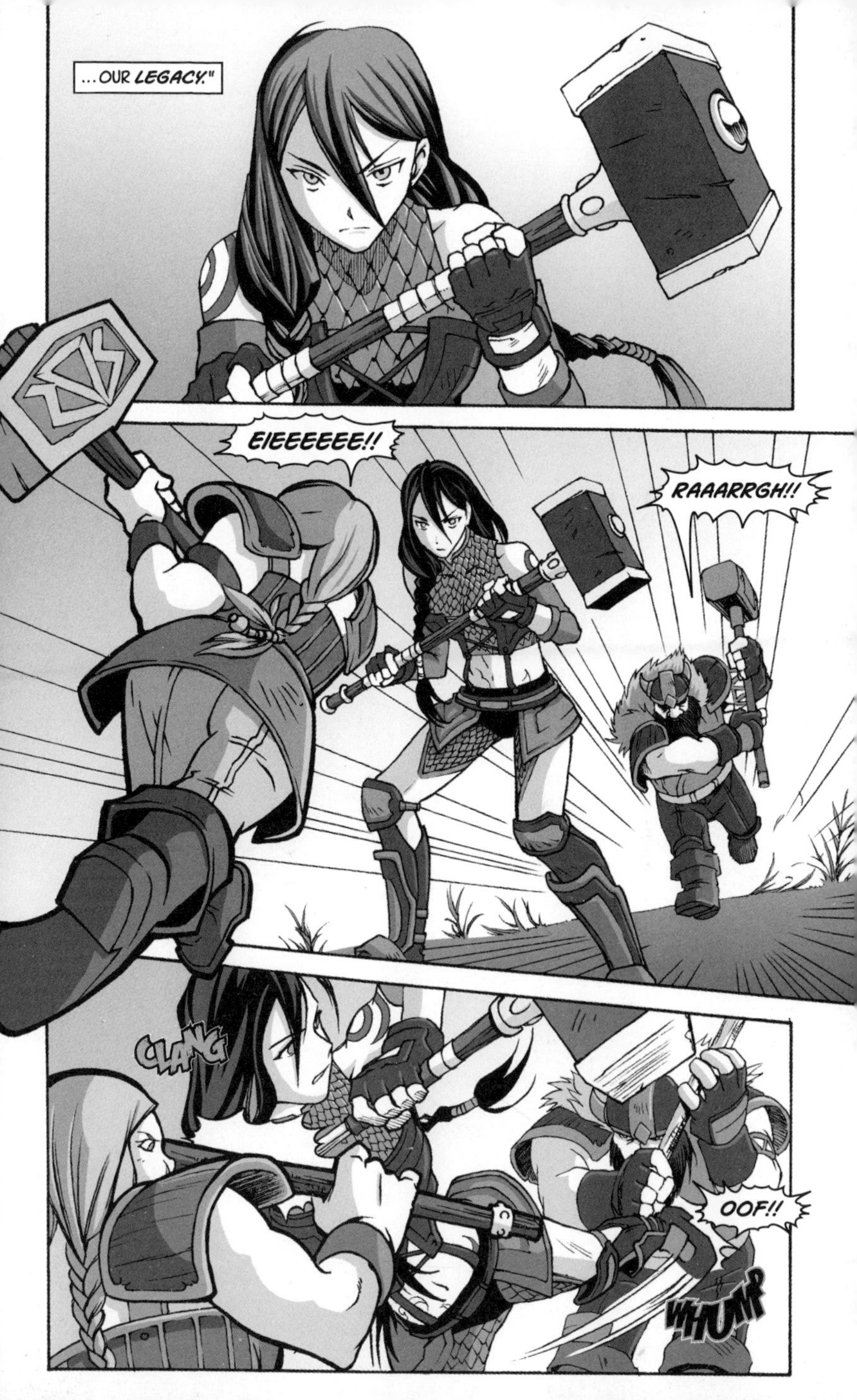
...OUR LEGACY."
EIEEEEEE!!
RAAARRGH!!
CLANG
OOF!!
WHUMP

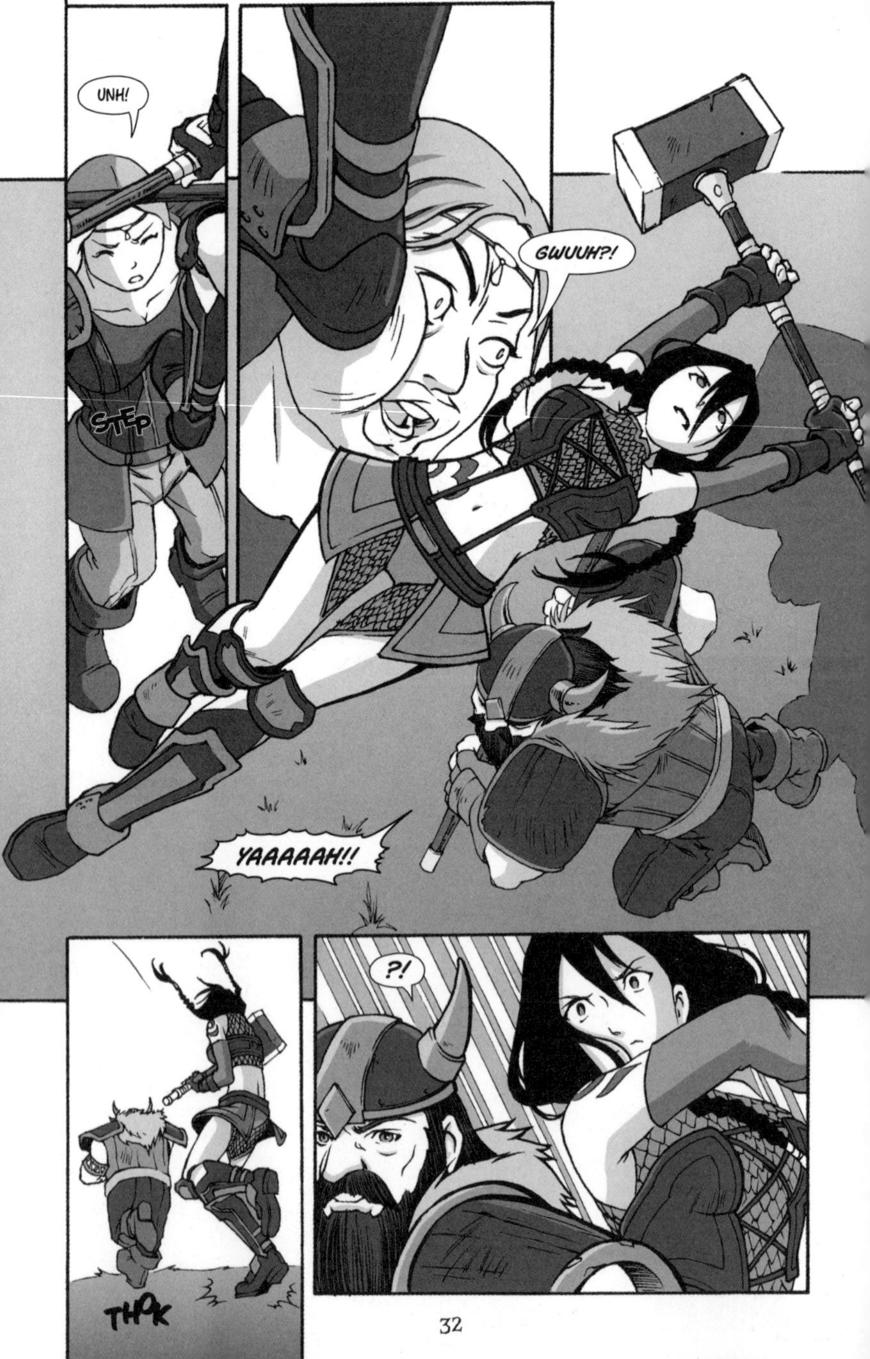
UNH!
STEP
GWUUH?!
YAAAAAH!!
THOK
?!

PWAANG

HA! I AM *TOO FAST* FOR YOU, LIEREN...!

YOU CANNOT GET THE JUMP ON *ME!!*

YES, KEERS...

CLAANG

...IT *APPEARS* YOU AND MOZZA HAVE BECOME *QUITE* SKILLED...!

HMPF!

UNNNH!

FWAAP

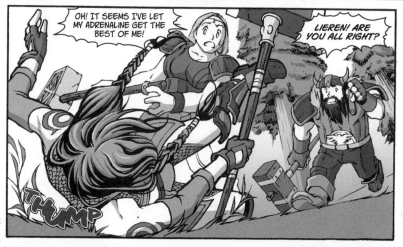

OH! IT SEEMS I'VE LET MY ADRENALINE GET THE BEST OF ME!

LIEREN! ARE YOU ALL RIGHT?

THUMP

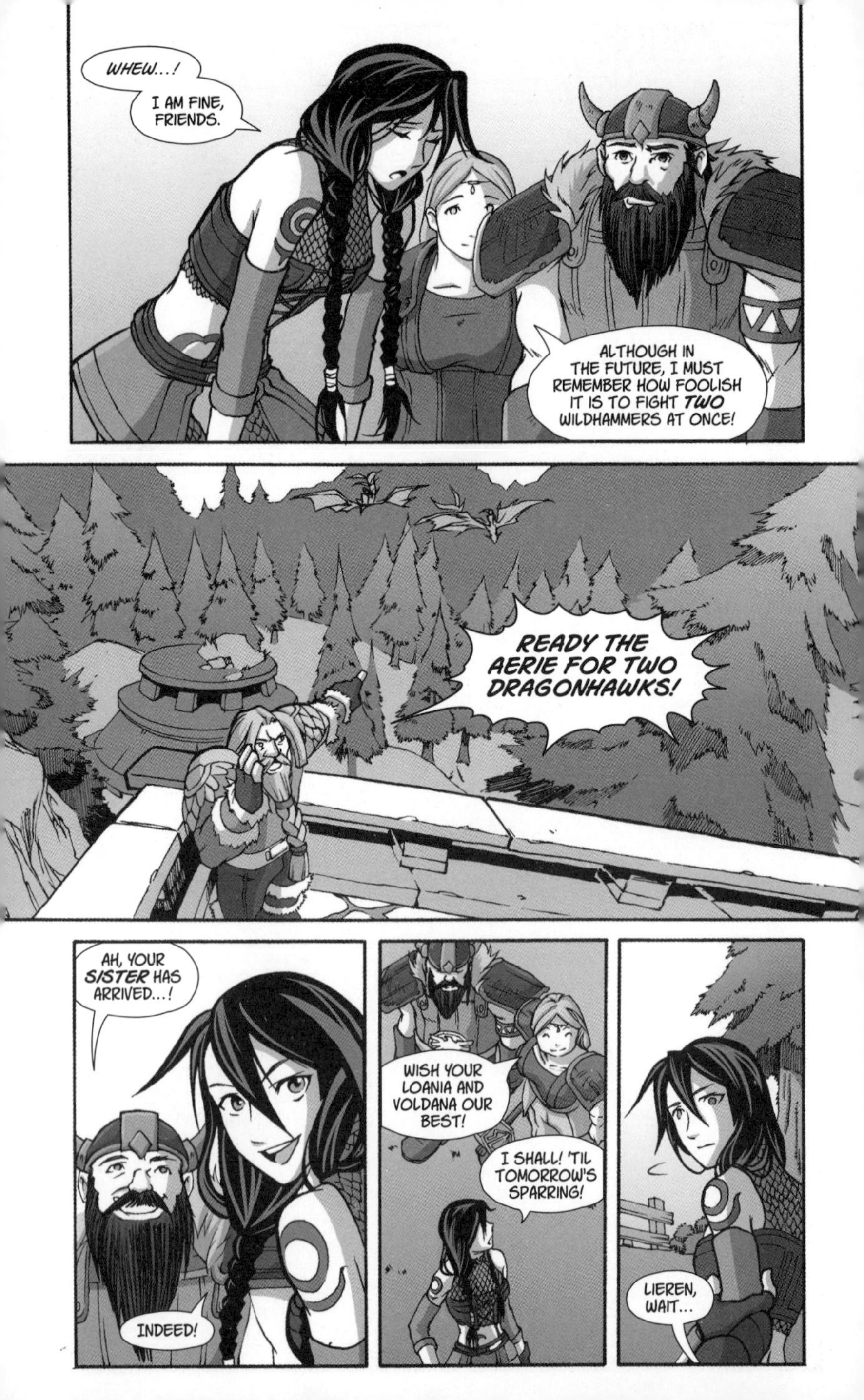
WHEW...!
I AM FINE, FRIENDS.
ALTHOUGH IN THE FUTURE, I MUST REMEMBER HOW FOOLISH IT IS TO FIGHT *TWO* WILDHAMMERS AT ONCE!
READY THE AERIE FOR TWO DRAGONHAWKS!
AH, YOUR *SISTER* HAS ARRIVED...!
INDEED!
WISH YOUR LOANIA AND VOLDANA OUR BEST!
I SHALL! 'TIL TOMORROW'S SPARRING!
LIEREN, WAIT...

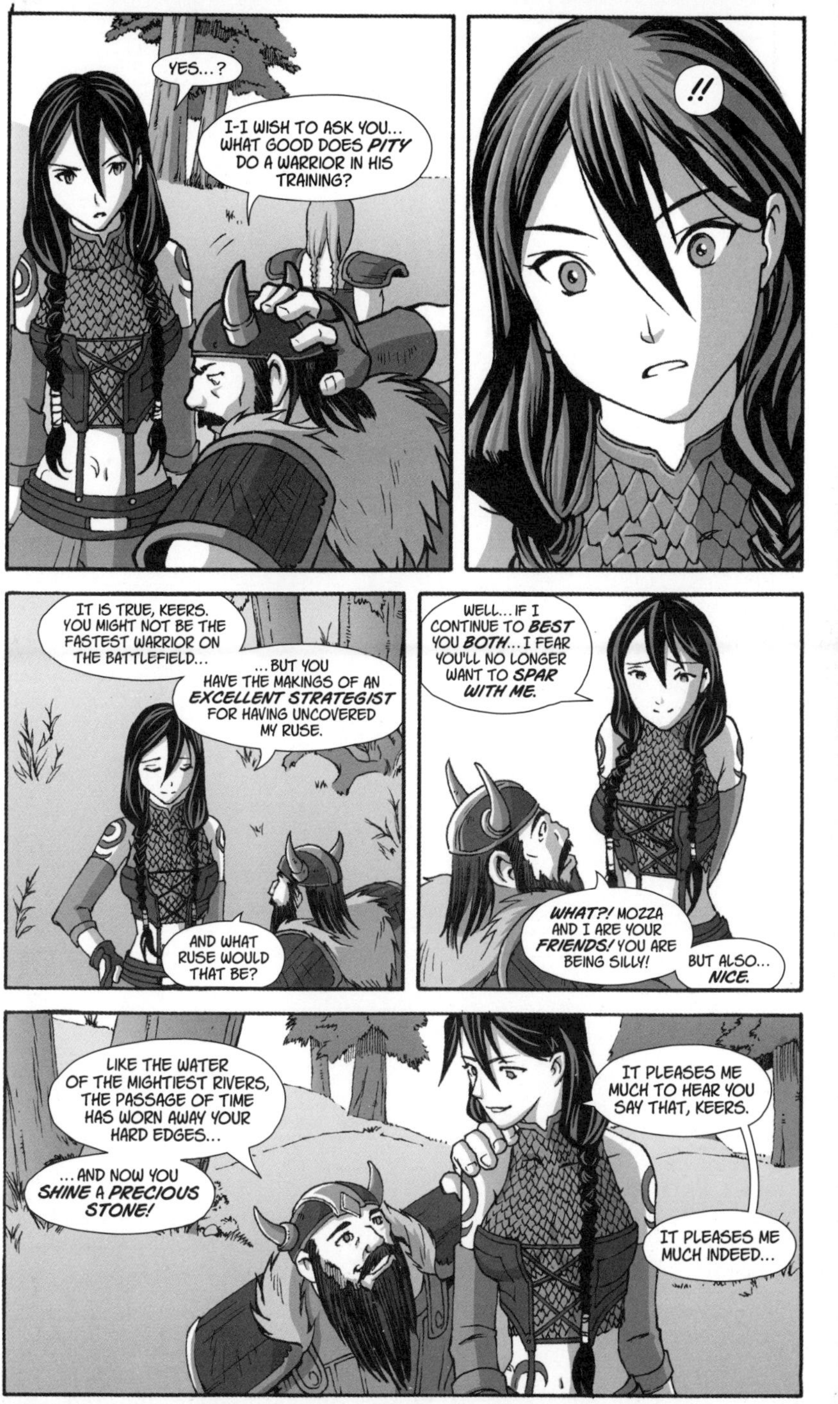
YES...?
I-I WISH TO ASK YOU... WHAT GOOD DOES *PITY* DO A WARRIOR IN HIS TRAINING?
!!
IT IS TRUE, KEERS. YOU MIGHT NOT BE THE FASTEST WARRIOR ON THE BATTLEFIELD...
...BUT YOU HAVE THE MAKINGS OF AN ***EXCELLENT STRATEGIST*** FOR HAVING UNCOVERED MY RUSE.
AND WHAT RUSE WOULD THAT BE?
WELL... IF I CONTINUE TO ***BEST*** YOU ***BOTH***... I FEAR YOU'LL NO LONGER WANT TO ***SPAR WITH ME.***
WHAT?! MOZZA AND I ARE YOUR ***FRIENDS!*** YOU ARE BEING SILLY!
BUT ALSO... ***NICE.***
LIKE THE WATER OF THE MIGHTIEST RIVERS, THE PASSAGE OF TIME HAS WORN AWAY YOUR HARD EDGES...
...AND NOW YOU ***SHINE*** A ***PRECIOUS STONE!***
IT PLEASES ME MUCH TO HEAR YOU SAY THAT, KEERS.
IT PLEASES ME MUCH INDEED...

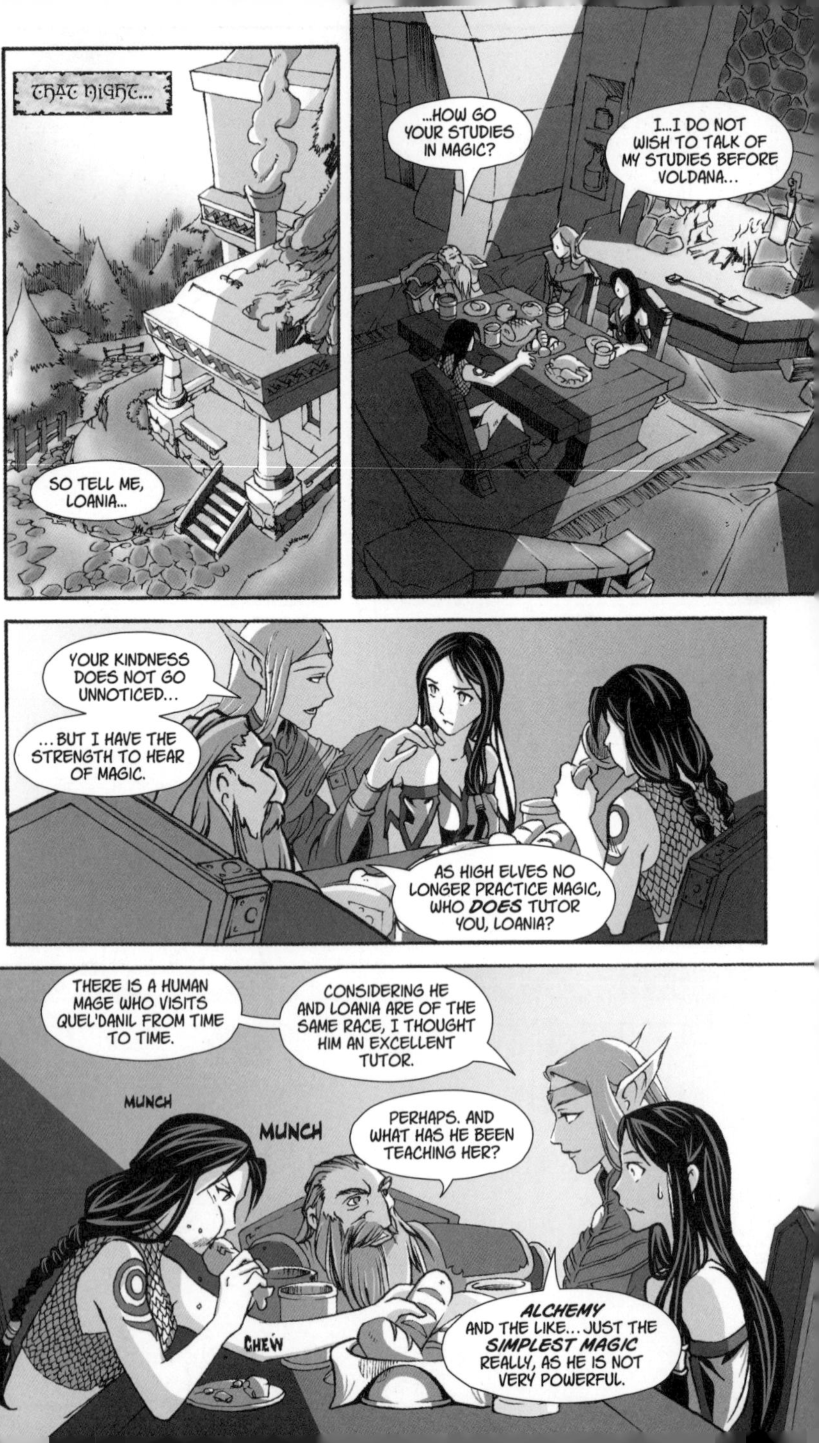
THAT NIGHT...
SO TELL ME, LOANIA...
...HOW GO YOUR STUDIES IN MAGIC?
I...I DO NOT WISH TO TALK OF MY STUDIES BEFORE VOLDANA...
YOUR KINDNESS DOES NOT GO UNNOTICED...
...BUT I HAVE THE STRENGTH TO HEAR OF MAGIC.
AS HIGH ELVES NO LONGER PRACTICE MAGIC, WHO ***DOES*** TUTOR YOU, LOANIA?
THERE IS A HUMAN MAGE WHO VISITS QUEL'DANIL FROM TIME TO TIME.
CONSIDERING HE AND LOANIA ARE OF THE SAME RACE, I THOUGHT HIM AN EXCELLENT TUTOR.
MUNCH
MUNCH
PERHAPS. AND WHAT HAS HE BEEN TEACHING HER?
CHEW
ALCHEMY AND THE LIKE... JUST THE ***SIMPLEST MAGIC*** REALLY, AS HE IS NOT VERY POWERFUL.

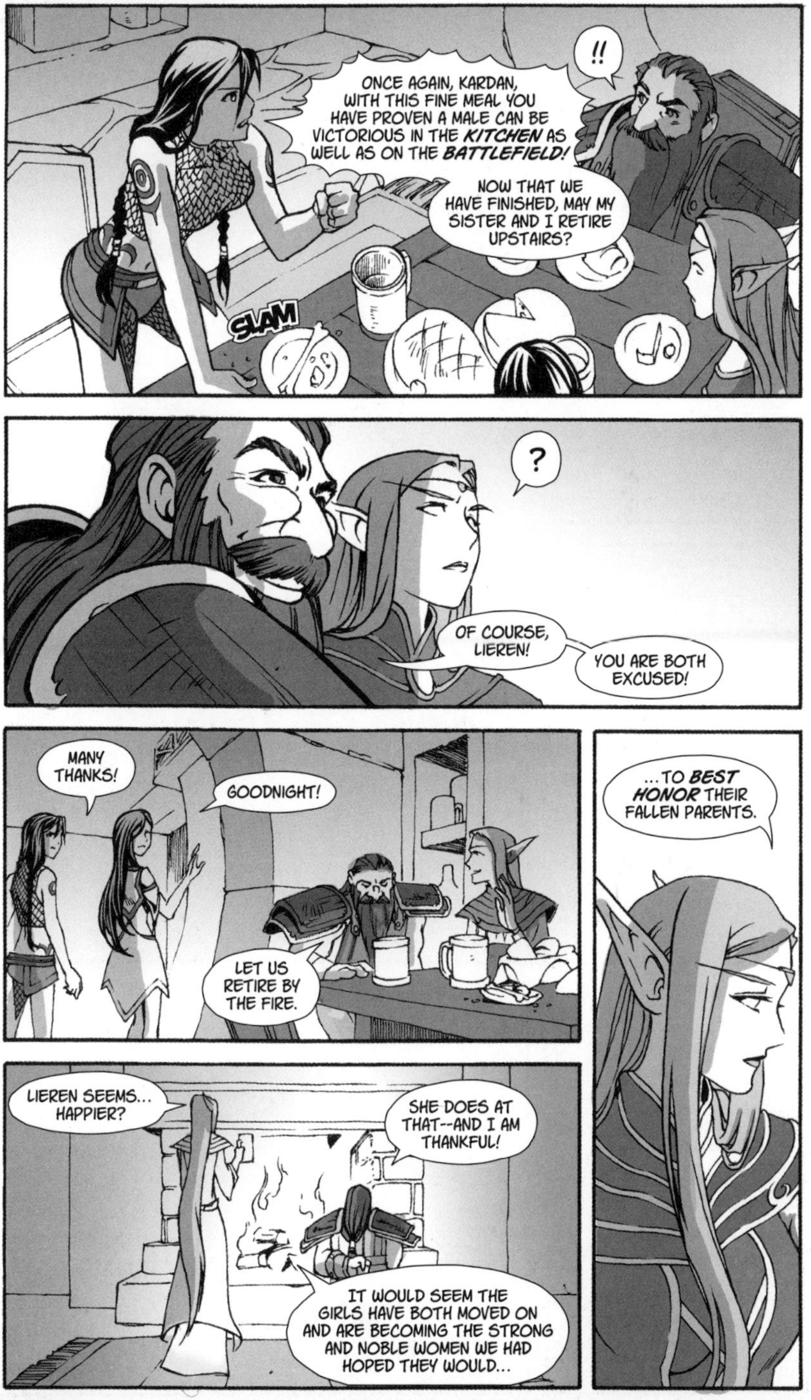
ONCE AGAIN, KARDAN, WITH THIS FINE MEAL YOU HAVE PROVEN A MALE CAN BE VICTORIOUS IN THE KITCHEN AS WELL AS ON THE BATTLEFIELD!
!!
SLAM
NOW THAT WE HAVE FINISHED, MAY MY SISTER AND I RETIRE UPSTAIRS?
?
OF COURSE, LIEREN!
YOU ARE BOTH EXCUSED!
MANY THANKS!
GOODNIGHT!
LET US RETIRE BY THE FIRE.
LIEREN SEEMS... HAPPIER?
SHE DOES AT THAT--AND I AM THANKFUL!
IT WOULD SEEM THE GIRLS HAVE BOTH MOVED ON AND ARE BECOMING THE STRONG AND NOBLE WOMEN WE HAD HOPED THEY WOULD...
...TO BEST HONOR THEIR FALLEN PARENTS.

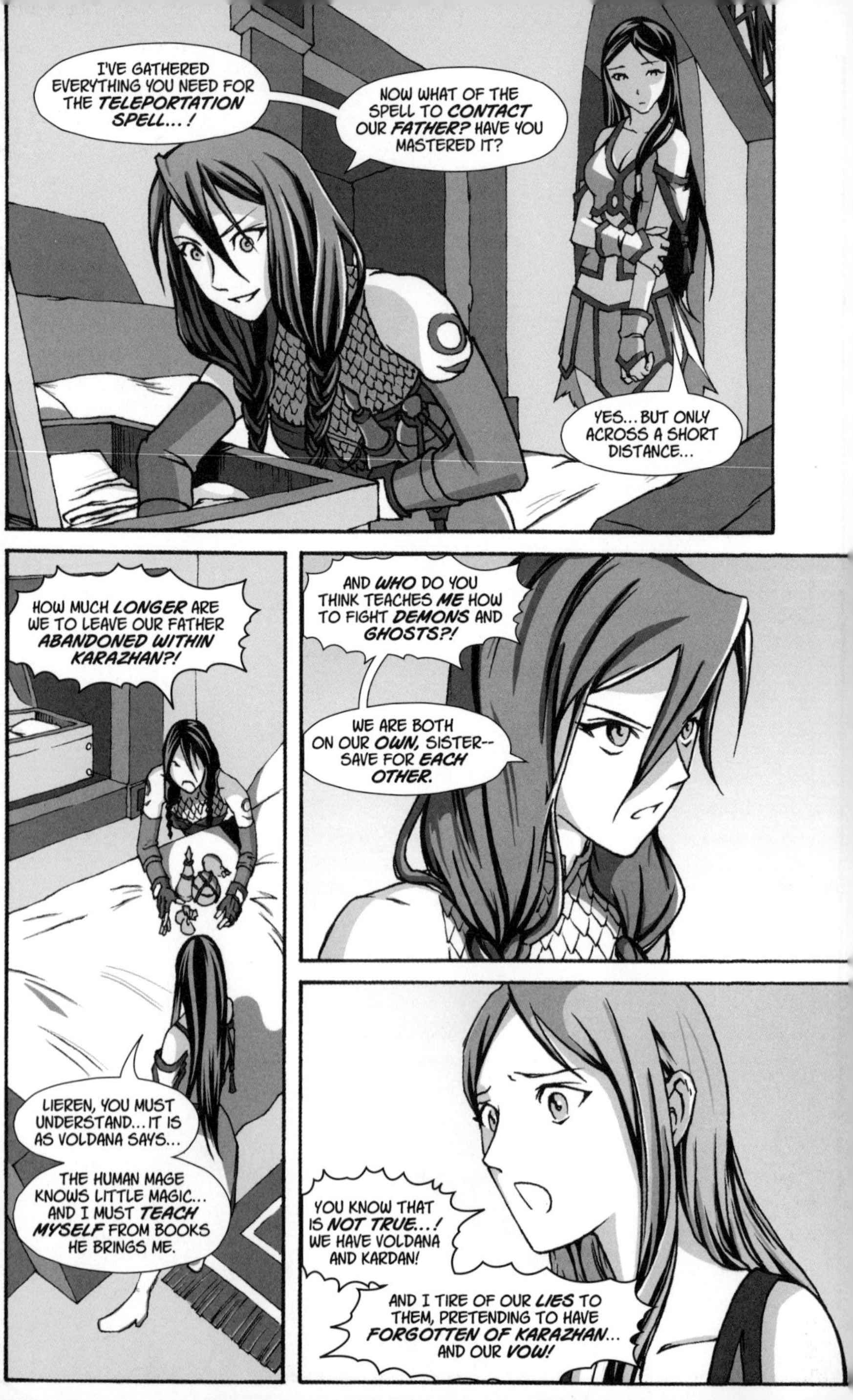
I'VE GATHERED EVERYTHING YOU NEED FOR THE ***TELEPORTATION SPELL...!***
NOW WHAT OF THE SPELL TO ***CONTACT*** OUR ***FATHER?*** HAVE YOU MASTERED IT?
YES... BUT ONLY ACROSS A SHORT DISTANCE...
HOW MUCH ***LONGER*** ARE WE TO LEAVE OUR FATHER ***ABANDONED WITHIN KARAZHAN?!***
LIEREN, YOU MUST UNDERSTAND... IT IS AS VOLDANA SAYS...
THE HUMAN MAGE KNOWS LITTLE MAGIC... AND I MUST ***TEACH MYSELF*** FROM BOOKS HE BRINGS ME.
AND ***WHO*** DO YOU THINK TEACHES ***ME*** HOW TO FIGHT ***DEMONS*** AND ***GHOSTS?!***
WE ARE BOTH ON OUR ***OWN,*** SISTER-- SAVE FOR ***EACH OTHER.***
YOU KNOW THAT IS ***NOT TRUE...!*** WE HAVE VOLDANA AND KARDAN!
AND I TIRE OF OUR ***LIES*** TO THEM, PRETENDING TO HAVE ***FORGOTTEN OF KARAZHAN...*** AND OUR ***VOW!***

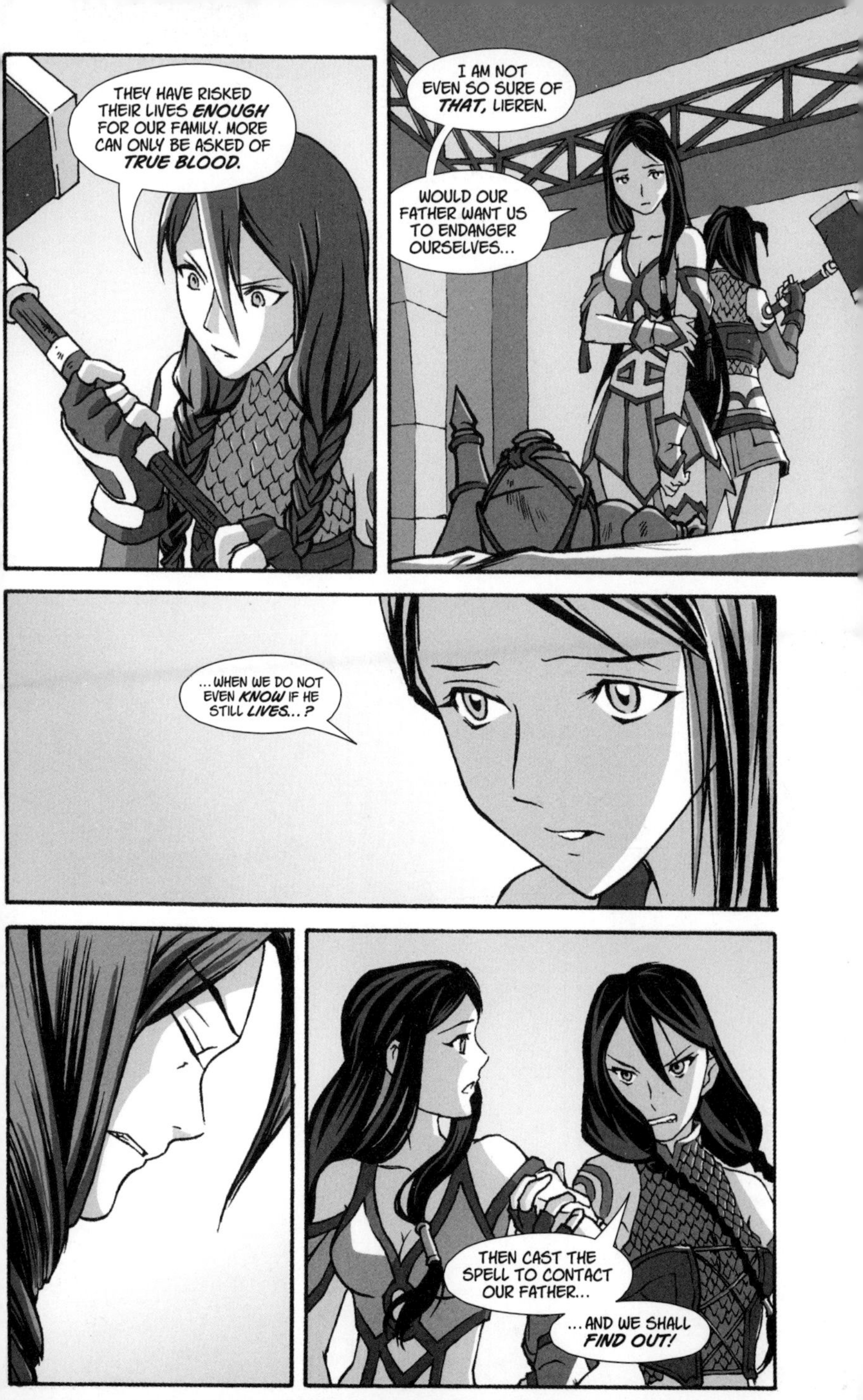
THEY HAVE RISKED THEIR LIVES ENOUGH FOR OUR FAMILY. MORE CAN ONLY BE ASKED OF TRUE BLOOD.
I AM NOT EVEN SO SURE OF THAT, LIEREN.
WOULD OUR FATHER WANT US TO ENDANGER OURSELVES...
...WHEN WE DO NOT EVEN KNOW IF HE STILL LIVES...?
THEN CAST THE SPELL TO CONTACT OUR FATHER...
...AND WE SHALL FIND OUT!

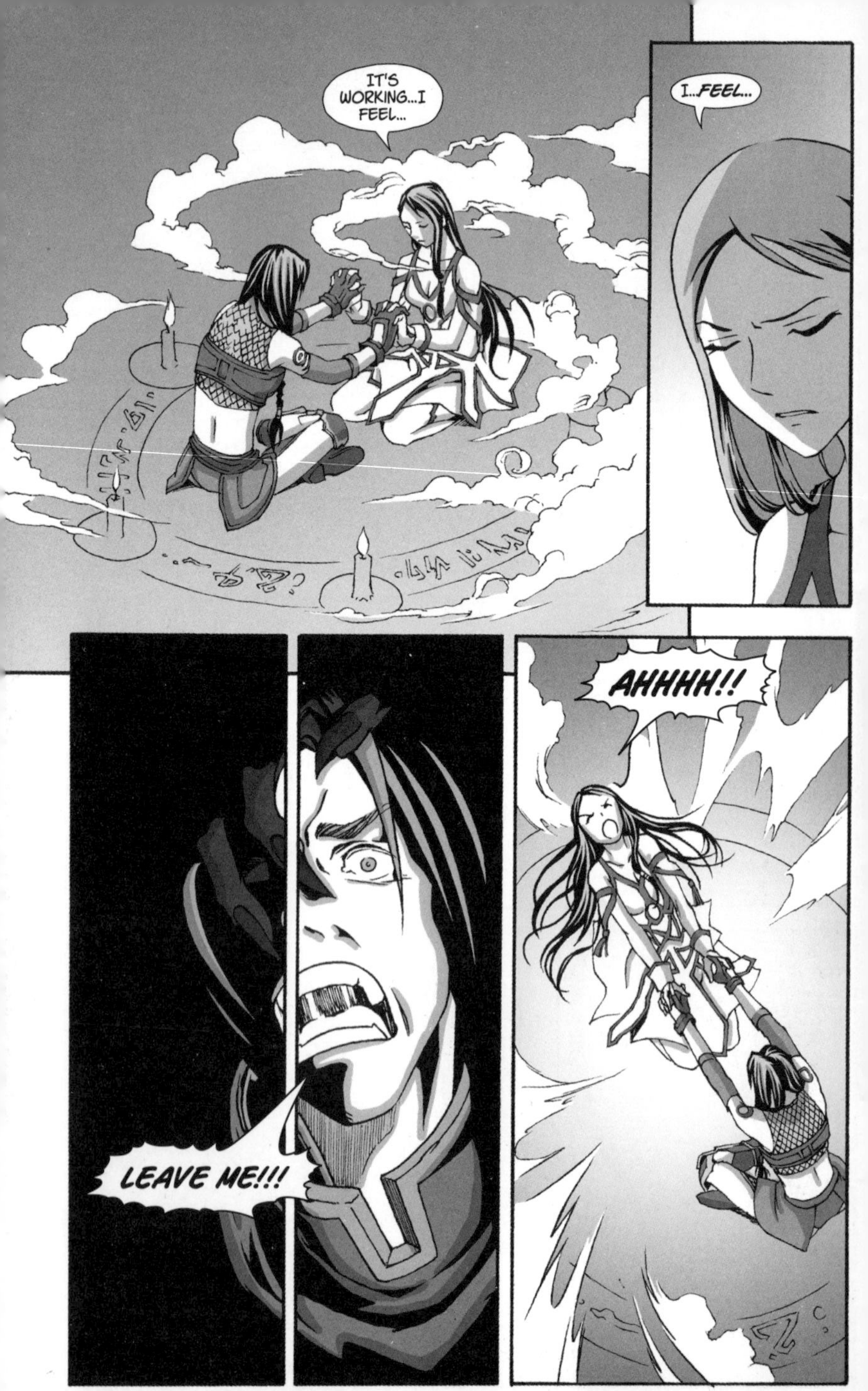
IT'S WORKING...I FEEL...
I...FEEL...
LEAVE ME!!!
AHHHH!!

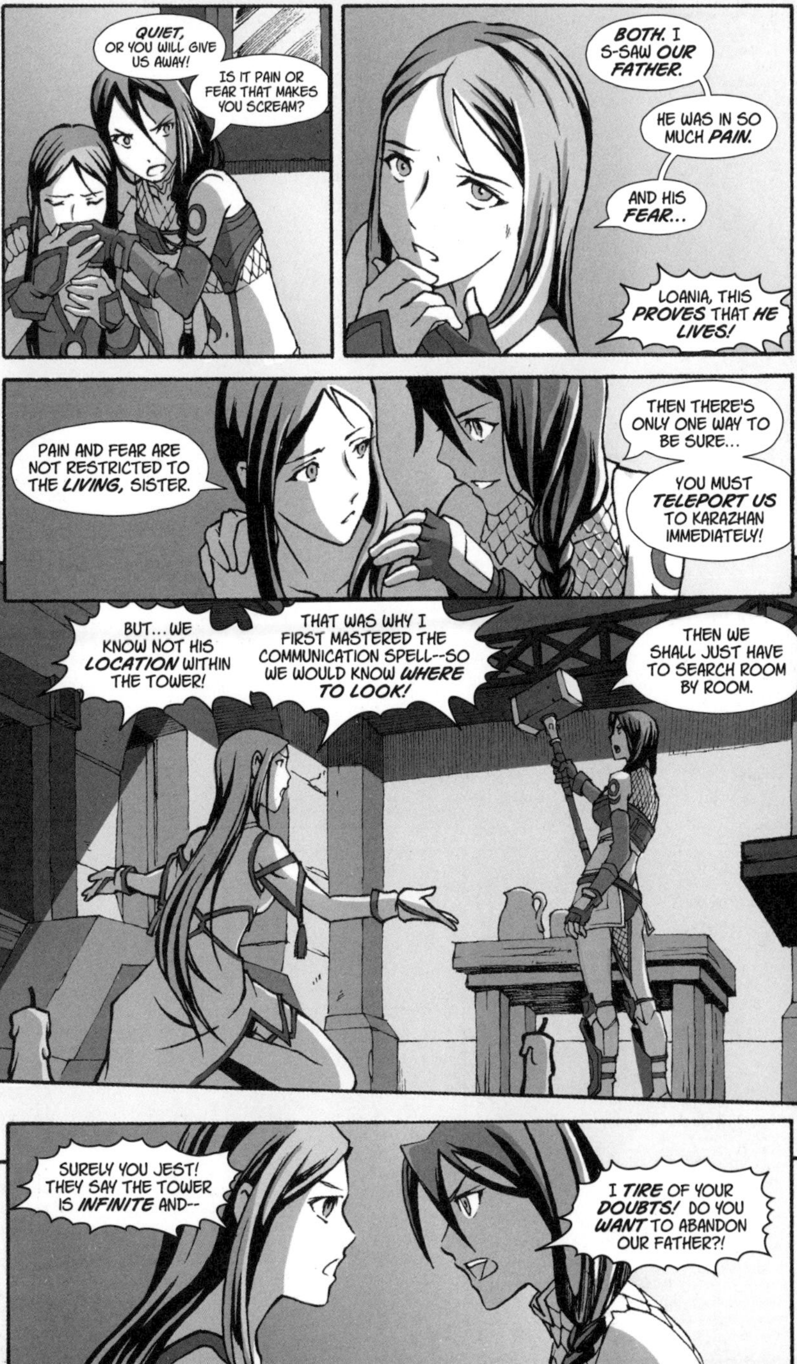
QUIET, OR YOU WILL GIVE US AWAY!
IS IT PAIN OR FEAR THAT MAKES YOU SCREAM?
BOTH. I S-SAW OUR FATHER.
HE WAS IN SO MUCH PAIN.
AND HIS FEAR...
LOANIA, THIS PROVES THAT HE LIVES!
PAIN AND FEAR ARE NOT RESTRICTED TO THE LIVING, SISTER.
THEN THERE'S ONLY ONE WAY TO BE SURE...
YOU MUST TELEPORT US TO KARAZHAN IMMEDIATELY!
BUT... WE KNOW NOT HIS LOCATION WITHIN THE TOWER!
THAT WAS WHY I FIRST MASTERED THE COMMUNICATION SPELL--SO WE WOULD KNOW WHERE TO LOOK!
THEN WE SHALL JUST HAVE TO SEARCH ROOM BY ROOM.
SURELY YOU JEST! THEY SAY THE TOWER IS INFINITE AND--
I TIRE OF YOUR DOUBTS! DO YOU WANT TO ABANDON OUR FATHER?!

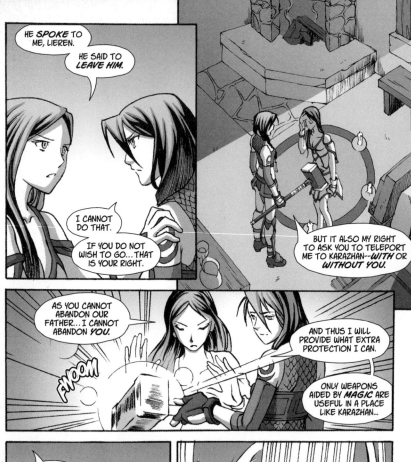

HE *SPOKE* TO ME, LIEREN.

HE SAID TO *LEAVE HIM.*

I CANNOT DO THAT.

IF YOU DO NOT WISH TO GO... THAT IS YOUR RIGHT.

BUT IT ALSO MY RIGHT TO ASK YOU TO TELEPORT ME TO KARAZHAN--*WITH* OR *WITHOUT YOU.*

AS YOU CANNOT ABANDON OUR FATHER... I CANNOT ABANDON *YOU.*

FWOOM

AND THUS I WILL PROVIDE WHAT EXTRA PROTECTION I CAN.

ONLY WEAPONS AIDED BY *MAGIC* ARE USEFUL IN A PLACE LIKE KARAZHAN...

READY?

YES.

FREEM

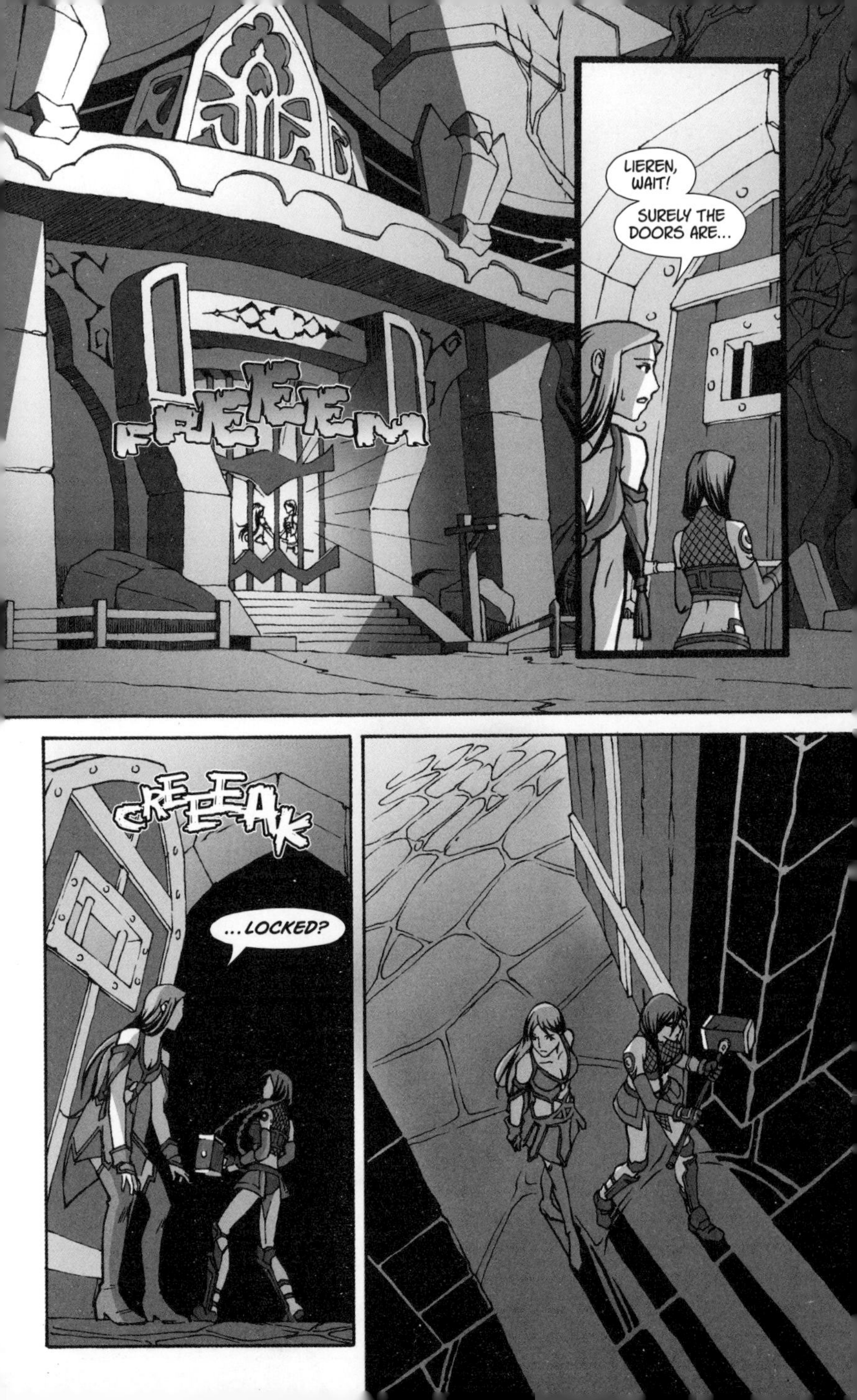
FREEEEM
LIEREN, WAIT!
SURELY THE DOORS ARE...
CREEEAK
...LOCKED?

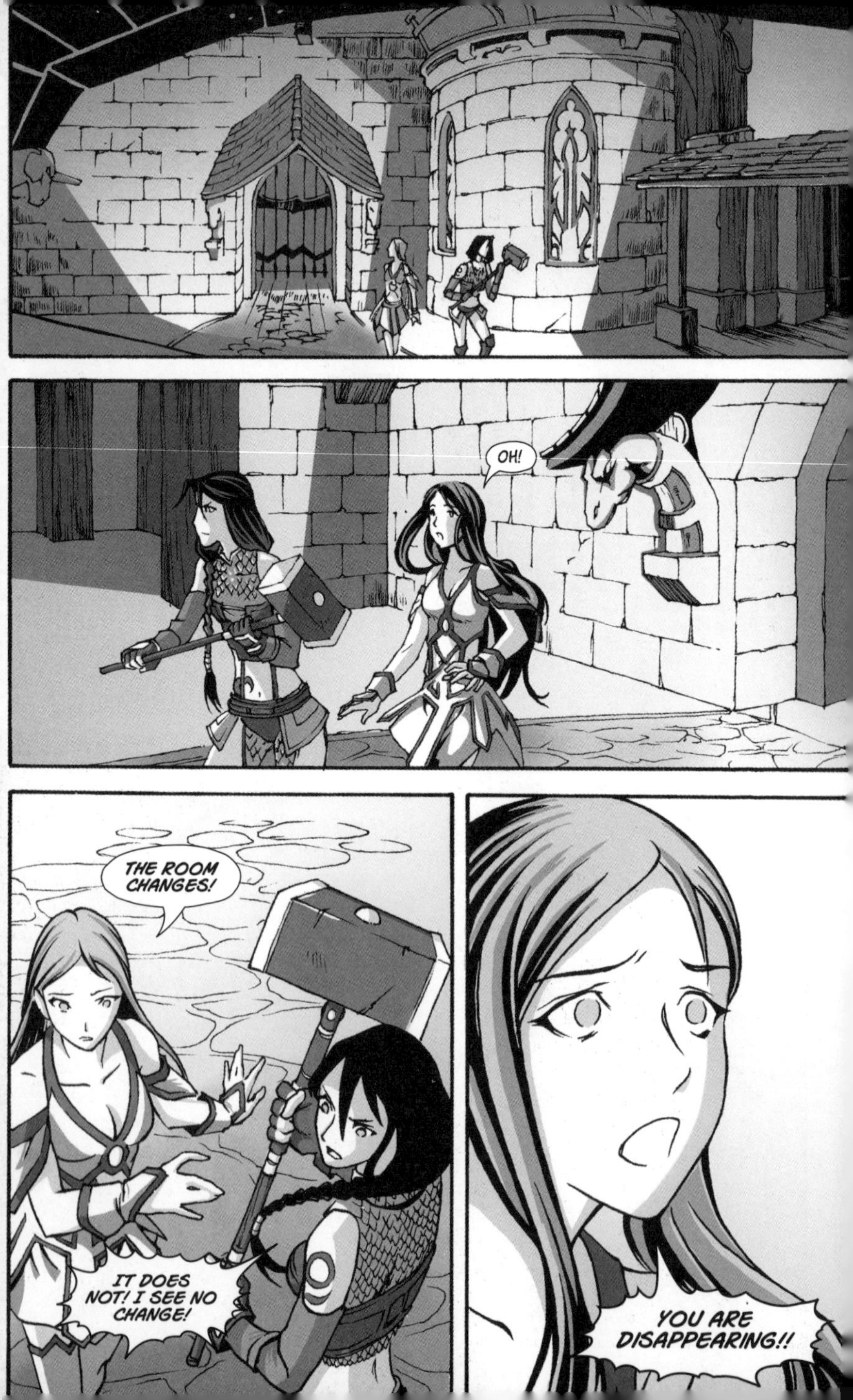
OH!
THE ROOM CHANGES!
IT DOES NOT! I SEE NO CHANGE!
YOU ARE DISAPPEARING!!

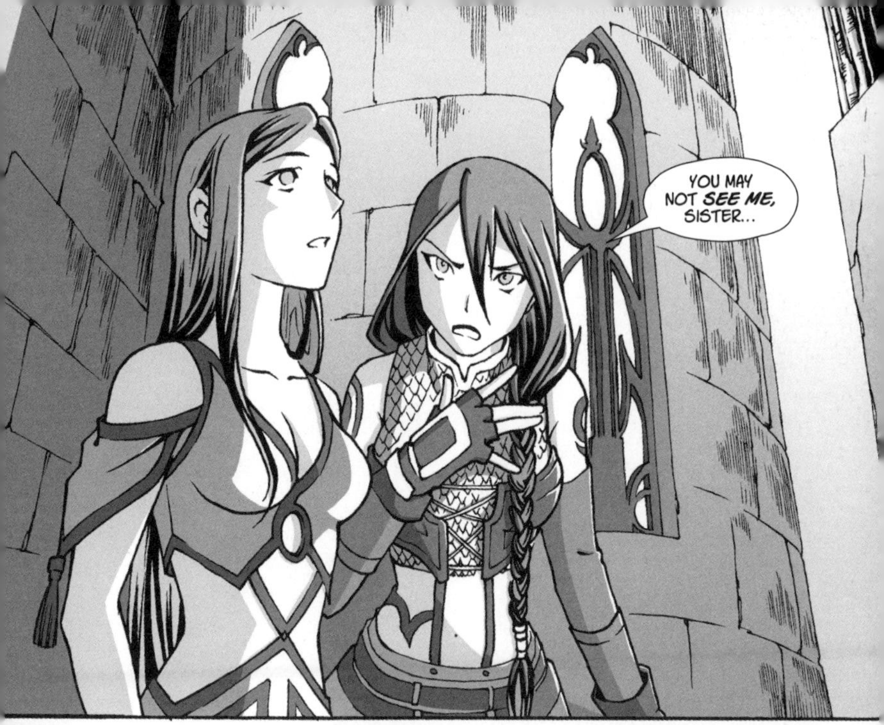
YOU MAY NOT SEE ME, SISTER...

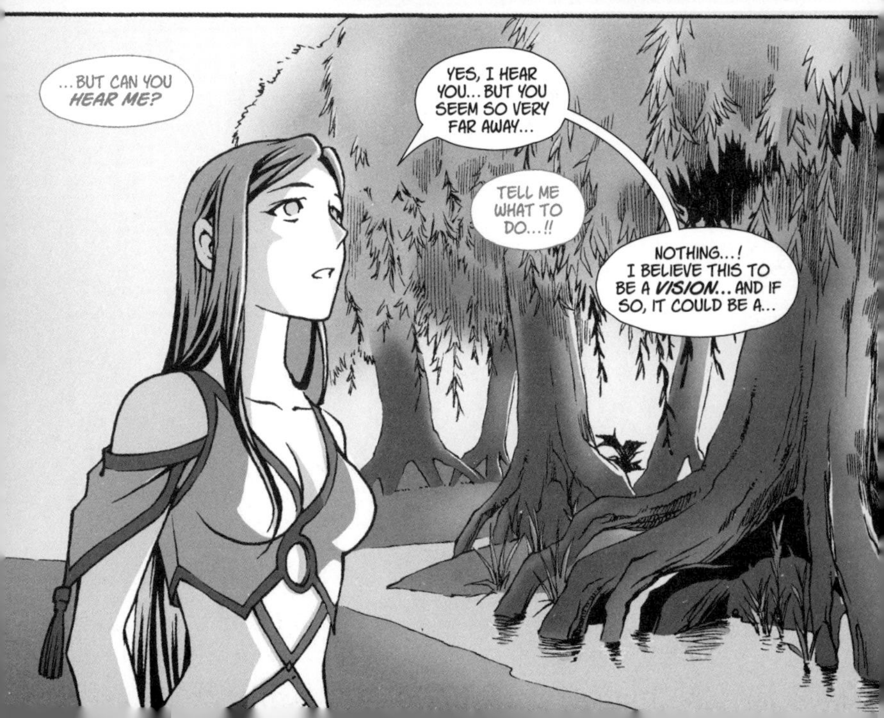
...BUT CAN YOU HEAR ME?
YES, I HEAR YOU... BUT YOU SEEM SO VERY FAR AWAY...
TELL ME WHAT TO DO...!!
NOTHING...! I BELIEVE THIS TO BE A VISION... AND IF SO, IT COULD BE A...

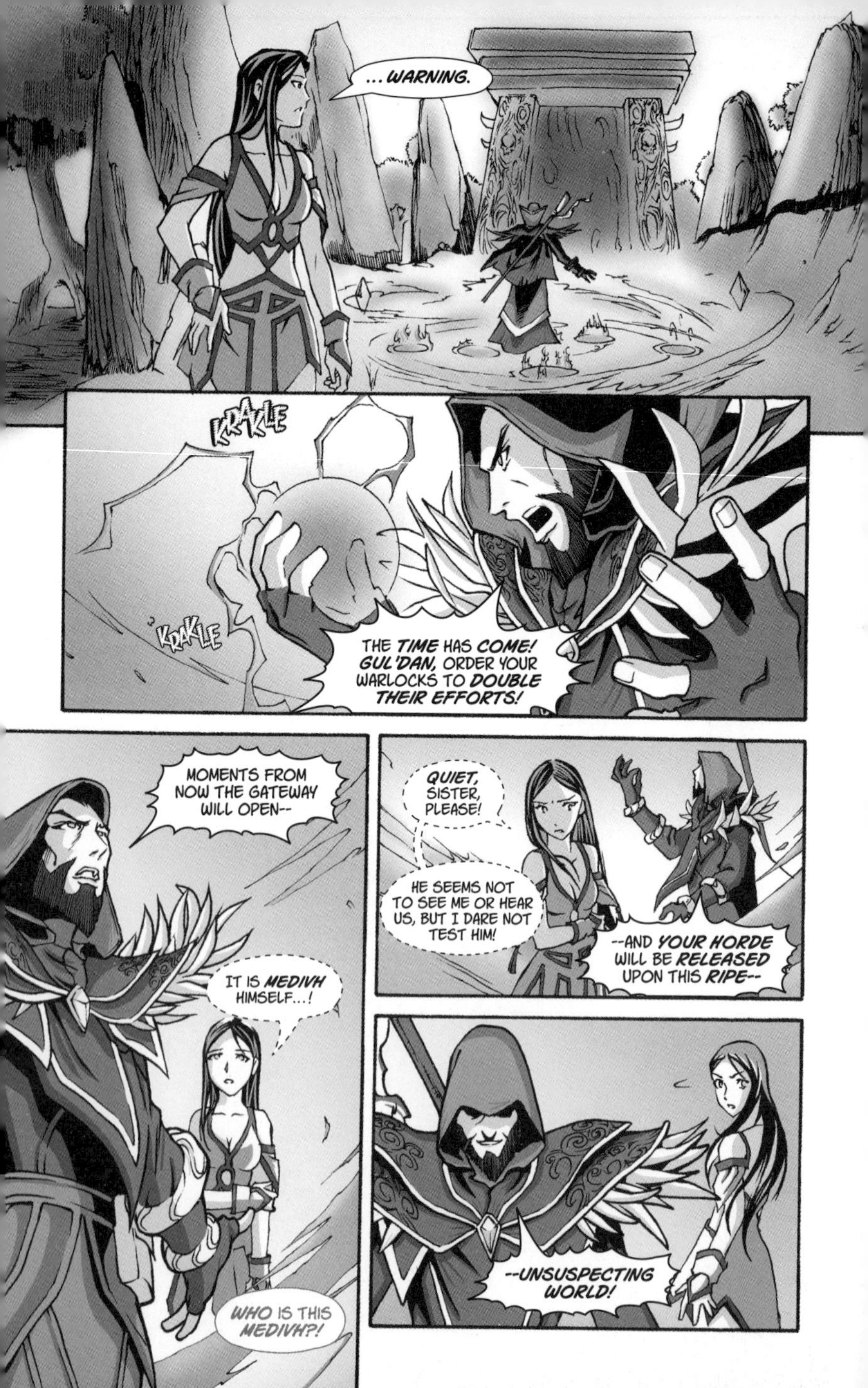
...WARNING.
KRAKLE
KRAKLE
THE TIME HAS COME! GUL'DAN, ORDER YOUR WARLOCKS TO DOUBLE THEIR EFFORTS!
MOMENTS FROM NOW THE GATEWAY WILL OPEN--
IT IS MEDIVH HIMSELF...!
WHO IS THIS MEDIVH?!
QUIET, SISTER, PLEASE!
HE SEEMS NOT TO SEE ME OR HEAR US, BUT I DARE NOT TEST HIM!
--AND YOUR HORDE WILL BE RELEASED UPON THIS RIPE--
--UNSUSPECTING WORLD!

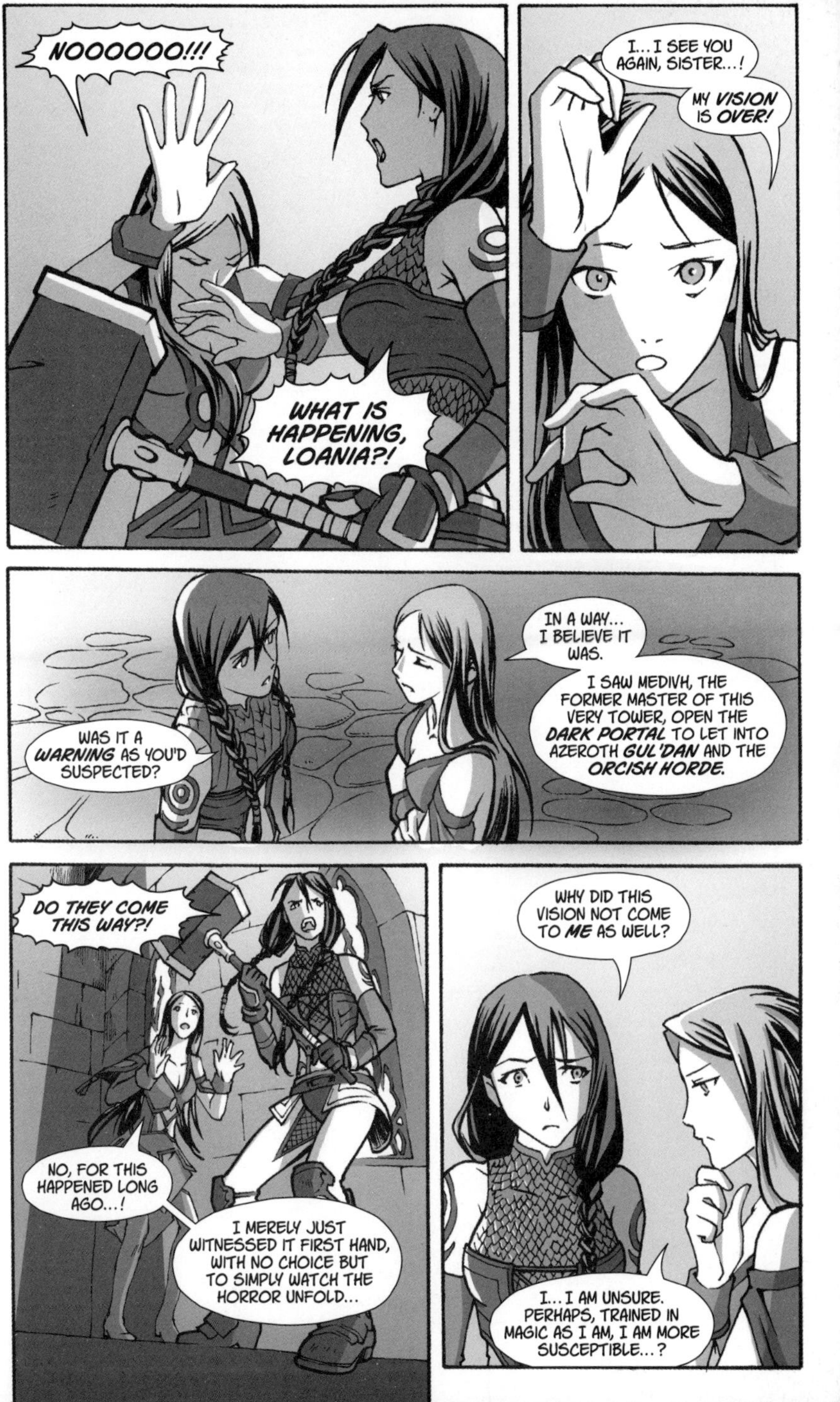
NOOOOOO!!!
WHAT IS HAPPENING, LOANIA?!
I... I SEE YOU AGAIN, SISTER...!
MY VISION IS OVER!
WAS IT A WARNING AS YOU'D SUSPECTED?
IN A WAY... I BELIEVE IT WAS.
I SAW MEDIVH, THE FORMER MASTER OF THIS VERY TOWER, OPEN THE DARK PORTAL TO LET INTO AZEROTH GUL'DAN AND THE ORCISH HORDE.
DO THEY COME THIS WAY?!
NO, FOR THIS HAPPENED LONG AGO...!
I MERELY JUST WITNESSED IT FIRST HAND, WITH NO CHOICE BUT TO SIMPLY WATCH THE HORROR UNFOLD...
WHY DID THIS VISION NOT COME TO ME AS WELL?
I... I AM UNSURE. PERHAPS, TRAINED IN MAGIC AS I AM, I AM MORE SUSCEPTIBLE...?

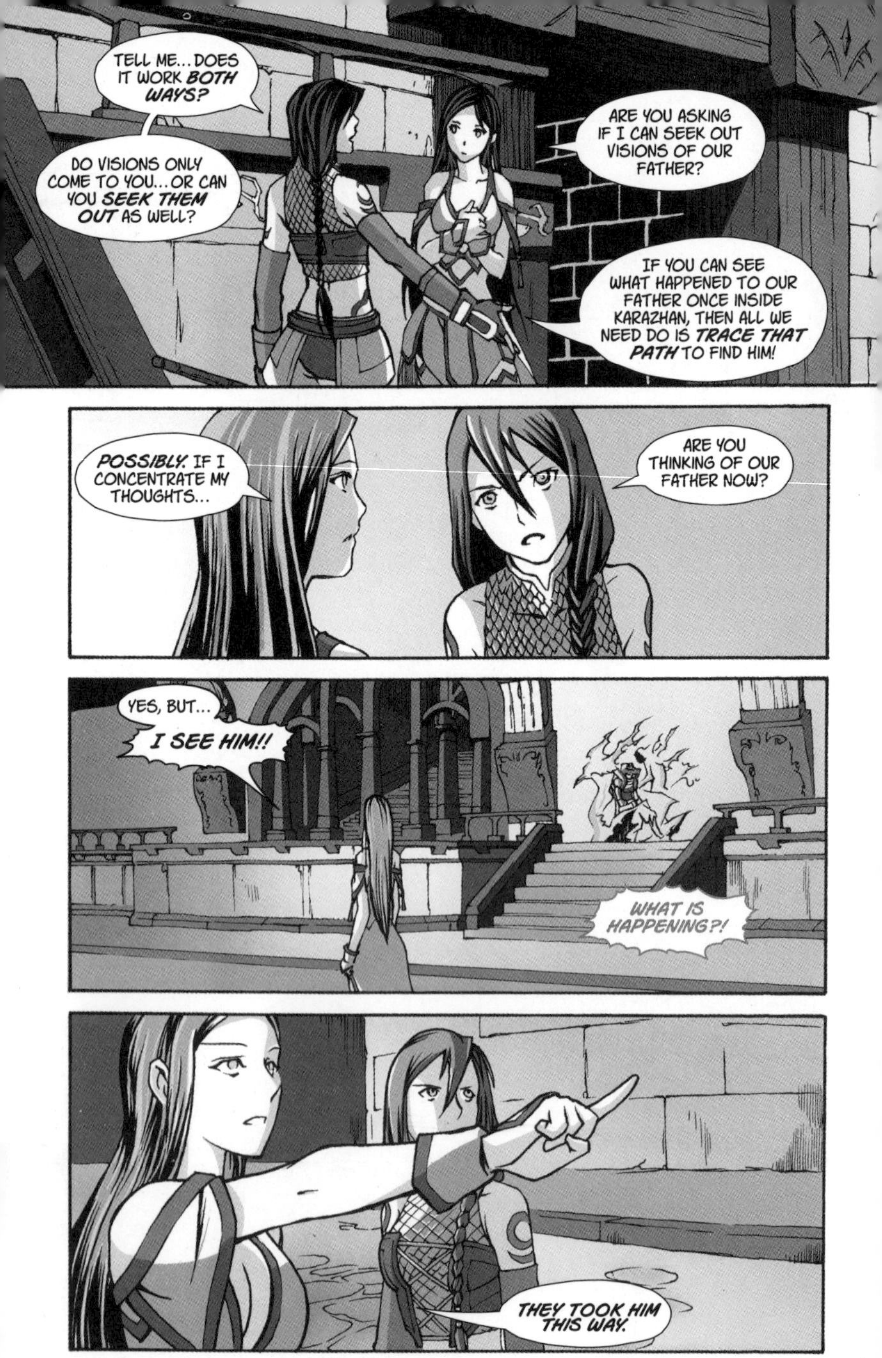
TELL ME... DOES IT WORK BOTH WAYS?
DO VISIONS ONLY COME TO YOU... OR CAN YOU SEEK THEM OUT AS WELL?
ARE YOU ASKING IF I CAN SEEK OUT VISIONS OF OUR FATHER?
IF YOU CAN SEE WHAT HAPPENED TO OUR FATHER ONCE INSIDE KARAZHAN, THEN ALL WE NEED DO IS TRACE THAT PATH TO FIND HIM!
POSSIBLY. IF I CONCENTRATE MY THOUGHTS...
ARE YOU THINKING OF OUR FATHER NOW?
YES, BUT...
I SEE HIM!!
WHAT IS HAPPENING?!
THEY TOOK HIM THIS WAY.

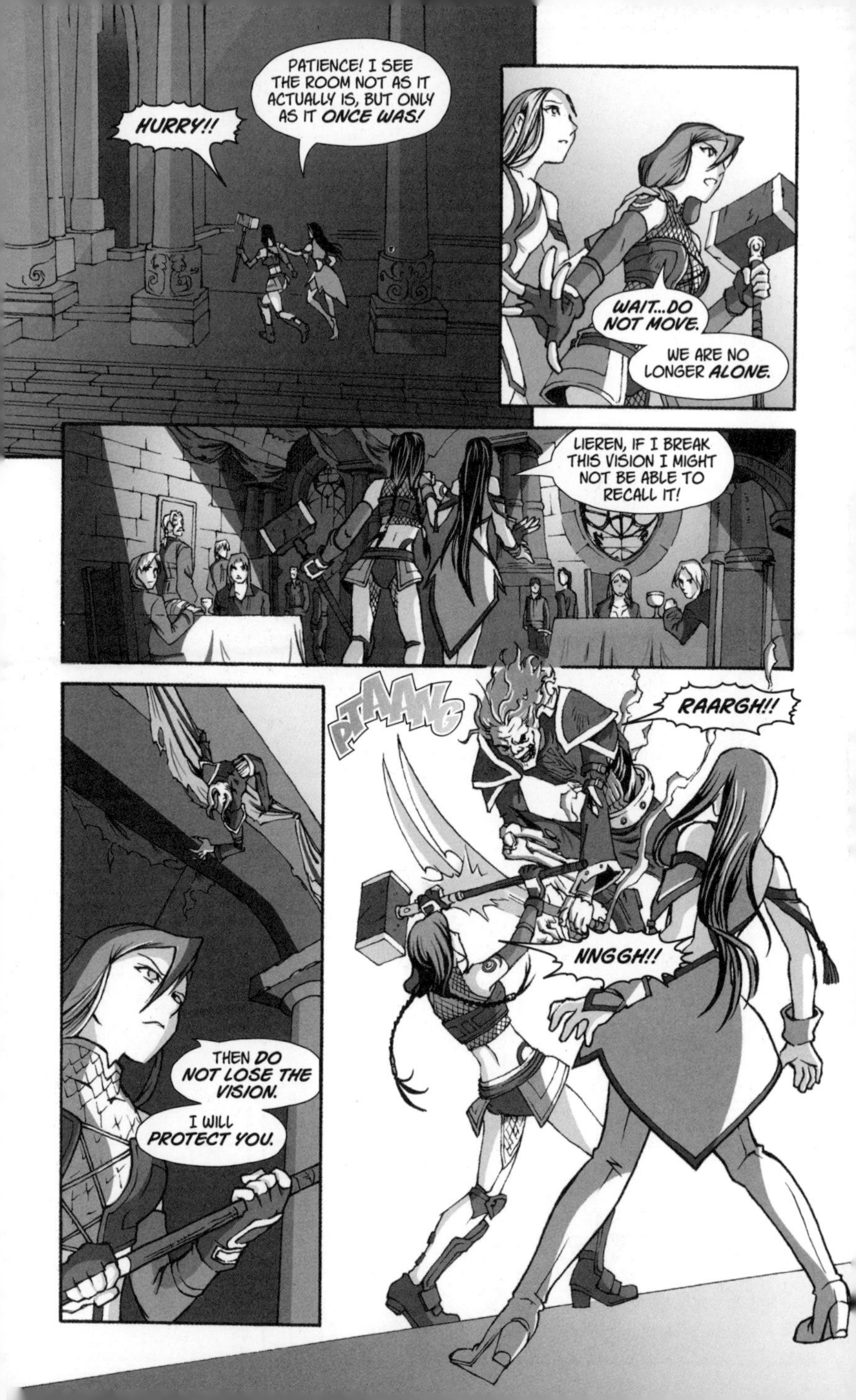
HURRY!!
PATIENCE! I SEE THE ROOM NOT AS IT ACTUALLY IS, BUT ONLY AS IT ONCE WAS!
WAIT...DO NOT MOVE.
WE ARE NO LONGER ALONE.
LIEREN, IF I BREAK THIS VISION I MIGHT NOT BE ABLE TO RECALL IT!
THEN DO NOT LOSE THE VISION.
I WILL PROTECT YOU.
PTAAANG
RAARGH!!
NNGGH!!

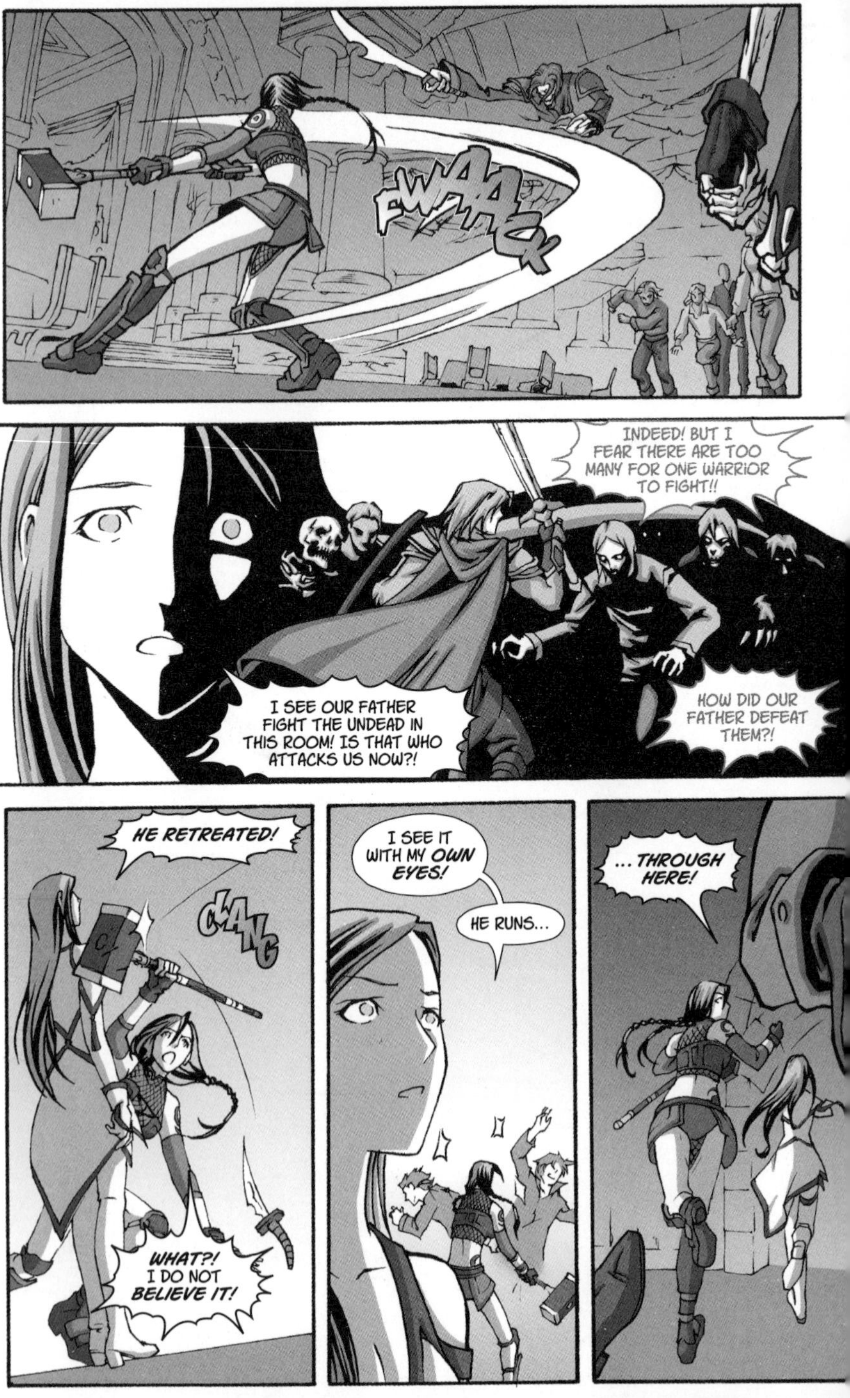
FWAACK
I SEE OUR FATHER FIGHT THE UNDEAD IN THIS ROOM! IS THAT WHO ATTACKS US NOW?!
INDEED! BUT I FEAR THERE ARE TOO MANY FOR ONE WARRIOR TO FIGHT!!
HOW DID OUR FATHER DEFEAT THEM?!
HE RETREATED!
CLANG
WHAT?! I DO NOT BELIEVE IT!
I SEE IT WITH MY OWN EYES!
HE RUNS...
... THROUGH HERE!

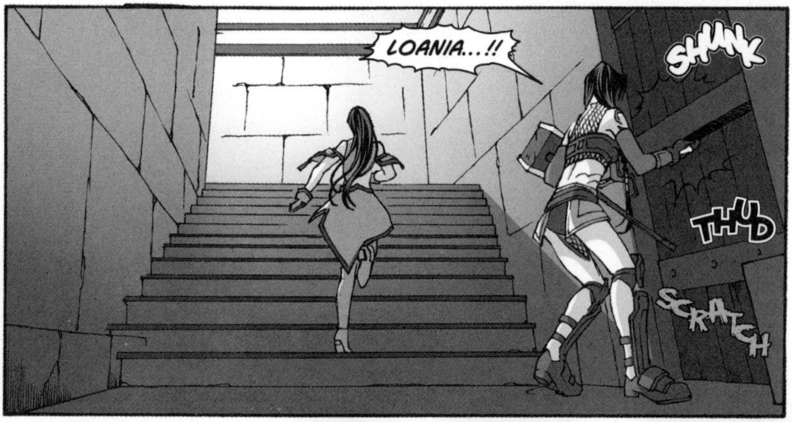
LOANIA...!!
SHUNK
THUD
SCRATCH

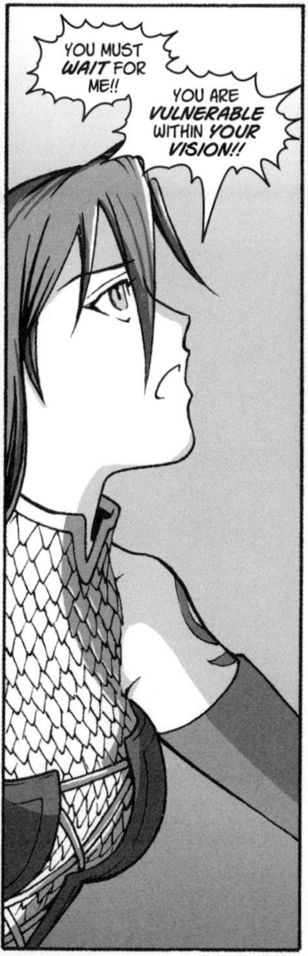
YOU MUST WAIT FOR ME!!
YOU ARE VULNERABLE WITHIN YOUR VISION!!

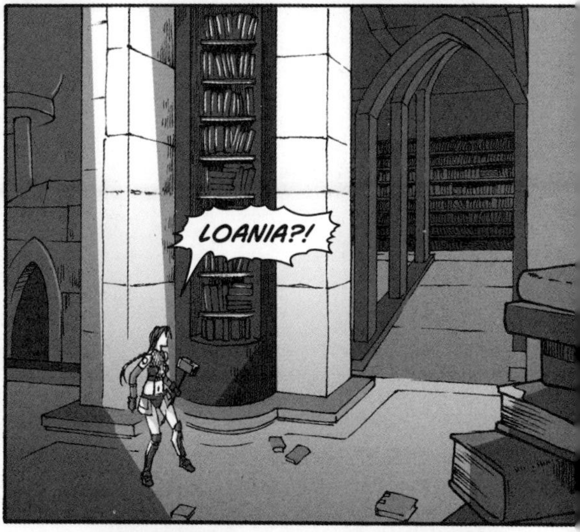
LOANIA?!

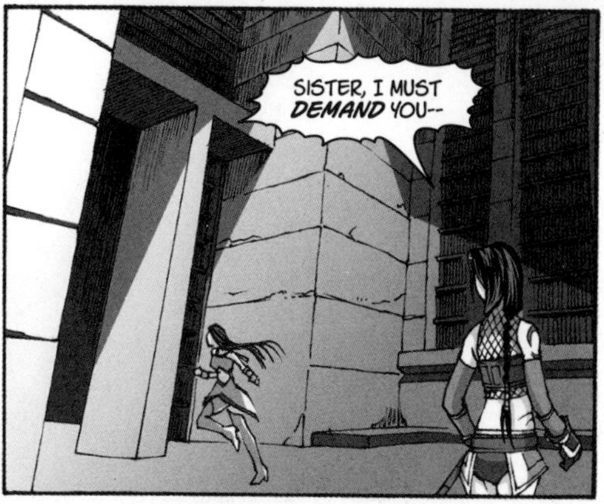
SISTER, I MUST DEMAND YOU--

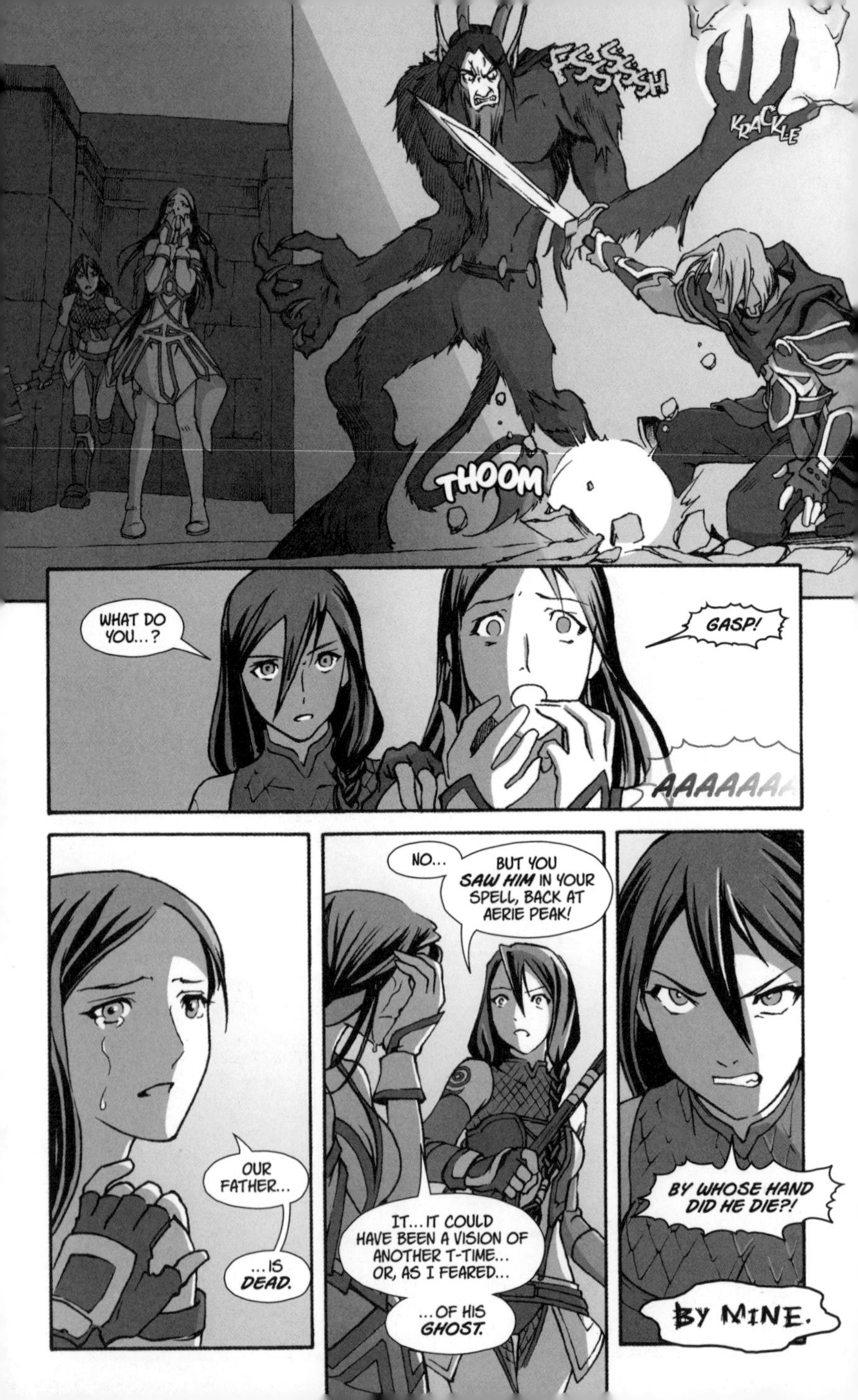
FSSSSH
KRACKLE
THOOM
WHAT DO YOU...?
GASP!
AAAAAAA
OUR FATHER...
...IS DEAD.
NO...
BUT YOU SAW HIM IN YOUR SPELL, BACK AT AERIE PEAK!
IT... IT COULD HAVE BEEN A VISION OF ANOTHER T-TIME... OR, AS I FEARED...
...OF HIS GHOST.
BY WHOSE HAND DID HE DIE?!
BY MINE.

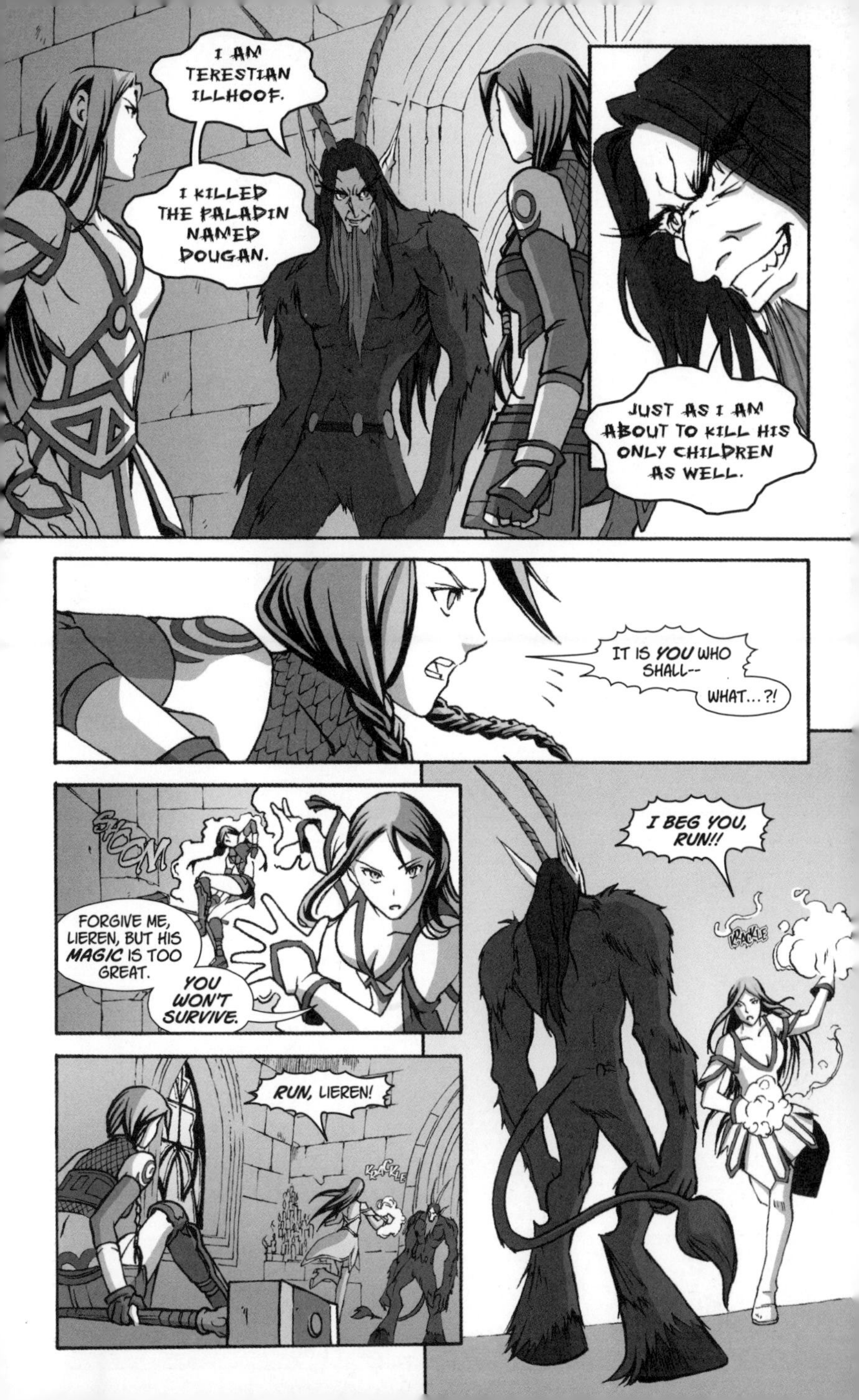
I AM TERESTIAN ILLHOOF.
I KILLED THE PALADIN NAMED DOUGAN.
JUST AS I AM ABOUT TO KILL HIS ONLY CHILDREN AS WELL.
IT IS *YOU* WHO SHALL--
WHAT...?!
SHOOM
FORGIVE ME, LIEREN, BUT HIS *MAGIC* IS TOO GREAT.
YOU WON'T SURVIVE.
I BEG YOU, RUN!!
KRACKLE
RUN, LIEREN!
KRACKLE

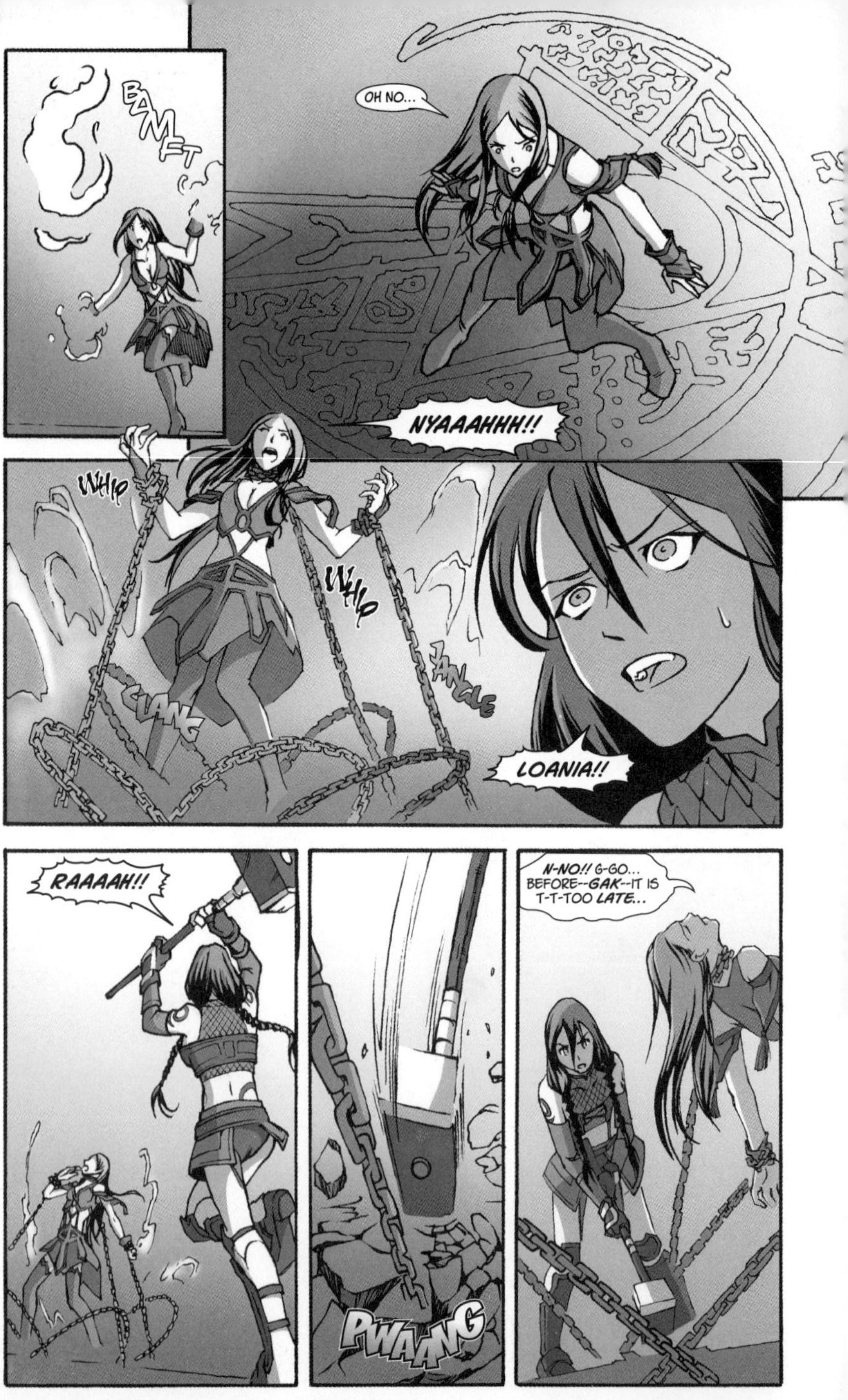
BAMFT
OH NO...
NYAAAHHH!!
WHIP
WHIP
CLANG
JANGLE
LOANIA!!
RAAAAH!!
PWAAANG
N-NO!! G-GO... BEFORE--GAK--IT IS T-T-TOO LATE...

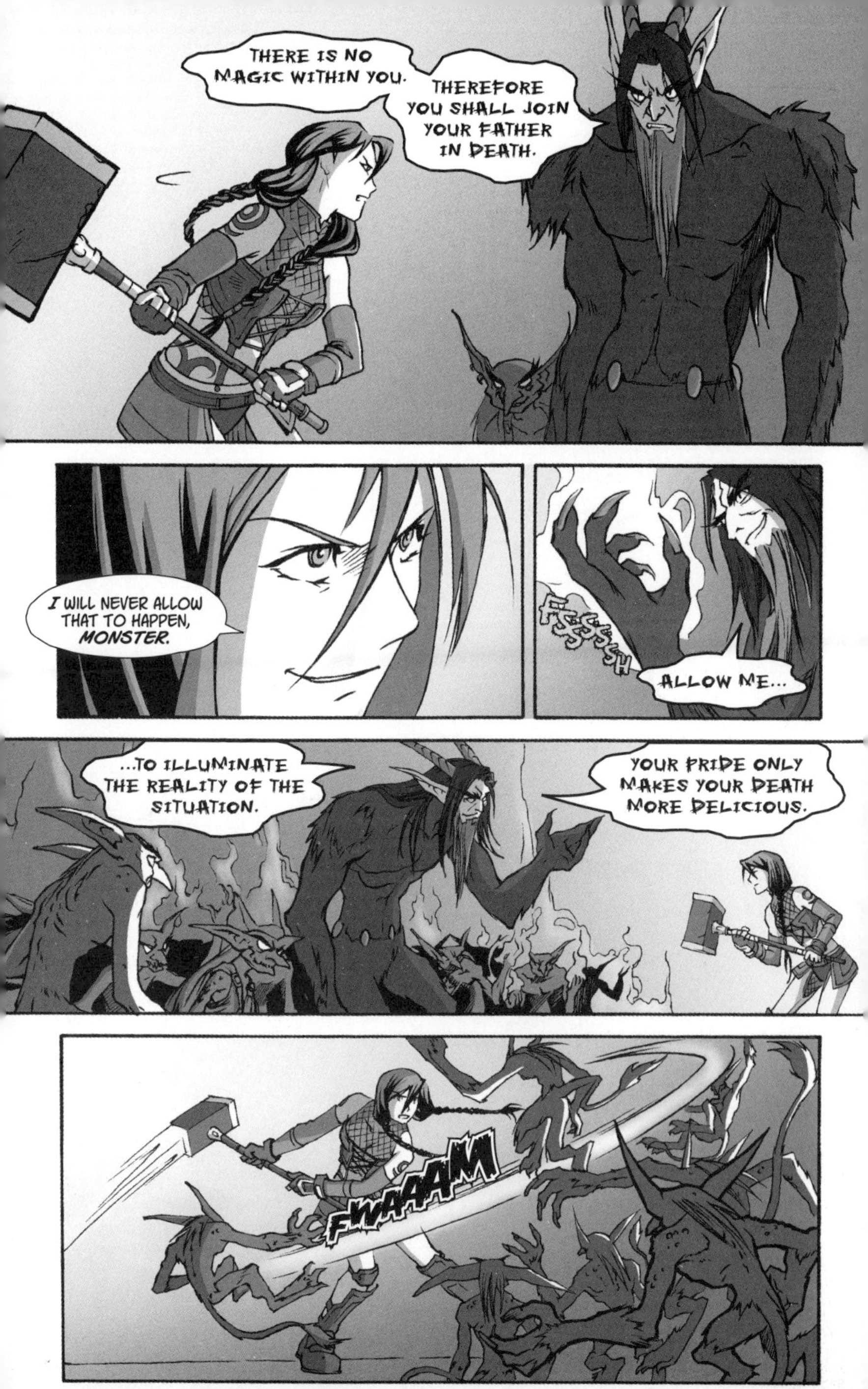
THERE IS NO MAGIC WITHIN YOU.
THEREFORE YOU SHALL JOIN YOUR FATHER IN DEATH.
I WILL NEVER ALLOW THAT TO HAPPEN, MONSTER.
FSSSSH
ALLOW ME...
...TO ILLUMINATE THE REALITY OF THE SITUATION.
YOUR PRIDE ONLY MAKES YOUR DEATH MORE DELICIOUS.
FWAAAM

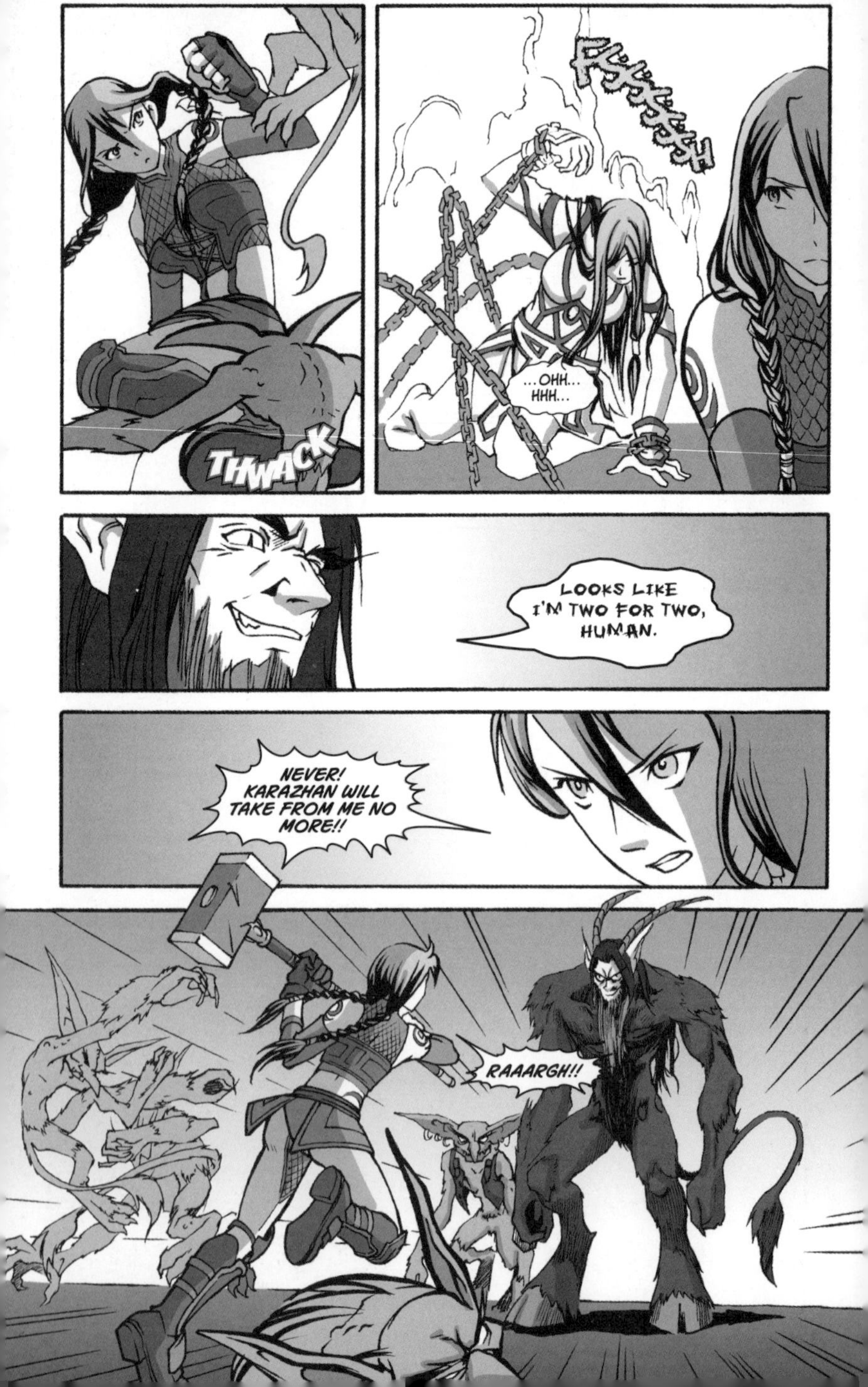
THWACK
FSSSSSH
...OHH... HHH...
LOOKS LIKE I'M TWO FOR TWO, HUMAN.
NEVER! KARAZHAN WILL TAKE FROM ME NO MORE!!
RAAARGH!!

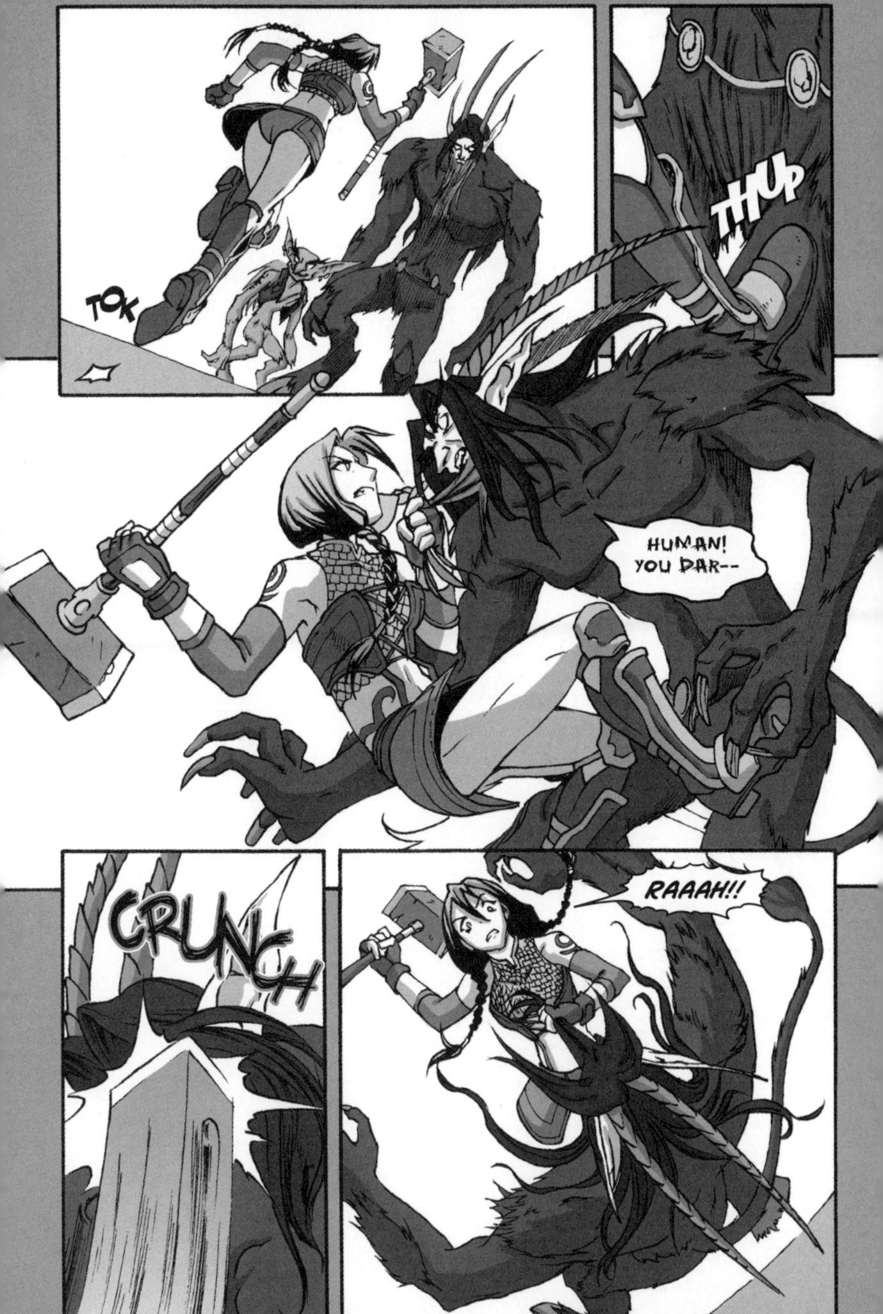
TOK
THUP
HUMAN! YOU DAR--
CRUNCH
RAAAH!!

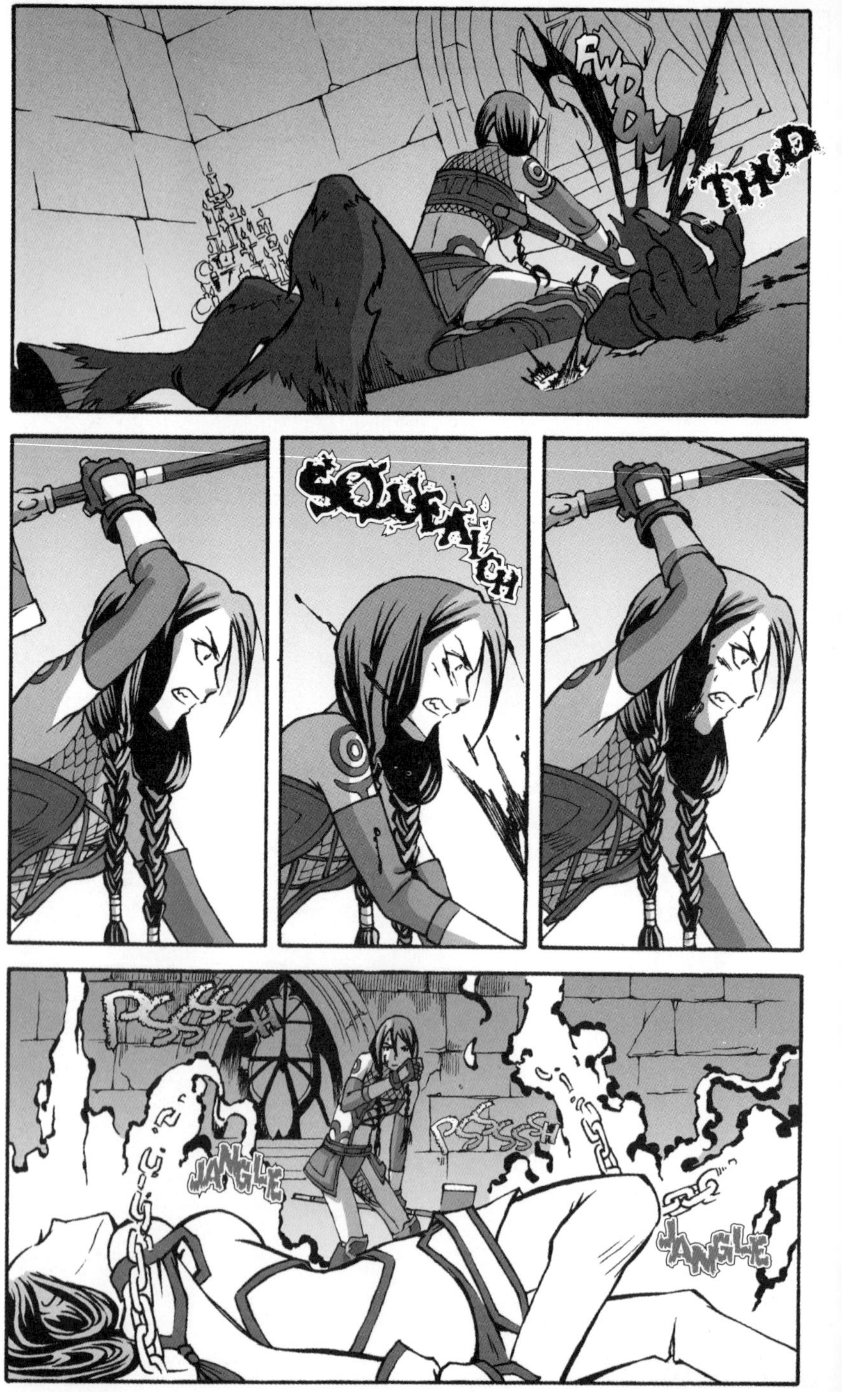
FWBOM
THUD
SQUEALCH
JANGLE
PSSSH
PSSSH
JANGLE

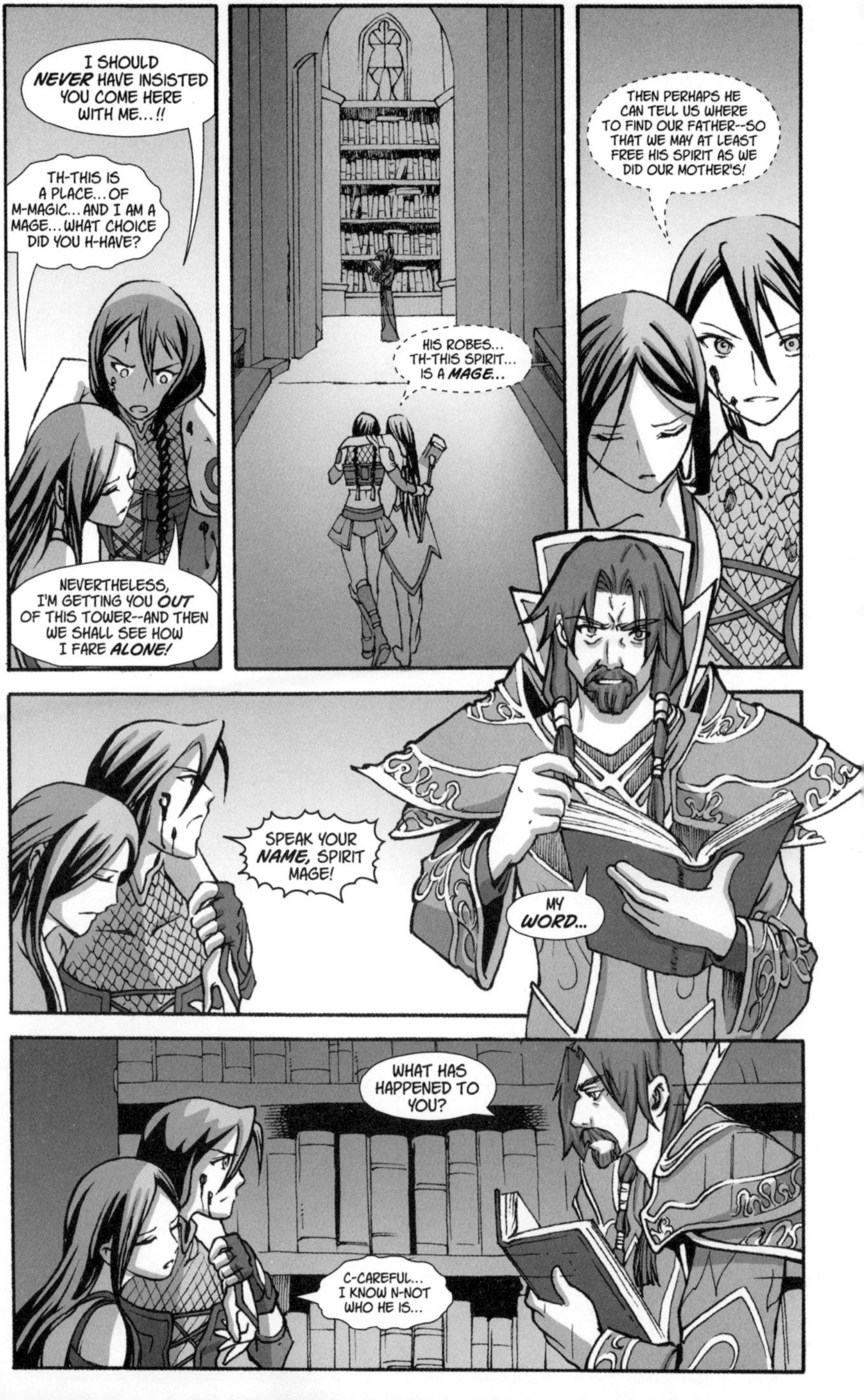
I SHOULD ***NEVER*** HAVE INSISTED YOU COME HERE WITH ME...!!
TH-THIS IS A PLACE... OF M-MAGIC... AND I AM A MAGE... WHAT CHOICE DID YOU H-HAVE?
NEVERTHELESS, I'M GETTING YOU ***OUT*** OF THIS TOWER--AND THEN WE SHALL SEE HOW I FARE ***ALONE!***
HIS ROBES... TH-THIS SPIRIT... IS A ***MAGE...***
THEN PERHAPS HE CAN TELL US WHERE TO FIND OUR FATHER--SO THAT WE MAY AT LEAST FREE HIS SPIRIT AS WE DID OUR MOTHER'S!
SPEAK YOUR ***NAME,*** SPIRIT MAGE!
MY ***WORD...***
WHAT HAS HAPPENED TO YOU?
C-CAREFUL... I KNOW N-NOT WHO HE IS...

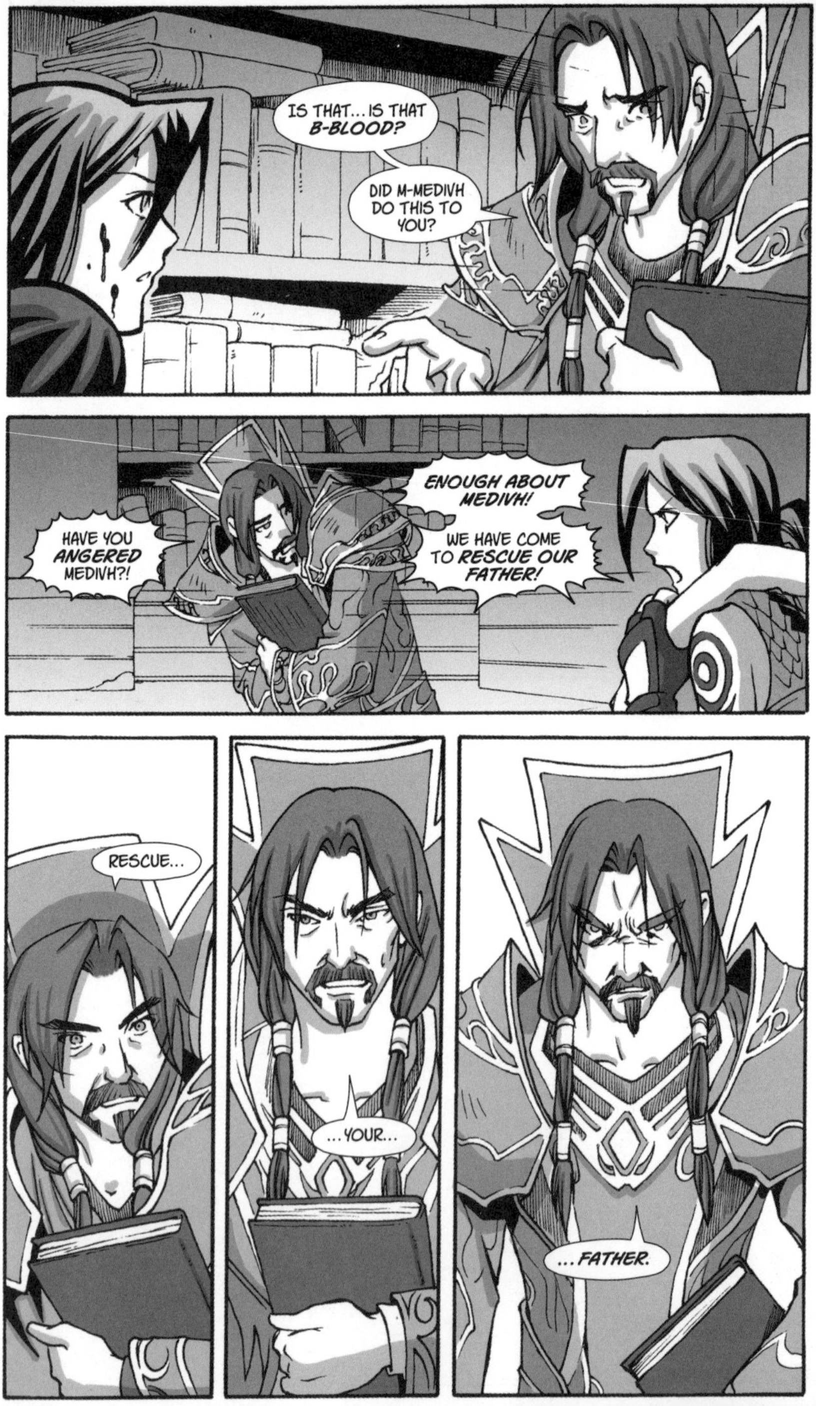
IS THAT... IS THAT B-BLOOD?
DID M-MEDIVH DO THIS TO YOU?
HAVE YOU ANGERED MEDIVH?!
ENOUGH ABOUT MEDIVH!
WE HAVE COME TO RESCUE OUR FATHER!
RESCUE...
...YOUR...
...FATHER.

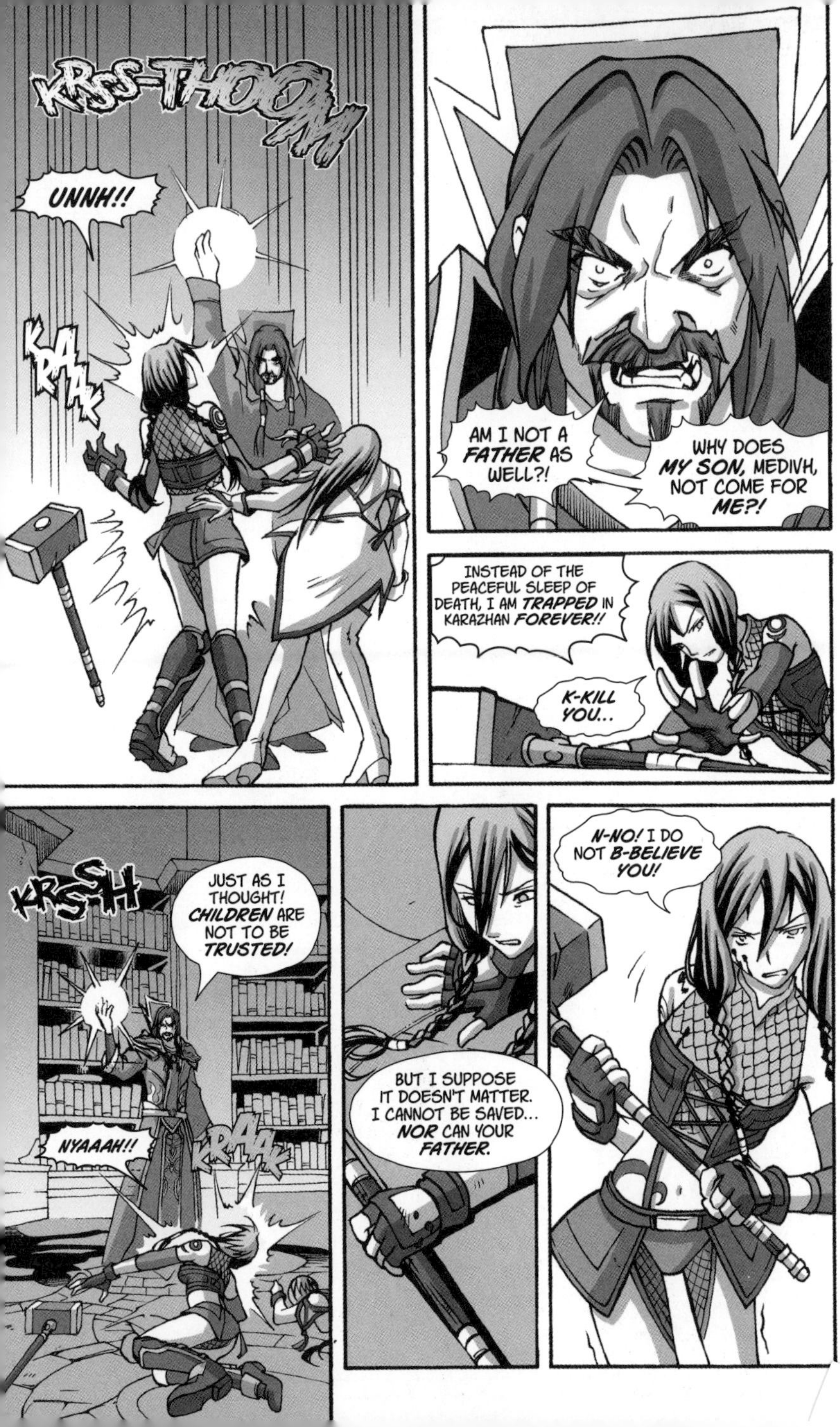
KRSS-THOOM
UNNH!!
KARAK
AM I NOT A FATHER AS WELL?!
WHY DOES MY SON, MEDIVH, NOT COME FOR ME?!
INSTEAD OF THE PEACEFUL SLEEP OF DEATH, I AM TRAPPED IN KARAZHAN FOREVER!!
K-KILL YOU...
KRSSH
JUST AS I THOUGHT! CHILDREN ARE NOT TO BE TRUSTED!
NYAAAH!!
KRAAK
BUT I SUPPOSE IT DOESN'T MATTER. I CANNOT BE SAVED... NOR CAN YOUR FATHER.
N-NO! I DO NOT B-BELIEVE YOU!

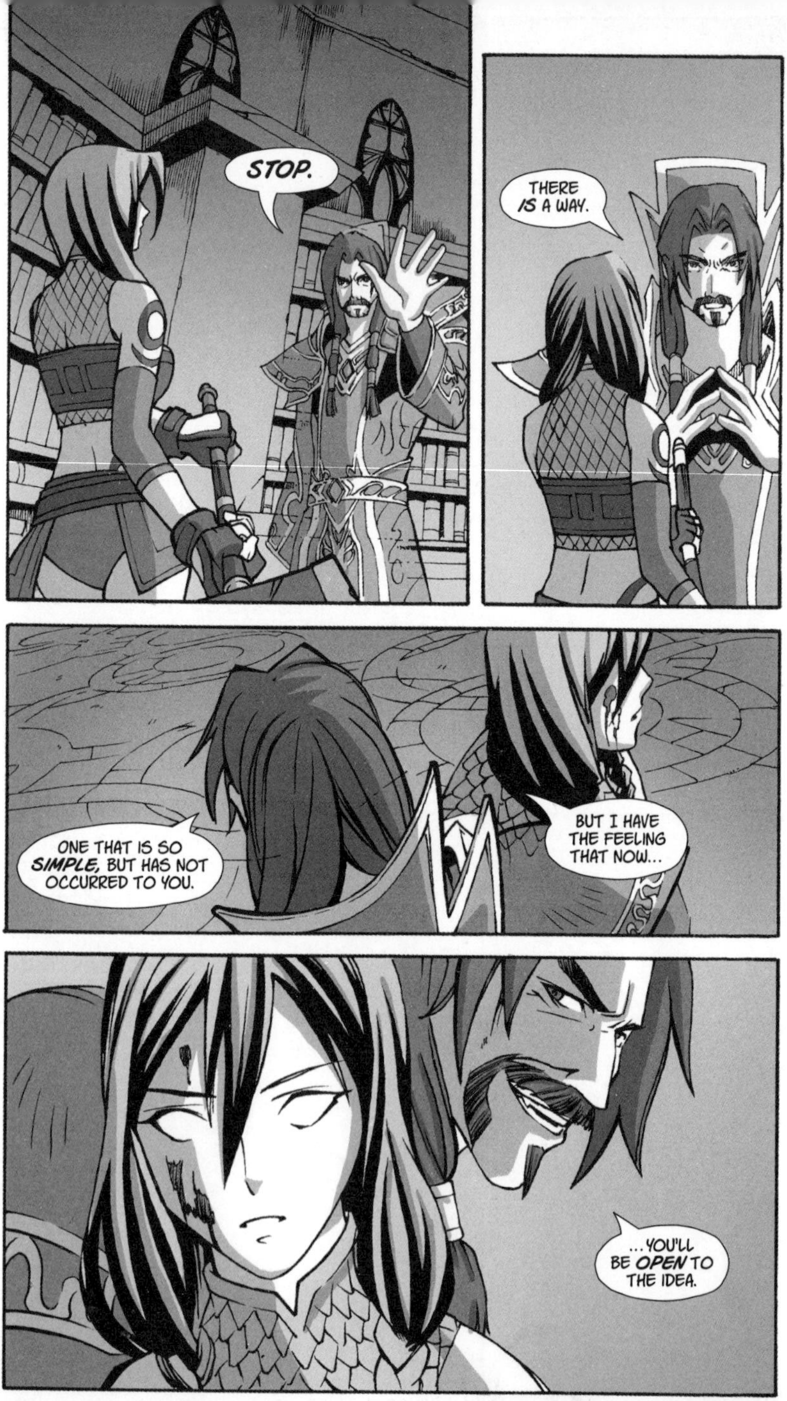
STOP.
THERE *IS* A WAY.
ONE THAT IS SO *SIMPLE,* BUT HAS NOT OCCURRED TO YOU.
BUT I HAVE THE FEELING THAT NOW...
...YOU'LL BE *OPEN* TO THE IDEA.

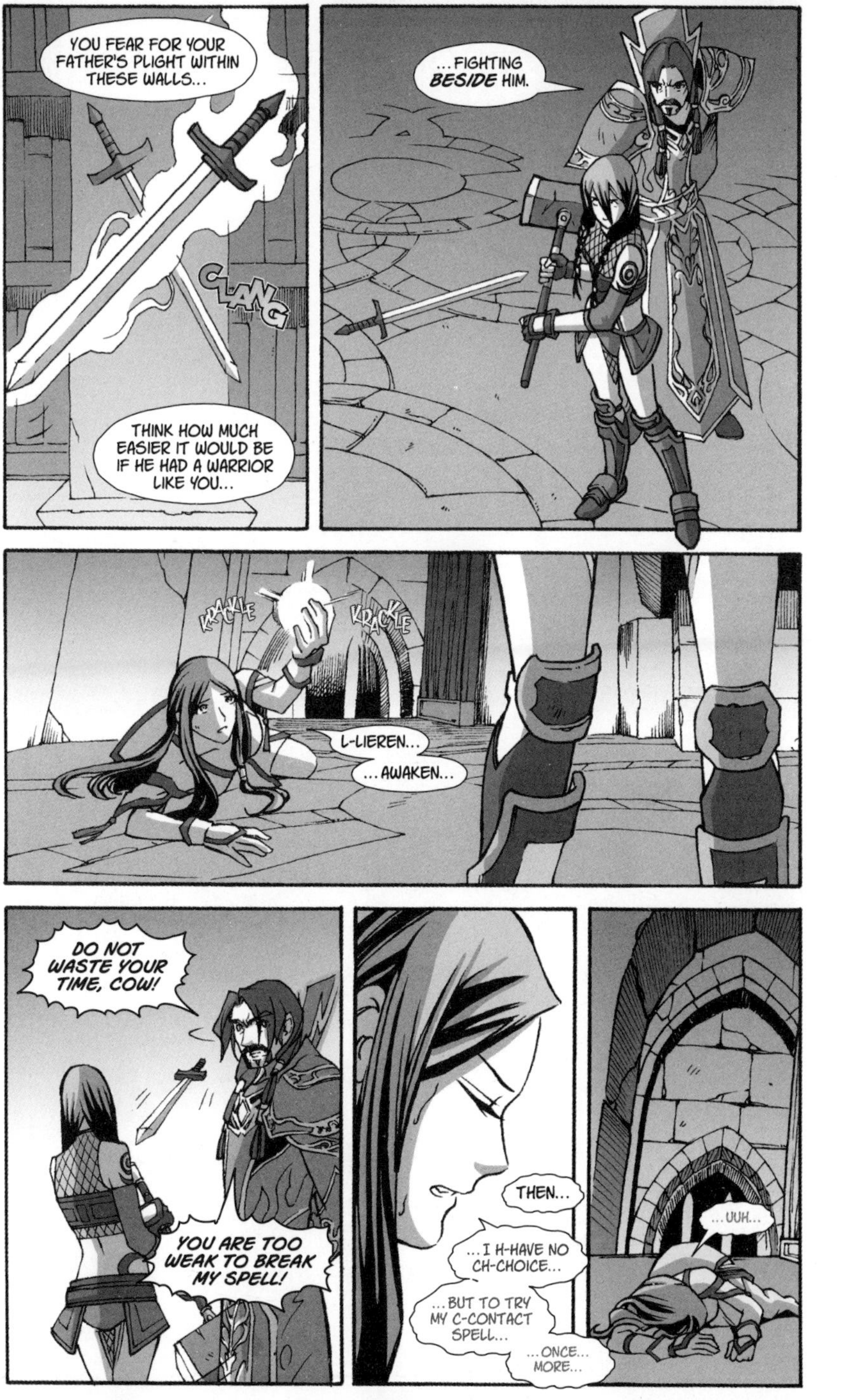
YOU FEAR FOR YOUR FATHER'S PLIGHT WITHIN THESE WALLS...
CLANG
THINK HOW MUCH EASIER IT WOULD BE IF HE HAD A WARRIOR LIKE YOU...
...FIGHTING *BESIDE* HIM.
KRACKLE
KRACKLE
L-LIEREN...
...AWAKEN...
DO NOT WASTE YOUR TIME, COW!
YOU ARE TOO WEAK TO BREAK MY SPELL!
THEN...
...I H-HAVE NO CH-CHOICE...
...BUT TO TRY MY C-CONTACT SPELL...
...ONCE... MORE...
...UUH...

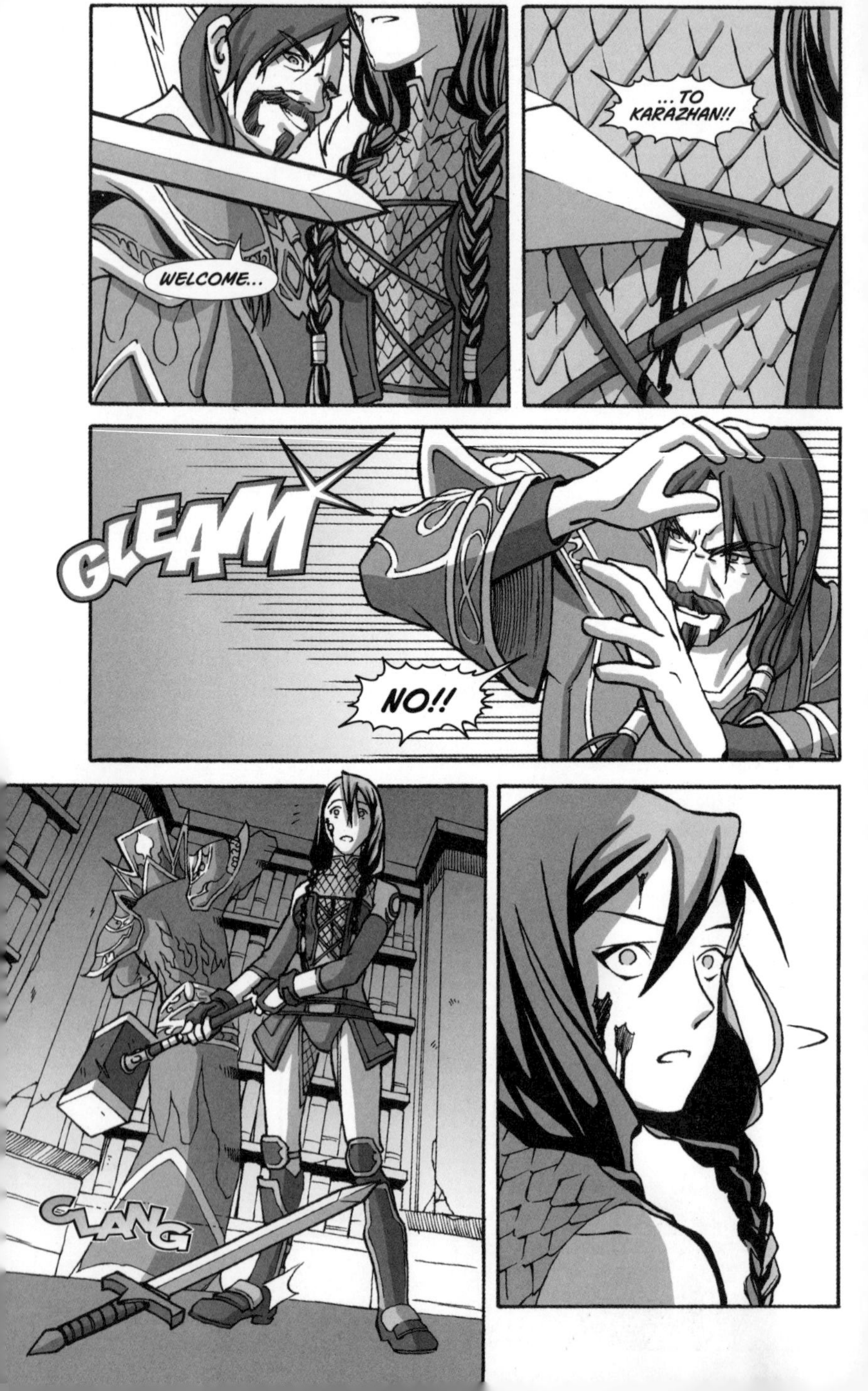
WELCOME...
...TO KARAZHAN!!
GLEAM
NO!!
CLANG

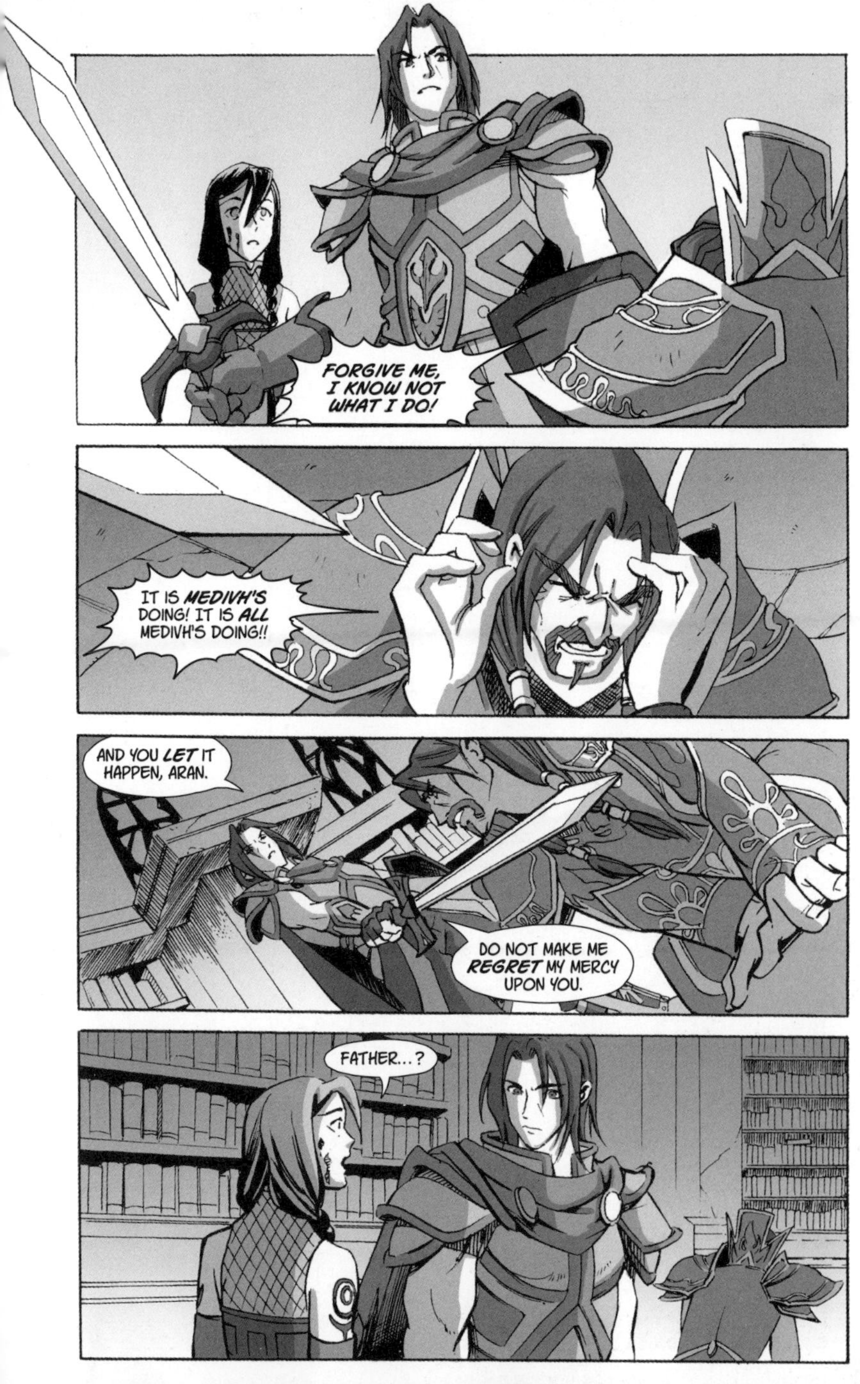
FORGIVE ME, I KNOW NOT WHAT I DO!
IT IS MEDIVH'S DOING! IT IS ALL MEDIVH'S DOING!!
AND YOU LET IT HAPPEN, ARAN.
DO NOT MAKE ME REGRET MY MERCY UPON YOU.
FATHER...?

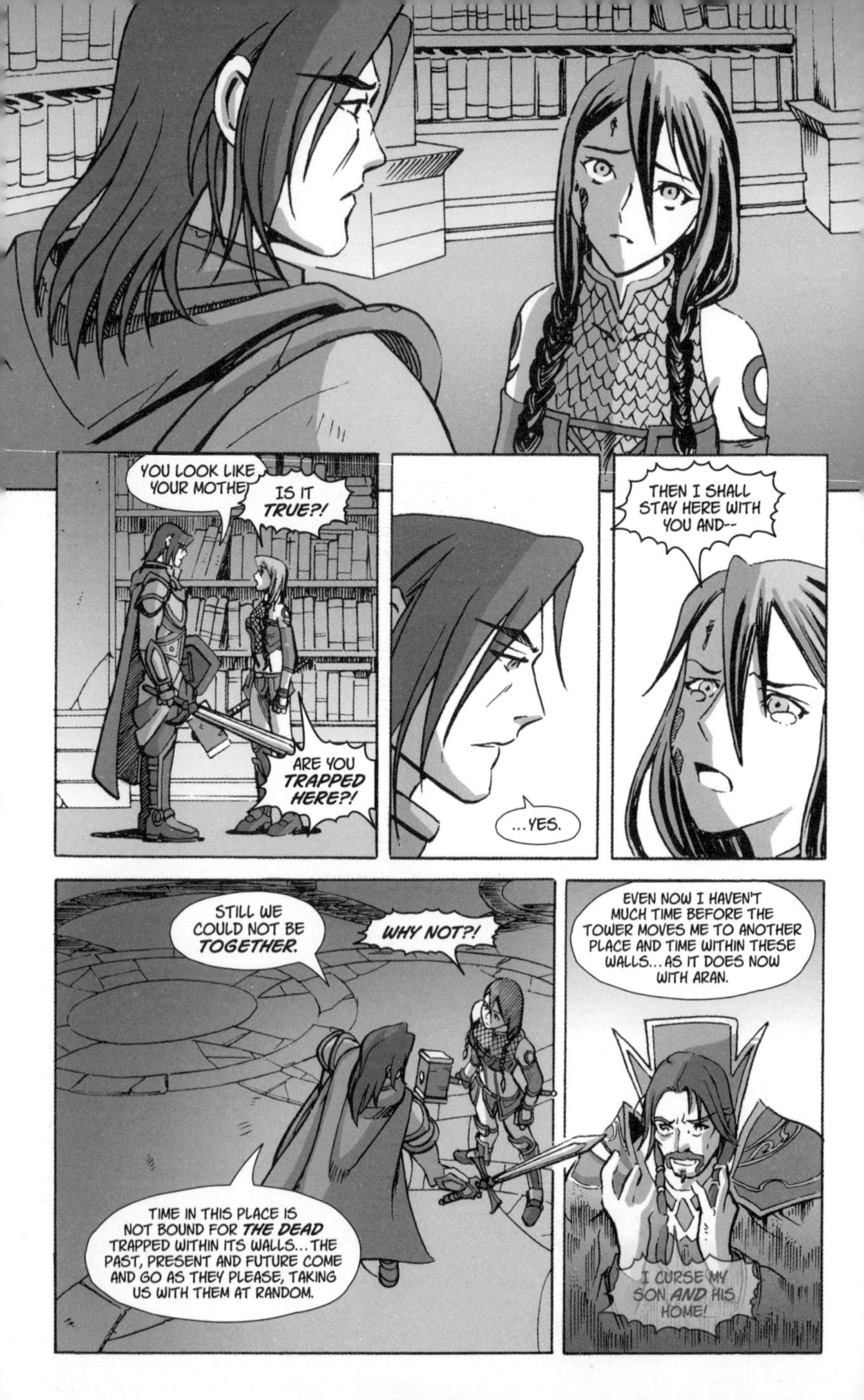
YOU LOOK LIKE YOUR MOTHE
IS IT *TRUE?!*
ARE YOU *TRAPPED HERE?!*
...YES.
THEN I SHALL STAY HERE WITH YOU AND--
STILL WE COULD NOT BE *TOGETHER.*
WHY NOT?!
TIME IN THIS PLACE IS NOT BOUND FOR *THE DEAD* TRAPPED WITHIN ITS WALLS... THE PAST, PRESENT AND FUTURE COME AND GO AS THEY PLEASE, TAKING US WITH THEM AT RANDOM.
EVEN NOW I HAVEN'T MUCH TIME BEFORE THE TOWER MOVES ME TO ANOTHER PLACE AND TIME WITHIN THESE WALLS... AS IT DOES NOW WITH ARAN.
I CURSE MY SON *AND* HIS HOME!

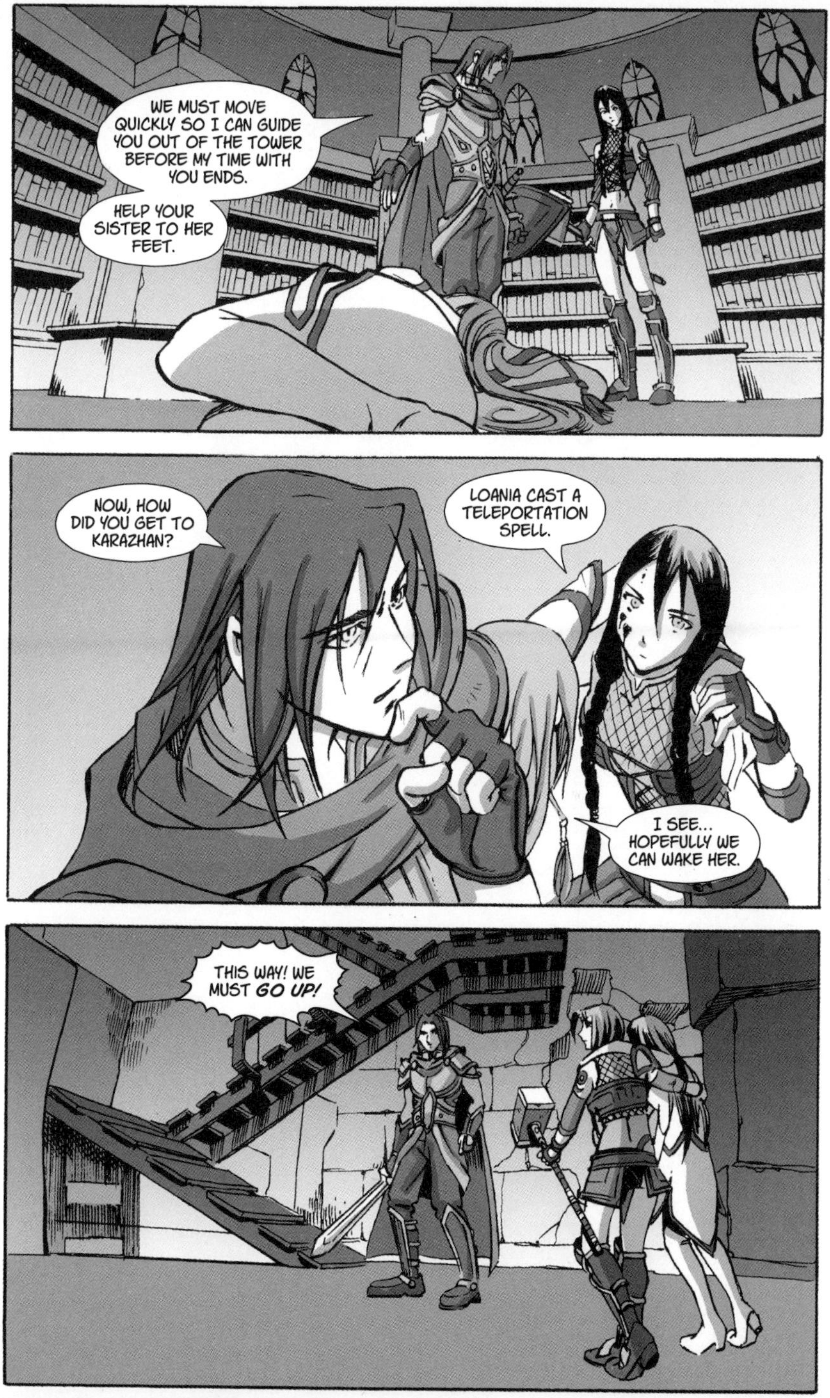
WE MUST MOVE QUICKLY SO I CAN GUIDE YOU OUT OF THE TOWER BEFORE MY TIME WITH YOU ENDS.
HELP YOUR SISTER TO HER FEET.
NOW, HOW DID YOU GET TO KARAZHAN?
LOANIA CAST A TELEPORTATION SPELL.
I SEE... HOPEFULLY WE CAN WAKE HER.
THIS WAY! WE MUST *GO UP!*

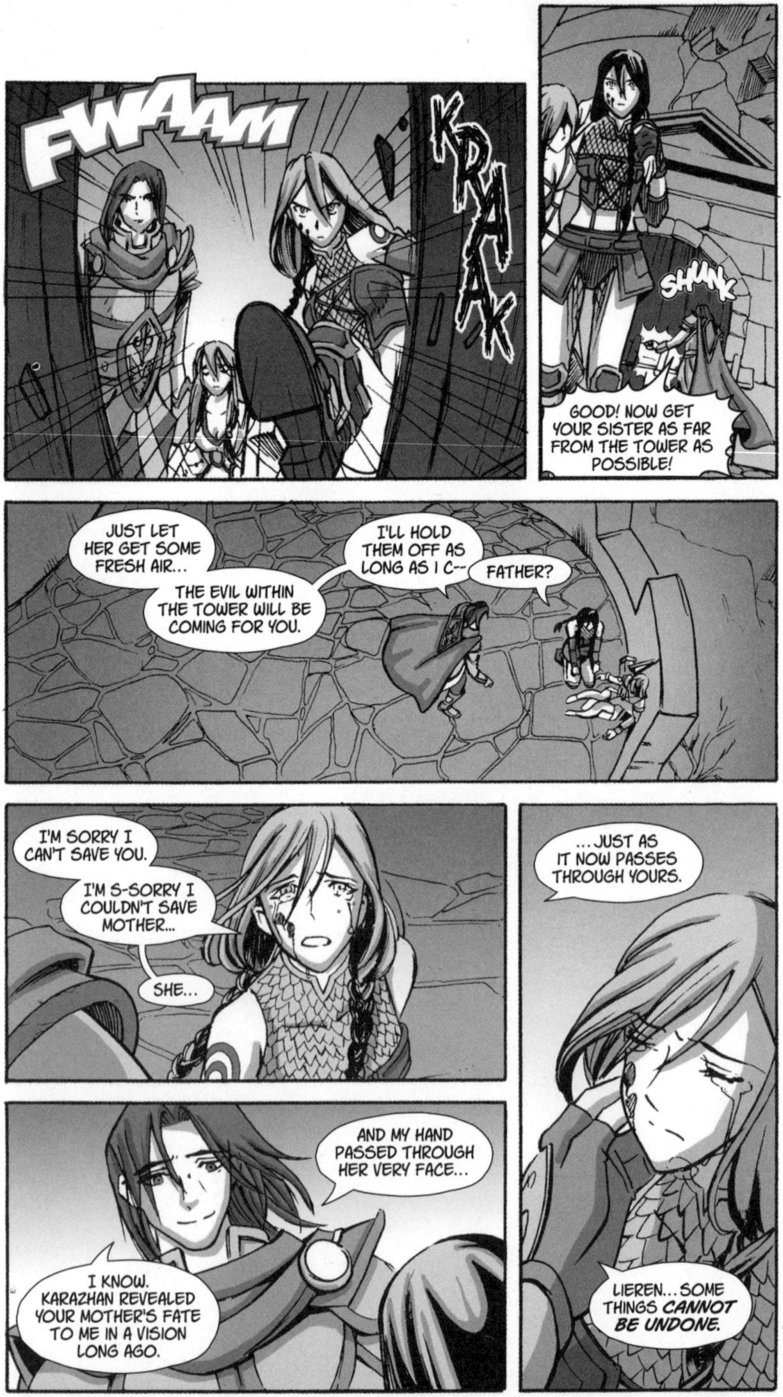
FWAAAM
KRAAK
SHUNK
GOOD! NOW GET YOUR SISTER AS FAR FROM THE TOWER AS POSSIBLE!
JUST LET HER GET SOME FRESH AIR...
THE EVIL WITHIN THE TOWER WILL BE COMING FOR YOU.
I'LL HOLD THEM OFF AS LONG AS I C--
FATHER?
I'M SORRY I CAN'T SAVE YOU.
I'M S-SORRY I COULDN'T SAVE MOTHER...
SHE...
AND MY HAND PASSED THROUGH HER VERY FACE...
I KNOW. KARAZHAN REVEALED YOUR MOTHER'S FATE TO ME IN A VISION LONG AGO.
...JUST AS IT NOW PASSES THROUGH YOURS.
LIEREN... SOME THINGS ***CANNOT BE UNDONE.***

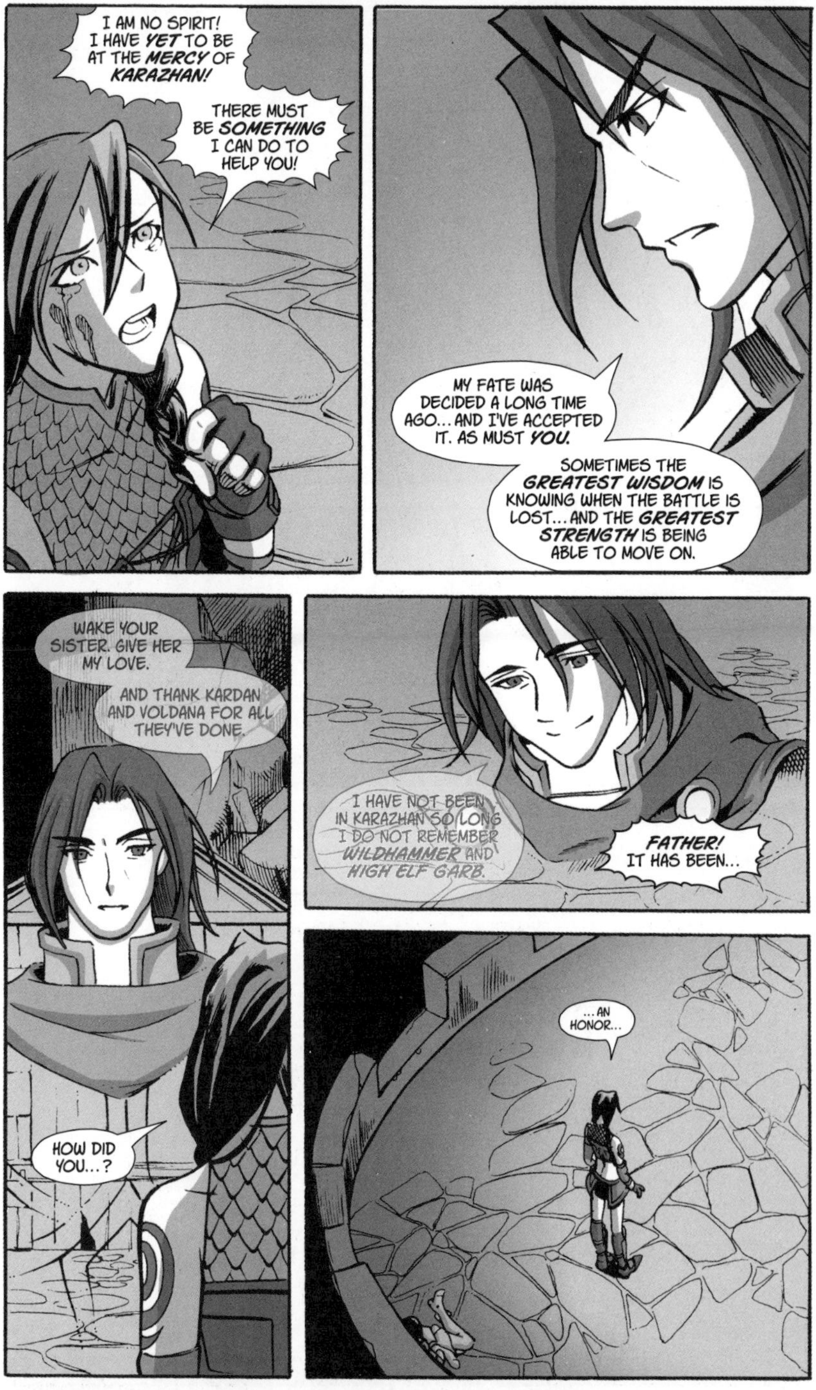

I AM NO SPIRIT! I HAVE *YET* TO BE AT THE *MERCY* OF *KARAZHAN!*
THERE MUST BE *SOMETHING* I CAN DO TO HELP YOU!
MY FATE WAS DECIDED A LONG TIME AGO... AND I'VE ACCEPTED IT. AS MUST *YOU.*
SOMETIMES THE *GREATEST WISDOM* IS KNOWING WHEN THE BATTLE IS LOST... AND THE *GREATEST STRENGTH* IS BEING ABLE TO MOVE ON.
WAKE YOUR SISTER. GIVE HER MY LOVE.
AND THANK KARDAN AND VOLDANA FOR ALL THEY'VE DONE.
HOW DID YOU...?
I HAVE NOT BEEN IN KARAZHAN SO LONG I DO NOT REMEMBER *WILDHAMMER* AND *HIGH ELF GARB.*
FATHER! IT HAS BEEN...
...AN HONOR...

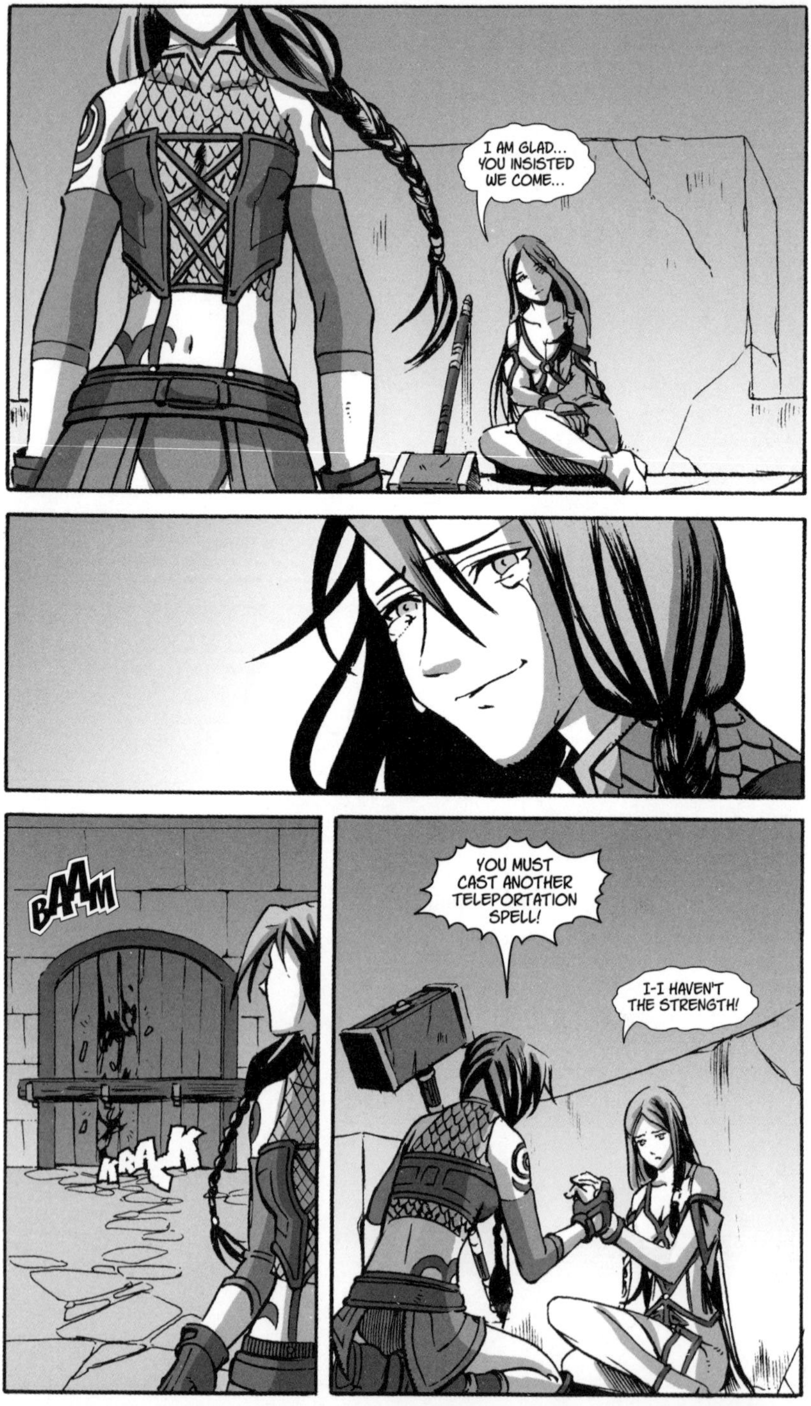
I AM GLAD... YOU INSISTED WE COME...
BAAM
KRAK
YOU MUST CAST ANOTHER TELEPORTATION SPELL!
I-I HAVEN'T THE STRENGTH!

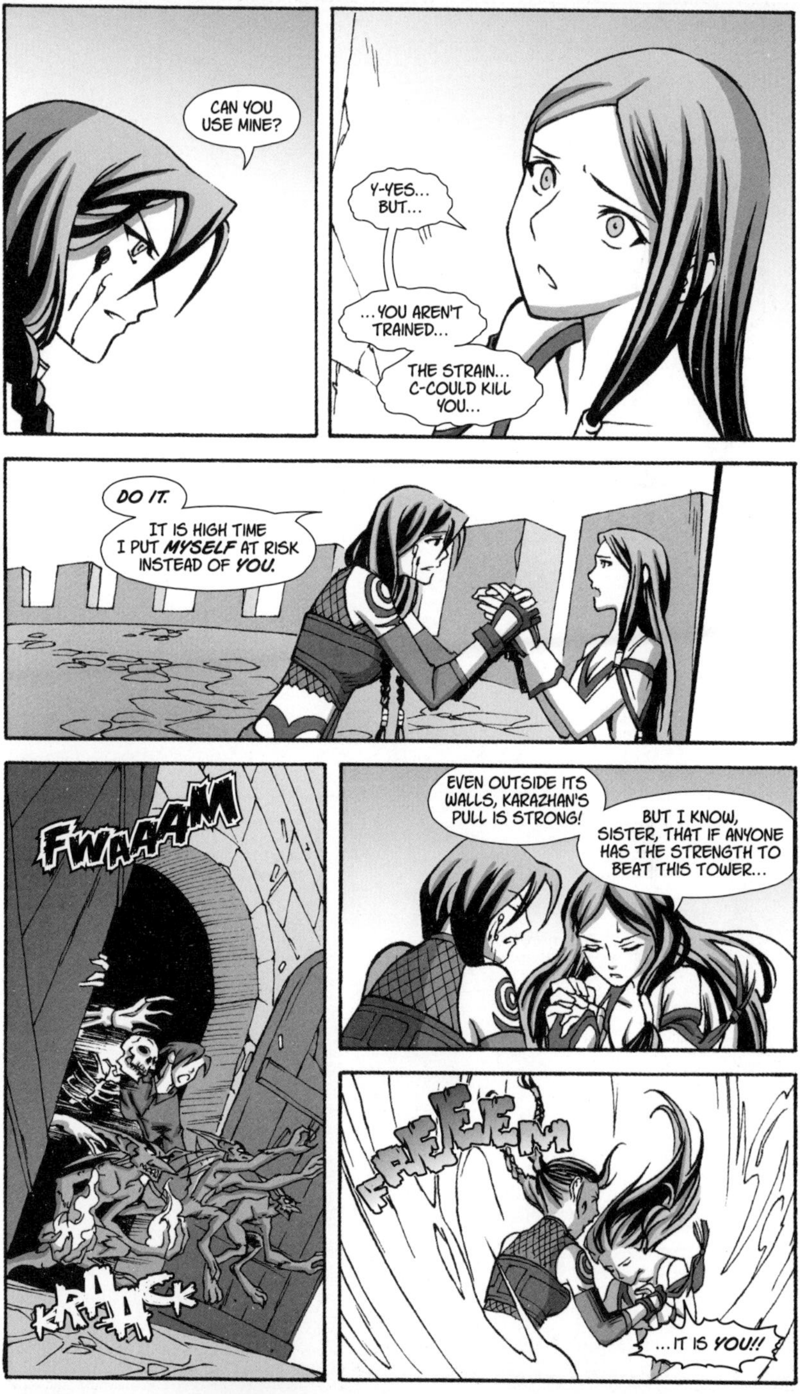
CAN YOU USE MINE?
Y-YES... BUT...
...YOU AREN'T TRAINED...
THE STRAIN... C-COULD KILL YOU...
DO IT.
IT IS HIGH TIME I PUT MYSELF AT RISK INSTEAD OF YOU.
FWAAAM
KRAACK
EVEN OUTSIDE ITS WALLS, KARAZHAN'S PULL IS STRONG!
BUT I KNOW, SISTER, THAT IF ANYONE HAS THE STRENGTH TO BEAT THIS TOWER...
FREEEM
...IT IS YOU!!

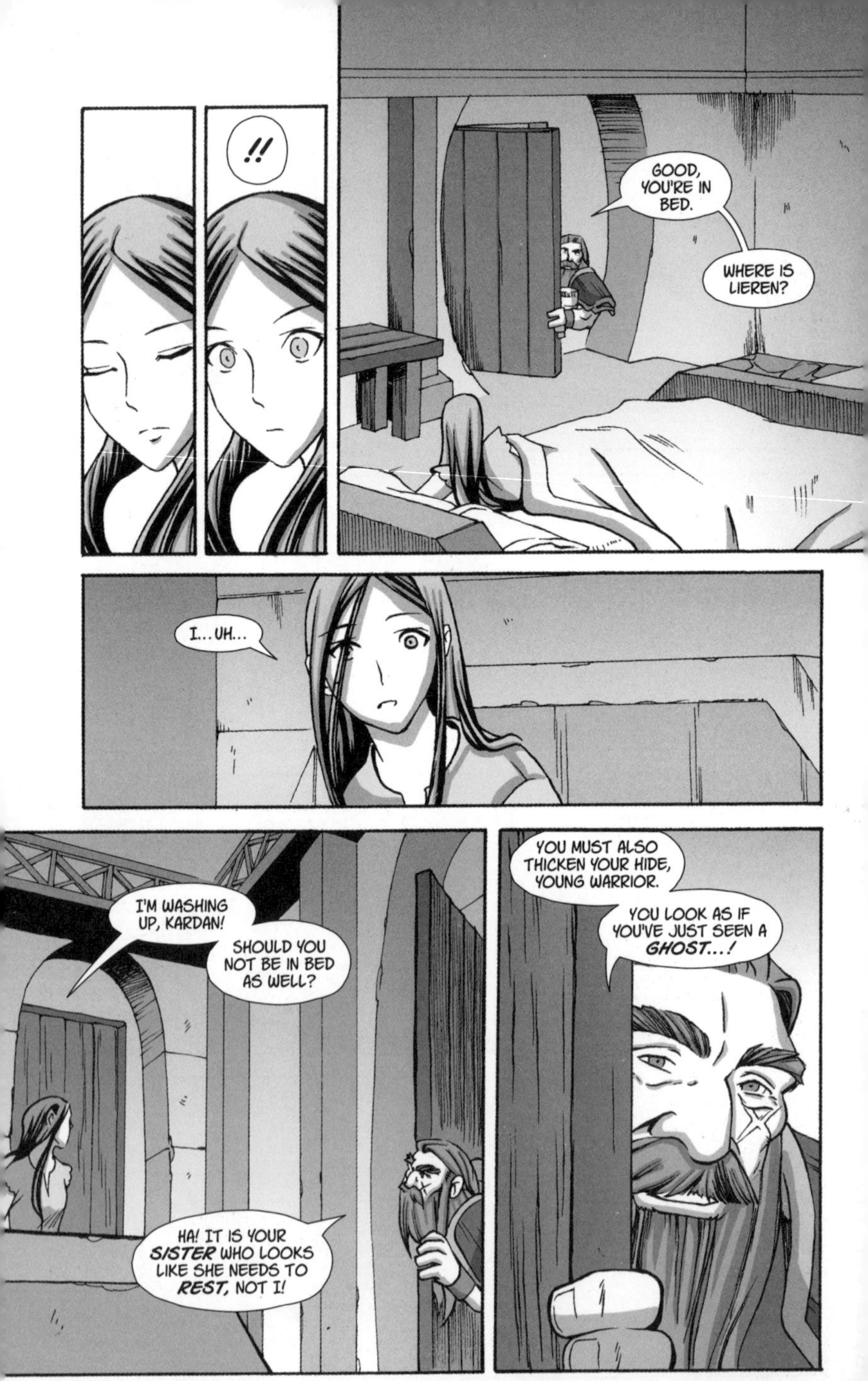
!!
GOOD, YOU'RE IN BED.
WHERE IS LIEREN?
I... UH...
I'M WASHING UP, KARDAN!
SHOULD YOU NOT BE IN BED AS WELL?
HA! IT IS YOUR SISTER WHO LOOKS LIKE SHE NEEDS TO REST, NOT I!
YOU MUST ALSO THICKEN YOUR HIDE, YOUNG WARRIOR.
YOU LOOK AS IF YOU'VE JUST SEEN A GHOST...!

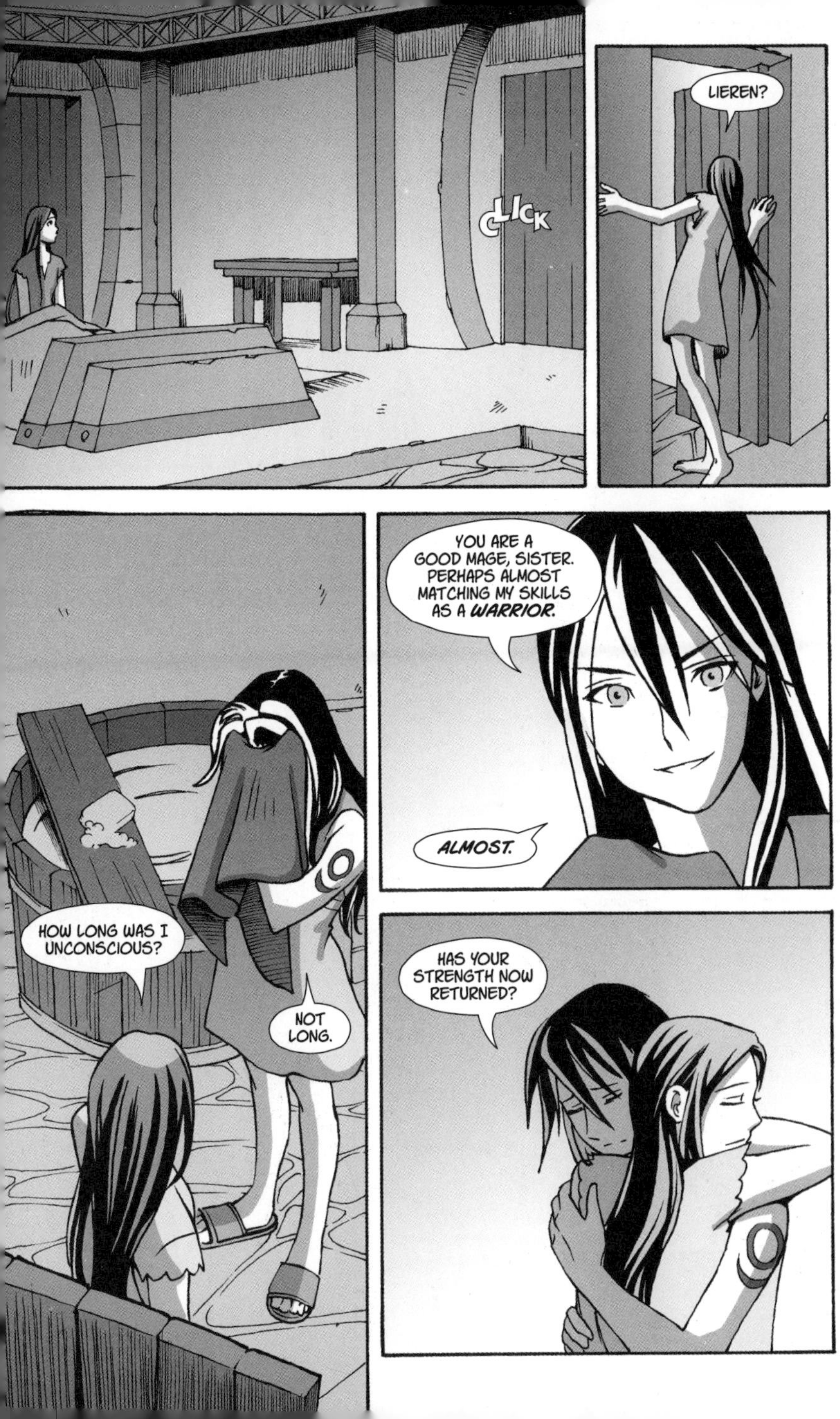
CLICK
LIEREN?
HOW LONG WAS I UNCONSCIOUS?
NOT LONG.
YOU ARE A GOOD MAGE, SISTER. PERHAPS ALMOST MATCHING MY SKILLS AS A *WARRIOR*.
ALMOST.
HAS YOUR STRENGTH NOW RETURNED?

COMPLETELY... THANKS TO YOUR SACRIFICE.

YOUR HAIR...IT'S *WHITE.* OH LIEREN...I'M SO SORRY. FOR MANY REASONS.

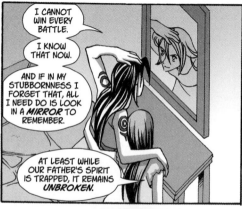

I CANNOT WIN EVERY BATTLE.

I KNOW THAT NOW.

AND IF IN MY STUBBORNNESS I FORGET THAT, ALL I NEED DO IS LOOK IN A *MIRROR* TO REMEMBER.

AT LEAST WHILE OUR FATHER'S SPIRIT IS TRAPPED, IT REMAINS *UNBROKEN.*

...AS DOES *OURS.*

AS DOES OURS, SISTER...

END

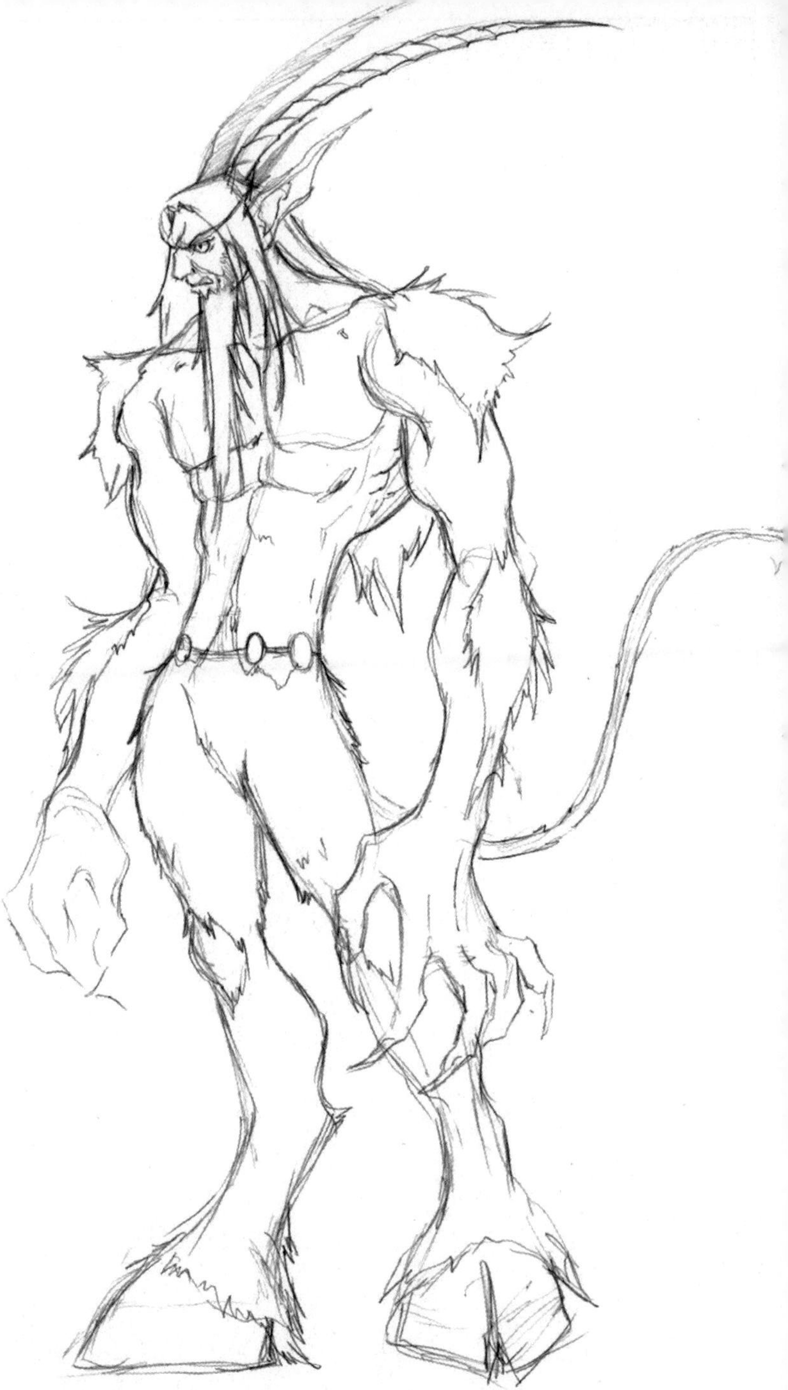

WarCraft®

LEGENDS™

VOLUME FIVE

THE FIRST GUARDIAN

WRITTEN BY LOUISE SIMONSON

PENCILS BY SEUNG-HUI KYE
INKS BY SEUNG-HUI KYE, ARIEL IACCI
& FERNANDO MELEK
TONES BY GONZALO DUARTE

Retouch Artist & Letterer: Michael Paolilli

DALARAN: A BRIEF HISTORY

Almost 3,000 years ago, a group of human magi, feeling fettered by strict laws governing magic in Strom, journeyed north to Lordaeron. On the southern shore of Lordamere Lake, these magi founded the city-state of Dalaran, where they hoped to practice their craft with less restraint.

The ruling archmagi, called Magocrats, eagerly devoted themselves to the arcane. They housed their growing libraries and research laboratories in the Violet Citadel, a towering spire raised by magic in the heart of the city.

Magi flocked to Dalaran in ever-increasing numbers to study at its schools, do research in its vast libraries and practice their craft freely in the company of their peers. Soon non-magical beings moved to Dalaran to provide necessary services for the residents of the thriving magocracy.

The citizens of Dalaran thought that their shining city was impregnable and that its glory would never end.

But, in time, the constant and ungoverned use of magic began to tear the fabric of reality around the city. These tears sent bright beacons out into the Twisting Nether and drew the attention of the banished denizens of the Burning Legion. Through these rents, demons began to slip back into Azeroth, bringing with them conflict and cruelty, misery and corruption.

Consulting the high elves, the Magocrats learned that as long as they used magic, they would need to protect their citizenry from the Legion's agents. Yet mankind could not be allowed to learn of this threat lest the people riot in fear. Thus, the elves and Magocrats formed a secret order known as the Council of Tirisfal.

The order began to experiment, trying to discover the most effective way to deal with the demon incursions.

One group held that the magi should work together as a team of equals. Another group believed that their magic should be funneled through a single head, though how that should be managed was another challenge.

In time, the solution was found by... THE FIRST GUARDIAN.

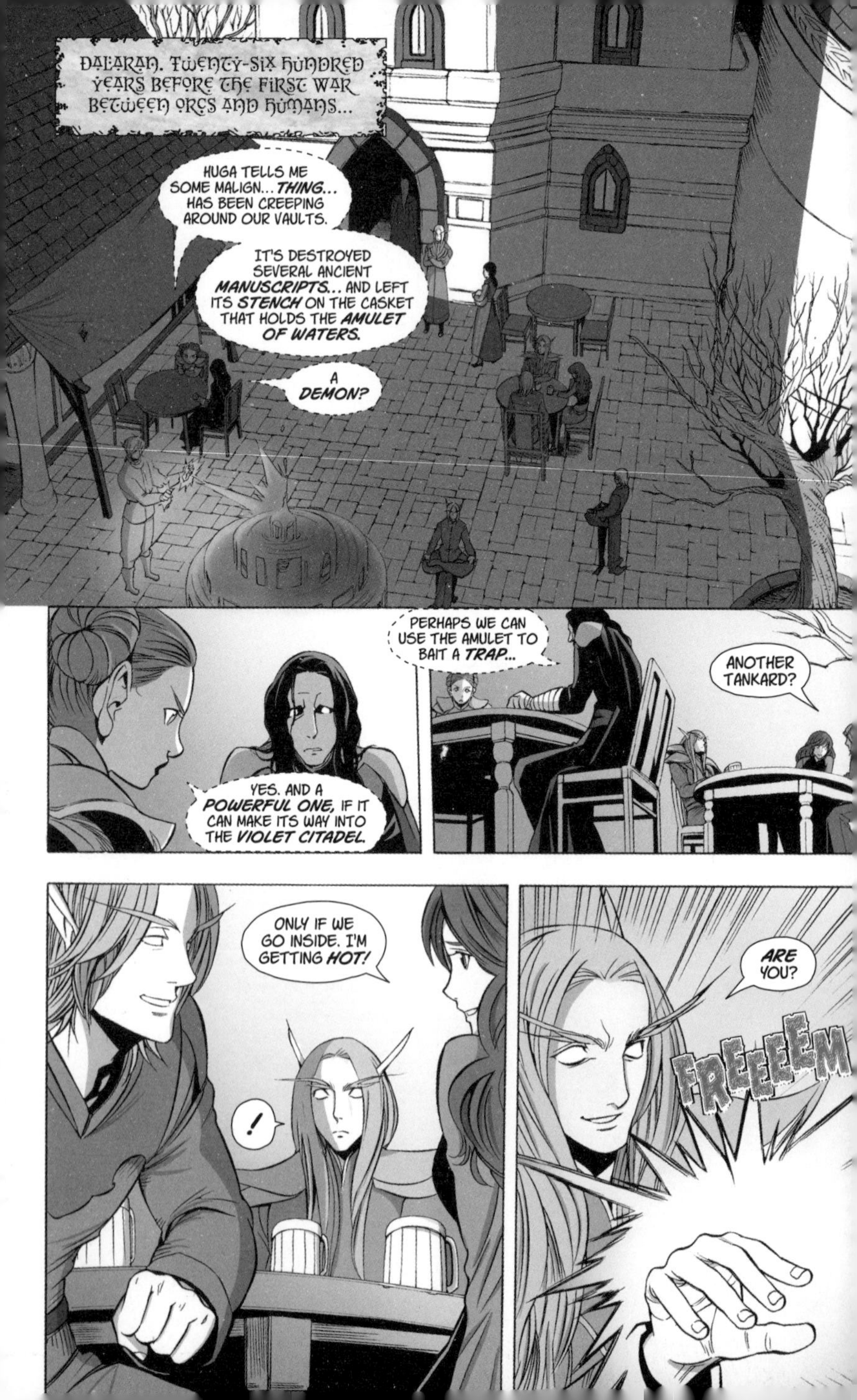
DALARAN. TWENTY-SIX HUNDRED YEARS BEFORE THE FIRST WAR BETWEEN ORCS AND HUMANS...
HUGA TELLS ME SOME MALIGN... THING... HAS BEEN CREEPING AROUND OUR VAULTS.
IT'S DESTROYED SEVERAL ANCIENT MANUSCRIPTS... AND LEFT ITS STENCH ON THE CASKET THAT HOLDS THE AMULET OF WATERS.
A DEMON?
YES. AND A POWERFUL ONE, IF IT CAN MAKE ITS WAY INTO THE VIOLET CITADEL.
PERHAPS WE CAN USE THE AMULET TO BAIT A TRAP...
ANOTHER TANKARD?
ONLY IF WE GO INSIDE. I'M GETTING HOT!
!
ARE YOU?
FREEEEM

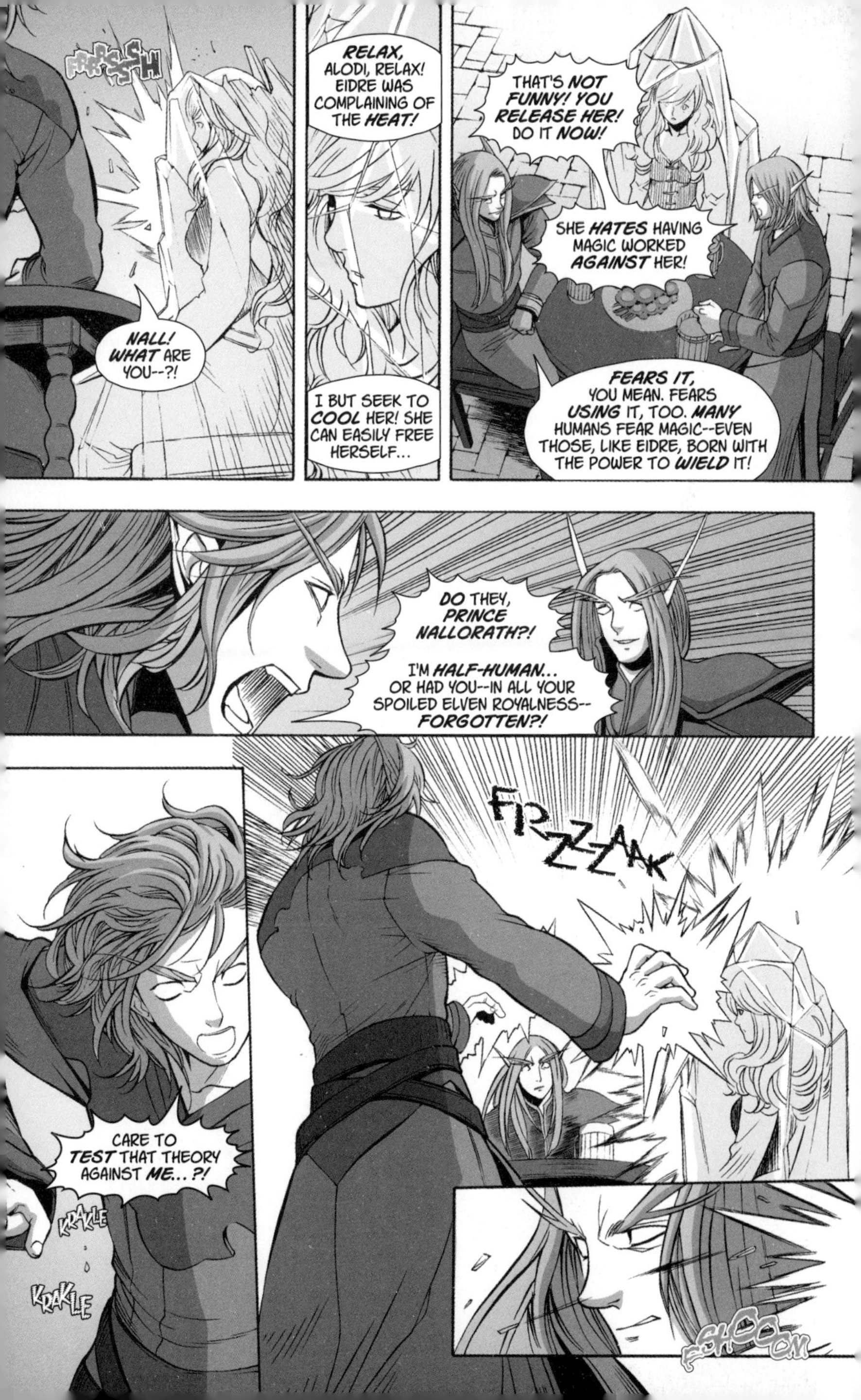

FRRSSSH
NALL! WHAT ARE YOU--?!
RELAX, ALODI, RELAX! EIDRE WAS COMPLAINING OF THE HEAT!
I BUT SEEK TO COOL HER! SHE CAN EASILY FREE HERSELF...
THAT'S NOT FUNNY! YOU RELEASE HER! DO IT NOW!
SHE HATES HAVING MAGIC WORKED AGAINST HER!
FEARS IT, YOU MEAN. FEARS USING IT, TOO. MANY HUMANS FEAR MAGIC--EVEN THOSE, LIKE EIDRE, BORN WITH THE POWER TO WIELD IT!
DO THEY, PRINCE NALLORATH?!
I'M HALF-HUMAN... OR HAD YOU--IN ALL YOUR SPOILED ELVEN ROYALNESS--FORGOTTEN?!
CARE TO TEST THAT THEORY AGAINST ME...?!
KRAKLE
KRAKLE
FRZZZAAK
FSHOOOM

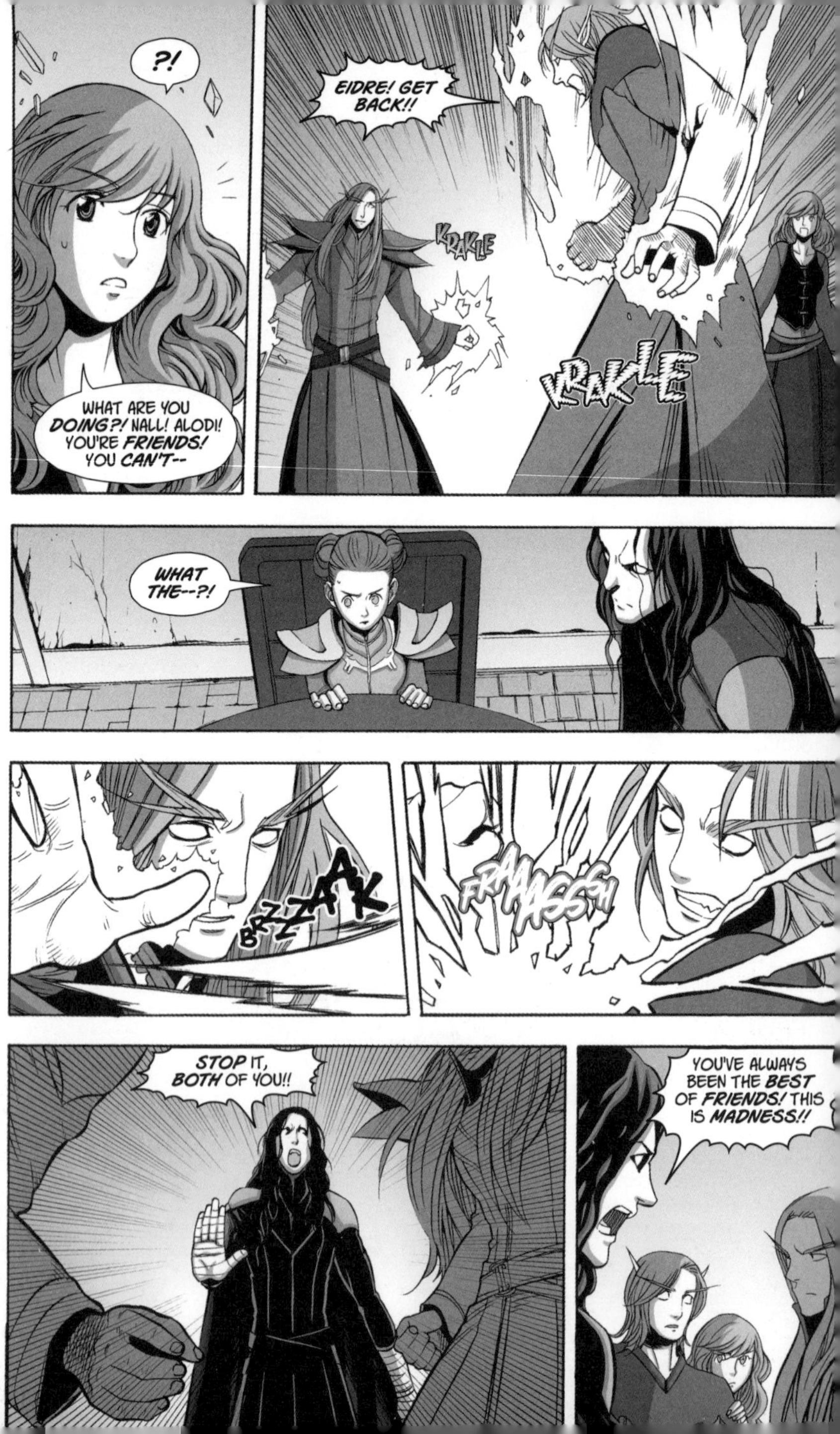
?!
WHAT ARE YOU DOING?! NALL! ALODI! YOU'RE FRIENDS! YOU CAN'T--
EIDRE! GET BACK!!
KRAKLE
KRAKLE
WHAT THE--?!
BRZZZAK
FRAAAASSSH
STOP IT, BOTH OF YOU!!
YOU'VE ALWAYS BEEN THE BEST OF FRIENDS! THIS IS MADNESS!!

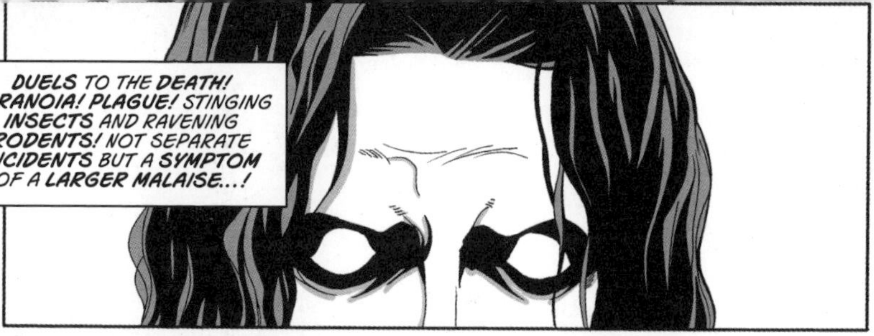
DUELS TO THE DEATH! PARANOIA! PLAGUE! STINGING INSECTS AND RAVENING RODENTS! NOT SEPARATE INCIDENTS BUT A SYMPTOM OF A LARGER MALAISE...!

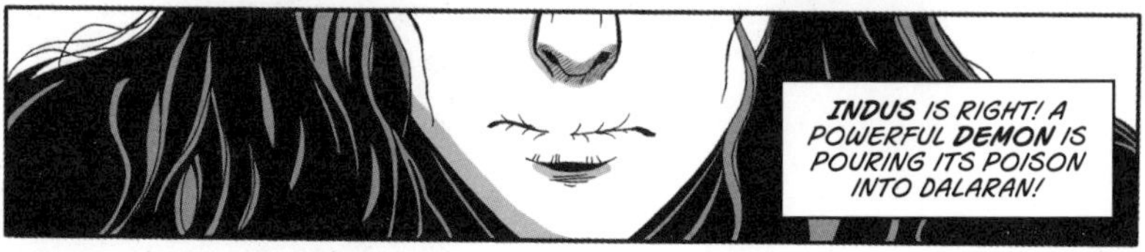
INDUS IS RIGHT! A POWERFUL DEMON IS POURING ITS POISON INTO DALARAN!

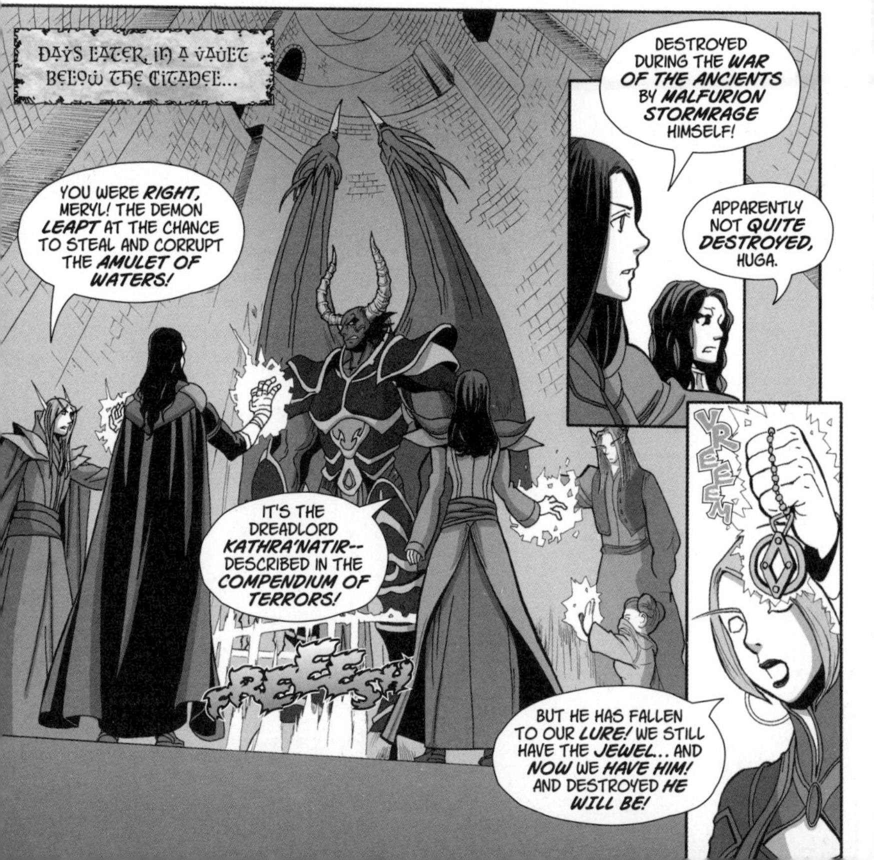
DAYS LATER, IN A VAULT BELOW THE CITADEL...
YOU WERE RIGHT, MERYL! THE DEMON LEAPT AT THE CHANCE TO STEAL AND CORRUPT THE AMULET OF WATERS!
IT'S THE DREADLORD KATHRA'NATIR-- DESCRIBED IN THE COMPENDIUM OF TERRORS!
FREEESH
DESTROYED DURING THE WAR OF THE ANCIENTS BY MALFURION STORMRAGE HIMSELF!
APPARENTLY NOT QUITE DESTROYED, HUGA.
VREEEM
BUT HE HAS FALLEN TO OUR LURE! WE STILL HAVE THE JEWEL... AND NOW WE HAVE HIM! AND DESTROYED HE WILL BE!

PZZAKKT

YEARRGHH!!

EH?

!!

ZZAKT!

ENOUGH
DISCUSSION!!

ZZAKKT

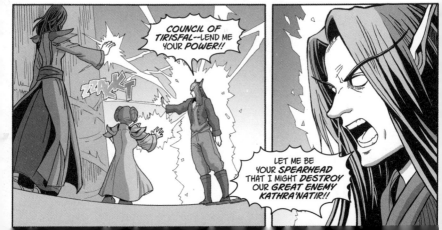
COUNCIL OF
TIRISFAL--LEND ME
YOUR *POWER*!!

ZZAKKT

LET ME BE
YOUR *SPEARHEAD*
THAT I MIGHT *DESTROY*
OUR GREAT ENEMY
KATHRA'NATIR!!

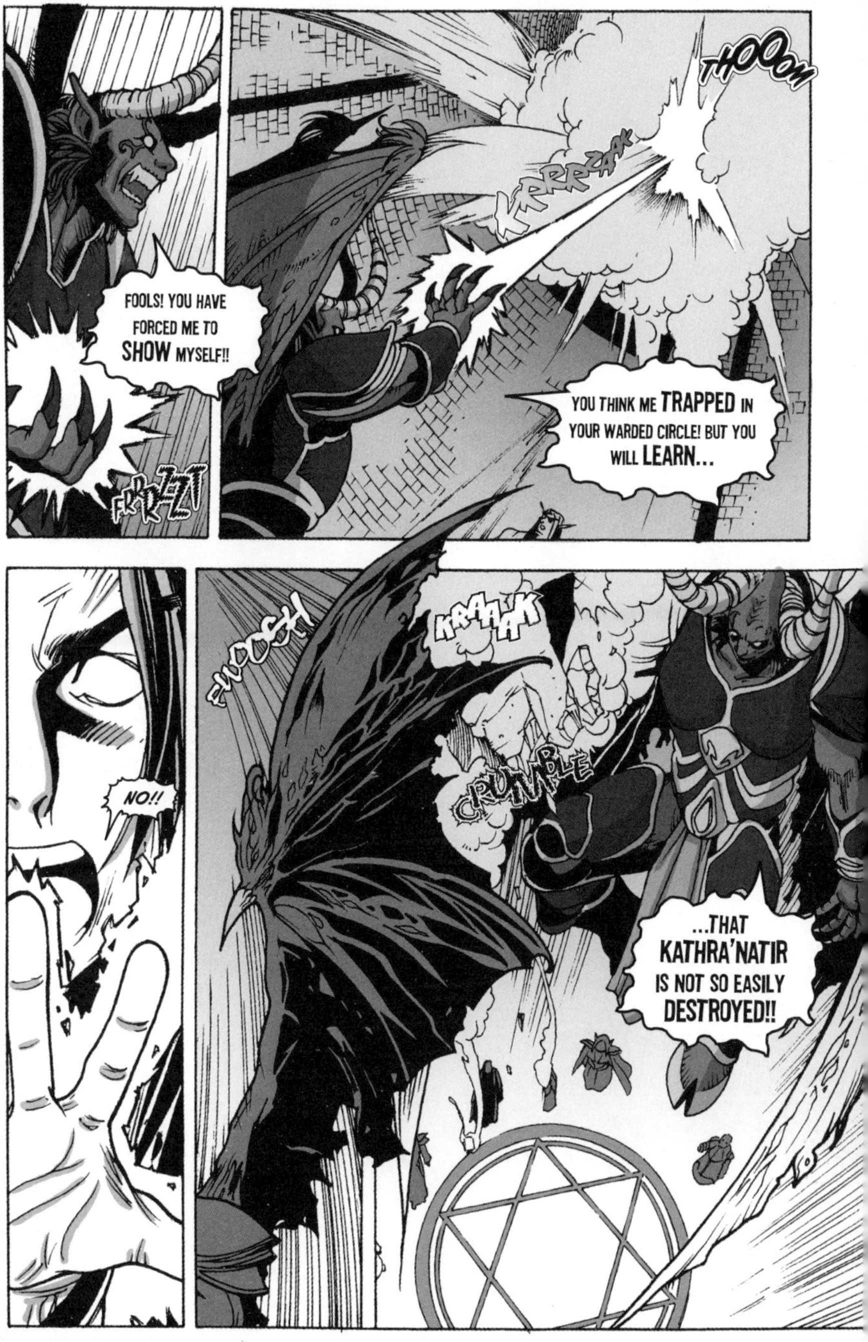
FOOLS! YOU HAVE FORCED ME TO SHOW MYSELF!!
FRRZZT
THOOOOM
KRRRZAAK
YOU THINK ME TRAPPED IN YOUR WARDED CIRCLE! BUT YOU WILL LEARN...
NO!!
FWOOSH
KRAAAAK
CRUMBLE
...THAT KATHRA'NATIR IS NOT SO EASILY DESTROYED!!

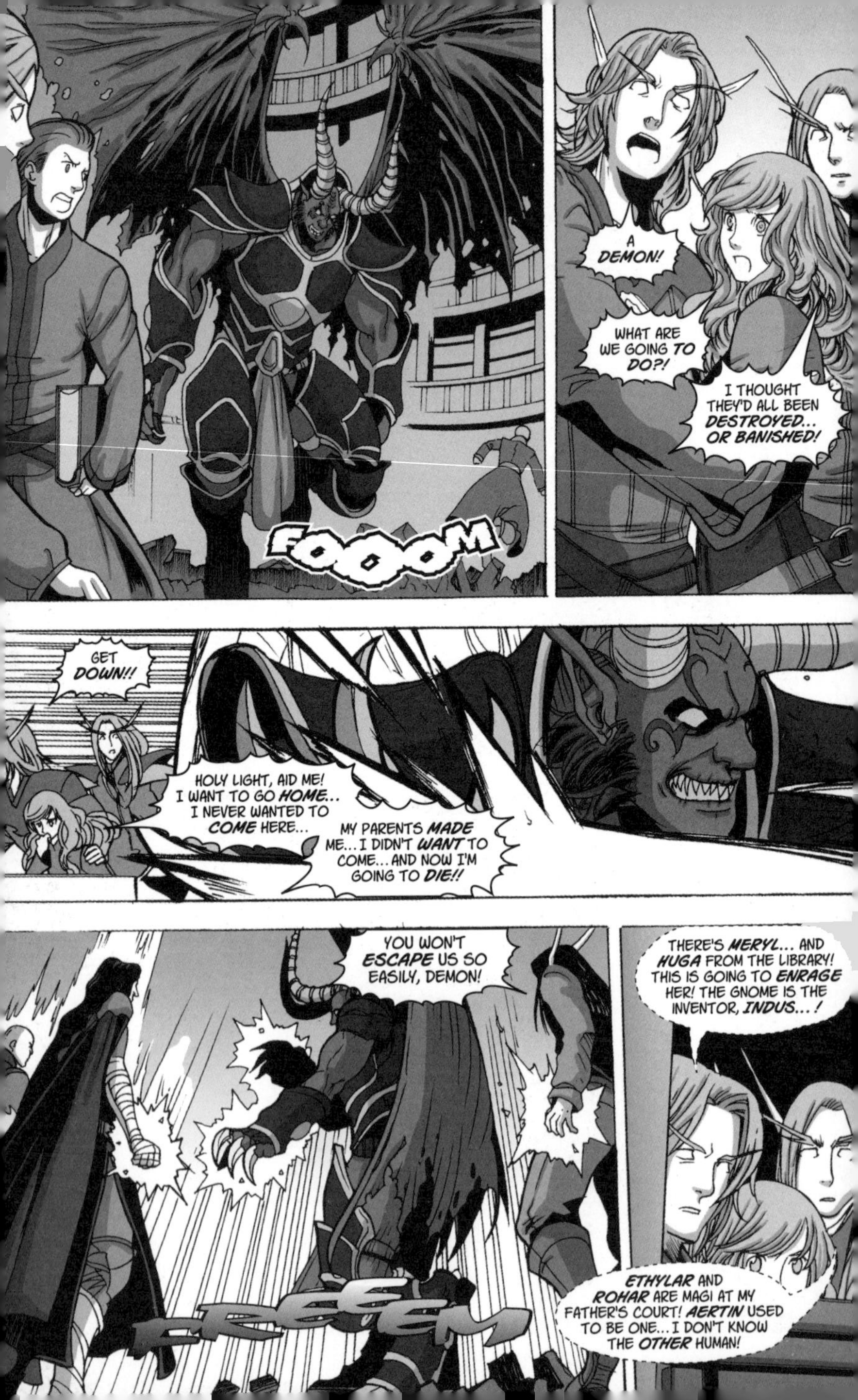
FOOOM
A DEMON!
WHAT ARE WE GOING TO DO?!
I THOUGHT THEY'D ALL BEEN DESTROYED... OR BANISHED!
GET DOWN!!
HOLY LIGHT, AID ME! I WANT TO GO HOME... I NEVER WANTED TO COME HERE...
MY PARENTS MADE ME... I DIDN'T WANT TO COME... AND NOW I'M GOING TO DIE!!
YOU WON'T ESCAPE US SO EASILY, DEMON!
THERE'S MERYL... AND HUGA FROM THE LIBRARY! THIS IS GOING TO ENRAGE HER! THE GNOME IS THE INVENTOR, INDUS...!
ETHYLAR AND ROHAR ARE MAGI AT MY FATHER'S COURT! AERTIN USED TO BE ONE... I DON'T KNOW THE OTHER HUMAN!

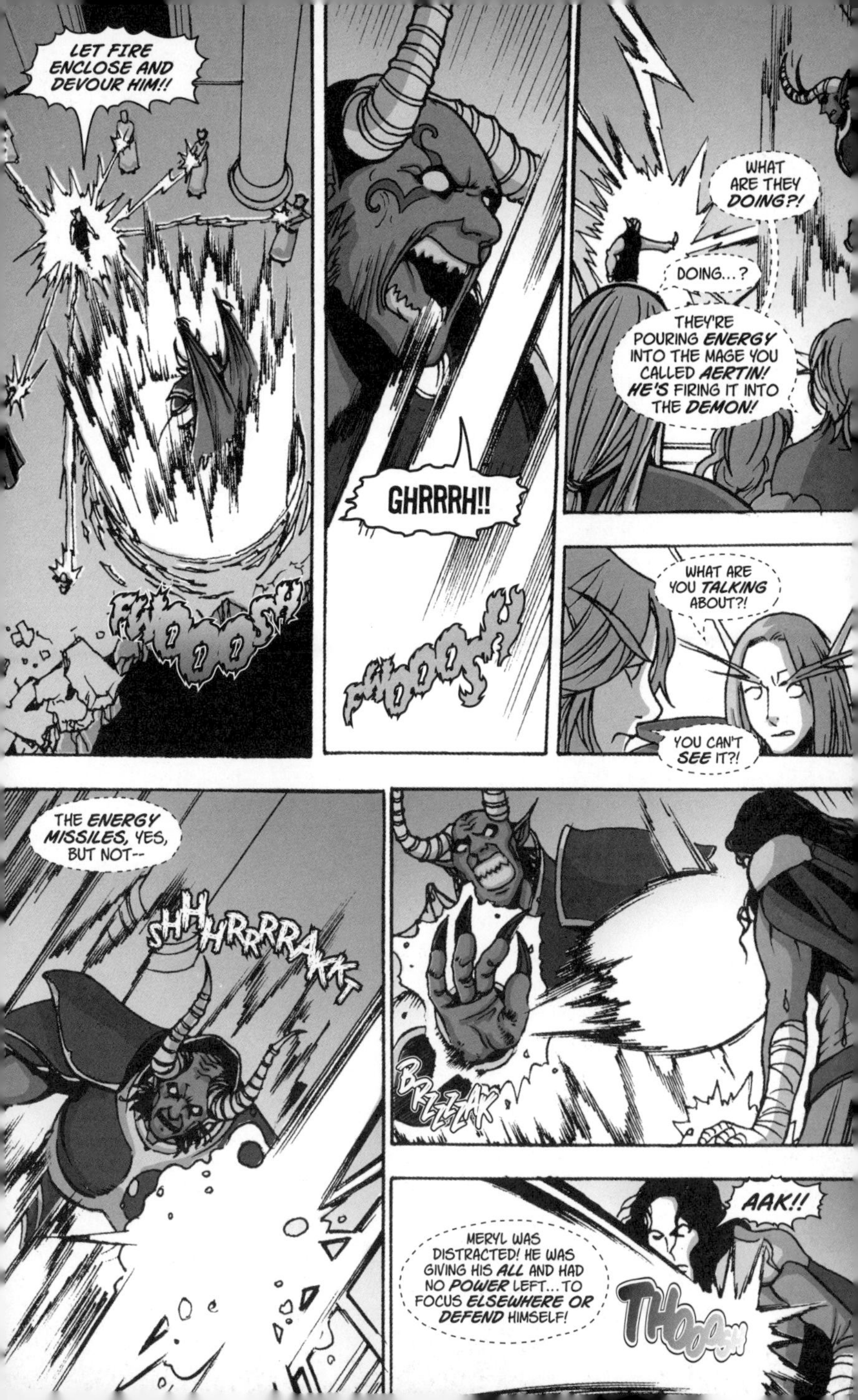
LET FIRE ENCLOSE AND DEVOUR HIM!!
GHRRRH!!
WHAT ARE THEY DOING?!
DOING...?
THEY'RE POURING ENERGY INTO THE MAGE YOU CALLED AERTIN! HE'S FIRING IT INTO THE DEMON!
WHAT ARE YOU TALKING ABOUT?!
YOU CAN'T SEE IT?!
THE ENERGY MISSILES, YES, BUT NOT--
SHHHRRRRAKKT
BRZZZAK
AAK!!
MERYL WAS DISTRACTED! HE WAS GIVING HIS ALL AND HAD NO POWER LEFT... TO FOCUS ELSEWHERE OR DEFEND HIMSELF!
THOOOSH

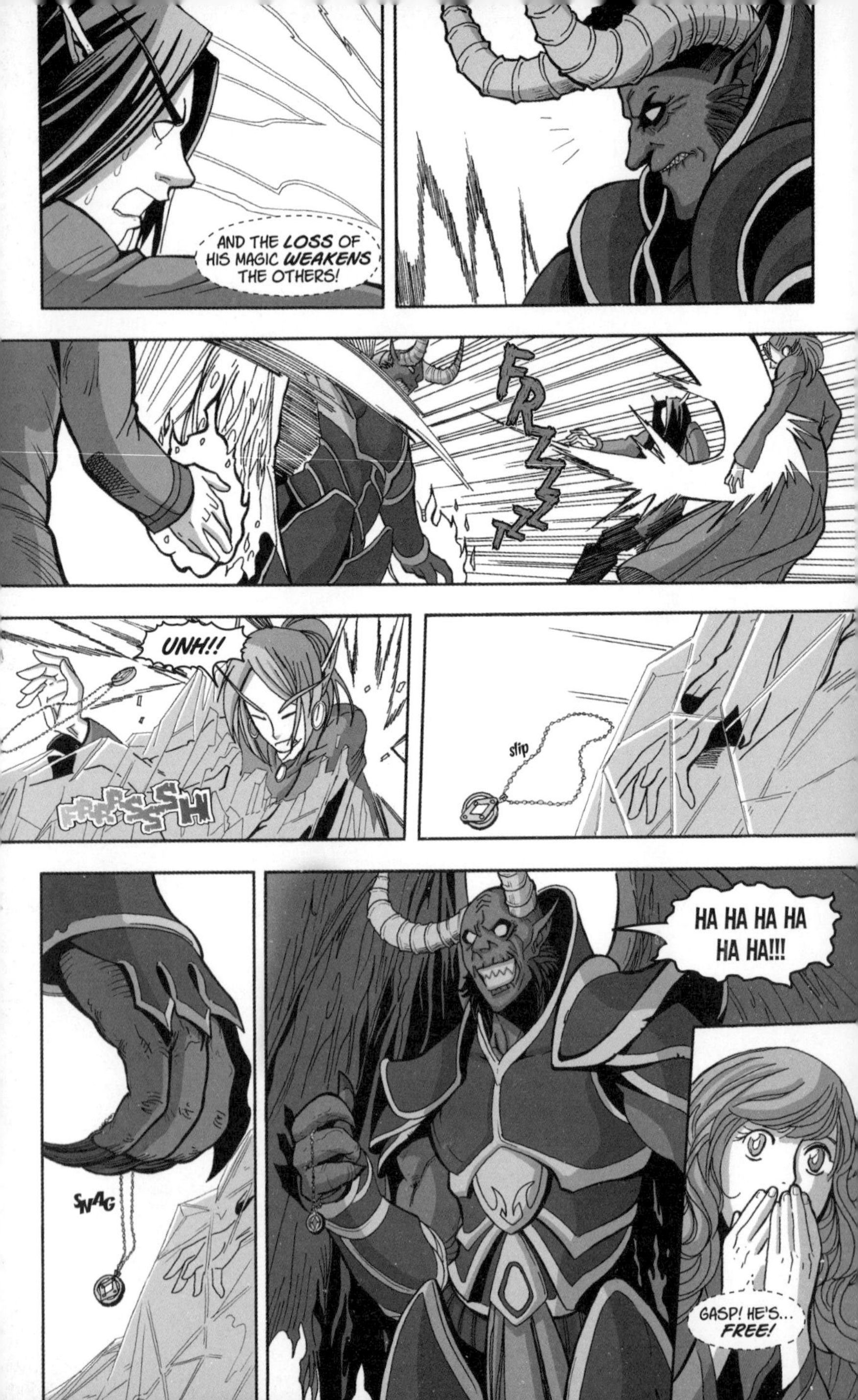
AND THE *LOSS* OF HIS MAGIC *WEAKENS* THE OTHERS!
FRZZZZT
UNH!!
FRRRSSSH
slip
SNAG
HA HA HA HA HA HA!!!
GASP! HE'S... *FREE!*

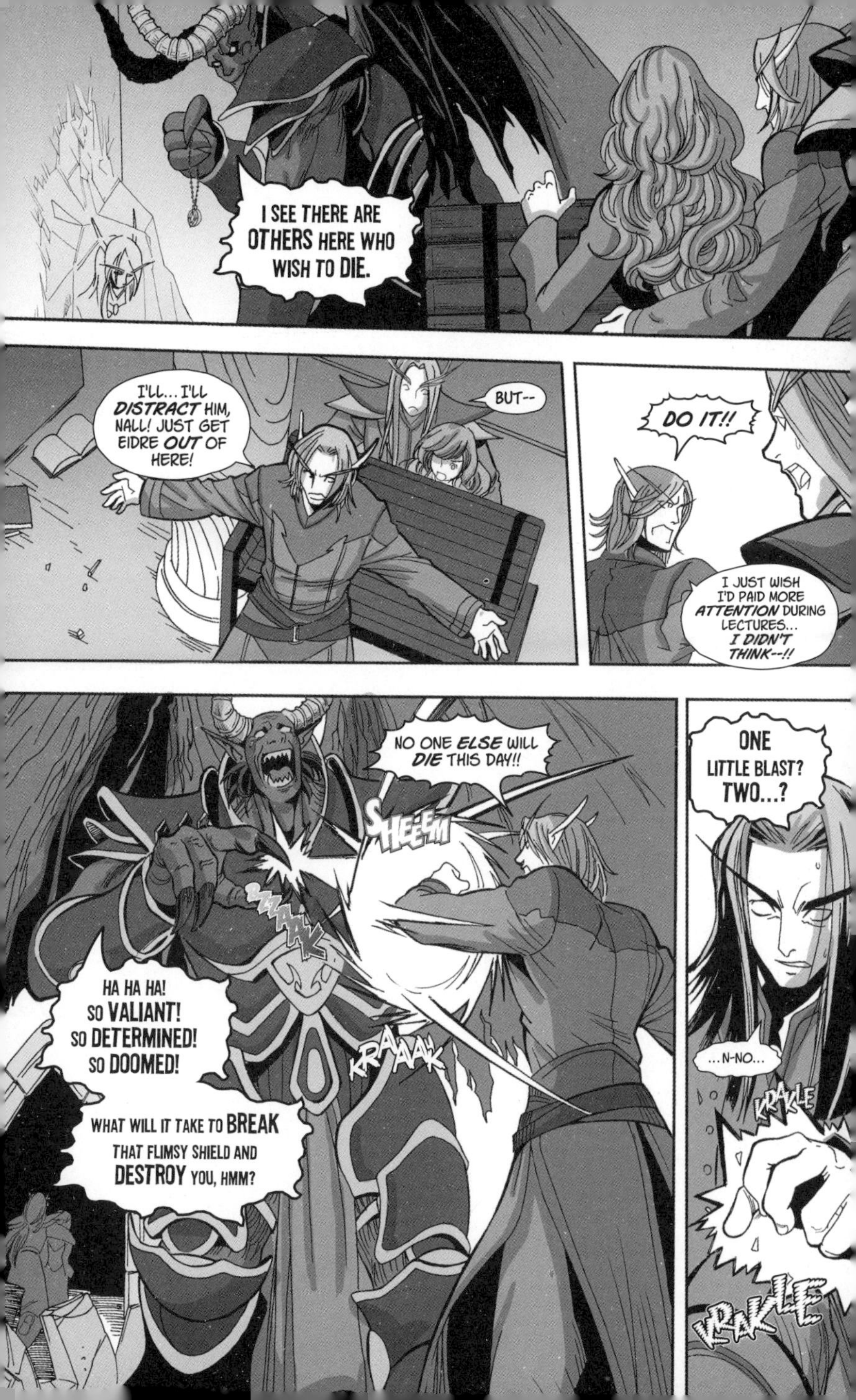
I SEE THERE ARE OTHERS HERE WHO WISH TO DIE.
I'LL... I'LL DISTRACT HIM, NALL! JUST GET EIDRE OUT OF HERE!
BUT--
DO IT!!
I JUST WISH I'D PAID MORE ATTENTION DURING LECTURES... I DIDN'T THINK--!!
NO ONE ELSE WILL DIE THIS DAY!!
SHEE-EM
BZZAAAK
HA HA HA! SO VALIANT! SO DETERMINED! SO DOOMED!
KRAAAAK
WHAT WILL IT TAKE TO BREAK THAT FLIMSY SHIELD AND DESTROY YOU, HMM?
ONE LITTLE BLAST? TWO...?
...N-NO...
KRAKLE
KRAKLE

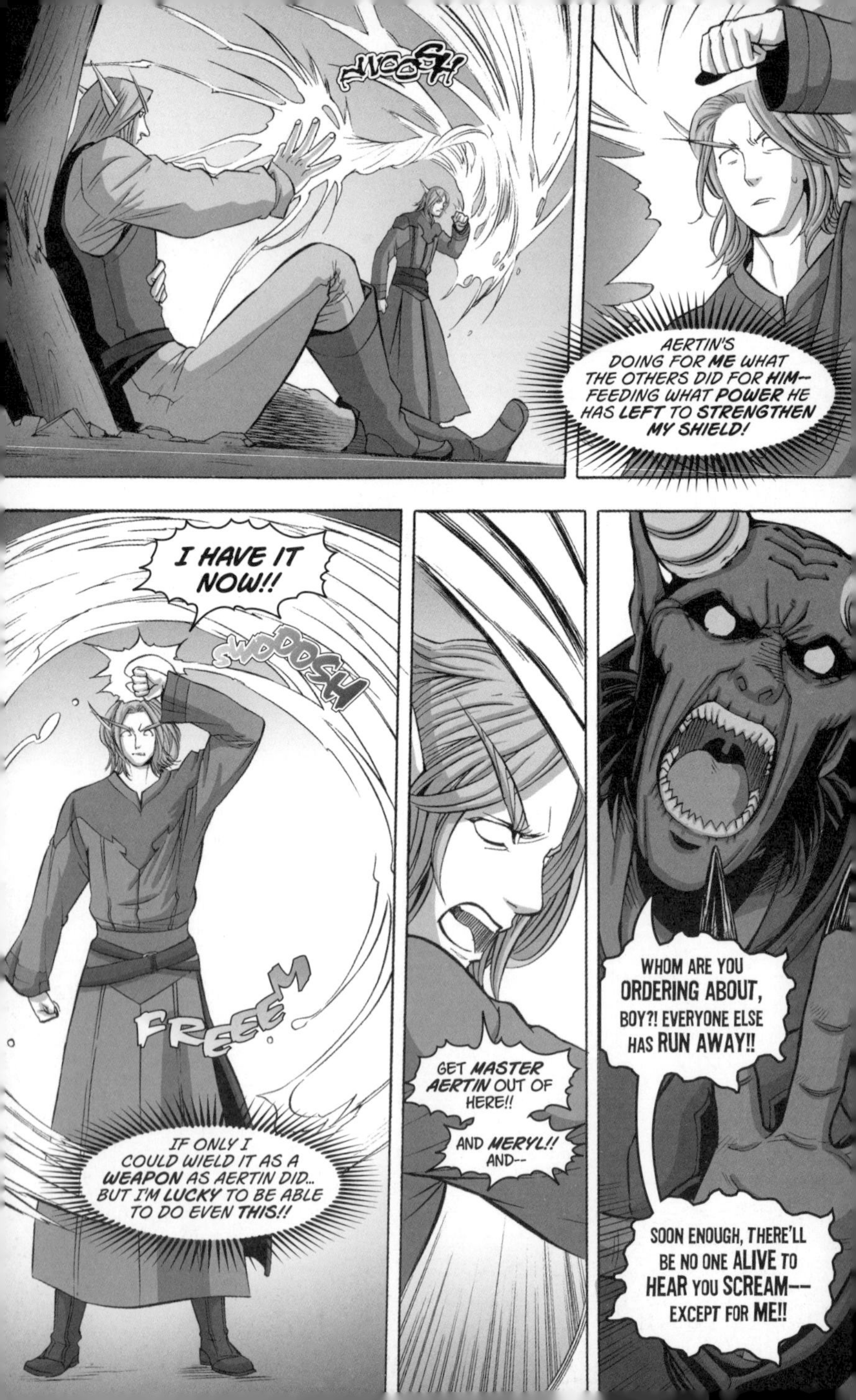
SWOOSH
AERTIN'S DOING FOR ME WHAT THE OTHERS DID FOR HIM-- FEEDING WHAT POWER HE HAS LEFT TO STRENGTHEN MY SHIELD!
I HAVE IT NOW!!
SWOOOSH
FREEEM
IF ONLY I COULD WIELD IT AS A WEAPON AS AERTIN DID... BUT I'M LUCKY TO BE ABLE TO DO EVEN THIS!!
GET MASTER AERTIN OUT OF HERE!!
AND MERYL!! AND--
WHOM ARE YOU ORDERING ABOUT, BOY?! EVERYONE ELSE HAS RUN AWAY!!
SOON ENOUGH, THERE'LL BE NO ONE ALIVE TO HEAR YOU SCREAM-- EXCEPT FOR ME!!

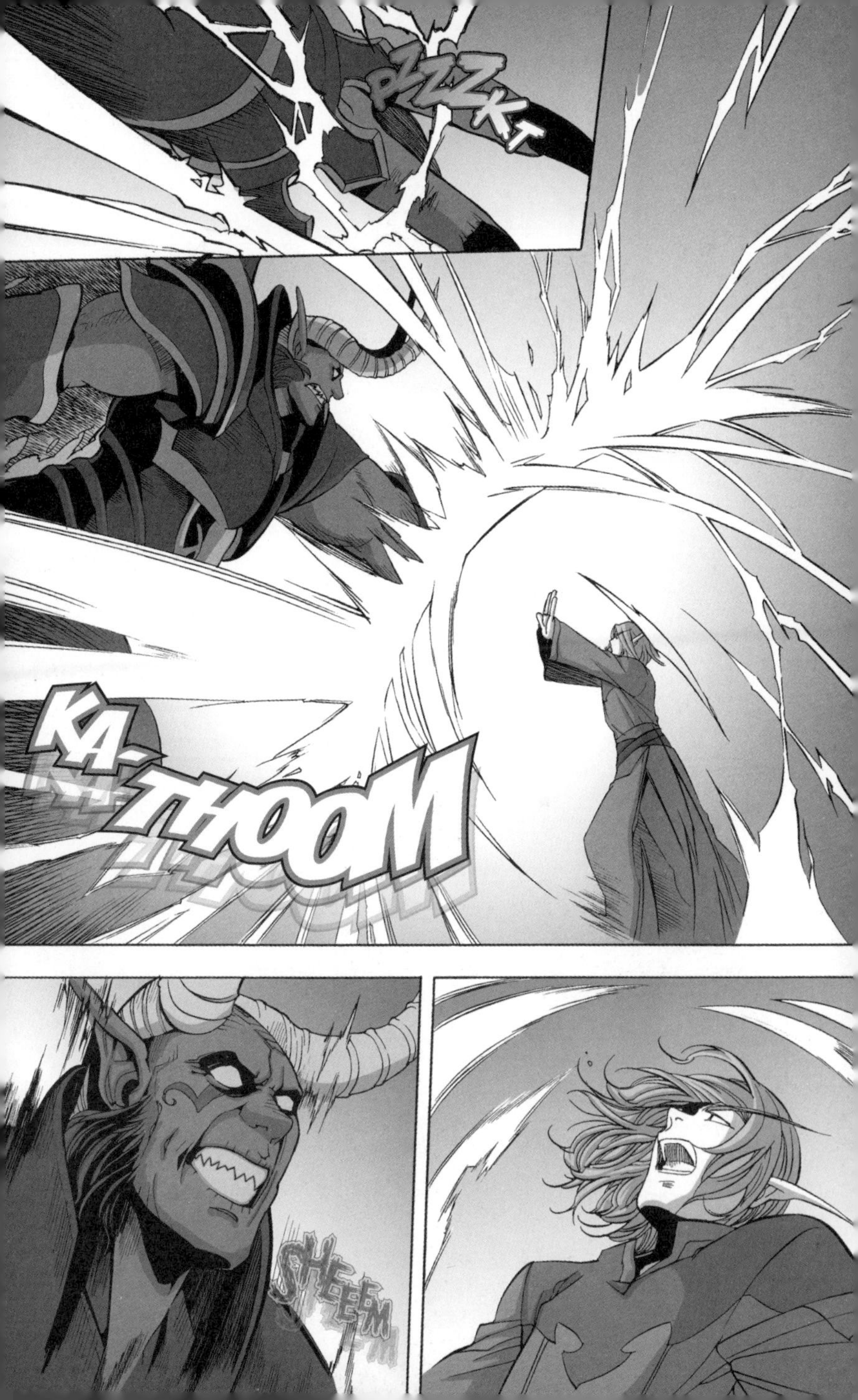
PZZZKT
KA-THOOM
SHEEEM

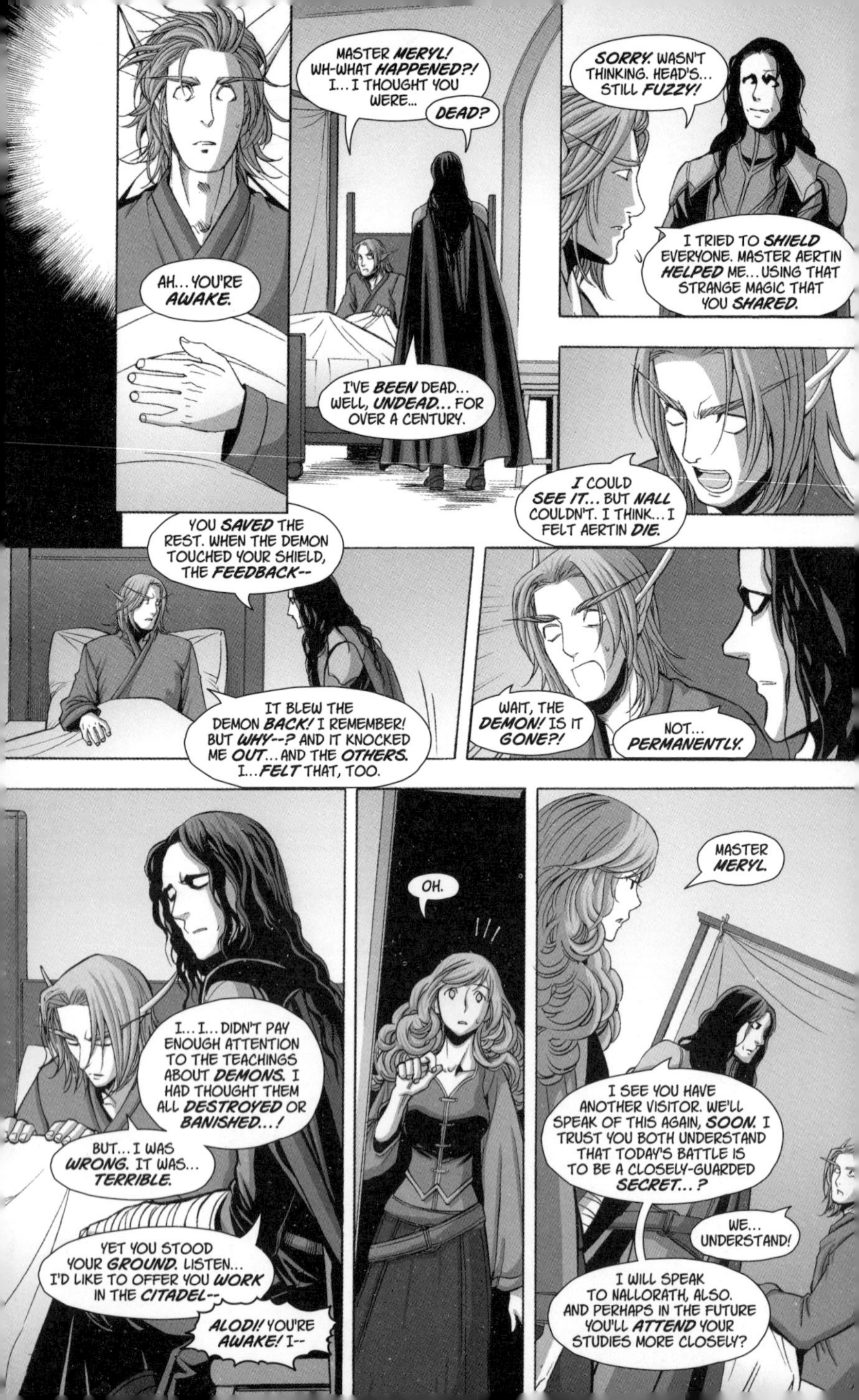
AH... YOU'RE AWAKE.
MASTER MERYL! WH-WHAT HAPPENED?! I... I THOUGHT YOU WERE...
DEAD?
I'VE BEEN DEAD... WELL, UNDEAD... FOR OVER A CENTURY.
SORRY. WASN'T THINKING. HEAD'S... STILL FUZZY!
I TRIED TO SHIELD EVERYONE. MASTER AERTIN HELPED ME... USING THAT STRANGE MAGIC THAT YOU SHARED.
I COULD SEE IT... BUT NALL COULDN'T. I THINK... I FELT AERTIN DIE.
YOU SAVED THE REST. WHEN THE DEMON TOUCHED YOUR SHIELD, THE FEEDBACK--
IT BLEW THE DEMON BACK! I REMEMBER! BUT WHY--? AND IT KNOCKED ME OUT... AND THE OTHERS. I... FELT THAT, TOO.
WAIT, THE DEMON! IS IT GONE?!
NOT... PERMANENTLY.
I... I... DIDN'T PAY ENOUGH ATTENTION TO THE TEACHINGS ABOUT DEMONS. I HAD THOUGHT THEM ALL DESTROYED OR BANISHED...!
BUT... I WAS WRONG. IT WAS... TERRIBLE.
YET YOU STOOD YOUR GROUND. LISTEN... I'D LIKE TO OFFER YOU WORK IN THE CITADEL--
ALODI! YOU'RE AWAKE! I--
OH.
MASTER MERYL.
I SEE YOU HAVE ANOTHER VISITOR. WE'LL SPEAK OF THIS AGAIN, SOON. I TRUST YOU BOTH UNDERSTAND THAT TODAY'S BATTLE IS TO BE A CLOSELY-GUARDED SECRET...?
WE... UNDERSTAND!
I WILL SPEAK TO NALLORATH, ALSO. AND PERHAPS IN THE FUTURE YOU'LL ATTEND YOUR STUDIES MORE CLOSELY?

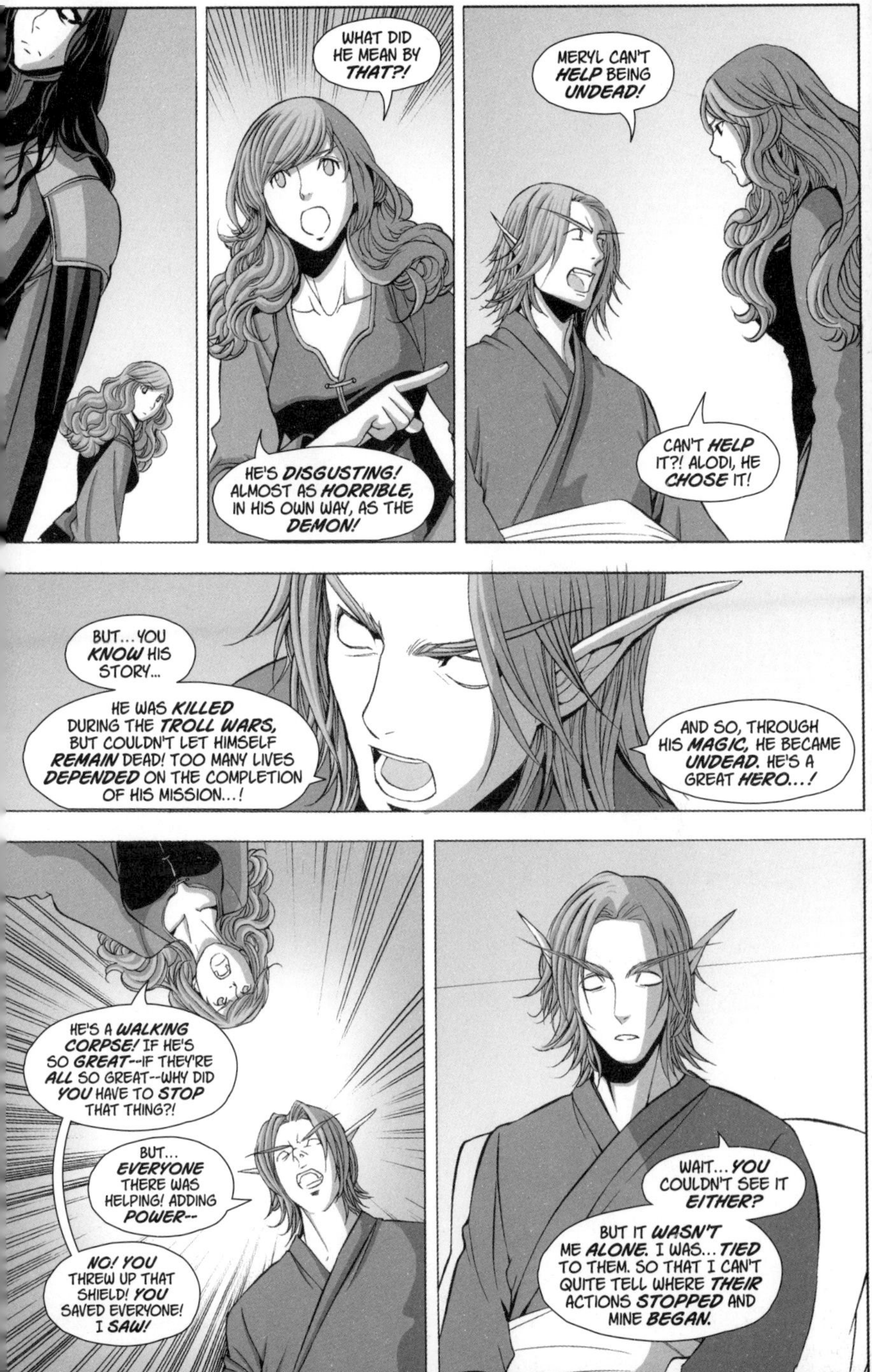
WHAT DID HE MEAN BY THAT?!
HE'S DISGUSTING! ALMOST AS HORRIBLE, IN HIS OWN WAY, AS THE DEMON!
MERYL CAN'T HELP BEING UNDEAD!
CAN'T HELP IT?! ALODI, HE CHOSE IT!
BUT... YOU KNOW HIS STORY...
HE WAS KILLED DURING THE TROLL WARS, BUT COULDN'T LET HIMSELF REMAIN DEAD! TOO MANY LIVES DEPENDED ON THE COMPLETION OF HIS MISSION...!
AND SO, THROUGH HIS MAGIC, HE BECAME UNDEAD. HE'S A GREAT HERO...!
HE'S A WALKING CORPSE! IF HE'S SO GREAT--IF THEY'RE ALL SO GREAT--WHY DID YOU HAVE TO STOP THAT THING?!
BUT... EVERYONE THERE WAS HELPING! ADDING POWER--
NO! YOU THREW UP THAT SHIELD! YOU SAVED EVERYONE! I SAW!
WAIT... YOU COULDN'T SEE IT EITHER?
BUT IT WASN'T ME ALONE. I WAS... TIED TO THEM. SO THAT I CAN'T QUITE TELL WHERE THEIR ACTIONS STOPPED AND MINE BEGAN.

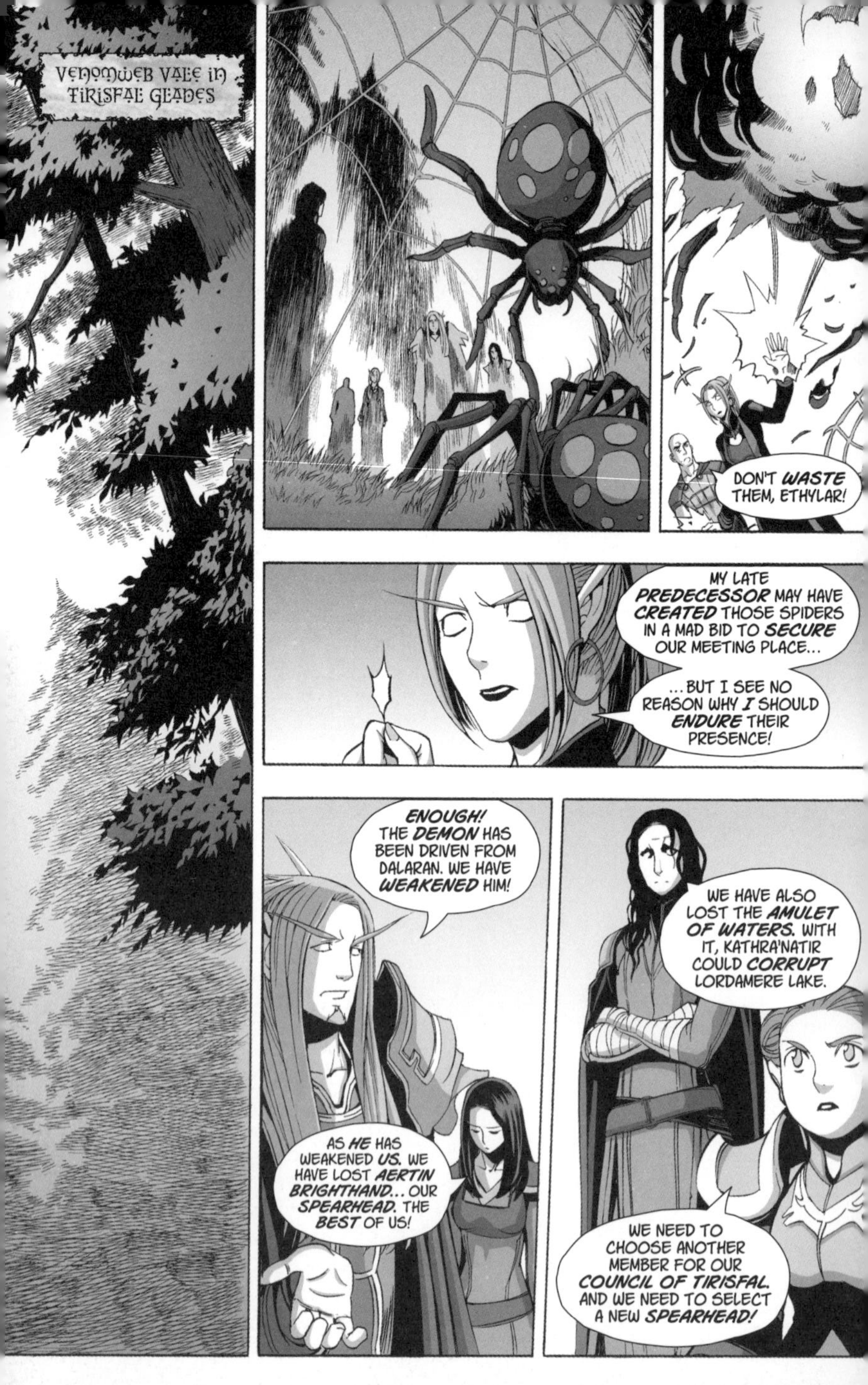
VENOMWEB VALE IN TIRISFAL GLADES
DON'T WASTE THEM, ETHYLAR!
MY LATE PREDECESSOR MAY HAVE CREATED THOSE SPIDERS IN A MAD BID TO SECURE OUR MEETING PLACE...
...BUT I SEE NO REASON WHY I SHOULD ENDURE THEIR PRESENCE!
ENOUGH! THE DEMON HAS BEEN DRIVEN FROM DALARAN. WE HAVE WEAKENED HIM!
AS HE HAS WEAKENED US. WE HAVE LOST AERTIN BRIGHTHAND... OUR SPEARHEAD. THE BEST OF US!
WE HAVE ALSO LOST THE AMULET OF WATERS. WITH IT, KATHRA'NATIR COULD CORRUPT LORDAMERE LAKE.
WE NEED TO CHOOSE ANOTHER MEMBER FOR OUR COUNCIL OF TIRISFAL. AND WE NEED TO SELECT A NEW SPEARHEAD!

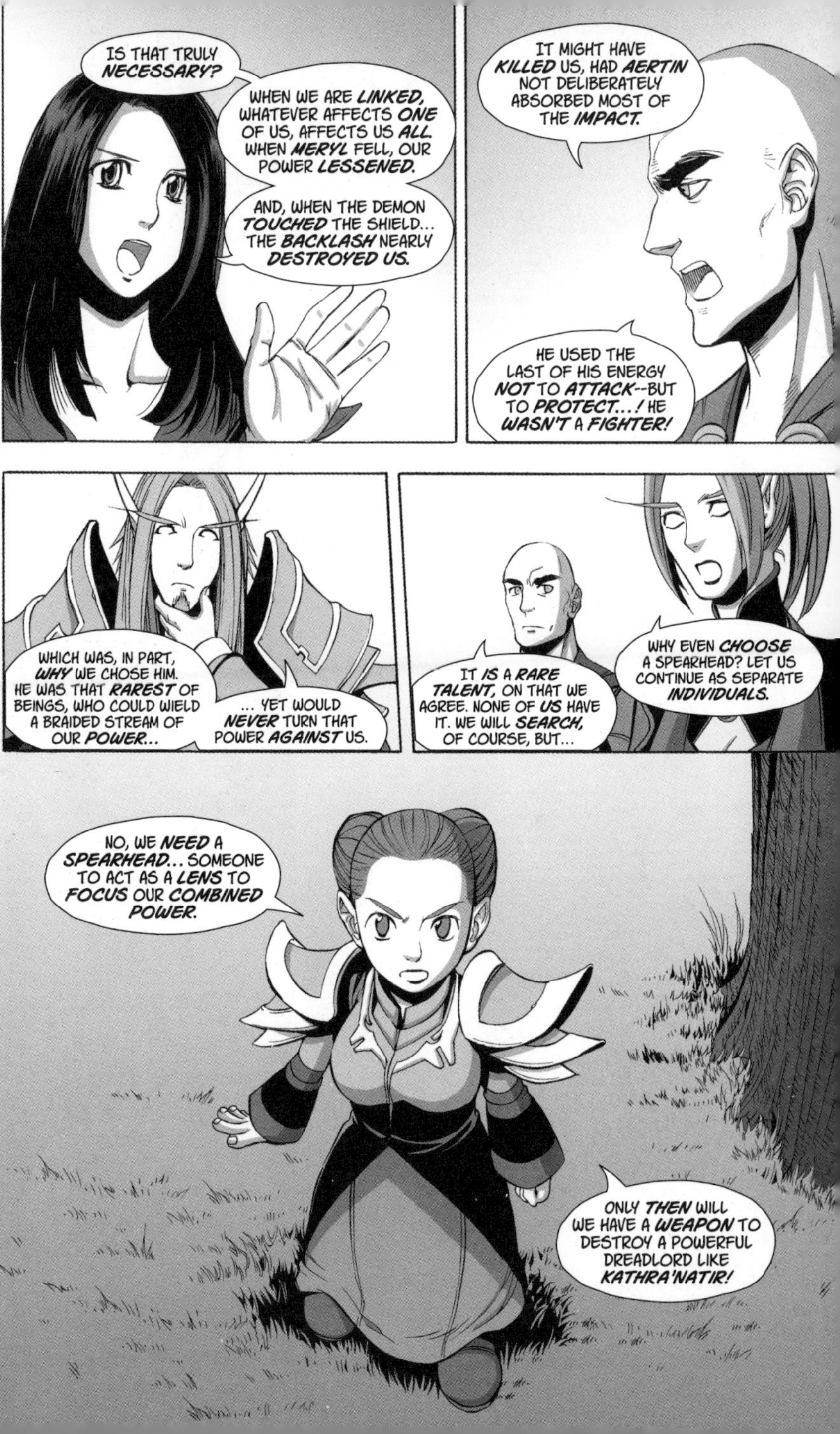
IS THAT TRULY NECESSARY?
WHEN WE ARE LINKED, WHATEVER AFFECTS ONE OF US, AFFECTS US ALL. WHEN MERYL FELL, OUR POWER LESSENED.
AND, WHEN THE DEMON TOUCHED THE SHIELD... THE BACKLASH NEARLY DESTROYED US.
IT MIGHT HAVE KILLED US, HAD AERTIN NOT DELIBERATELY ABSORBED MOST OF THE IMPACT.
HE USED THE LAST OF HIS ENERGY NOT TO ATTACK--BUT TO PROTECT...! HE WASN'T A FIGHTER!
WHICH WAS, IN PART, WHY WE CHOSE HIM. HE WAS THAT RAREST OF BEINGS, WHO COULD WIELD A BRAIDED STREAM OF OUR POWER...
... YET WOULD NEVER TURN THAT POWER AGAINST US.
IT IS A RARE TALENT, ON THAT WE AGREE. NONE OF US HAVE IT. WE WILL SEARCH, OF COURSE, BUT...
WHY EVEN CHOOSE A SPEARHEAD? LET US CONTINUE AS SEPARATE INDIVIDUALS.
NO, WE NEED A SPEARHEAD... SOMEONE TO ACT AS A LENS TO FOCUS OUR COMBINED POWER.
ONLY THEN WILL WE HAVE A WEAPON TO DESTROY A POWERFUL DREADLORD LIKE KATHRA'NATIR!

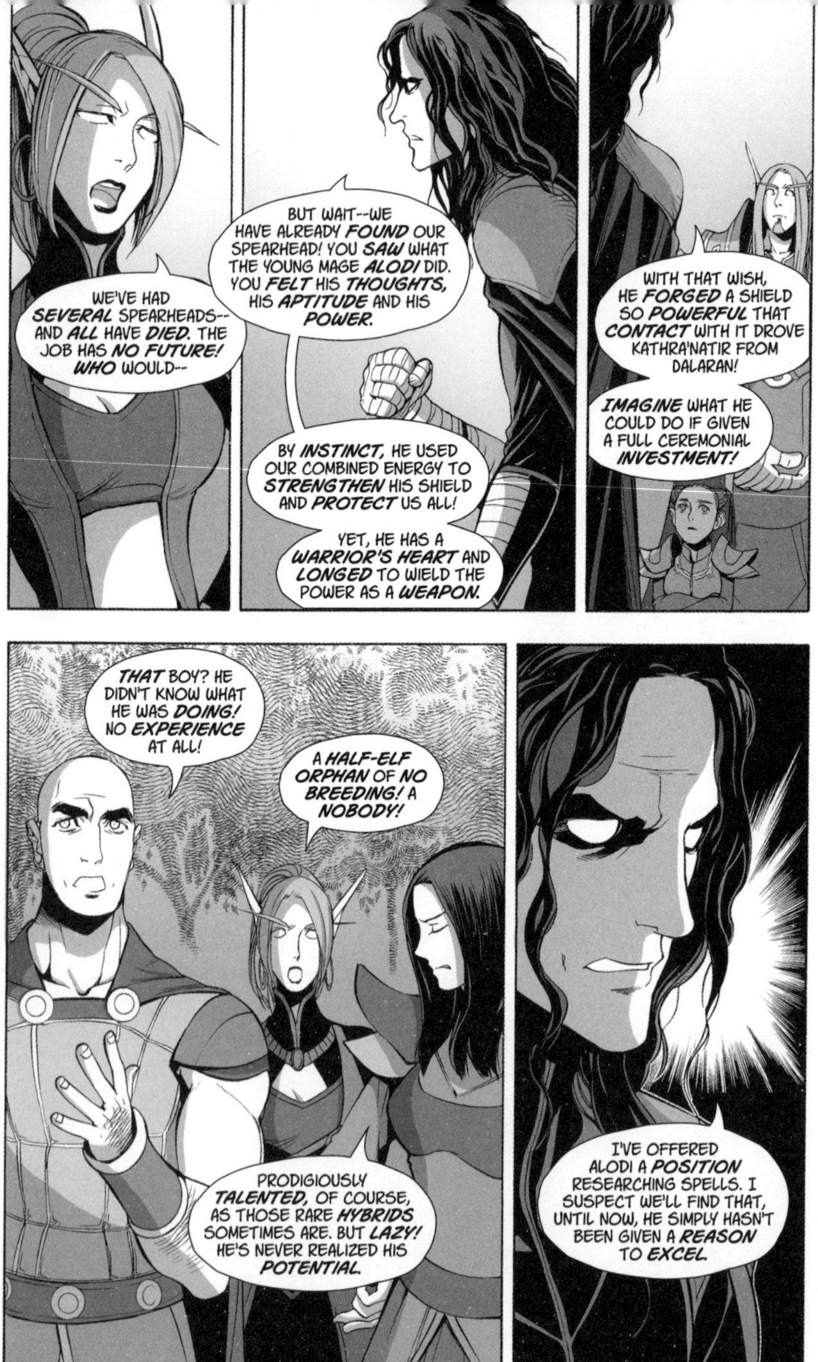
WE'VE HAD SEVERAL SPEARHEADS-- AND ALL HAVE DIED. THE JOB HAS NO FUTURE! WHO WOULD--
BUT WAIT--WE HAVE ALREADY FOUND OUR SPEARHEAD! YOU SAW WHAT THE YOUNG MAGE ALODI DID. YOU FELT HIS THOUGHTS, HIS APTITUDE AND HIS POWER.
BY INSTINCT, HE USED OUR COMBINED ENERGY TO STRENGTHEN HIS SHIELD AND PROTECT US ALL!
YET, HE HAS A WARRIOR'S HEART AND LONGED TO WIELD THE POWER AS A WEAPON.
WITH THAT WISH, HE FORGED A SHIELD SO POWERFUL THAT CONTACT WITH IT DROVE KATHRA'NATIR FROM DALARAN!
IMAGINE WHAT HE COULD DO IF GIVEN A FULL CEREMONIAL INVESTMENT!
THAT BOY? HE DIDN'T KNOW WHAT HE WAS DOING! NO EXPERIENCE AT ALL!
A HALF-ELF ORPHAN OF NO BREEDING! A NOBODY!
PRODIGIOUSLY TALENTED, OF COURSE, AS THOSE RARE HYBRIDS SOMETIMES ARE. BUT LAZY! HE'S NEVER REALIZED HIS POTENTIAL.
I'VE OFFERED ALODI A POSITION RESEARCHING SPELLS. I SUSPECT WE'LL FIND THAT, UNTIL NOW, HE SIMPLY HASN'T BEEN GIVEN A REASON TO EXCEL.

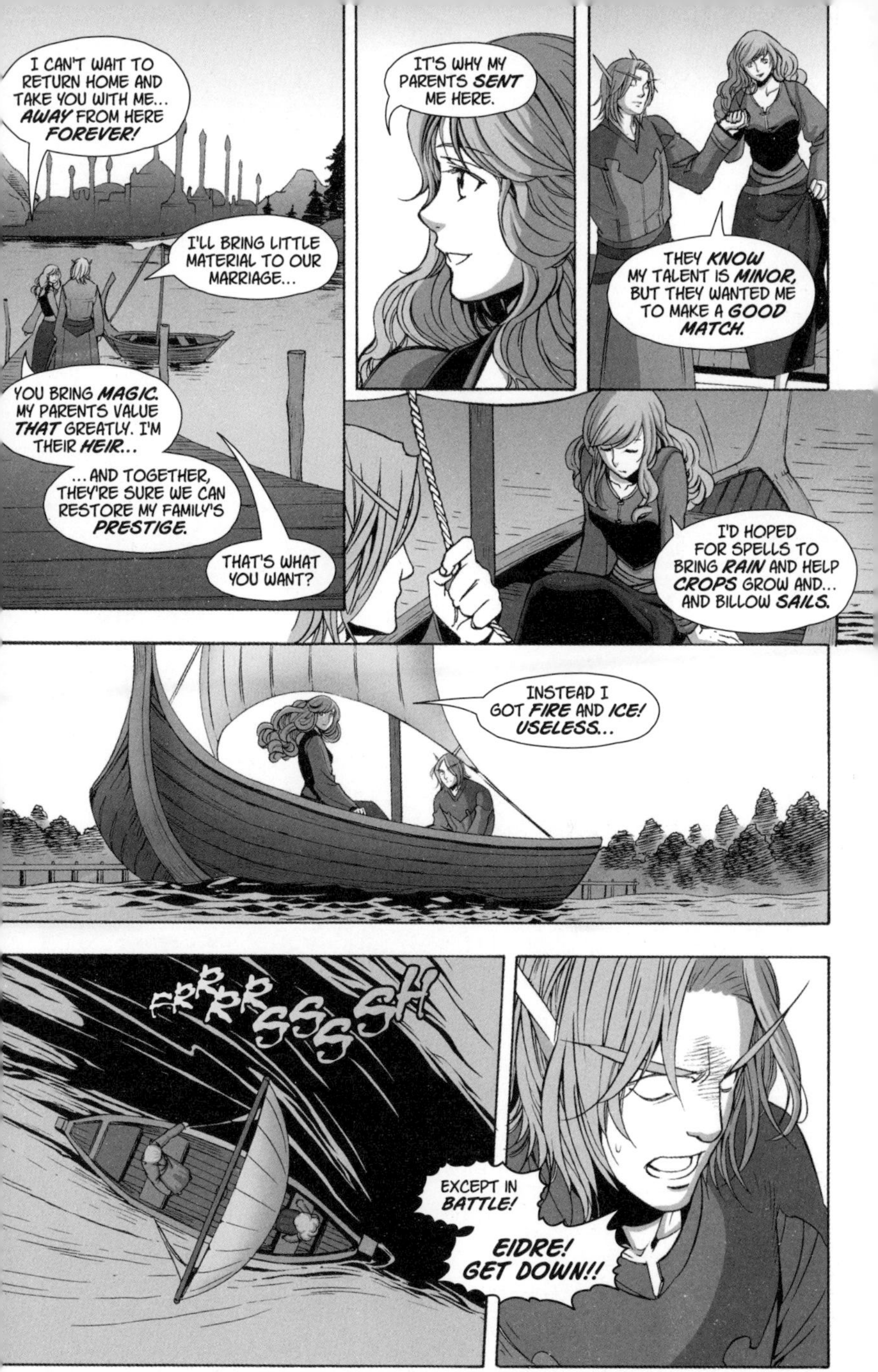
I CAN'T WAIT TO RETURN HOME AND TAKE YOU WITH ME... AWAY FROM HERE FOREVER!
I'LL BRING LITTLE MATERIAL TO OUR MARRIAGE...
YOU BRING MAGIC. MY PARENTS VALUE THAT GREATLY. I'M THEIR HEIR...
...AND TOGETHER, THEY'RE SURE WE CAN RESTORE MY FAMILY'S PRESTIGE.
THAT'S WHAT YOU WANT?
IT'S WHY MY PARENTS SENT ME HERE.
THEY KNOW MY TALENT IS MINOR, BUT THEY WANTED ME TO MAKE A GOOD MATCH.
I'D HOPED FOR SPELLS TO BRING RAIN AND HELP CROPS GROW AND... AND BILLOW SAILS.
INSTEAD I GOT FIRE AND ICE! USELESS...
FRRRRSSSSSH
EXCEPT IN BATTLE!
EIDRE! GET DOWN!!

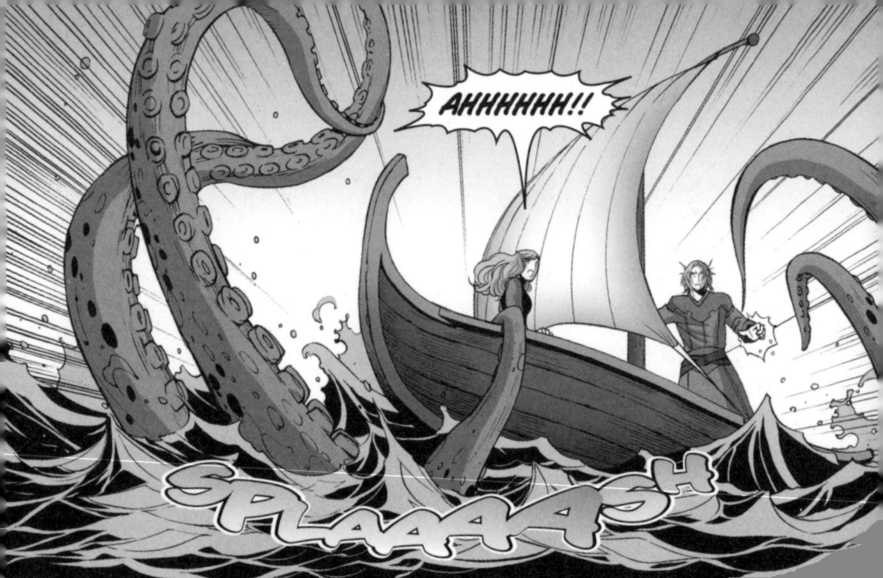
AHHHHHH!!
SPLAAAASH

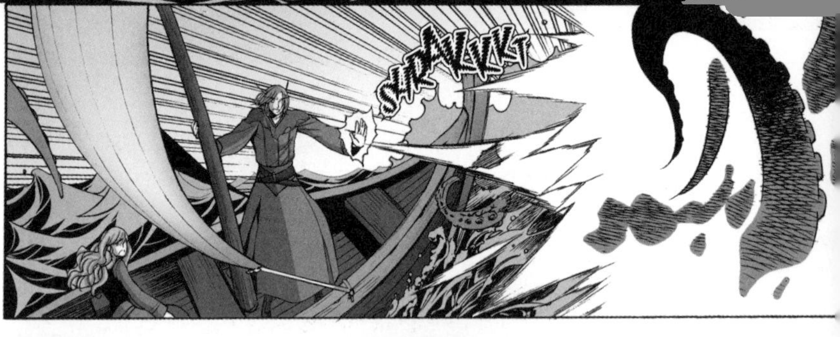

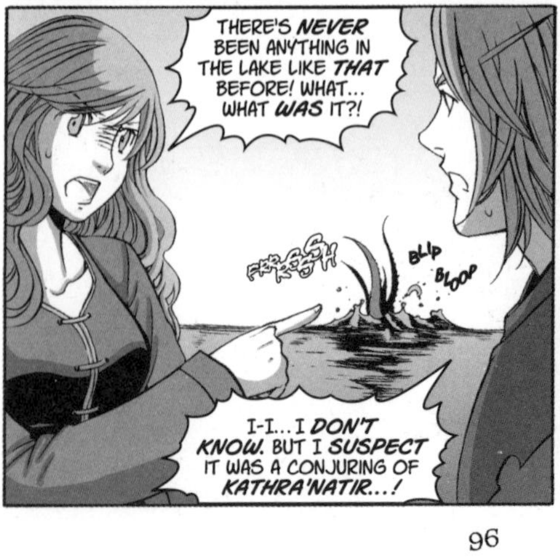
THERE'S **NEVER** BEEN ANYTHING IN THE LAKE LIKE **THAT** BEFORE! WHAT... WHAT **WAS** IT?!
BLIP
BLOOP
I-I... I **DON'T KNOW.** BUT I **SUSPECT** IT WAS A CONJURING OF **KATHRA'NATIR...!**

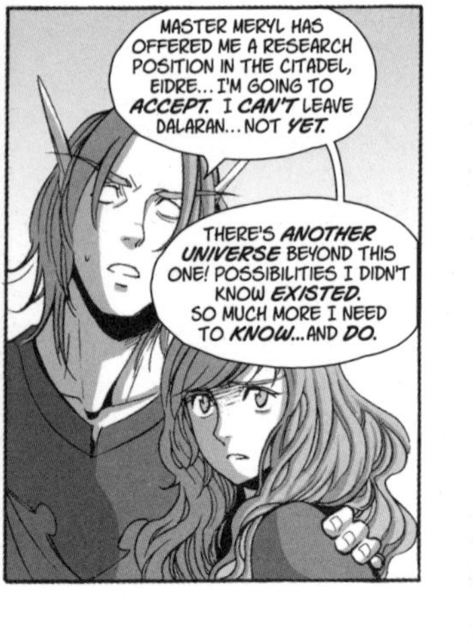
MASTER MERYL HAS OFFERED ME A RESEARCH POSITION IN THE CITADEL, EIDRE... I'M GOING TO **ACCEPT.** I **CAN'T** LEAVE DALARAN... NOT **YET.**
THERE'S **ANOTHER UNIVERSE** BEYOND THIS ONE! POSSIBILITIES I DIDN'T KNOW **EXISTED.** SO MUCH MORE I NEED TO **KNOW...** AND **DO.**

THIS CAMPAIGN TO RID THE LAKE OF KATHRA'NATIR'S TAINT WILL BE A *FAIR TEST.*

THE COUNCIL MAY WELL SUCCEED *WITHOUT* A SPEARHEAD.

WE'RE *READY,* INDUS...!

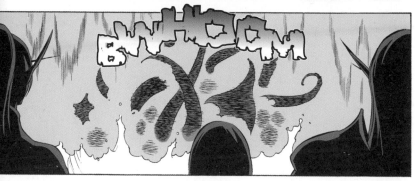

B-WHOOM

HA! YOU SEE HOW *EASILY* WE DESTROY THESE MONSTERS...!

TAKE HEED... THEY ARE THE DEMON'S *PETS,* IRAR--NOT THE DEMON *HIMSELF.* KATHRA'NATIR HAS *LEFT* DALARAN TO SPREAD HIS MISERY ACROSS *ARATHOR.*

97

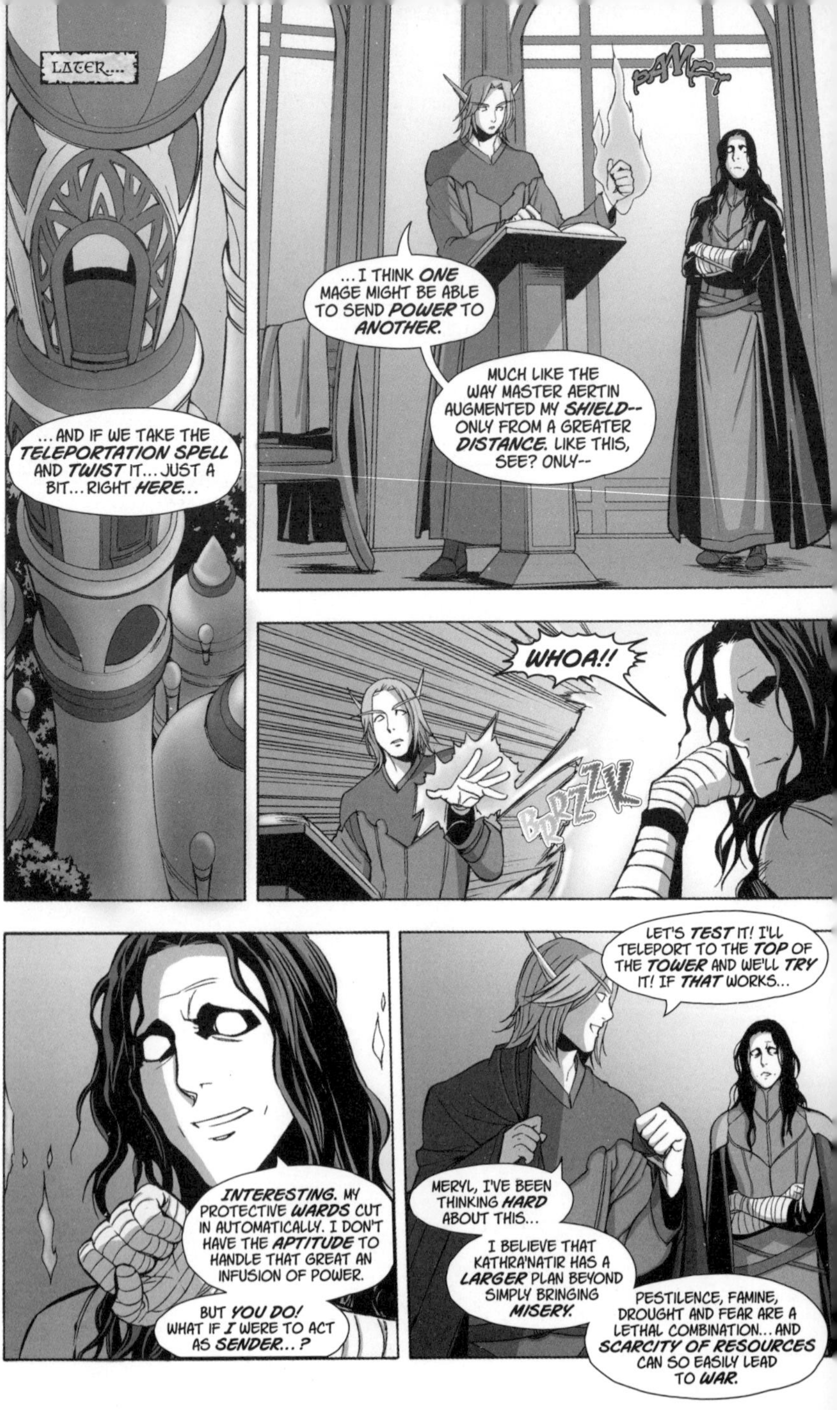
LATER....
...AND IF WE TAKE THE TELEPORTATION SPELL AND TWIST IT... JUST A BIT... RIGHT HERE...
...I THINK ONE MAGE MIGHT BE ABLE TO SEND POWER TO ANOTHER.
MUCH LIKE THE WAY MASTER AERTIN AUGMENTED MY SHIELD-- ONLY FROM A GREATER DISTANCE. LIKE THIS, SEE? ONLY--
WHOA!!
INTERESTING. MY PROTECTIVE WARDS CUT IN AUTOMATICALLY. I DON'T HAVE THE APTITUDE TO HANDLE THAT GREAT AN INFUSION OF POWER.
BUT YOU DO! WHAT IF I WERE TO ACT AS SENDER...?
LET'S TEST IT! I'LL TELEPORT TO THE TOP OF THE TOWER AND WE'LL TRY IT! IF THAT WORKS...
MERYL, I'VE BEEN THINKING HARD ABOUT THIS...
I BELIEVE THAT KATHRA'NATIR HAS A LARGER PLAN BEYOND SIMPLY BRINGING MISERY.
PESTILENCE, FAMINE, DROUGHT AND FEAR ARE A LETHAL COMBINATION... AND SCARCITY OF RESOURCES CAN SO EASILY LEAD TO WAR.

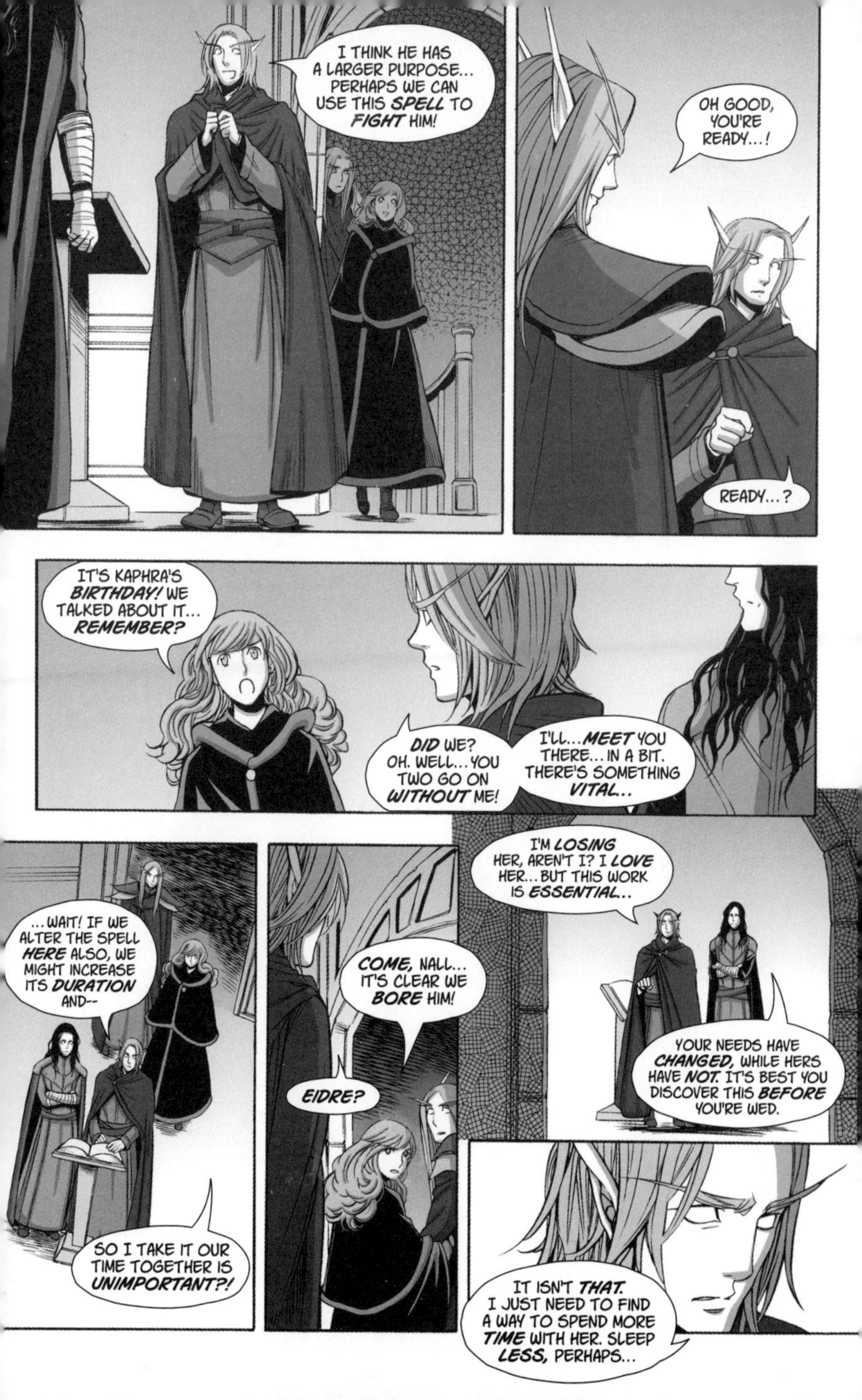
I THINK HE HAS A LARGER PURPOSE... PERHAPS WE CAN USE THIS SPELL TO FIGHT HIM!
OH GOOD, YOU'RE READY...!
READY...?
IT'S KAPHRA'S BIRTHDAY! WE TALKED ABOUT IT... REMEMBER?
DID WE? OH. WELL... YOU TWO GO ON WITHOUT ME!
I'LL... MEET YOU THERE... IN A BIT. THERE'S SOMETHING VITAL...
...WAIT! IF WE ALTER THE SPELL HERE ALSO, WE MIGHT INCREASE ITS DURATION AND--
SO I TAKE IT OUR TIME TOGETHER IS UNIMPORTANT?!
COME, NALL... IT'S CLEAR WE BORE HIM!
EIDRE?
I'M LOSING HER, AREN'T I? I LOVE HER... BUT THIS WORK IS ESSENTIAL...
YOUR NEEDS HAVE CHANGED, WHILE HERS HAVE NOT. IT'S BEST YOU DISCOVER THIS BEFORE YOU'RE WED.
IT ISN'T THAT. I JUST NEED TO FIND A WAY TO SPEND MORE TIME WITH HER. SLEEP LESS, PERHAPS...

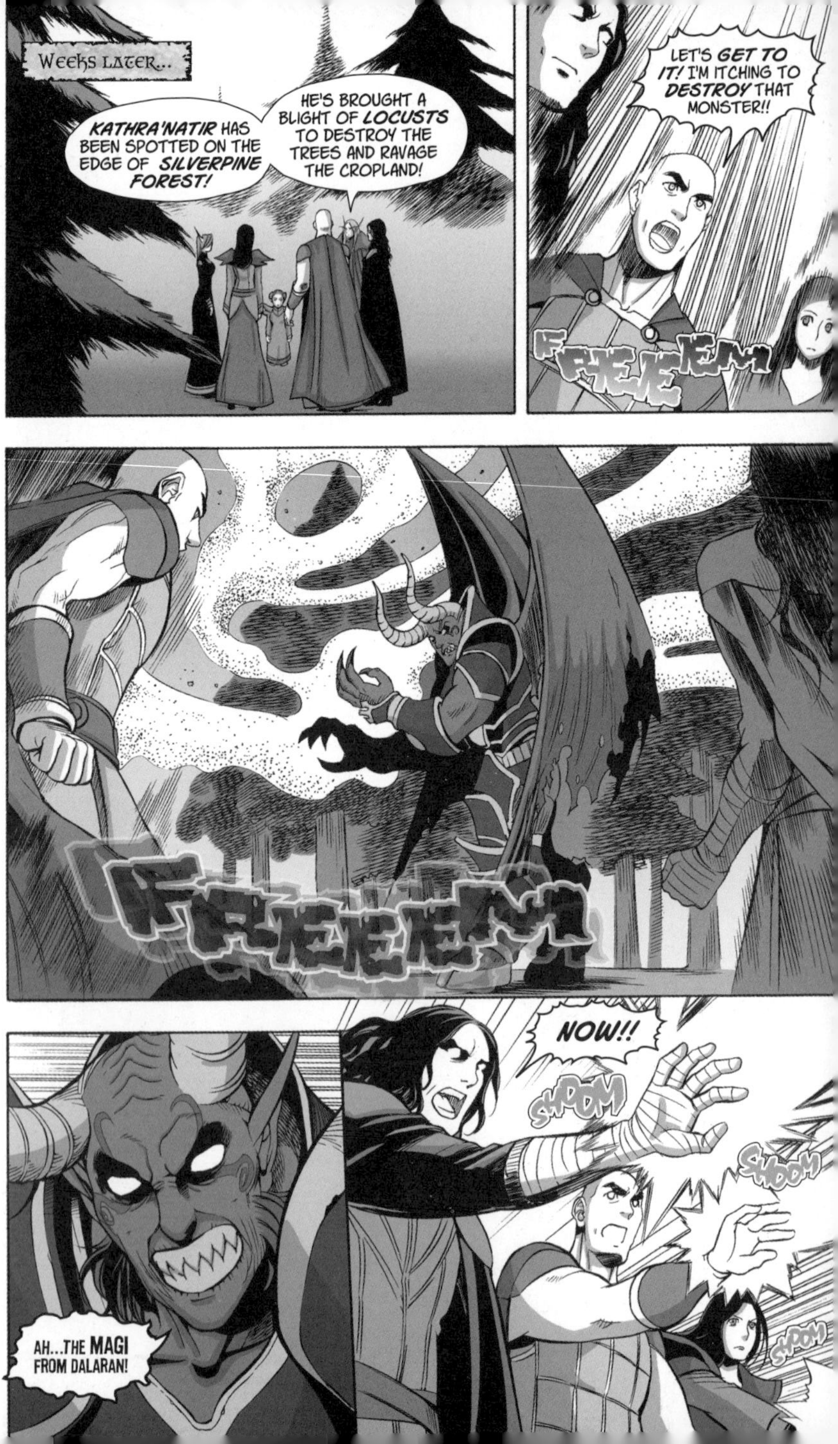
Weeks later...
KATHRA'NATIR HAS BEEN SPOTTED ON THE EDGE OF *SILVERPINE FOREST!*
HE'S BROUGHT A BLIGHT OF *LOCUSTS* TO DESTROY THE TREES AND RAVAGE THE CROPLAND!
LET'S *GET TO IT!* I'M ITCHING TO *DESTROY* THAT MONSTER!!
FREEEM
FREEEM
AH...THE **MAGI** FROM DALARAN!
NOW!!
SHOOM
SHOOM
SHOOM

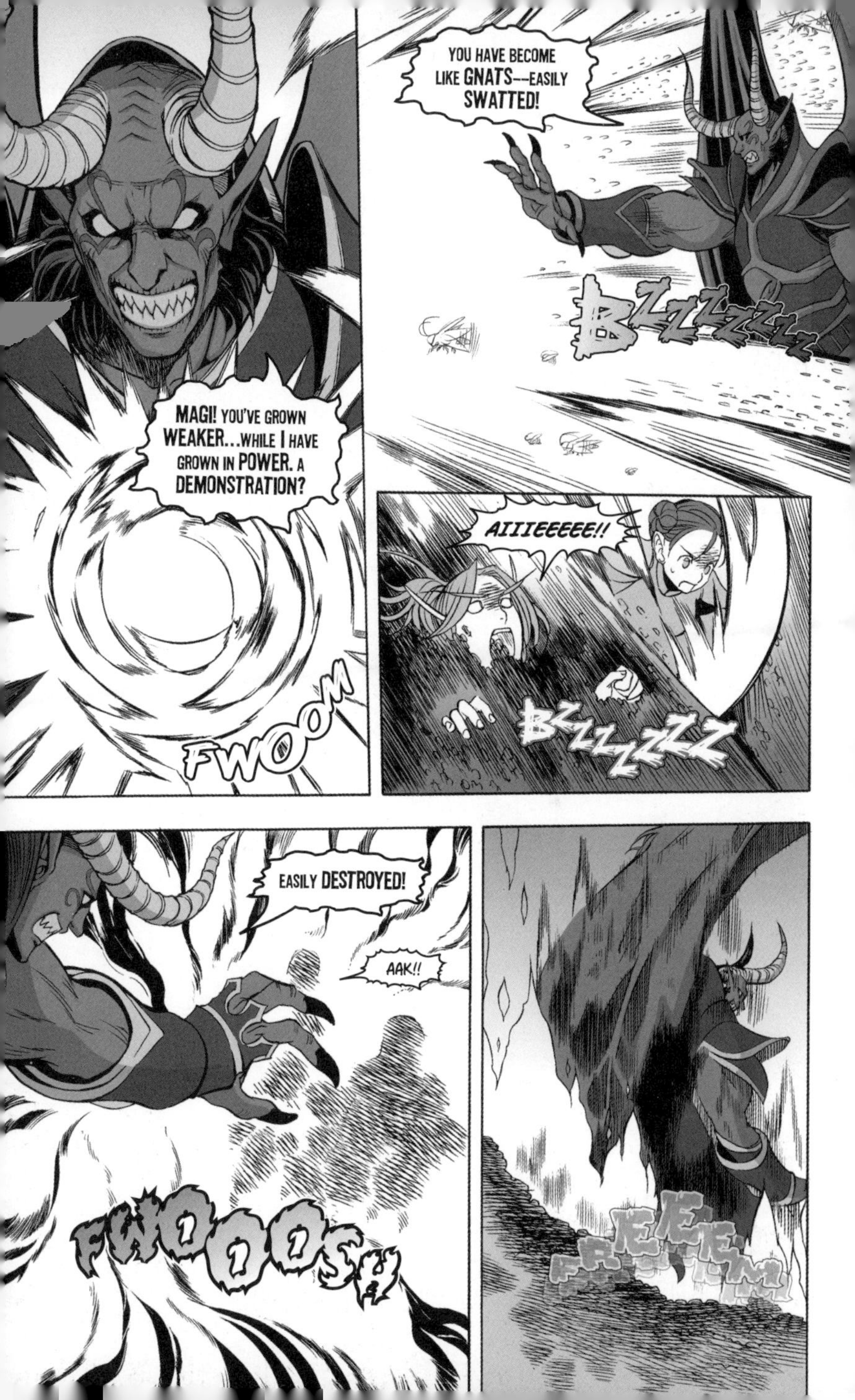
MAGI! YOU'VE GROWN WEAKER...WHILE I HAVE GROWN IN POWER. A DEMONSTRATION?
FWOOM
YOU HAVE BECOME LIKE GNATS--EASILY SWATTED!
AIIIEEEEE!!
EASILY DESTROYED!
AAK!!
FWOOOSH

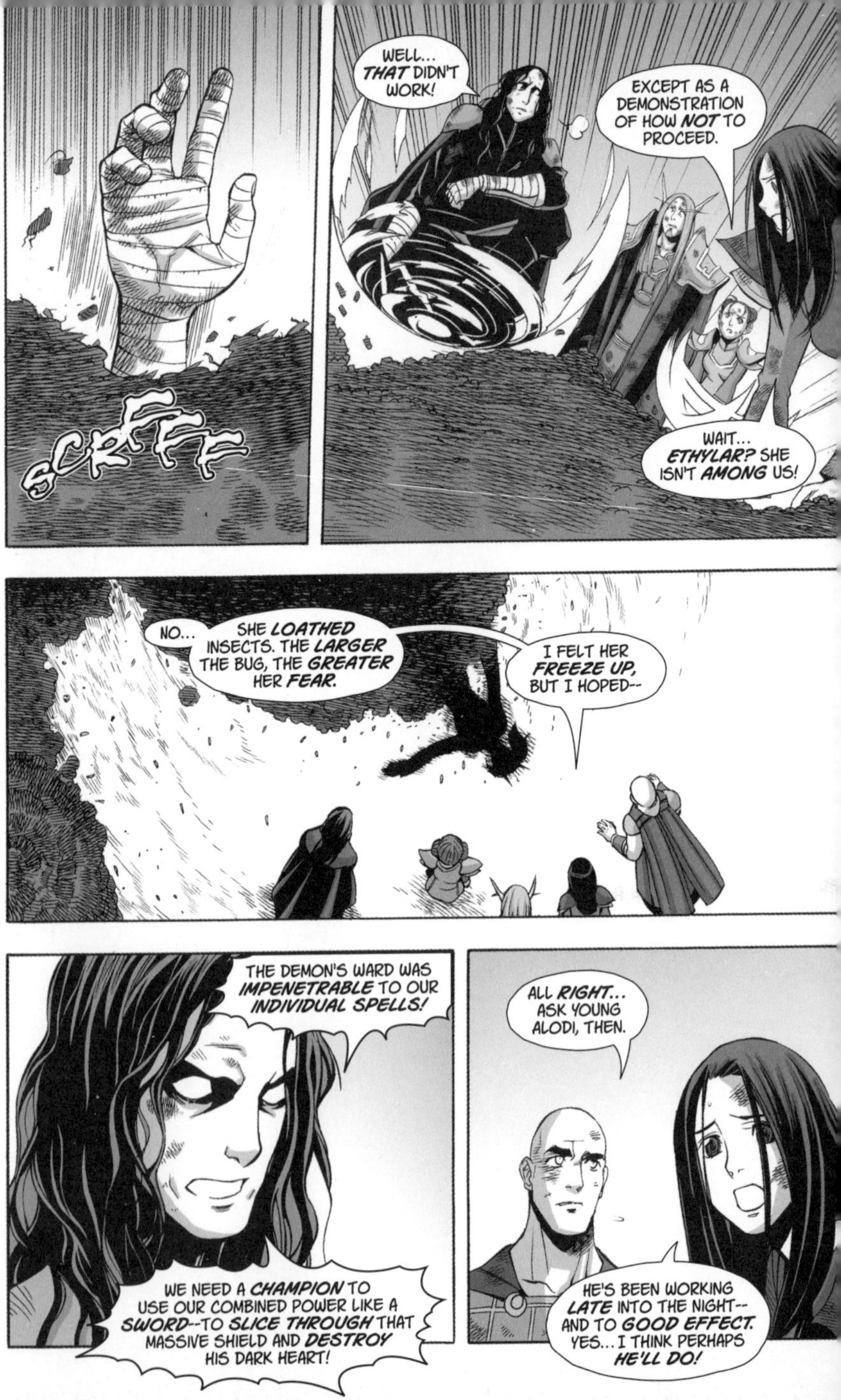
SCRFFF
WELL... THAT DIDN'T WORK!
EXCEPT AS A DEMONSTRATION OF HOW NOT TO PROCEED.
WAIT... ETHYLAR? SHE ISN'T AMONG US!
NO...
SHE LOATHED INSECTS. THE LARGER THE BUG, THE GREATER HER FEAR.
I FELT HER FREEZE UP, BUT I HOPED--
THE DEMON'S WARD WAS IMPENETRABLE TO OUR INDIVIDUAL SPELLS!
WE NEED A CHAMPION TO USE OUR COMBINED POWER LIKE A SWORD--TO SLICE THROUGH THAT MASSIVE SHIELD AND DESTROY HIS DARK HEART!
ALL RIGHT... ASK YOUNG ALODI, THEN.
HE'S BEEN WORKING LATE INTO THE NIGHT-- AND TO GOOD EFFECT. YES... I THINK PERHAPS HE'LL DO!

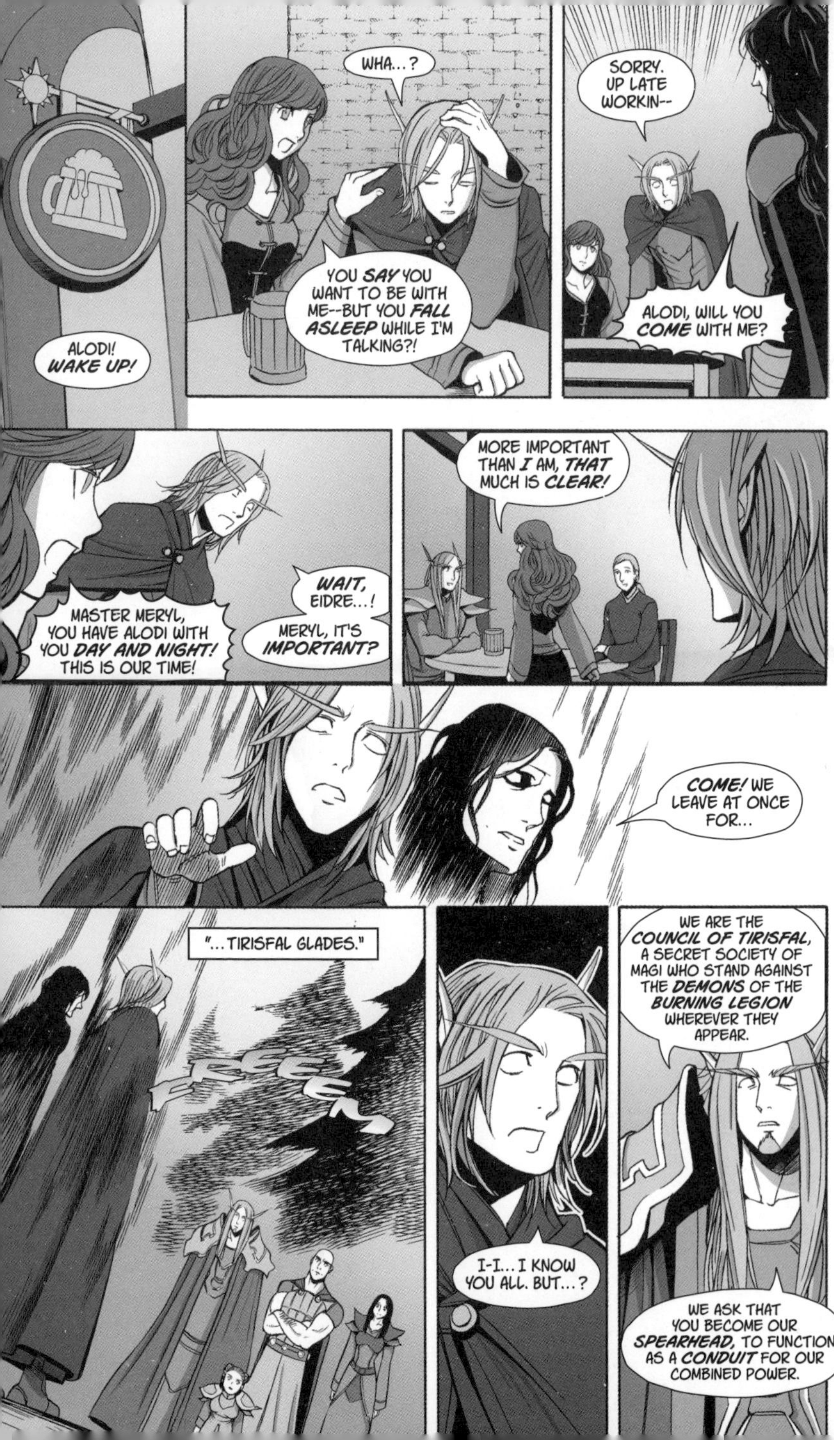
ALODI! WAKE UP!
WHA...?
YOU SAY YOU WANT TO BE WITH ME--BUT YOU FALL ASLEEP WHILE I'M TALKING?!
SORRY. UP LATE WORKIN--
ALODI, WILL YOU COME WITH ME?
MASTER MERYL, YOU HAVE ALODI WITH YOU DAY AND NIGHT! THIS IS OUR TIME!
WAIT, EIDRE...!
MERYL, IT'S IMPORTANT?
MORE IMPORTANT THAN I AM, THAT MUCH IS CLEAR!
COME! WE LEAVE AT ONCE FOR...
"...TIRISFAL GLADES."
FREEEEM
I-I... I KNOW YOU ALL. BUT...?
WE ARE THE COUNCIL OF TIRISFAL, A SECRET SOCIETY OF MAGI WHO STAND AGAINST THE DEMONS OF THE BURNING LEGION WHEREVER THEY APPEAR.
WE ASK THAT YOU BECOME OUR SPEARHEAD, TO FUNCTION AS A CONDUIT FOR OUR COMBINED POWER.

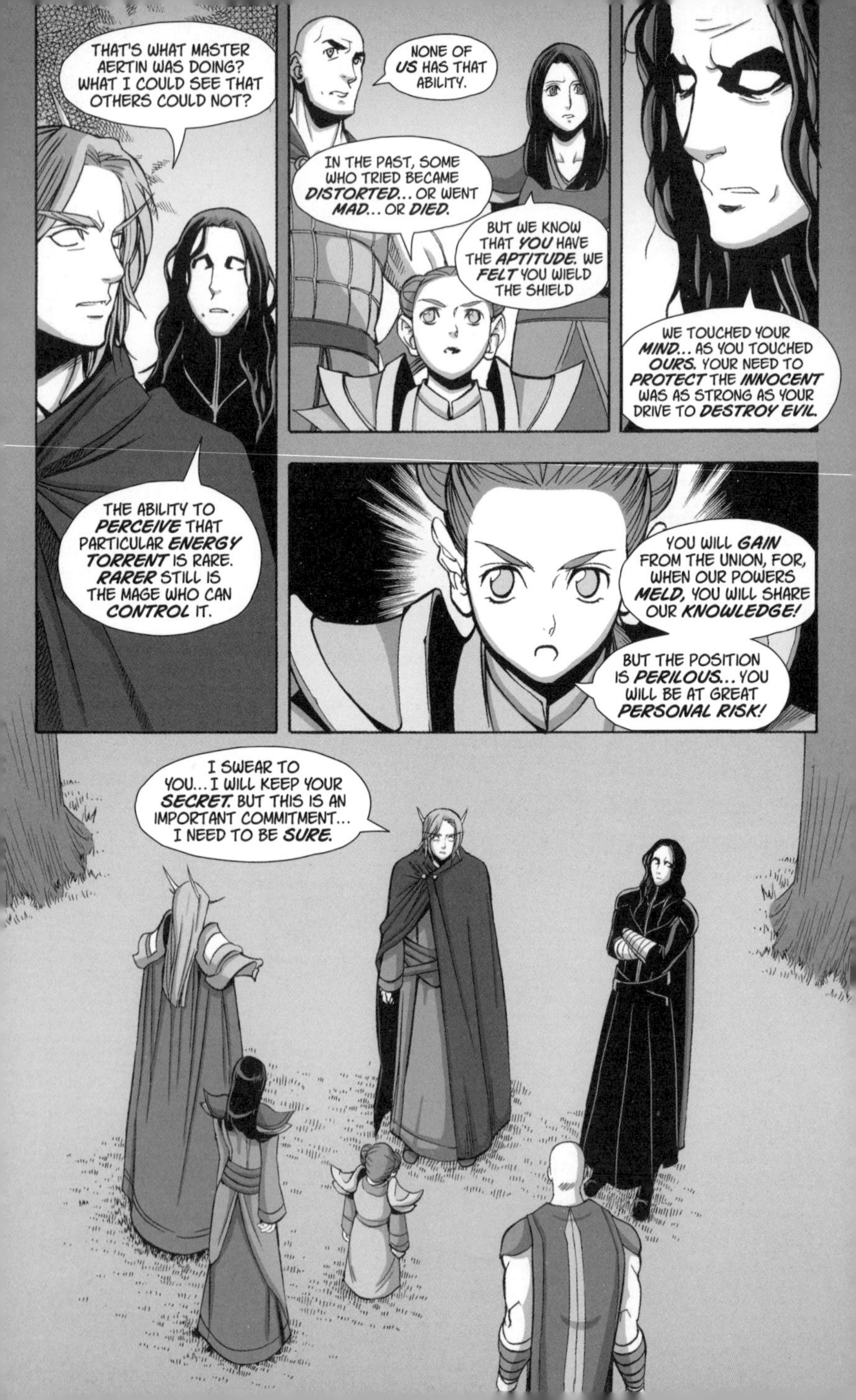
THAT'S WHAT MASTER AERTIN WAS DOING? WHAT I COULD SEE THAT OTHERS COULD NOT?
THE ABILITY TO PERCEIVE THAT PARTICULAR ENERGY TORRENT IS RARE. RARER STILL IS THE MAGE WHO CAN CONTROL IT.
NONE OF US HAS THAT ABILITY.
IN THE PAST, SOME WHO TRIED BECAME DISTORTED... OR WENT MAD... OR DIED.
BUT WE KNOW THAT YOU HAVE THE APTITUDE. WE FELT YOU WIELD THE SHIELD
WE TOUCHED YOUR MIND... AS YOU TOUCHED OURS. YOUR NEED TO PROTECT THE INNOCENT WAS AS STRONG AS YOUR DRIVE TO DESTROY EVIL.
YOU WILL GAIN FROM THE UNION, FOR, WHEN OUR POWERS MELD, YOU WILL SHARE OUR KNOWLEDGE!
BUT THE POSITION IS PERILOUS... YOU WILL BE AT GREAT PERSONAL RISK!
I SWEAR TO YOU... I WILL KEEP YOUR SECRET. BUT THIS IS AN IMPORTANT COMMITMENT... I NEED TO BE SURE.

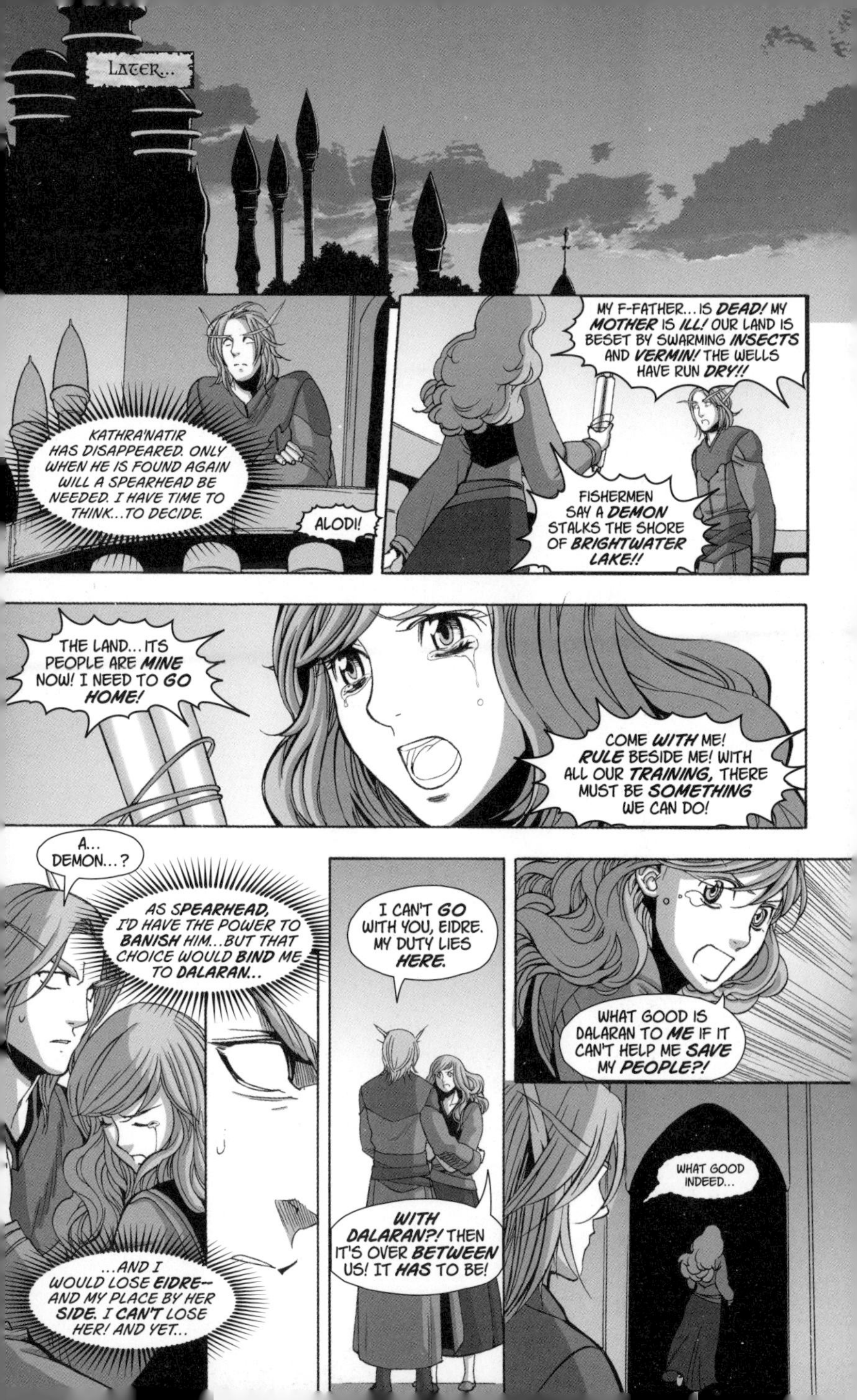
LATER...
KATHRA'NATIR HAS DISAPPEARED. ONLY WHEN HE IS FOUND AGAIN WILL A SPEARHEAD BE NEEDED. I HAVE TIME TO THINK...TO DECIDE.
ALODI!
MY F-FATHER... IS DEAD! MY MOTHER IS ILL! OUR LAND IS BESET BY SWARMING INSECTS AND VERMIN! THE WELLS HAVE RUN DRY!!
FISHERMEN SAY A DEMON STALKS THE SHORE OF BRIGHTWATER LAKE!!
THE LAND... ITS PEOPLE ARE MINE NOW! I NEED TO GO HOME!
COME WITH ME! RULE BESIDE ME! WITH ALL OUR TRAINING, THERE MUST BE SOMETHING WE CAN DO!
A... DEMON...?
AS SPEARHEAD, I'D HAVE THE POWER TO BANISH HIM...BUT THAT CHOICE WOULD BIND ME TO DALARAN...
...AND I WOULD LOSE EIDRE-- AND MY PLACE BY HER SIDE. I CAN'T LOSE HER! AND YET...
I CAN'T GO WITH YOU, EIDRE. MY DUTY LIES HERE.
WITH DALARAN?! THEN IT'S OVER BETWEEN US! IT HAS TO BE!
WHAT GOOD IS DALARAN TO ME IF IT CAN'T HELP ME SAVE MY PEOPLE?!
WHAT GOOD INDEED...

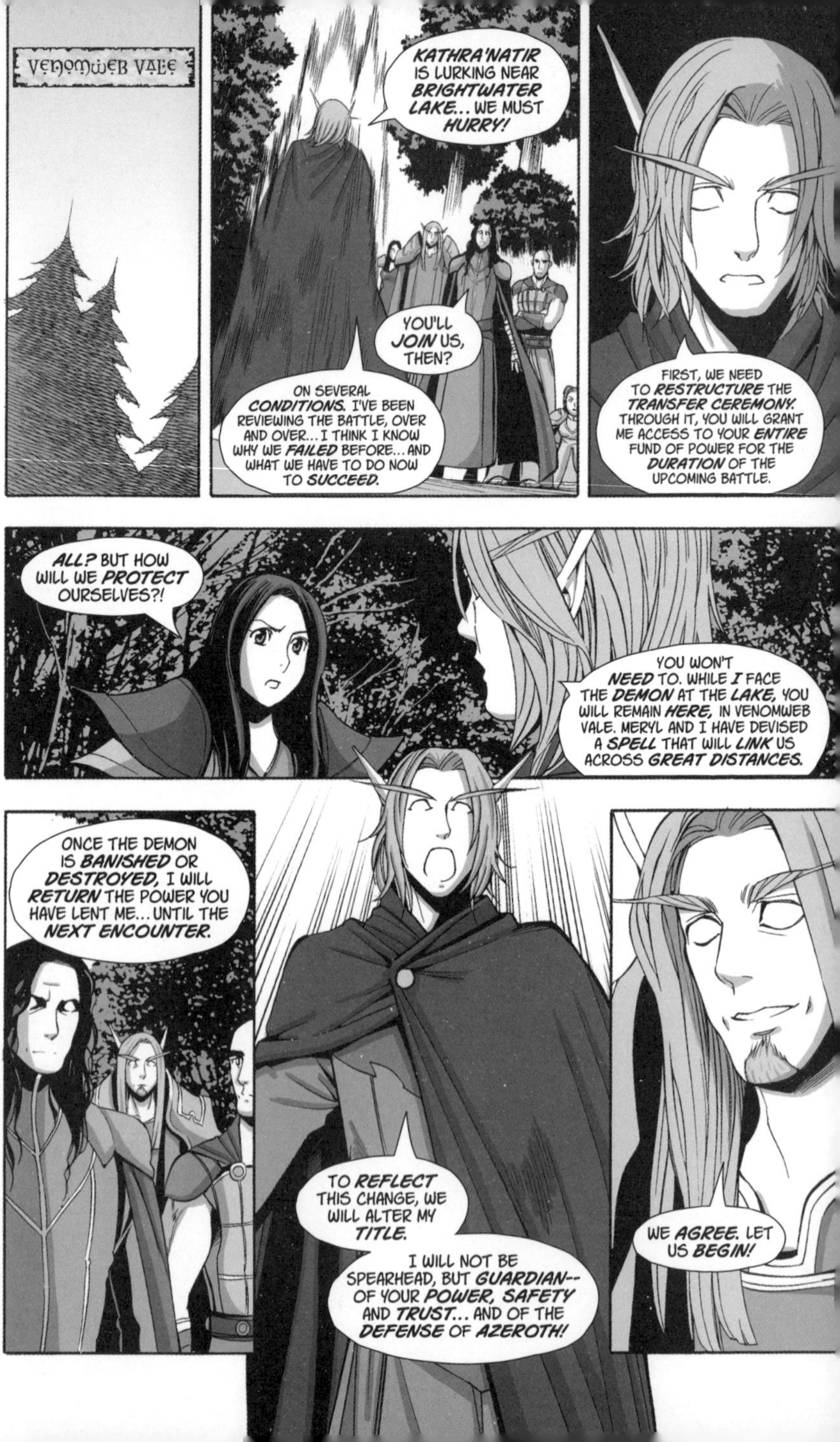
VENOMWEB VALE
KATHRA'NATIR IS LURKING NEAR BRIGHTWATER LAKE... WE MUST HURRY!
YOU'LL JOIN US, THEN?
ON SEVERAL CONDITIONS. I'VE BEEN REVIEWING THE BATTLE, OVER AND OVER... I THINK I KNOW WHY WE FAILED BEFORE... AND WHAT WE HAVE TO DO NOW TO SUCCEED.
FIRST, WE NEED TO RESTRUCTURE THE TRANSFER CEREMONY. THROUGH IT, YOU WILL GRANT ME ACCESS TO YOUR ENTIRE FUND OF POWER FOR THE DURATION OF THE UPCOMING BATTLE.
ALL? BUT HOW WILL WE PROTECT OURSELVES?!
YOU WON'T NEED TO. WHILE I FACE THE DEMON AT THE LAKE, YOU WILL REMAIN HERE, IN VENOMWEB VALE. MERYL AND I HAVE DEVISED A SPELL THAT WILL LINK US ACROSS GREAT DISTANCES.
ONCE THE DEMON IS BANISHED OR DESTROYED, I WILL RETURN THE POWER YOU HAVE LENT ME... UNTIL THE NEXT ENCOUNTER.
TO REFLECT THIS CHANGE, WE WILL ALTER MY TITLE.
I WILL NOT BE SPEARHEAD, BUT GUARDIAN-- OF YOUR POWER, SAFETY AND TRUST... AND OF THE DEFENSE OF AZEROTH!
WE AGREE. LET US BEGIN!

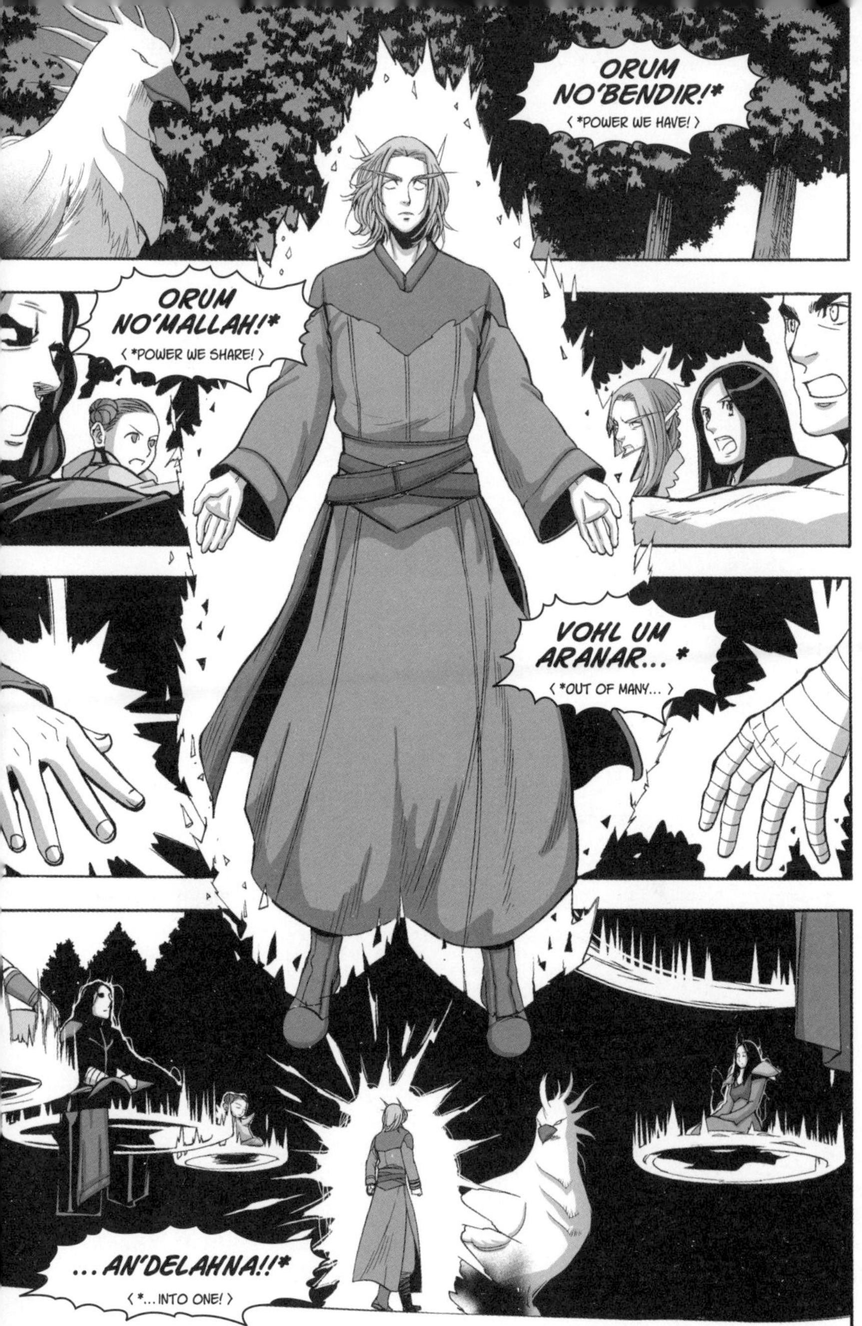
ORUM NO'BENDIR!* ⟨ *POWER WE HAVE! ⟩
ORUM NO'MALLAH!* ⟨ *POWER WE SHARE! ⟩
VOHL UM ARANAR...* ⟨ *OUT OF MANY... ⟩
...AN'DELAHNA!!* ⟨ *...INTO ONE! ⟩

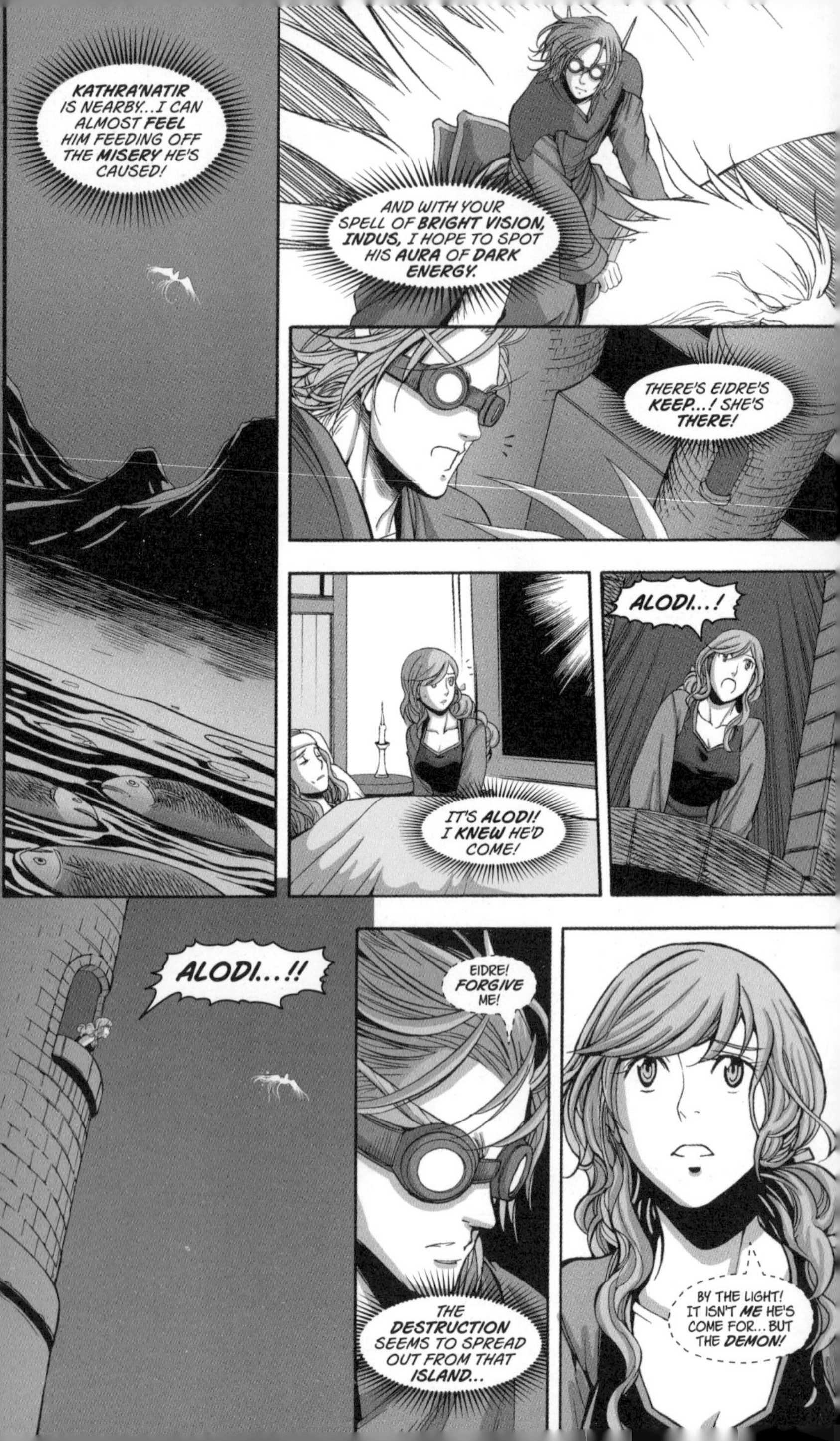
KATHRA'NATIR IS NEARBY...I CAN ALMOST FEEL HIM FEEDING OFF THE MISERY HE'S CAUSED!
AND WITH YOUR SPELL OF BRIGHT VISION, INDUS, I HOPE TO SPOT HIS AURA OF DARK ENERGY.
THERE'S EIDRE'S KEEP...! SHE'S THERE!
IT'S ALODI! I KNEW HE'D COME!
ALODI...!
ALODI...!!
EIDRE! FORGIVE ME!
THE DESTRUCTION SEEMS TO SPREAD OUT FROM THAT ISLAND...
BY THE LIGHT! IT ISN'T ME HE'S COME FOR... BUT THE DEMON!

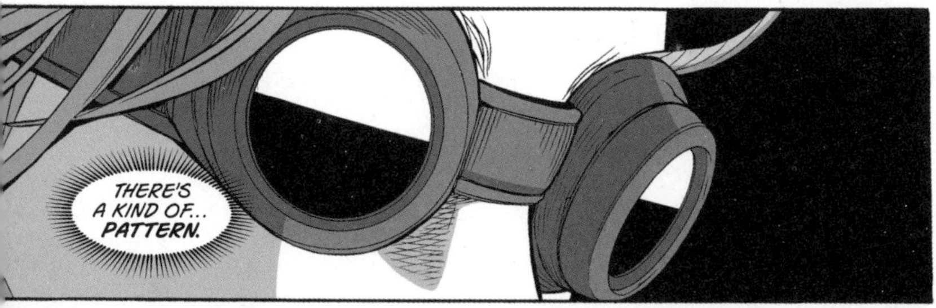
THERE'S A KIND OF... PATTERN.

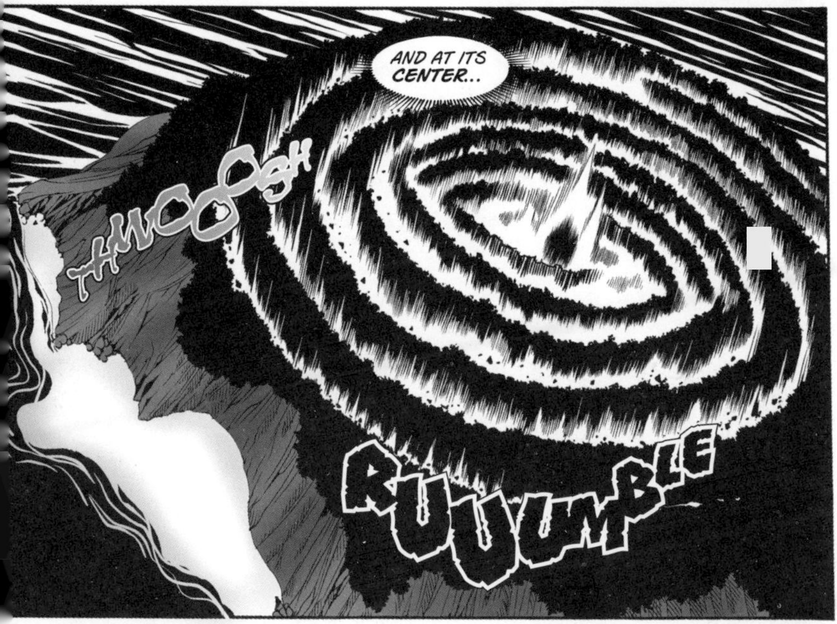
AND AT ITS CENTER...
THWOOOSH
RUUUMBLE

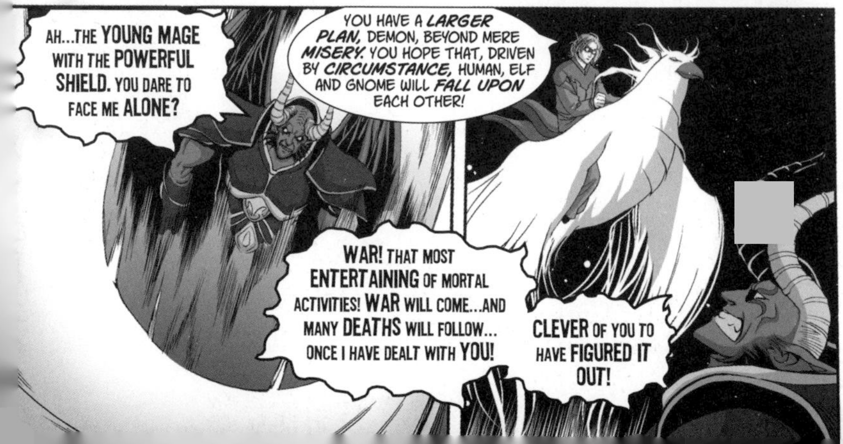
AH...THE YOUNG MAGE WITH THE POWERFUL SHIELD. YOU DARE TO FACE ME ALONE?
YOU HAVE A LARGER PLAN, DEMON, BEYOND MERE MISERY. YOU HOPE THAT, DRIVEN BY CIRCUMSTANCE, HUMAN, ELF AND GNOME WILL FALL UPON EACH OTHER!
CLEVER OF YOU TO HAVE FIGURED IT OUT!
WAR! THAT MOST ENTERTAINING OF MORTAL ACTIVITIES! WAR WILL COME...AND MANY DEATHS WILL FOLLOW... ONCE I HAVE DEALT WITH YOU!

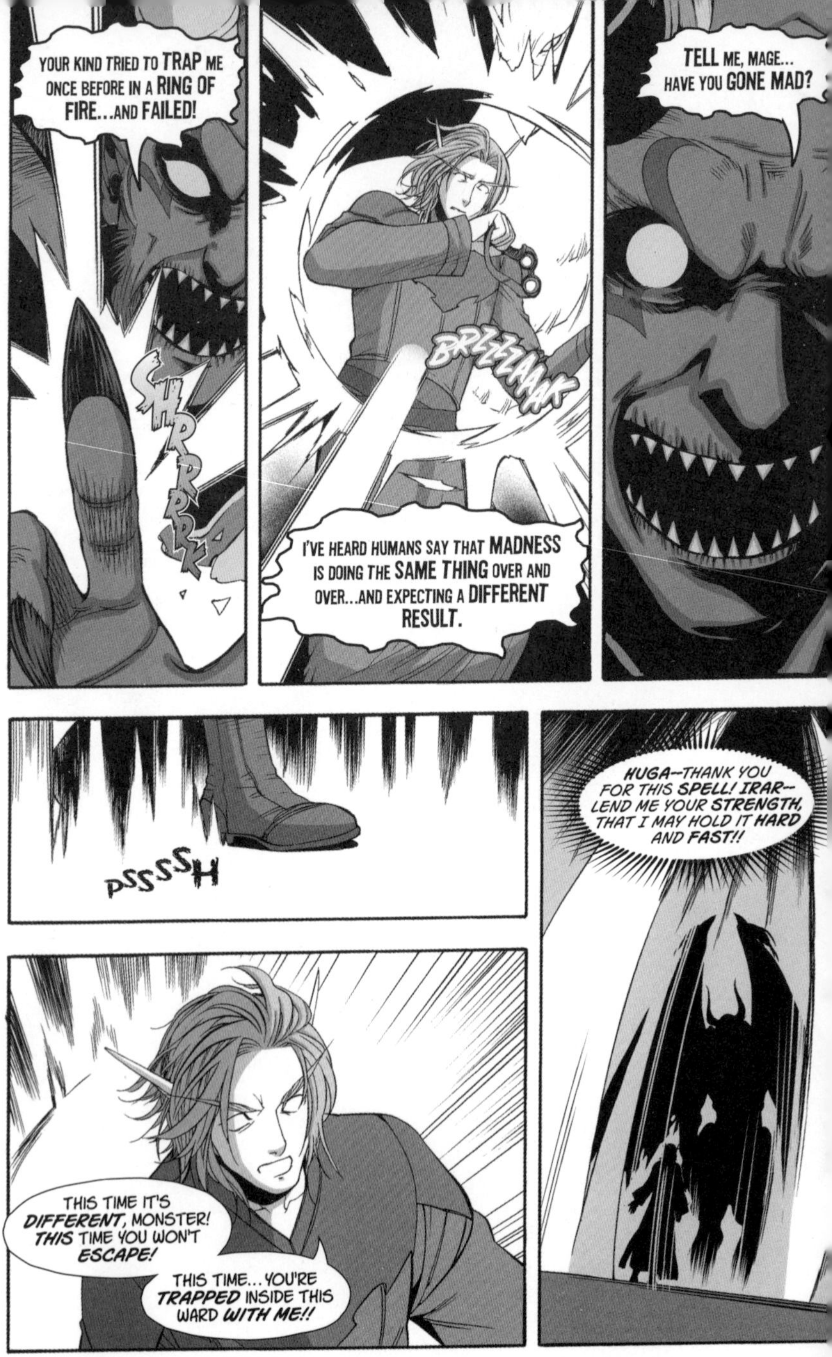
YOUR KIND TRIED TO TRAP ME ONCE BEFORE IN A RING OF FIRE...AND FAILED!
SHRRRRK
BRZZZAAAK
I'VE HEARD HUMANS SAY THAT MADNESS IS DOING THE SAME THING OVER AND OVER...AND EXPECTING A DIFFERENT RESULT.
TELL ME, MAGE... HAVE YOU GONE MAD?
PSSSSH
THIS TIME IT'S DIFFERENT, MONSTER! THIS TIME YOU WON'T ESCAPE!
THIS TIME...YOU'RE TRAPPED INSIDE THIS WARD WITH ME!!
HUGA--THANK YOU FOR THIS SPELL! IRAR--LEND ME YOUR STRENGTH, THAT I MAY HOLD IT HARD AND FAST!!

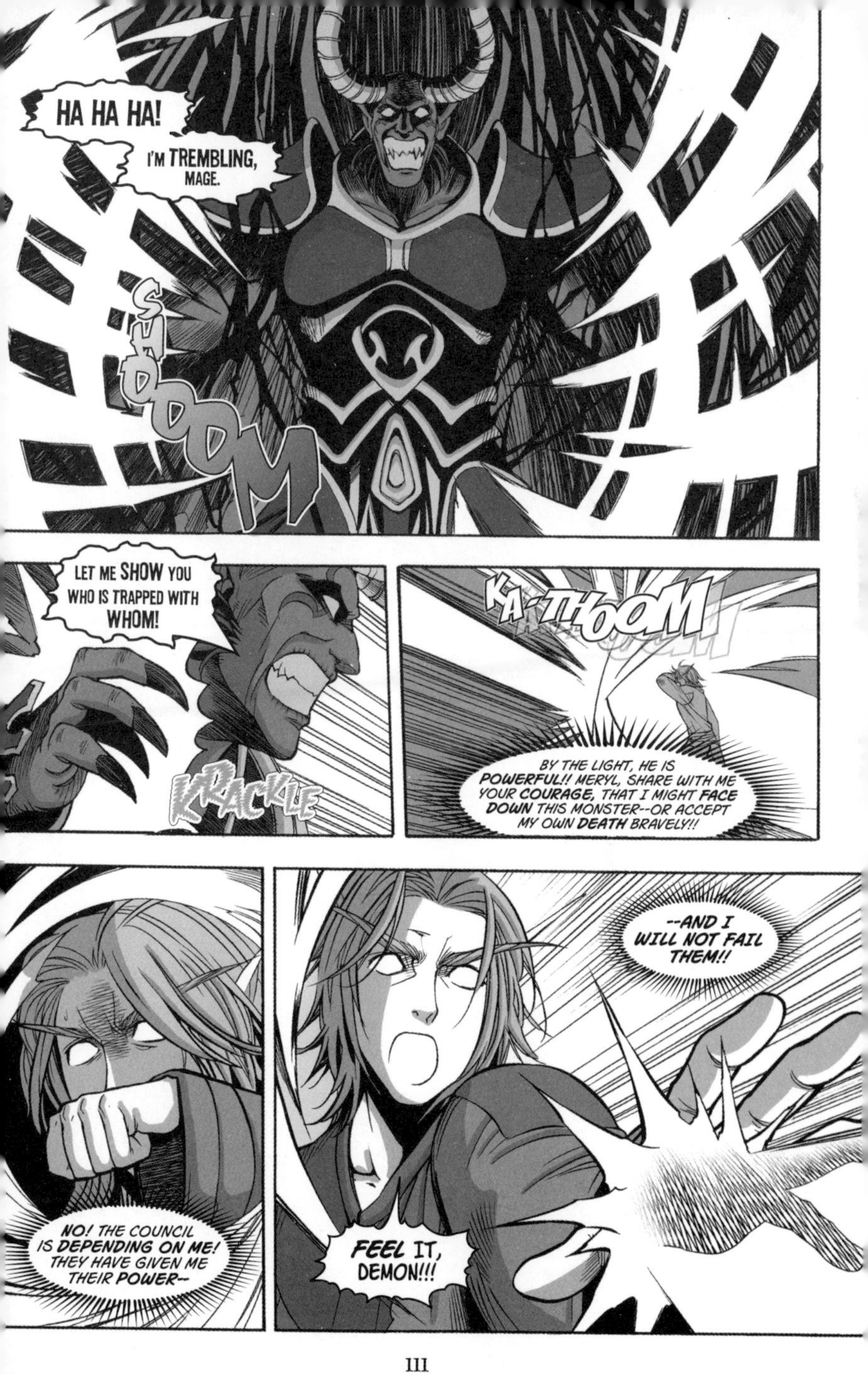
HA HA HA!
I'M TREMBLING, MAGE.
SHOOOOM
LET ME SHOW YOU WHO IS TRAPPED WITH WHOM!
KRACKLE
KA-THOOM
BY THE LIGHT, HE IS POWERFUL!! MERYL, SHARE WITH ME YOUR COURAGE, THAT I MIGHT FACE DOWN THIS MONSTER--OR ACCEPT MY OWN DEATH BRAVELY!!
NO! THE COUNCIL IS DEPENDING ON ME! THEY HAVE GIVEN ME THEIR POWER--
--AND I WILL NOT FAIL THEM!!
FEEL IT, DEMON!!!

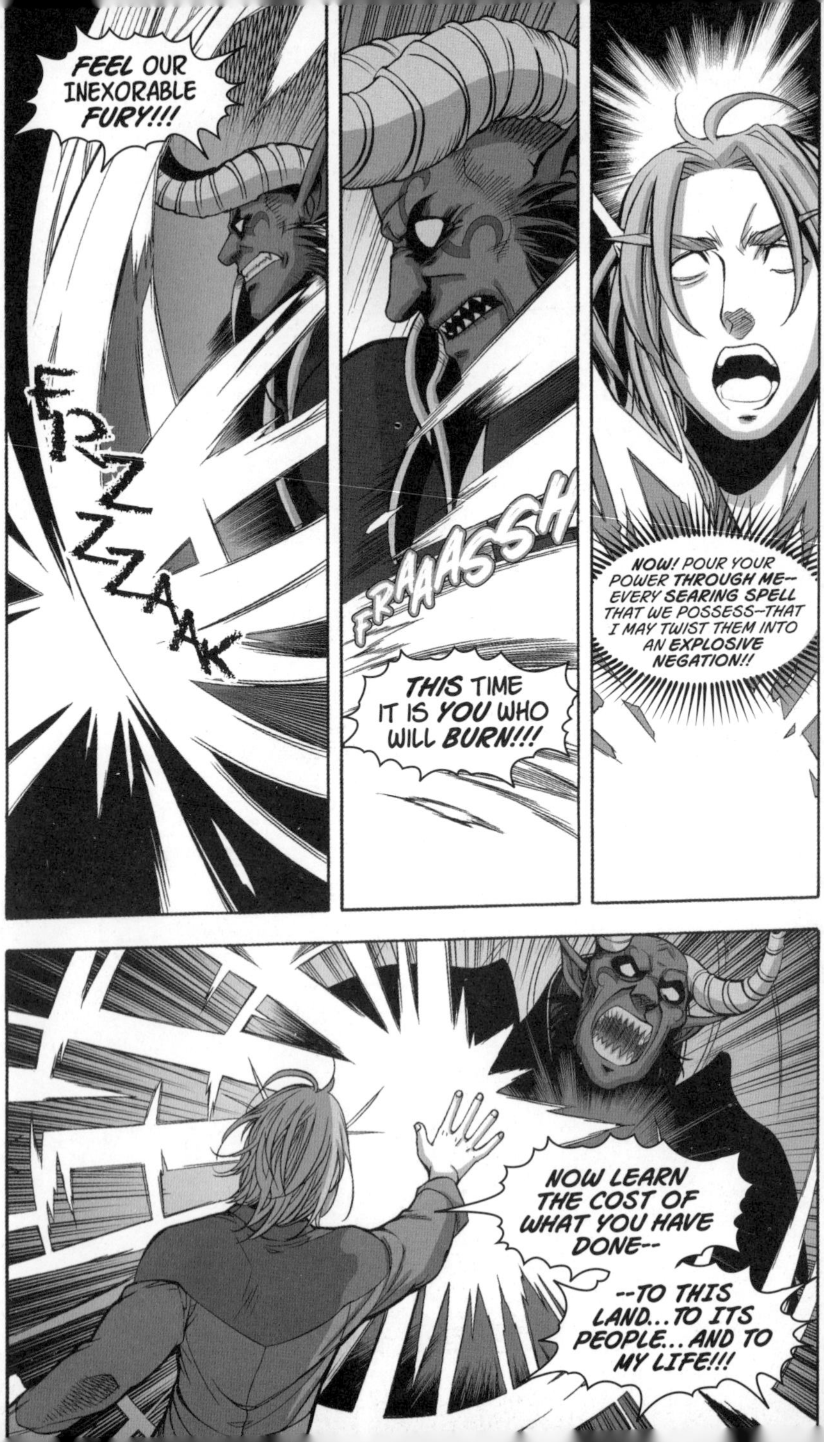
FEEL OUR INEXORABLE FURY!!!
FRZZZZAAK
FRAAAASSSH
THIS TIME IT IS YOU WHO WILL BURN!!!
NOW! POUR YOUR POWER THROUGH ME-- EVERY SEARING SPELL THAT WE POSSESS--THAT I MAY TWIST THEM INTO AN EXPLOSIVE NEGATION!!
NOW LEARN THE COST OF WHAT YOU HAVE DONE--
--TO THIS LAND...TO ITS PEOPLE...AND TO MY LIFE!!!

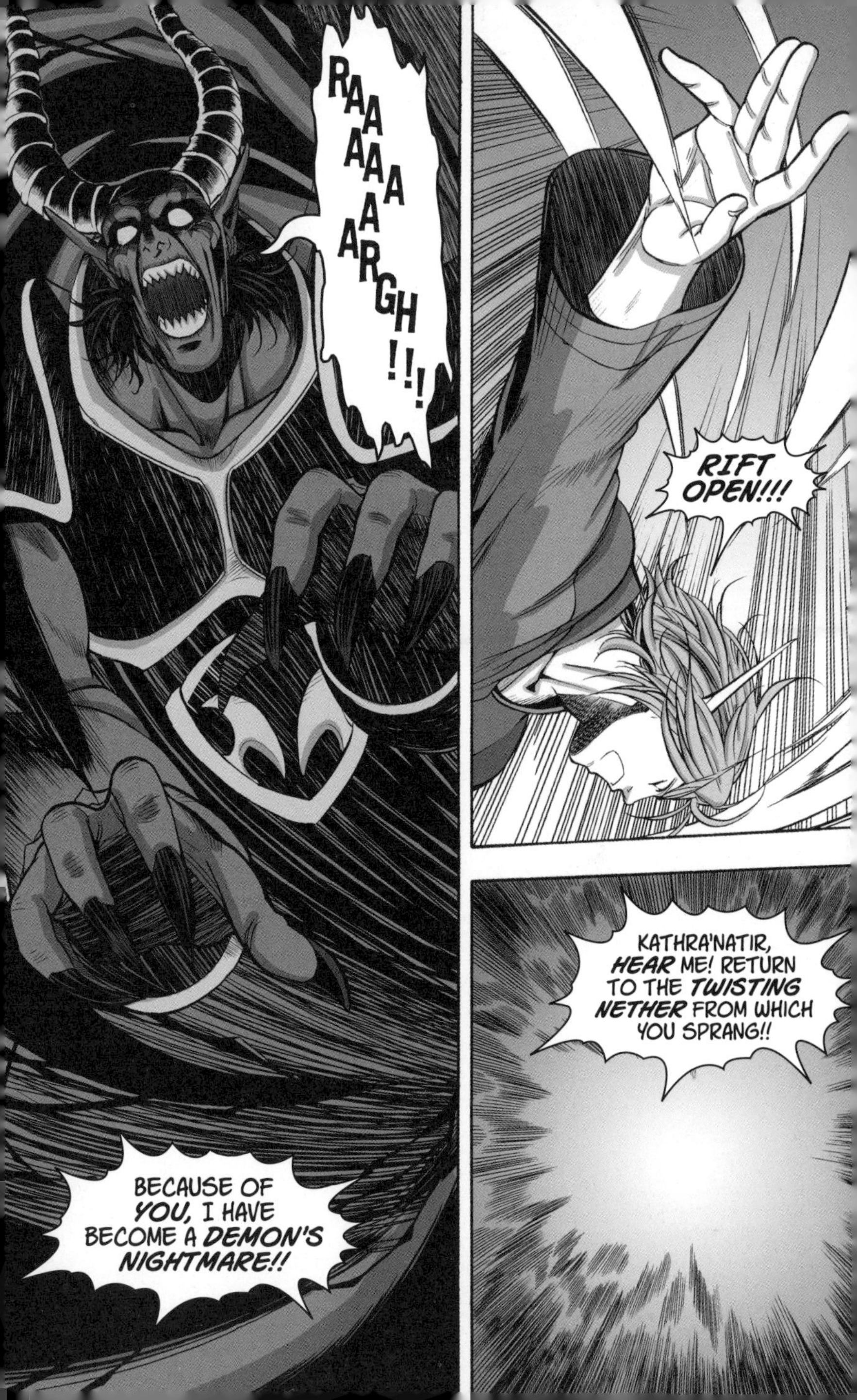
RIFT OPEN!!!
KATHRA'NATIR, HEAR ME! RETURN TO THE TWISTING NETHER FROM WHICH YOU SPRANG!!
RAAAAAAAARGH!!!
BECAUSE OF YOU, I HAVE BECOME A DEMON'S NIGHTMARE!!

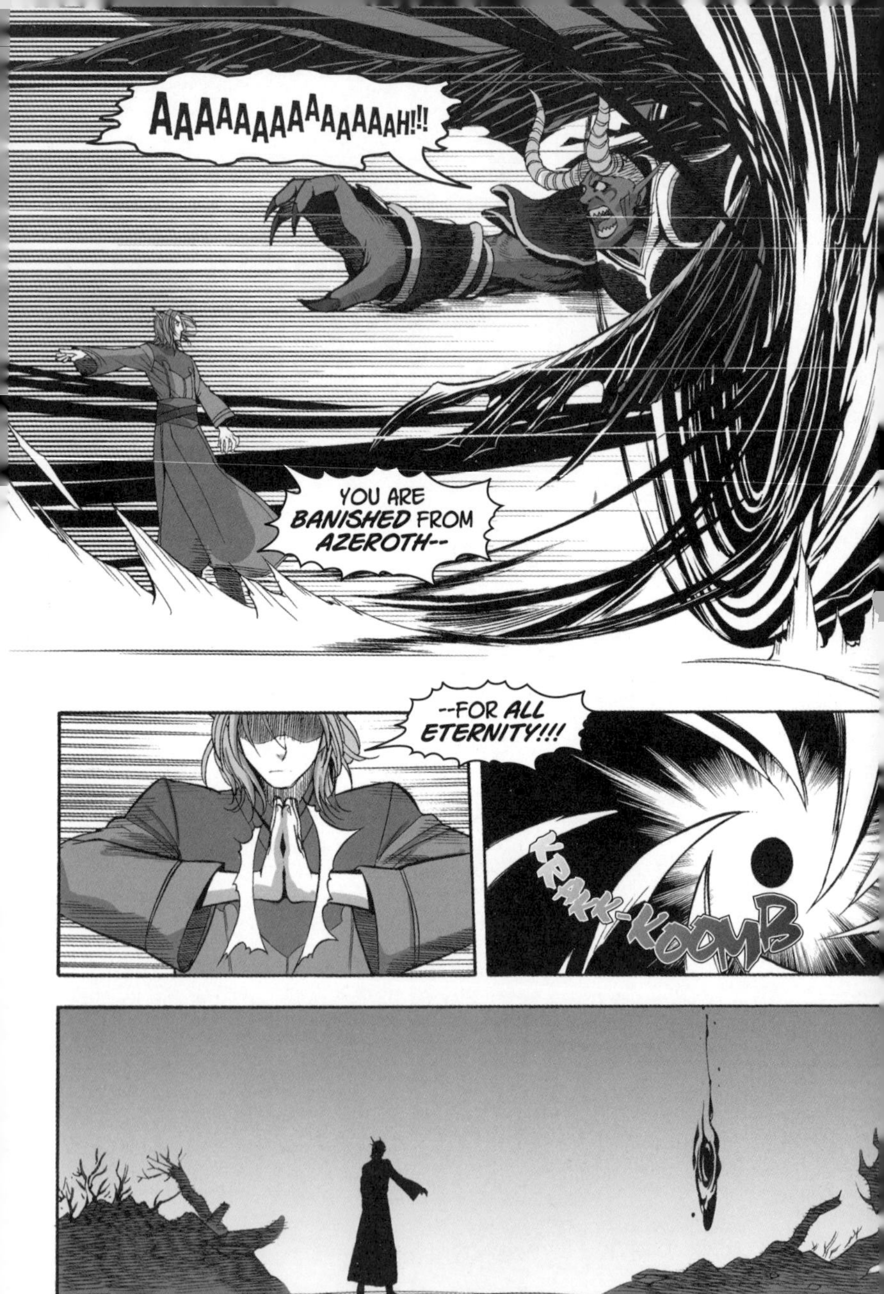
AAAAAAAAAAAAAAH!!!
YOU ARE BANISHED FROM AZEROTH--
--FOR ALL ETERNITY!!!
KRAKK-KOOMB

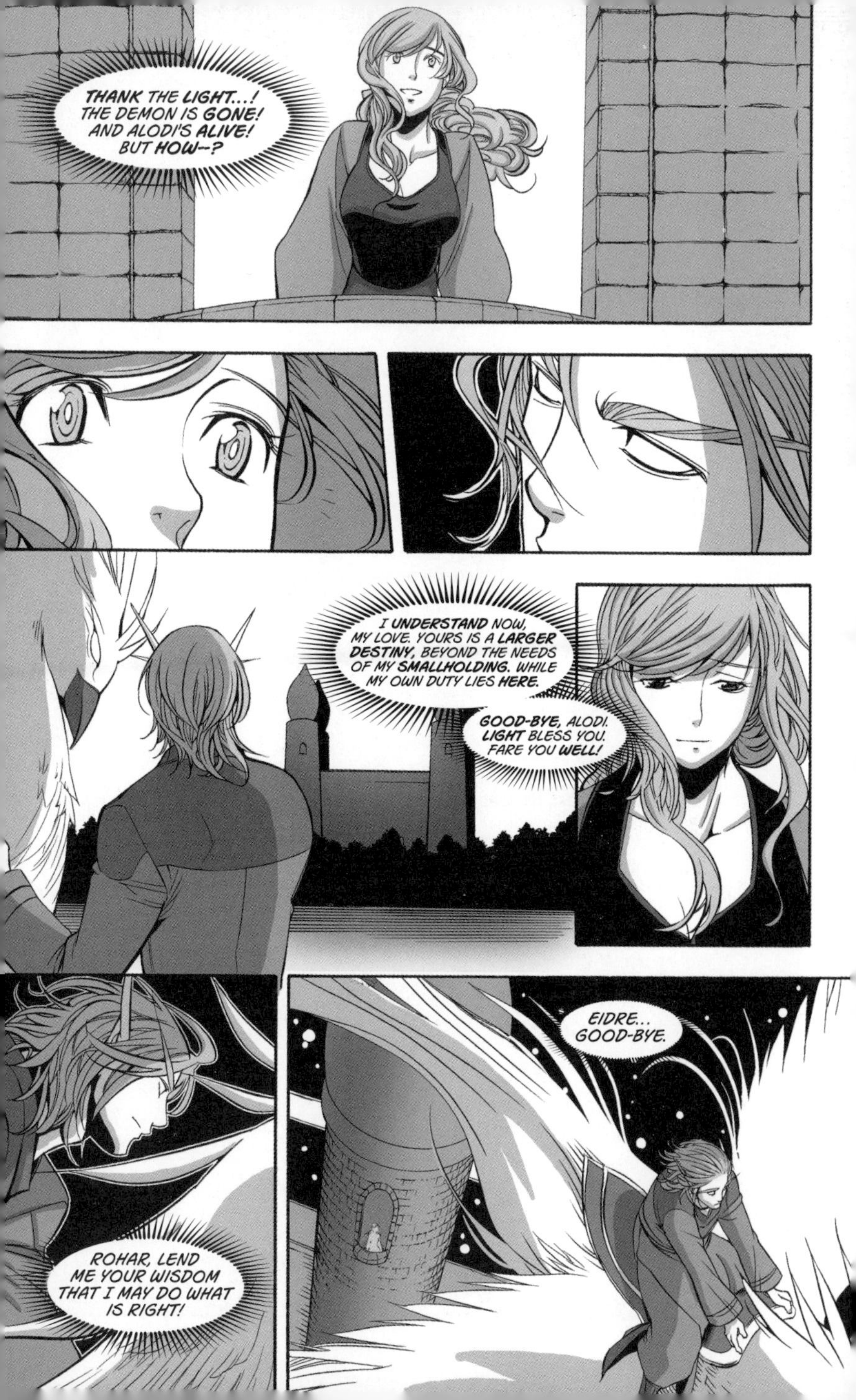
THANK THE LIGHT...! THE DEMON IS GONE! AND ALODI'S ALIVE! BUT HOW--?
I UNDERSTAND NOW, MY LOVE. YOURS IS A LARGER DESTINY, BEYOND THE NEEDS OF MY SMALLHOLDING. WHILE MY OWN DUTY LIES HERE.
GOOD-BYE, ALODI. LIGHT BLESS YOU. FARE YOU WELL!
ROHAR, LEND ME YOUR WISDOM THAT I MAY DO WHAT IS RIGHT!
EIDRE... GOOD-BYE.

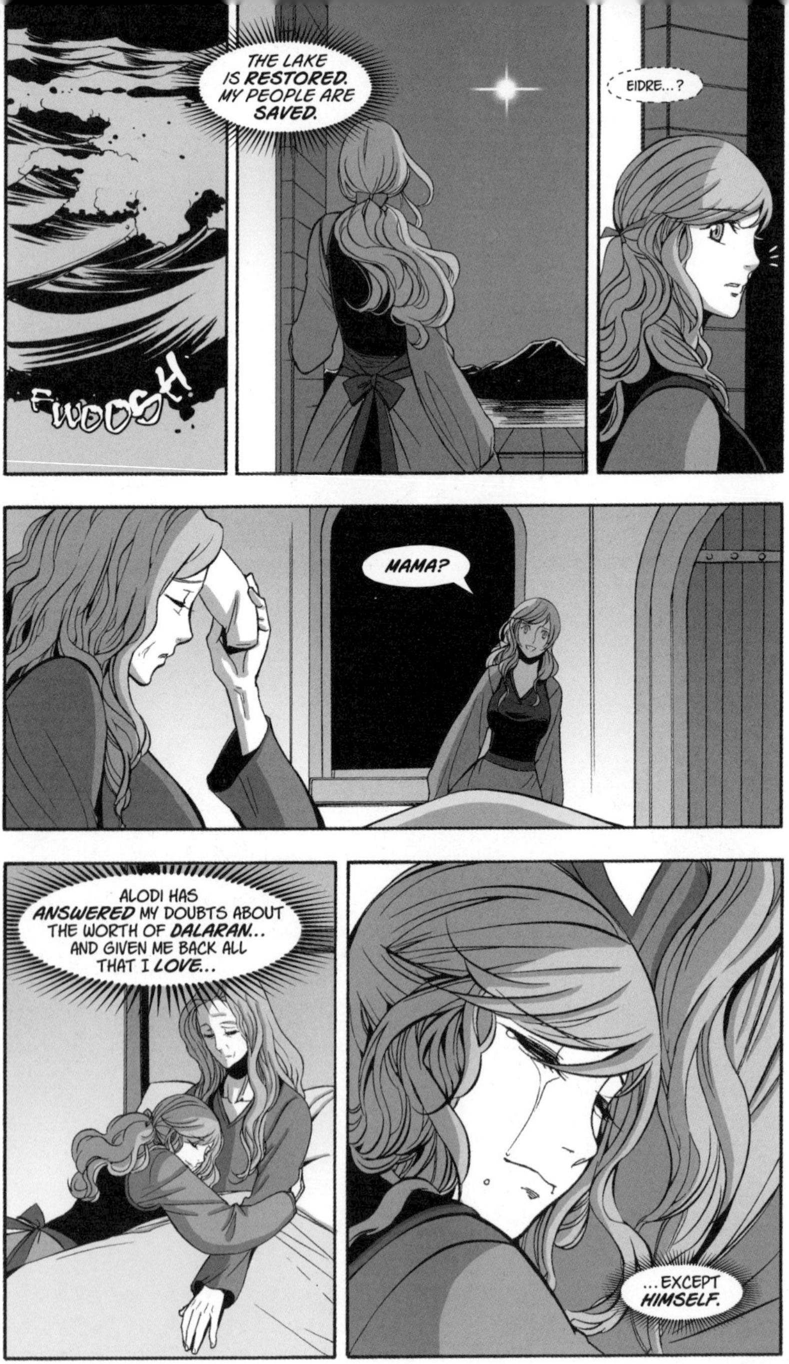
FWOOSH!
THE LAKE IS **RESTORED.** MY PEOPLE ARE **SAVED.**
EIDRE...?
MAMA?
ALODI HAS **ANSWERED** MY DOUBTS ABOUT THE WORTH OF **DALARAN...** AND GIVEN ME BACK ALL THAT I **LOVE...**
...EXCEPT **HIMSELF.**

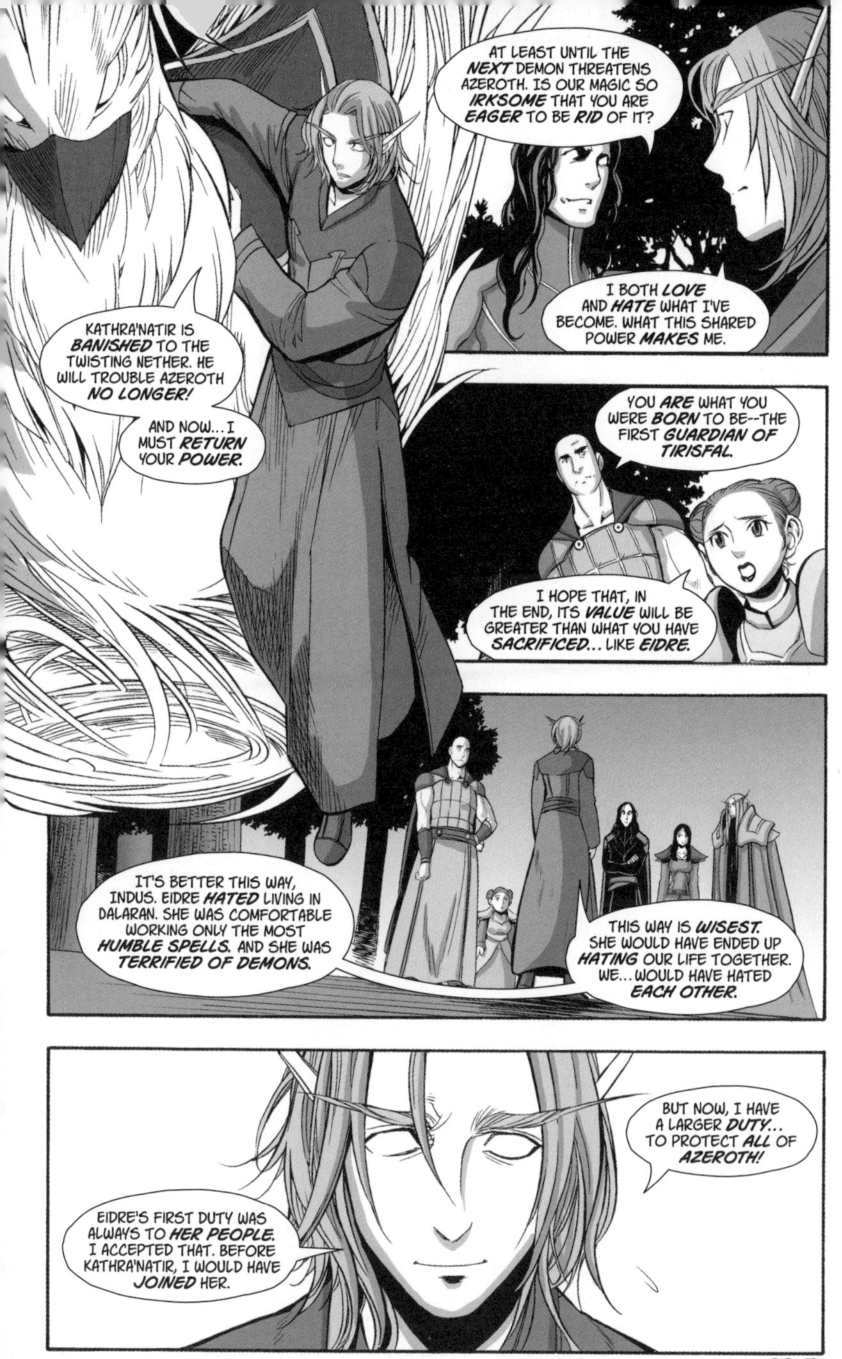
KATHRA'NATIR IS BANISHED TO THE TWISTING NETHER. HE WILL TROUBLE AZEROTH NO LONGER!
AND NOW... I MUST RETURN YOUR POWER.
AT LEAST UNTIL THE NEXT DEMON THREATENS AZEROTH. IS OUR MAGIC SO IRKSOME THAT YOU ARE EAGER TO BE RID OF IT?
I BOTH LOVE AND HATE WHAT I'VE BECOME. WHAT THIS SHARED POWER MAKES ME.
YOU ARE WHAT YOU WERE BORN TO BE--THE FIRST GUARDIAN OF TIRISFAL.
I HOPE THAT, IN THE END, ITS VALUE WILL BE GREATER THAN WHAT YOU HAVE SACRIFICED... LIKE EIDRE.
IT'S BETTER THIS WAY, INDUS. EIDRE HATED LIVING IN DALARAN. SHE WAS COMFORTABLE WORKING ONLY THE MOST HUMBLE SPELLS. AND SHE WAS TERRIFIED OF DEMONS.
THIS WAY IS WISEST. SHE WOULD HAVE ENDED UP HATING OUR LIFE TOGETHER. WE... WOULD HAVE HATED EACH OTHER.
EIDRE'S FIRST DUTY WAS ALWAYS TO HER PEOPLE. I ACCEPTED THAT. BEFORE KATHRA'NATIR, I WOULD HAVE JOINED HER.
BUT NOW, I HAVE A LARGER DUTY... TO PROTECT ALL OF AZEROTH!

END

WARCRAFT®

LEGENDS™

VOLUME FIVE

A CLEANSING FIRE

WRITTEN BY EVELYN FREDERICKSEN

PENCILS & TONES BY RYO KAWAKAMI
INKS BY FERNANDO MELEK

LETTERER: MICHAEL PAOLILLI

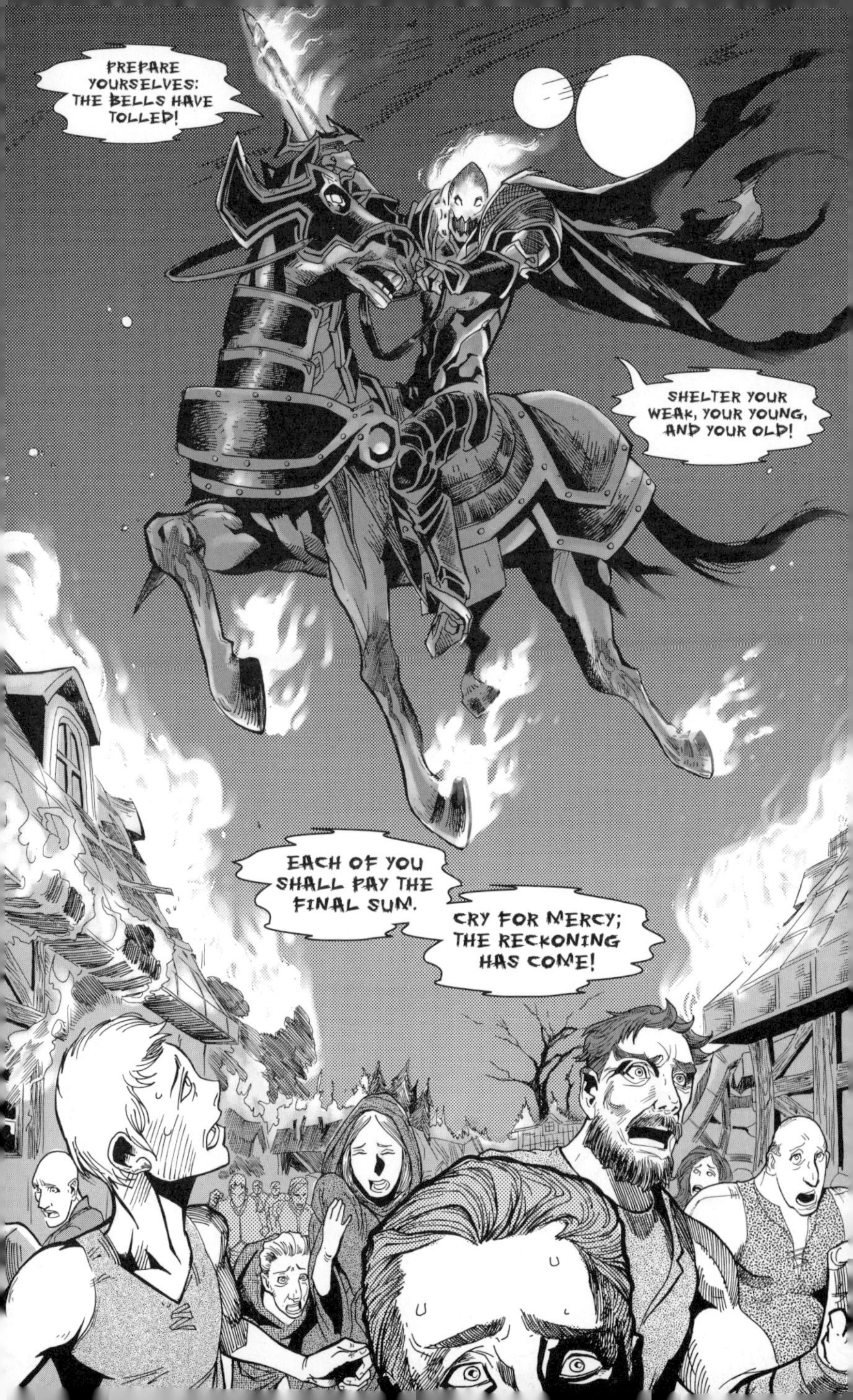
PREPARE YOURSELVES: THE BELLS HAVE TOLLED!
SHELTER YOUR WEAK, YOUR YOUNG, AND YOUR OLD!
EACH OF YOU SHALL PAY THE FINAL SUM.
CRY FOR MERCY; THE RECKONING HAS COME!

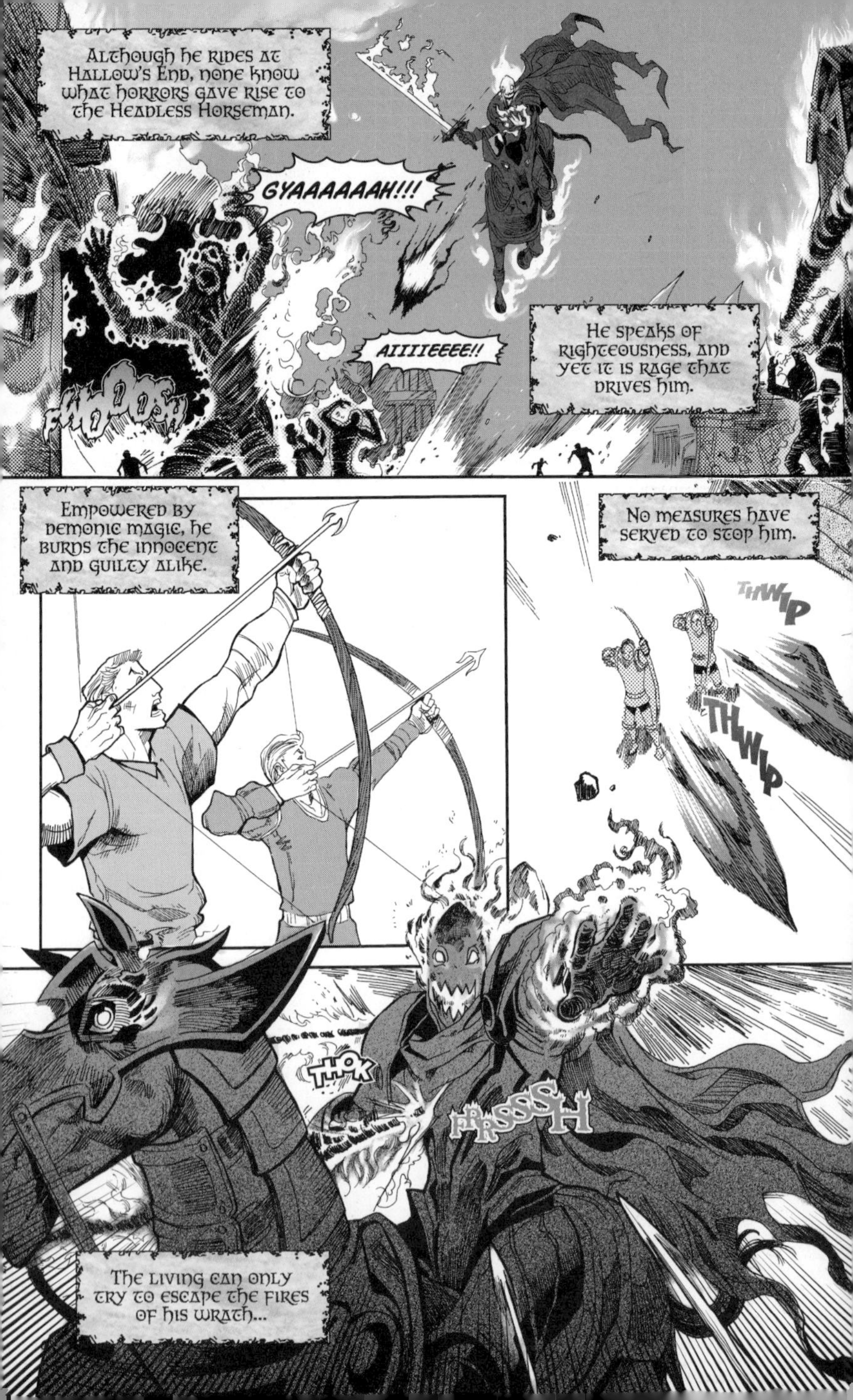
Although he rides at Hallow's End, none know what horrors gave rise to the Headless Horseman.
GYAAAAAAH!!!
FWOOSH
AIIIIEEEE!!
He speaks of righteousness, and yet it is rage that drives him.
Empowered by demonic magic, he burns the innocent and guilty alike.
No measures have served to stop him.
THWIP
THWIP
THOK
FRRSSSH
The living can only try to escape the fires of his wrath...

...AND PRAY TO THE LIGHT FOR DELIVERANCE.

A VILLAGE IN LORDAERON--YEAR 20.

IN THE DAYS SINCE PRINCE ARTHAS TOOK THE FLEET TO NORTHREND, THE SILVER HAND HAS BEEN STRETCHED THIN FIGHTING THE **SPREAD** OF THIS **TERRIBLE PLAGUE.**

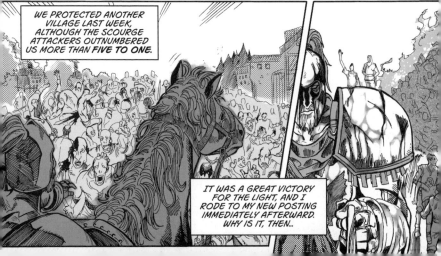

WE PROTECTED ANOTHER VILLAGE LAST WEEK, ALTHOUGH THE SCOURGE ATTACKERS OUTNUMBERED US MORE THAN **FIVE TO ONE.**

IT WAS A GREAT VICTORY FOR THE LIGHT, AND I RODE TO MY NEW POSTING IMMEDIATELY AFTERWARD. WHY IS IT, THEN...

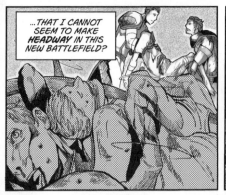

...THAT I CANNOT SEEM TO MAKE **HEADWAY** IN THIS NEW BATTLEFIELD?

WHEN THE PRINCE ORDERED US TO PURGE STRATHOLME, I NEVER HAD A MOMENT'S **DOUBT** THAT IT WAS A **MISTAKE**.

SUCH A DEED WOULD HAVE DEFILED OUR SACRED CHARGE--**PROTECTING THE PEOPLE OF LORDAERON**.

LORD UTHER WAS RIGHT: THERE **HAD** TO BE ANOTHER WAY.

STILL, FOR ALL MY **PRAYERS**, THE PEOPLE IN THIS TOWN ARE **DYING**.

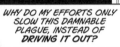

WHY DO MY EFFORTS ONLY SLOW THIS DAMNABLE PLAGUE, INSTEAD OF **DRIVING IT OUT**?

NOW OUR SUPPLIES GROW SHORT, FOR WE CANNOT RELY ON GRAIN FROM ANDORHAL. THE SICK AND THE HEALTHY SUFFER ALIKE.

THEIR SUFFERING **MUST** HAVE SOME **HIGHER PURPOSE**, BUT I CANNOT **SEE** IT.

O LIGHT, GUIDE MY WAY. HELP ME **UNDERSTAND**.

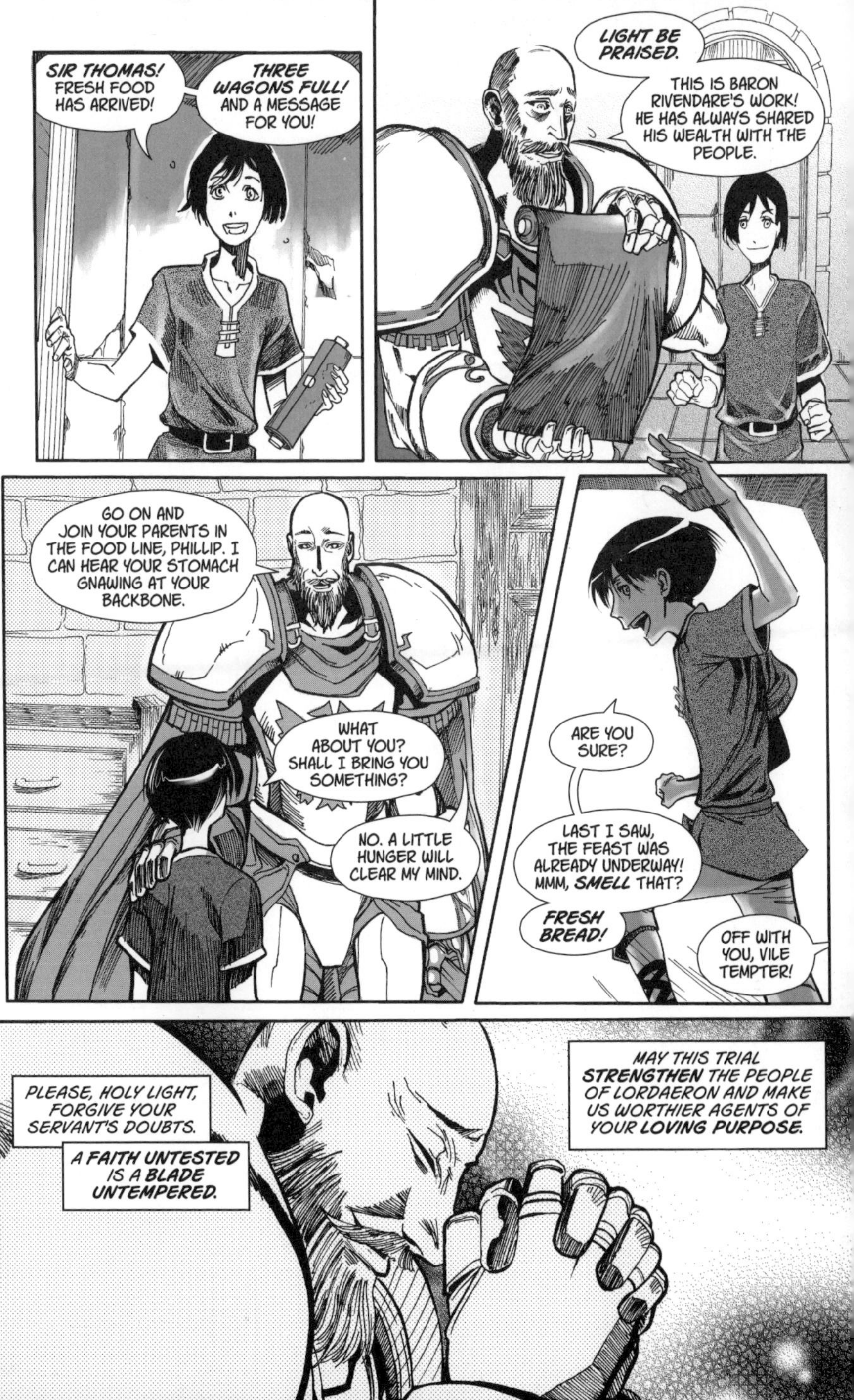
SIR THOMAS! FRESH FOOD HAS ARRIVED!
THREE WAGONS FULL! AND A MESSAGE FOR YOU!
LIGHT BE PRAISED.
THIS IS BARON RIVENDARE'S WORK! HE HAS ALWAYS SHARED HIS WEALTH WITH THE PEOPLE.
GO ON AND JOIN YOUR PARENTS IN THE FOOD LINE, PHILLIP. I CAN HEAR YOUR STOMACH GNAWING AT YOUR BACKBONE.
WHAT ABOUT YOU? SHALL I BRING YOU SOMETHING?
NO. A LITTLE HUNGER WILL CLEAR MY MIND.
ARE YOU SURE?
LAST I SAW, THE FEAST WAS ALREADY UNDERWAY! MMM, SMELL THAT?
FRESH BREAD!
OFF WITH YOU, VILE TEMPTER!
PLEASE, HOLY LIGHT, FORGIVE YOUR SERVANT'S DOUBTS.
A FAITH UNTESTED IS A BLADE UNTEMPERED.
MAY THIS TRIAL STRENGTHEN THE PEOPLE OF LORDAERON AND MAKE US WORTHIER AGENTS OF YOUR LOVING PURPOSE.

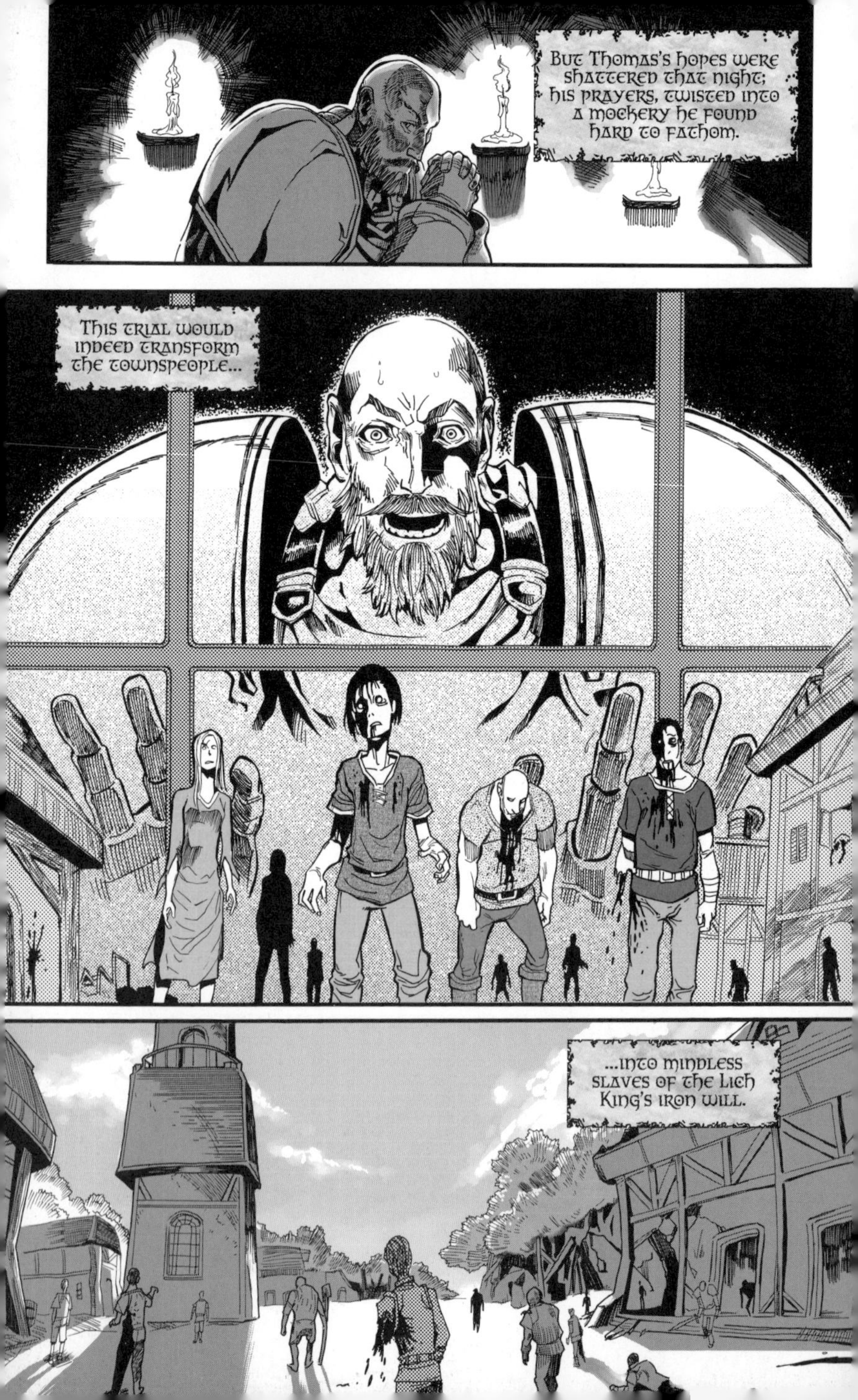
But Thomas's hopes were shattered that night; his prayers, twisted into a mockery he found hard to fathom.
This trial would indeed transform the townspeople...
...into mindless slaves of the Lich King's iron will.

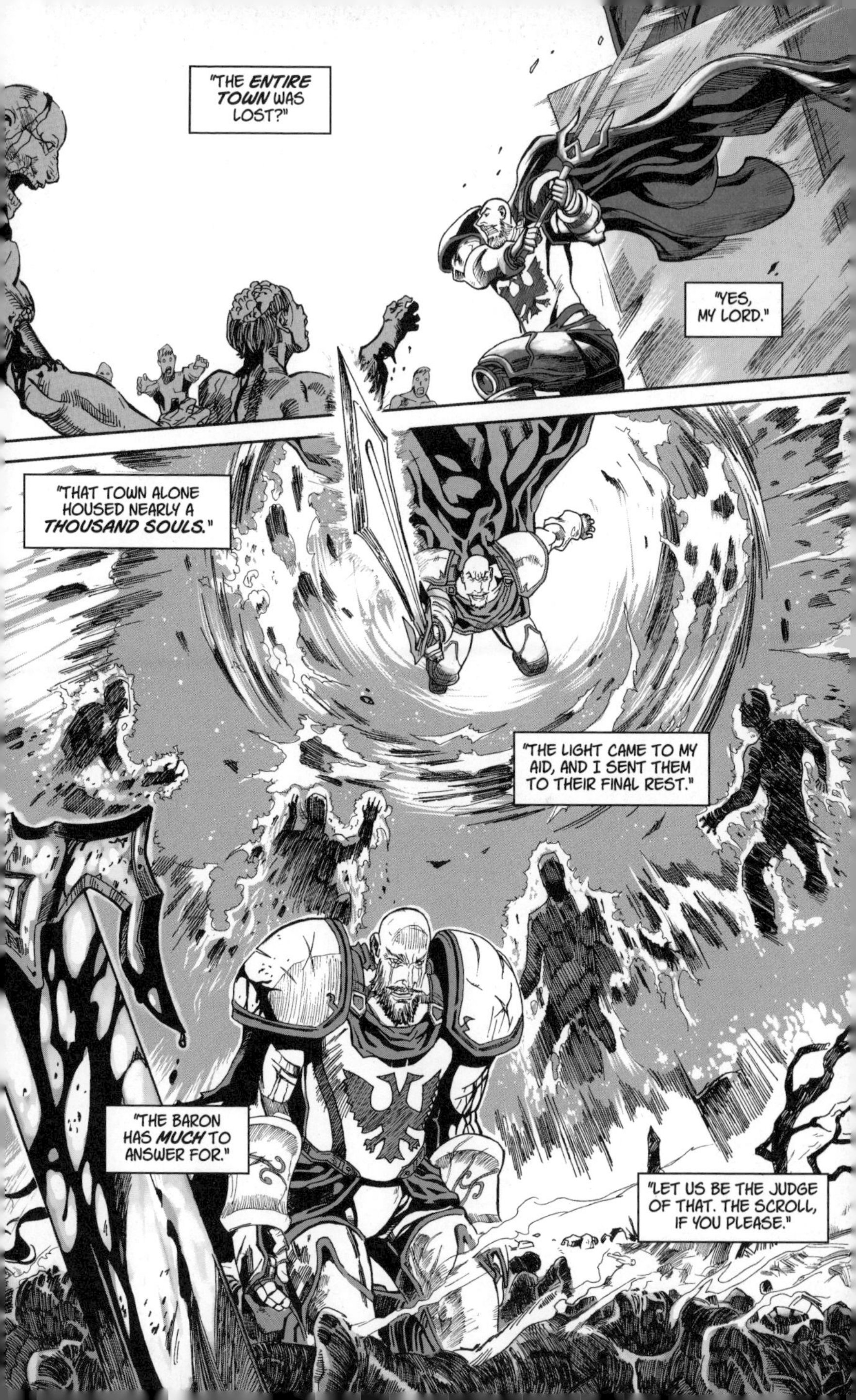
"THE ENTIRE TOWN WAS LOST?"
"YES, MY LORD."
"THAT TOWN ALONE HOUSED NEARLY A THOUSAND SOULS."
"THE LIGHT CAME TO MY AID, AND I SENT THEM TO THEIR FINAL REST."
"THE BARON HAS MUCH TO ANSWER FOR."
"LET US BE THE JUDGE OF THAT. THE SCROLL, IF YOU PLEASE."

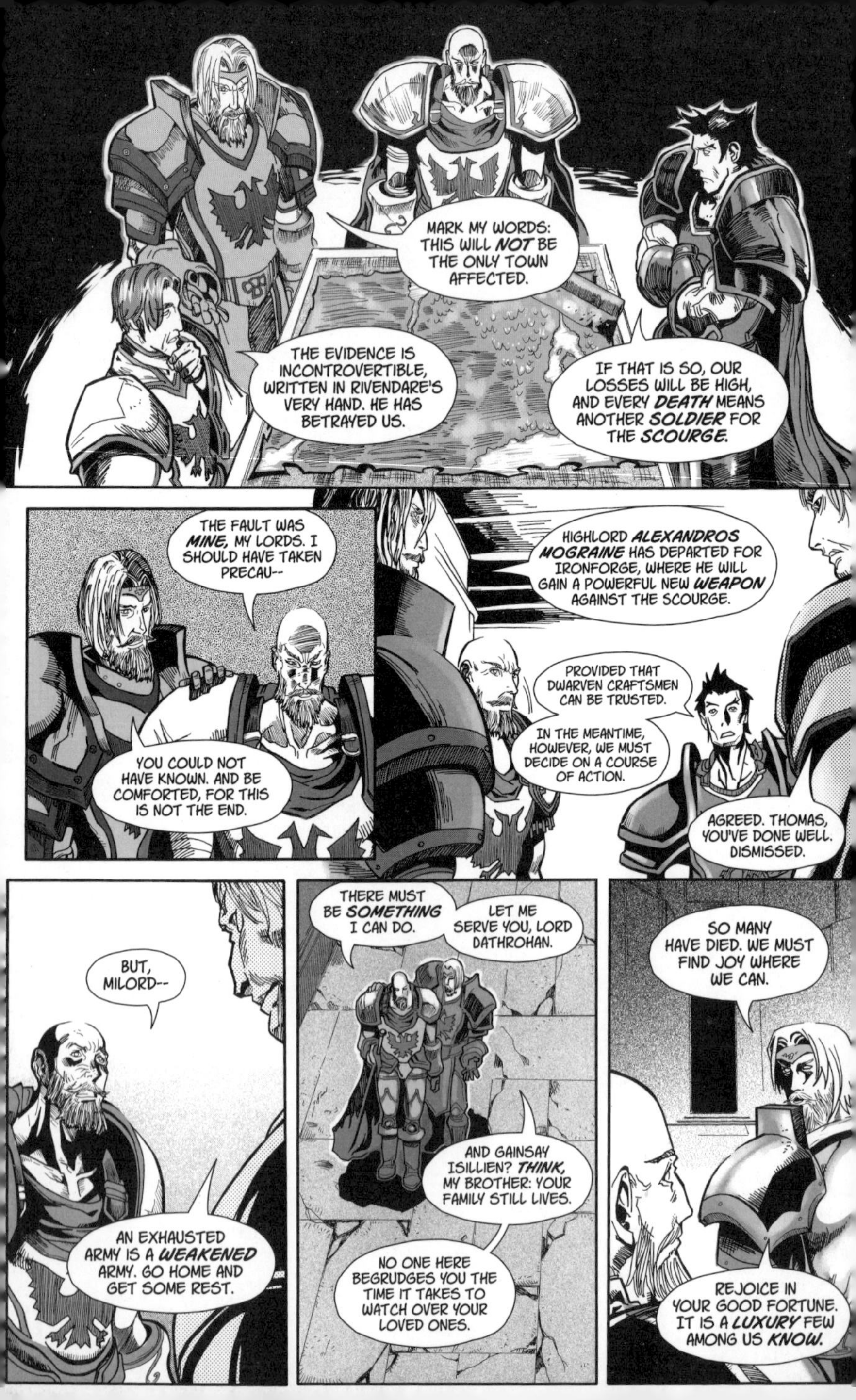
MARK MY WORDS: THIS WILL NOT BE THE ONLY TOWN AFFECTED.
THE EVIDENCE IS INCONTROVERTIBLE, WRITTEN IN RIVENDARE'S VERY HAND. HE HAS BETRAYED US.
IF THAT IS SO, OUR LOSSES WILL BE HIGH, AND EVERY DEATH MEANS ANOTHER SOLDIER FOR THE SCOURGE.
THE FAULT WAS MINE, MY LORDS. I SHOULD HAVE TAKEN PRECAU--
YOU COULD NOT HAVE KNOWN. AND BE COMFORTED, FOR THIS IS NOT THE END.
HIGHLORD ALEXANDROS MOGRAINE HAS DEPARTED FOR IRONFORGE, WHERE HE WILL GAIN A POWERFUL NEW WEAPON AGAINST THE SCOURGE.
PROVIDED THAT DWARVEN CRAFTSMEN CAN BE TRUSTED.
IN THE MEANTIME, HOWEVER, WE MUST DECIDE ON A COURSE OF ACTION.
AGREED. THOMAS, YOU'VE DONE WELL. DISMISSED.
BUT, MILORD--
AN EXHAUSTED ARMY IS A WEAKENED ARMY. GO HOME AND GET SOME REST.
THERE MUST BE SOMETHING I CAN DO.
LET ME SERVE YOU, LORD DATHROHAN.
AND GAINSAY ISILLIEN? THINK, MY BROTHER: YOUR FAMILY STILL LIVES.
NO ONE HERE BEGRUDGES YOU THE TIME IT TAKES TO WATCH OVER YOUR LOVED ONES.
SO MANY HAVE DIED. WE MUST FIND JOY WHERE WE CAN.
REJOICE IN YOUR GOOD FORTUNE. IT IS A LUXURY FEW AMONG US KNOW.

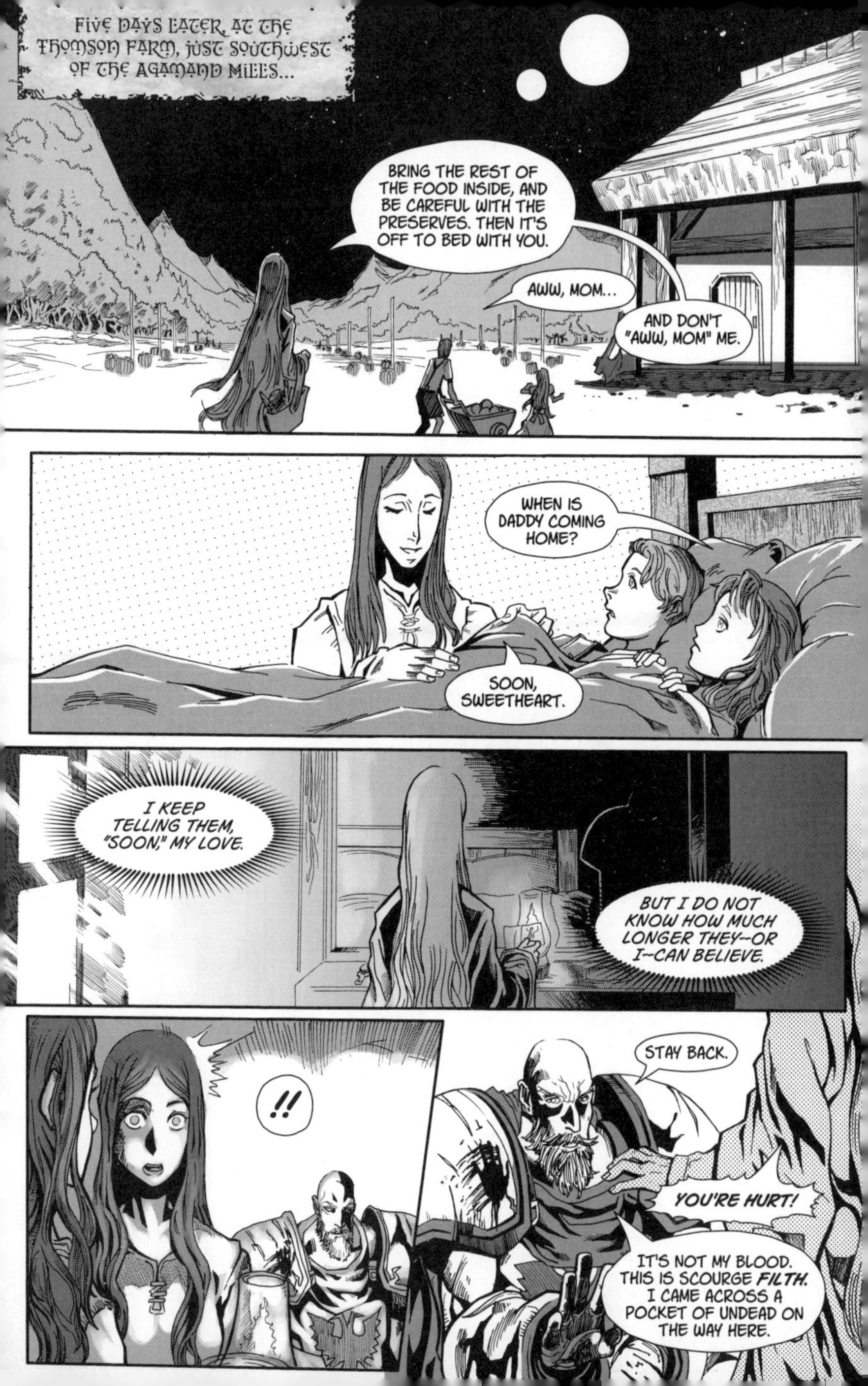
FIVE DAYS LATER, AT THE THOMSON FARM, JUST SOUTHWEST OF THE AGAMAND MILLS...
BRING THE REST OF THE FOOD INSIDE, AND BE CAREFUL WITH THE PRESERVES. THEN IT'S OFF TO BED WITH YOU.
AWW, MOM...
AND DON'T "AWW, MOM" ME.
WHEN IS DADDY COMING HOME?
SOON, SWEETHEART.
I KEEP TELLING THEM, "SOON," MY LOVE.
BUT I DO NOT KNOW HOW MUCH LONGER THEY--OR I--CAN BELIEVE.
!!
STAY BACK.
YOU'RE HURT!
IT'S NOT MY BLOOD. THIS IS SCOURGE ***FILTH.*** I CAME ACROSS A POCKET OF UNDEAD ON THE WAY HERE.

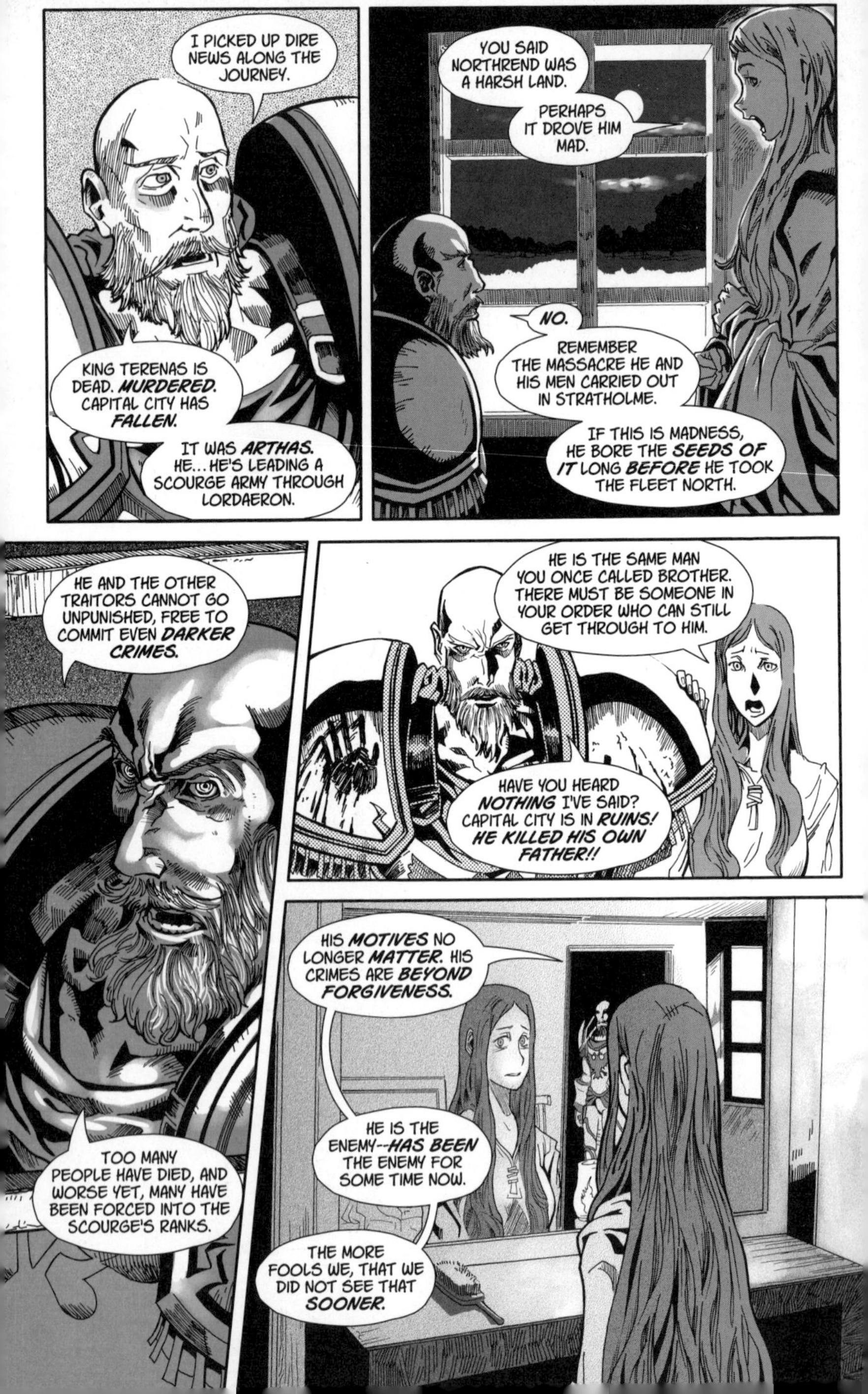

I PICKED UP DIRE NEWS ALONG THE JOURNEY.
KING TERENAS IS DEAD. ***MURDERED.*** CAPITAL CITY HAS ***FALLEN.***
IT WAS ***ARTHAS.*** HE... HE'S LEADING A SCOURGE ARMY THROUGH LORDAERON.
YOU SAID NORTHREND WAS A HARSH LAND.
PERHAPS IT DROVE HIM MAD.
NO.
REMEMBER THE MASSACRE HE AND HIS MEN CARRIED OUT IN STRATHOLME.
IF THIS IS MADNESS, HE BORE THE ***SEEDS OF IT*** LONG ***BEFORE*** HE TOOK THE FLEET NORTH.
HE AND THE OTHER TRAITORS CANNOT GO UNPUNISHED, FREE TO COMMIT EVEN ***DARKER CRIMES.***
TOO MANY PEOPLE HAVE DIED, AND WORSE YET, MANY HAVE BEEN FORCED INTO THE SCOURGE'S RANKS.
HE IS THE SAME MAN YOU ONCE CALLED BROTHER. THERE MUST BE SOMEONE IN YOUR ORDER WHO CAN STILL GET THROUGH TO HIM.
HAVE YOU HEARD ***NOTHING*** I'VE SAID? CAPITAL CITY IS IN ***RUINS! HE KILLED HIS OWN FATHER!!***
HIS ***MOTIVES*** NO LONGER ***MATTER.*** HIS CRIMES ARE ***BEYOND FORGIVENESS.***
HE IS THE ENEMY--***HAS BEEN*** THE ENEMY FOR SOME TIME NOW.
THE MORE FOOLS WE, THAT WE DID NOT SEE THAT ***SOONER.***

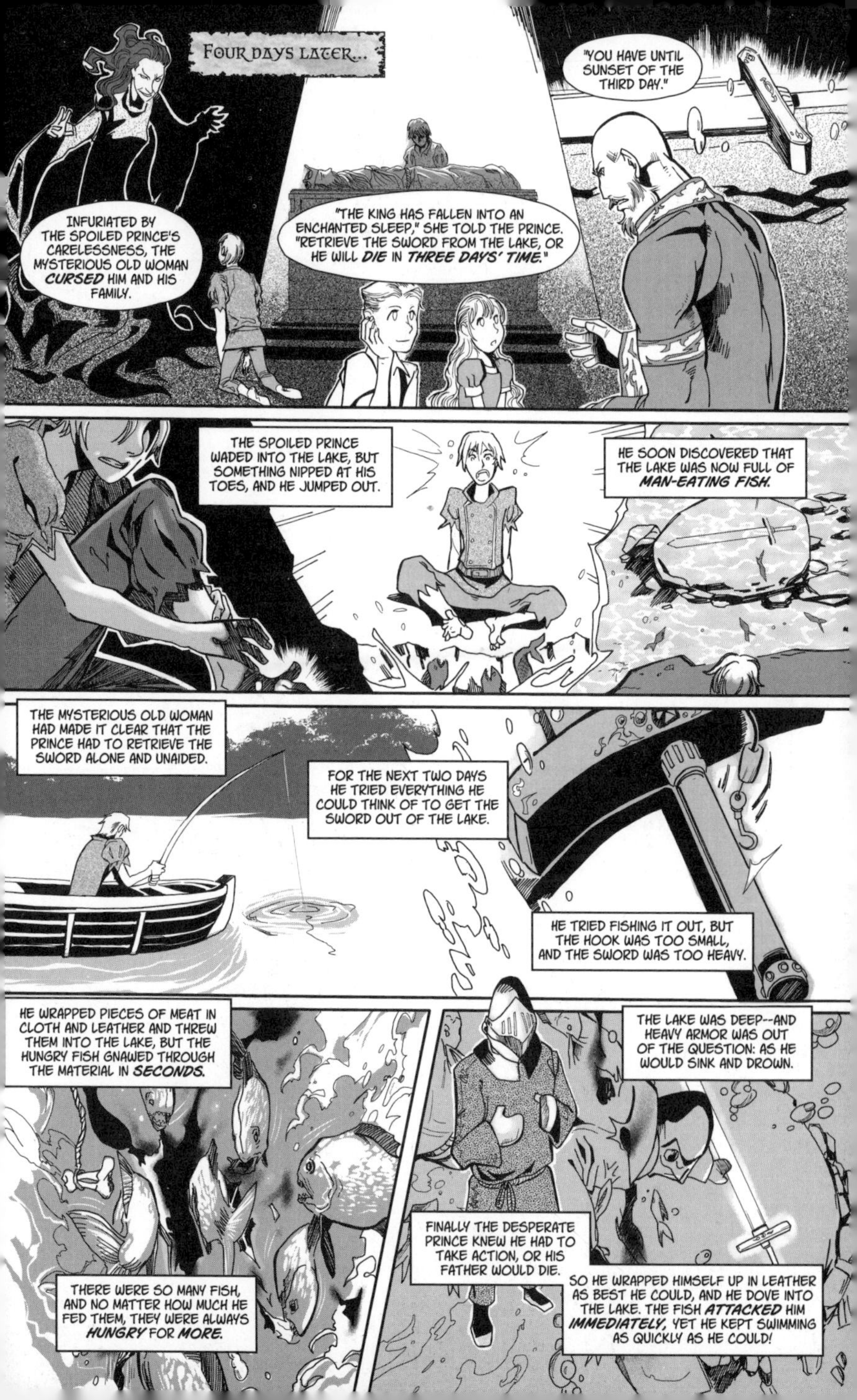
FOUR DAYS LATER...
INFURIATED BY THE SPOILED PRINCE'S CARELESSNESS, THE MYSTERIOUS OLD WOMAN CURSED HIM AND HIS FAMILY.
"THE KING HAS FALLEN INTO AN ENCHANTED SLEEP," SHE TOLD THE PRINCE. "RETRIEVE THE SWORD FROM THE LAKE, OR HE WILL DIE IN THREE DAYS' TIME."
"YOU HAVE UNTIL SUNSET OF THE THIRD DAY."
THE SPOILED PRINCE WADED INTO THE LAKE, BUT SOMETHING NIPPED AT HIS TOES, AND HE JUMPED OUT.
HE SOON DISCOVERED THAT THE LAKE WAS NOW FULL OF MAN-EATING FISH.
THE MYSTERIOUS OLD WOMAN HAD MADE IT CLEAR THAT THE PRINCE HAD TO RETRIEVE THE SWORD ALONE AND UNAIDED.
FOR THE NEXT TWO DAYS HE TRIED EVERYTHING HE COULD THINK OF TO GET THE SWORD OUT OF THE LAKE.
HE TRIED FISHING IT OUT, BUT THE HOOK WAS TOO SMALL, AND THE SWORD WAS TOO HEAVY.
HE WRAPPED PIECES OF MEAT IN CLOTH AND LEATHER AND THREW THEM INTO THE LAKE, BUT THE HUNGRY FISH GNAWED THROUGH THE MATERIAL IN SECONDS.
THERE WERE SO MANY FISH, AND NO MATTER HOW MUCH HE FED THEM, THEY WERE ALWAYS HUNGRY FOR MORE.
THE LAKE WAS DEEP--AND HEAVY ARMOR WAS OUT OF THE QUESTION: AS HE WOULD SINK AND DROWN.
FINALLY THE DESPERATE PRINCE KNEW HE HAD TO TAKE ACTION, OR HIS FATHER WOULD DIE.
SO HE WRAPPED HIMSELF UP IN LEATHER AS BEST HE COULD, AND HE DOVE INTO THE LAKE. THE FISH ATTACKED HIM IMMEDIATELY, YET HE KEPT SWIMMING AS QUICKLY AS HE COULD!

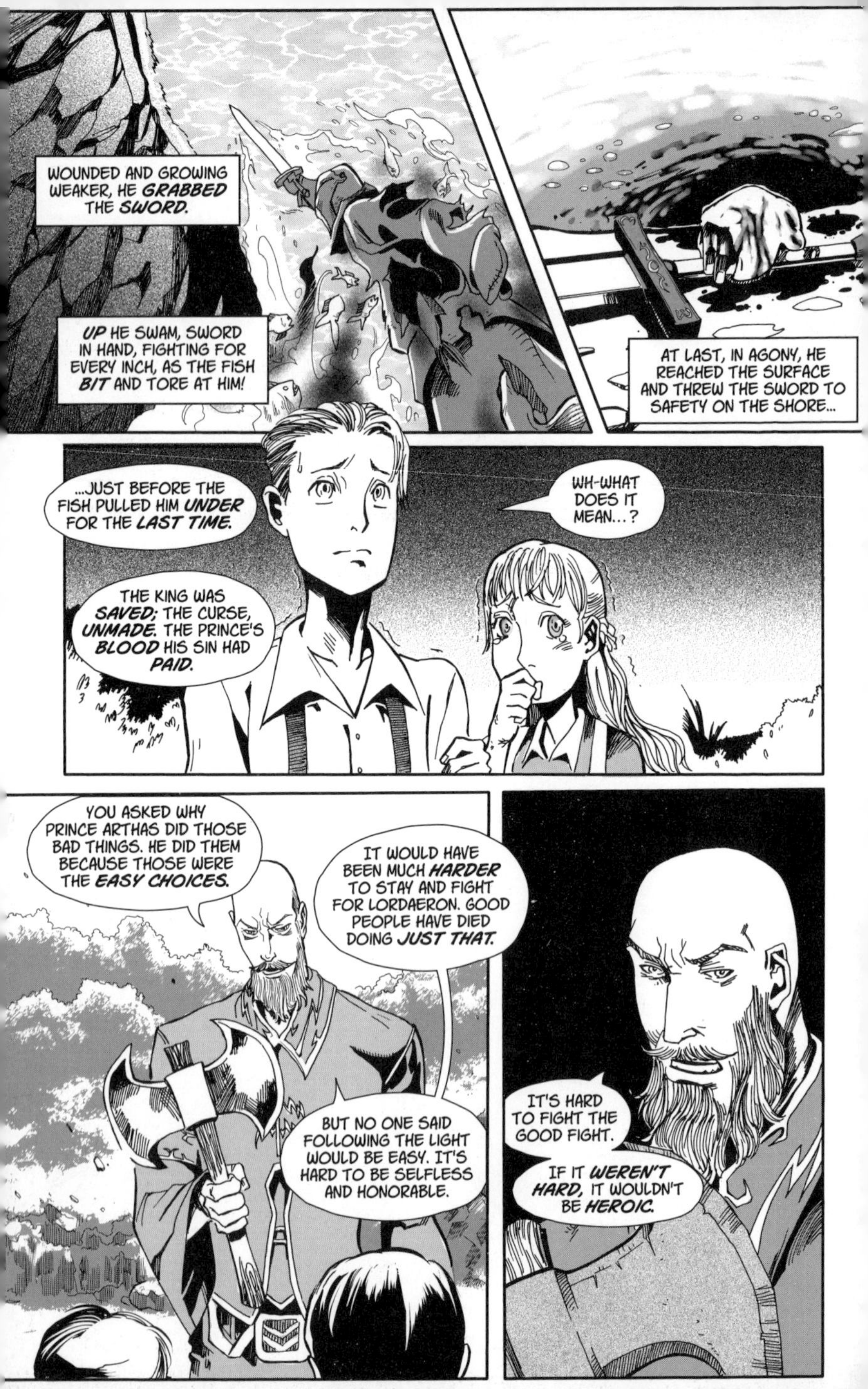
WOUNDED AND GROWING WEAKER, HE *GRABBED* THE *SWORD.*
UP HE SWAM, SWORD IN HAND, FIGHTING FOR EVERY INCH, AS THE FISH *BIT* AND TORE AT HIM!
AT LAST, IN AGONY, HE REACHED THE SURFACE AND THREW THE SWORD TO SAFETY ON THE SHORE...
...JUST BEFORE THE FISH PULLED HIM *UNDER* FOR THE *LAST TIME.*
THE KING WAS *SAVED;* THE CURSE, *UNMADE.* THE PRINCE'S *BLOOD* HIS SIN HAD *PAID.*
WH-WHAT DOES IT MEAN...?
YOU ASKED WHY PRINCE ARTHAS DID THOSE BAD THINGS. HE DID THEM BECAUSE THOSE WERE THE *EASY CHOICES.*
IT WOULD HAVE BEEN MUCH *HARDER* TO STAY AND FIGHT FOR LORDAERON. GOOD PEOPLE HAVE DIED DOING *JUST THAT.*
BUT NO ONE SAID FOLLOWING THE LIGHT WOULD BE EASY. IT'S HARD TO BE SELFLESS AND HONORABLE.
IT'S HARD TO FIGHT THE GOOD FIGHT.
IF IT *WEREN'T HARD,* IT WOULDN'T BE *HEROIC.*

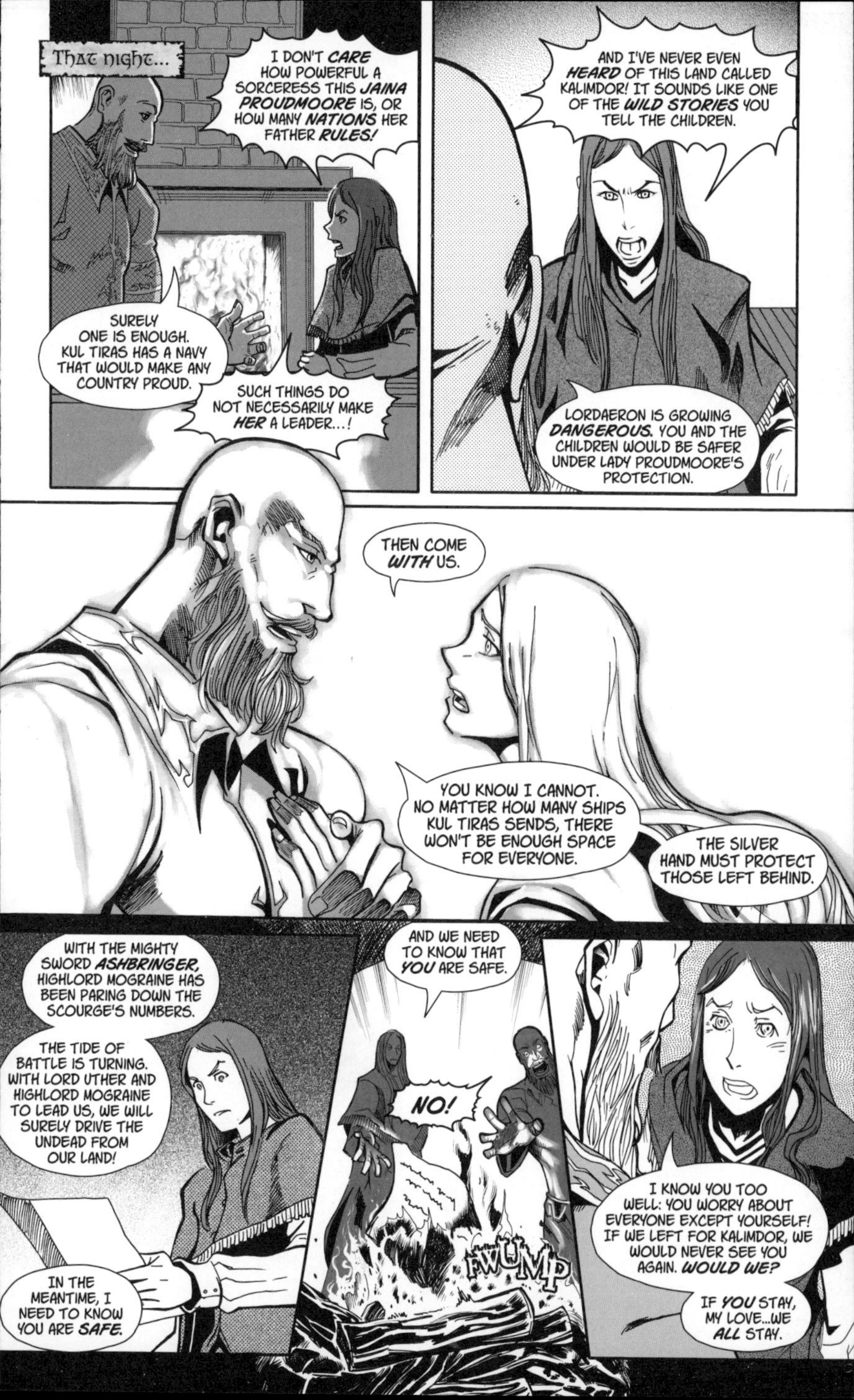
That night...
I DON'T CARE HOW POWERFUL A SORCERESS THIS JAINA PROUDMOORE IS, OR HOW MANY NATIONS HER FATHER RULES!
SURELY ONE IS ENOUGH. KUL TIRAS HAS A NAVY THAT WOULD MAKE ANY COUNTRY PROUD.
SUCH THINGS DO NOT NECESSARILY MAKE HER A LEADER...!
AND I'VE NEVER EVEN HEARD OF THIS LAND CALLED KALIMDOR! IT SOUNDS LIKE ONE OF THE WILD STORIES YOU TELL THE CHILDREN.
LORDAERON IS GROWING DANGEROUS. YOU AND THE CHILDREN WOULD BE SAFER UNDER LADY PROUDMOORE'S PROTECTION.
THEN COME WITH US.
YOU KNOW I CANNOT. NO MATTER HOW MANY SHIPS KUL TIRAS SENDS, THERE WON'T BE ENOUGH SPACE FOR EVERYONE.
THE SILVER HAND MUST PROTECT THOSE LEFT BEHIND.
WITH THE MIGHTY SWORD ASHBRINGER, HIGHLORD MOGRAINE HAS BEEN PARING DOWN THE SCOURGE'S NUMBERS.
THE TIDE OF BATTLE IS TURNING. WITH LORD UTHER AND HIGHLORD MOGRAINE TO LEAD US, WE WILL SURELY DRIVE THE UNDEAD FROM OUR LAND!
IN THE MEANTIME, I NEED TO KNOW YOU ARE SAFE.
AND WE NEED TO KNOW THAT YOU ARE SAFE.
NO!
FWUMP
I KNOW YOU TOO WELL: YOU WORRY ABOUT EVERYONE EXCEPT YOURSELF! IF WE LEFT FOR KALIMDOR, WE WOULD NEVER SEE YOU AGAIN. WOULD WE?
IF YOU STAY, MY LOVE...WE ALL STAY.

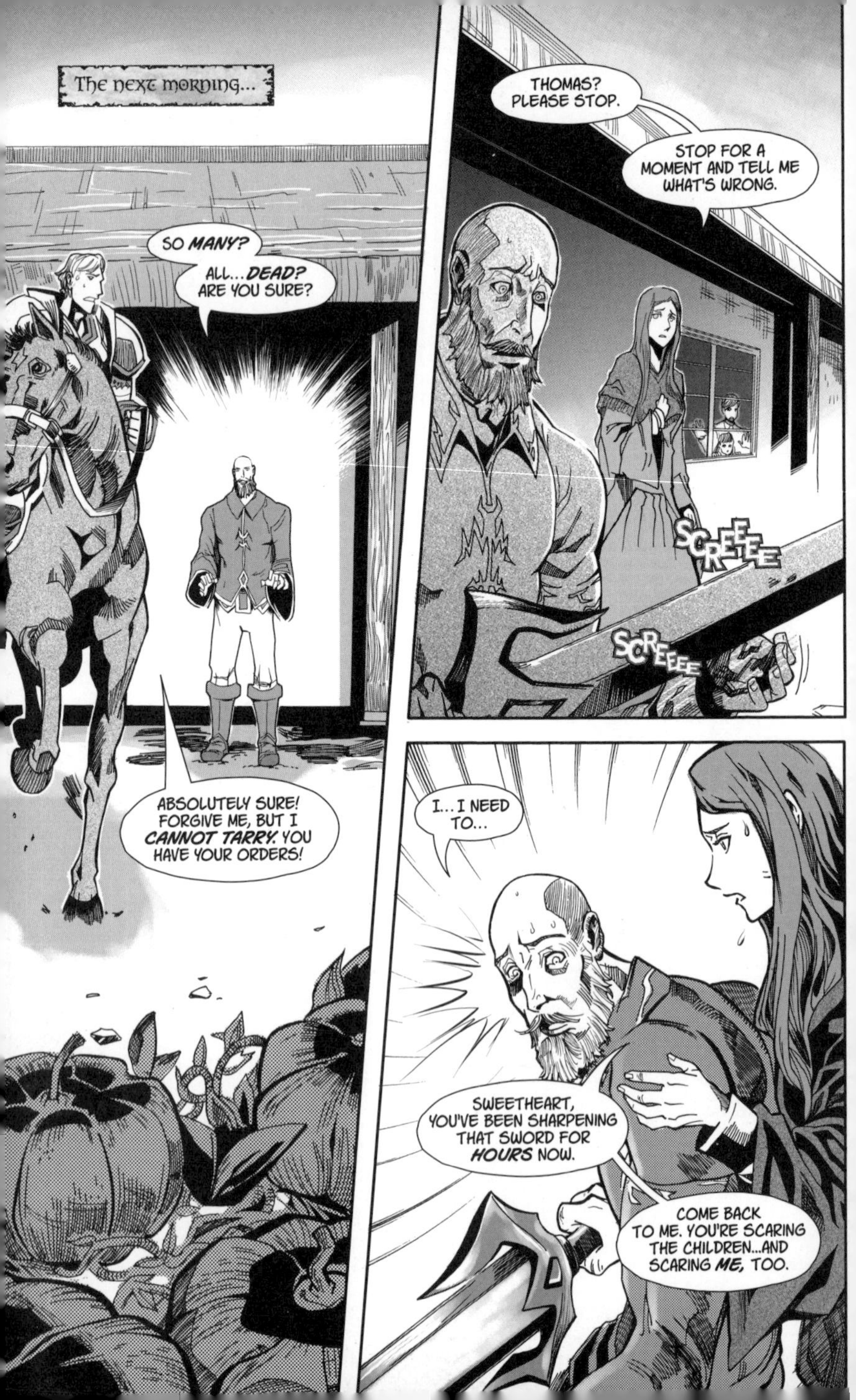
The next morning...
SO MANY?
ALL... DEAD? ARE YOU SURE?
ABSOLUTELY SURE! FORGIVE ME, BUT I CANNOT TARRY. YOU HAVE YOUR ORDERS!
THOMAS? PLEASE STOP.
STOP FOR A MOMENT AND TELL ME WHAT'S WRONG.
SCREEEE
SCREEEE
I... I NEED TO...
SWEETHEART, YOU'VE BEEN SHARPENING THAT SWORD FOR HOURS NOW.
COME BACK TO ME. YOU'RE SCARING THE CHILDREN...AND SCARING ME, TOO.

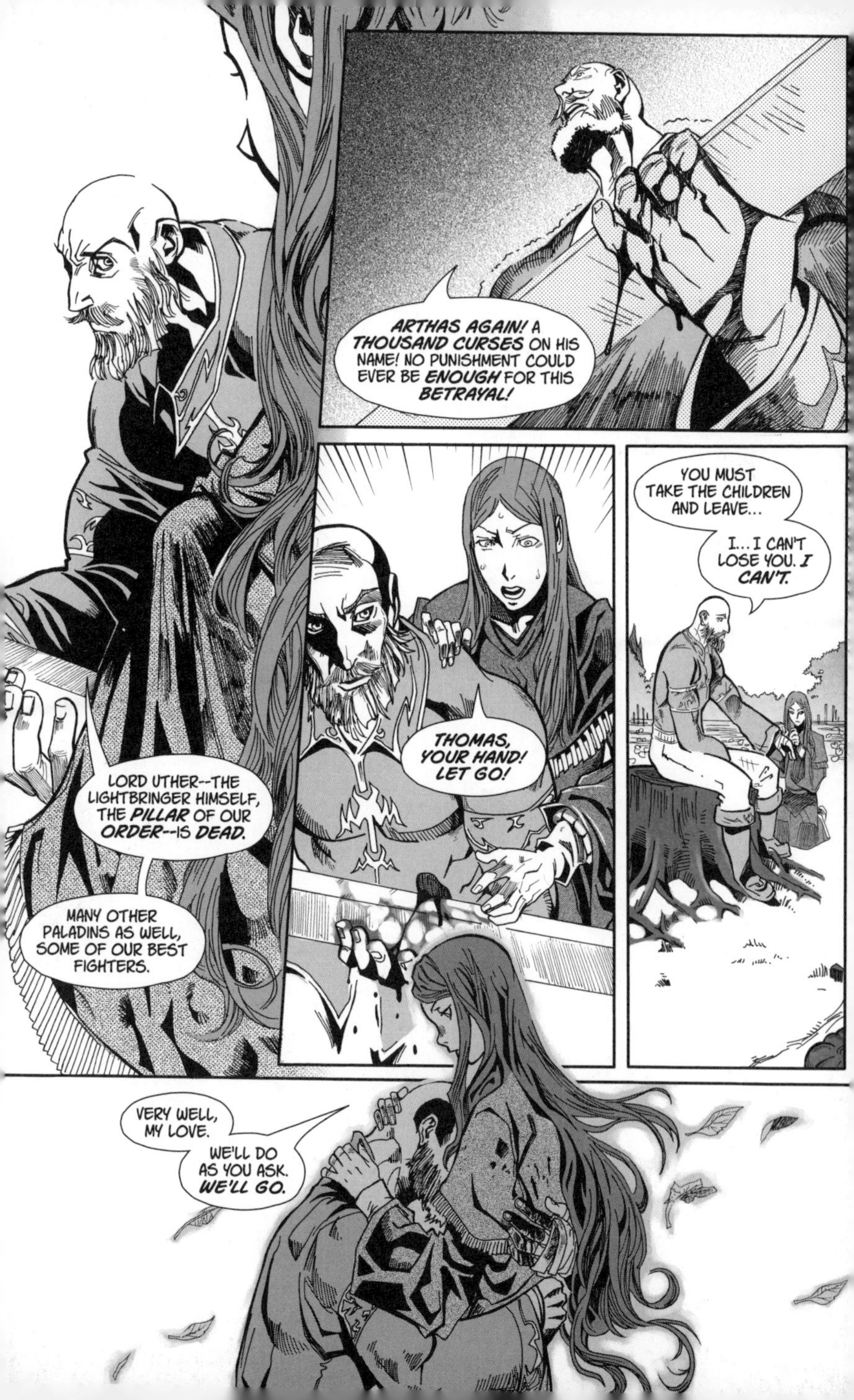
LORD UTHER--THE LIGHTBRINGER HIMSELF, THE PILLAR OF OUR ORDER--IS DEAD.
MANY OTHER PALADINS AS WELL, SOME OF OUR BEST FIGHTERS.
ARTHAS AGAIN! A THOUSAND CURSES ON HIS NAME! NO PUNISHMENT COULD EVER BE ENOUGH FOR THIS BETRAYAL!
THOMAS, YOUR HAND! LET GO!
YOU MUST TAKE THE CHILDREN AND LEAVE...
I... I CAN'T LOSE YOU. I CAN'T.
VERY WELL, MY LOVE.
WE'LL DO AS YOU ASK. WE'LL GO.

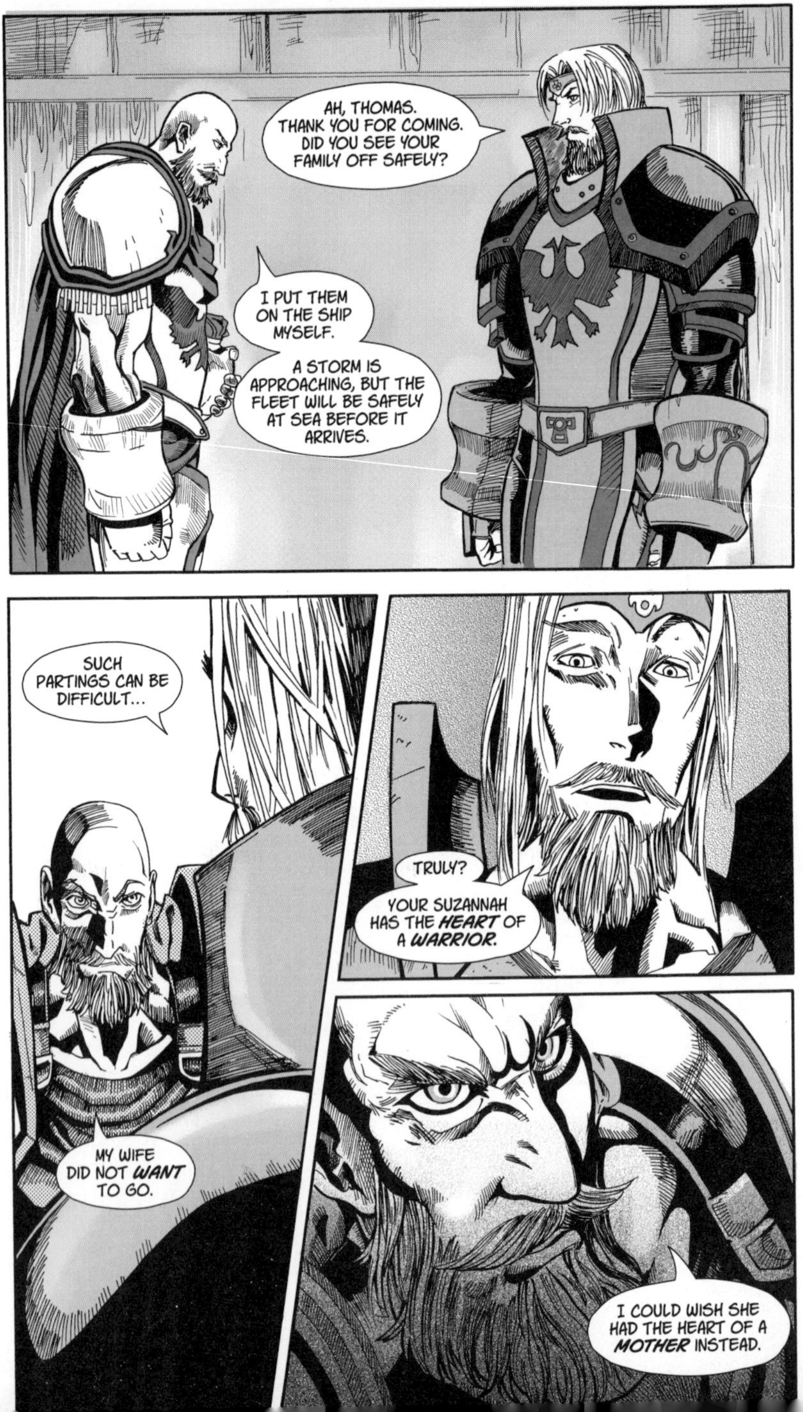
AH, THOMAS. THANK YOU FOR COMING. DID YOU SEE YOUR FAMILY OFF SAFELY?
I PUT THEM ON THE SHIP MYSELF.
A STORM IS APPROACHING, BUT THE FLEET WILL BE SAFELY AT SEA BEFORE IT ARRIVES.
SUCH PARTINGS CAN BE DIFFICULT...
MY WIFE DID NOT *WANT* TO GO.
TRULY?
YOUR SUZANNAH HAS THE *HEART* OF A *WARRIOR*.
I COULD WISH SHE HAD THE HEART OF A *MOTHER* INSTEAD.

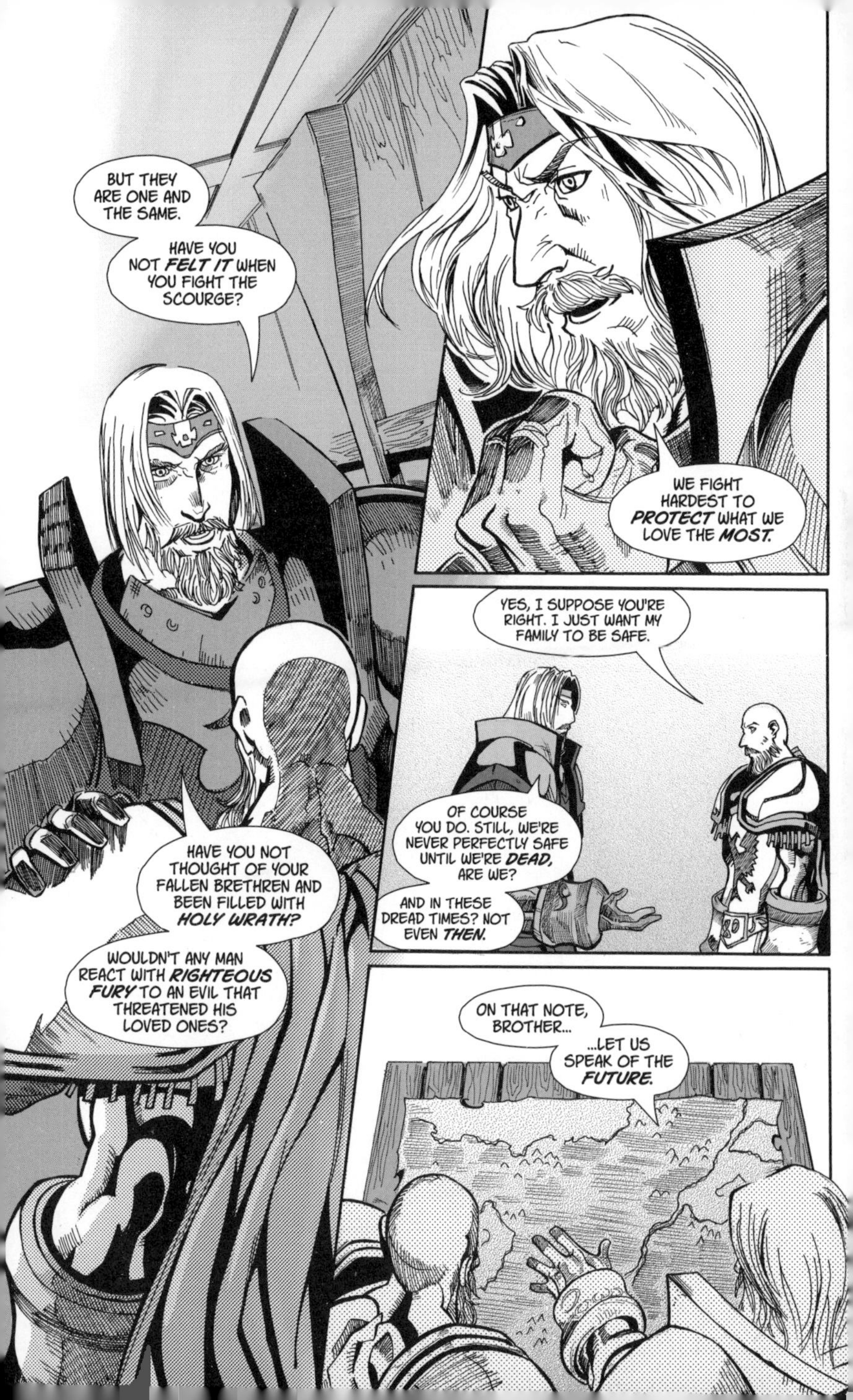
BUT THEY ARE ONE AND THE SAME.
HAVE YOU NOT *FELT IT* WHEN YOU FIGHT THE SCOURGE?
HAVE YOU NOT THOUGHT OF YOUR FALLEN BRETHREN AND BEEN FILLED WITH *HOLY WRATH?*
WOULDN'T ANY MAN REACT WITH *RIGHTEOUS FURY* TO AN EVIL THAT THREATENED HIS LOVED ONES?
WE FIGHT HARDEST TO *PROTECT* WHAT WE LOVE THE *MOST.*
YES, I SUPPOSE YOU'RE RIGHT. I JUST WANT MY FAMILY TO BE SAFE.
OF COURSE YOU DO. STILL, WE'RE NEVER PERFECTLY SAFE UNTIL WE'RE *DEAD,* ARE WE?
AND IN THESE DREAD TIMES? NOT EVEN *THEN.*
ON THAT NOTE, BROTHER...
...LET US SPEAK OF THE *FUTURE.*

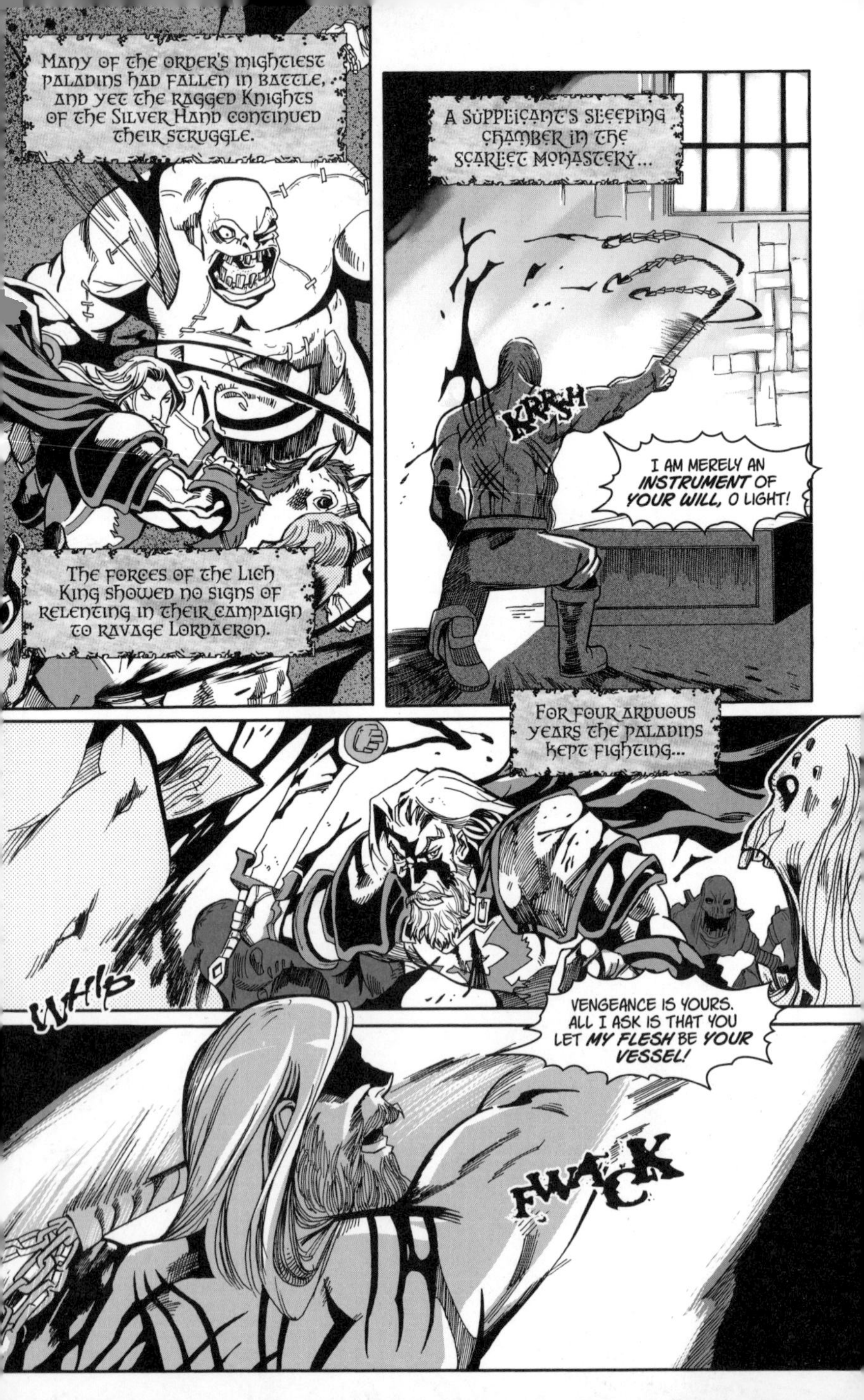
Many of the order's mightiest paladins had fallen in battle, and yet the ragged Knights of the Silver Hand continued their struggle.
The forces of the Lich King showed no signs of relenting in their campaign to ravage Lordaeron.
A supplicant's sleeping chamber in the Scarlet Monastery...
KRRSH
I AM MERELY AN *INSTRUMENT* OF *YOUR WILL,* O LIGHT!
For four arduous years the paladins kept fighting...
WHIP
VENGEANCE IS YOURS. ALL I ASK IS THAT YOU LET *MY FLESH* BE *YOUR VESSEL!*
FWACK

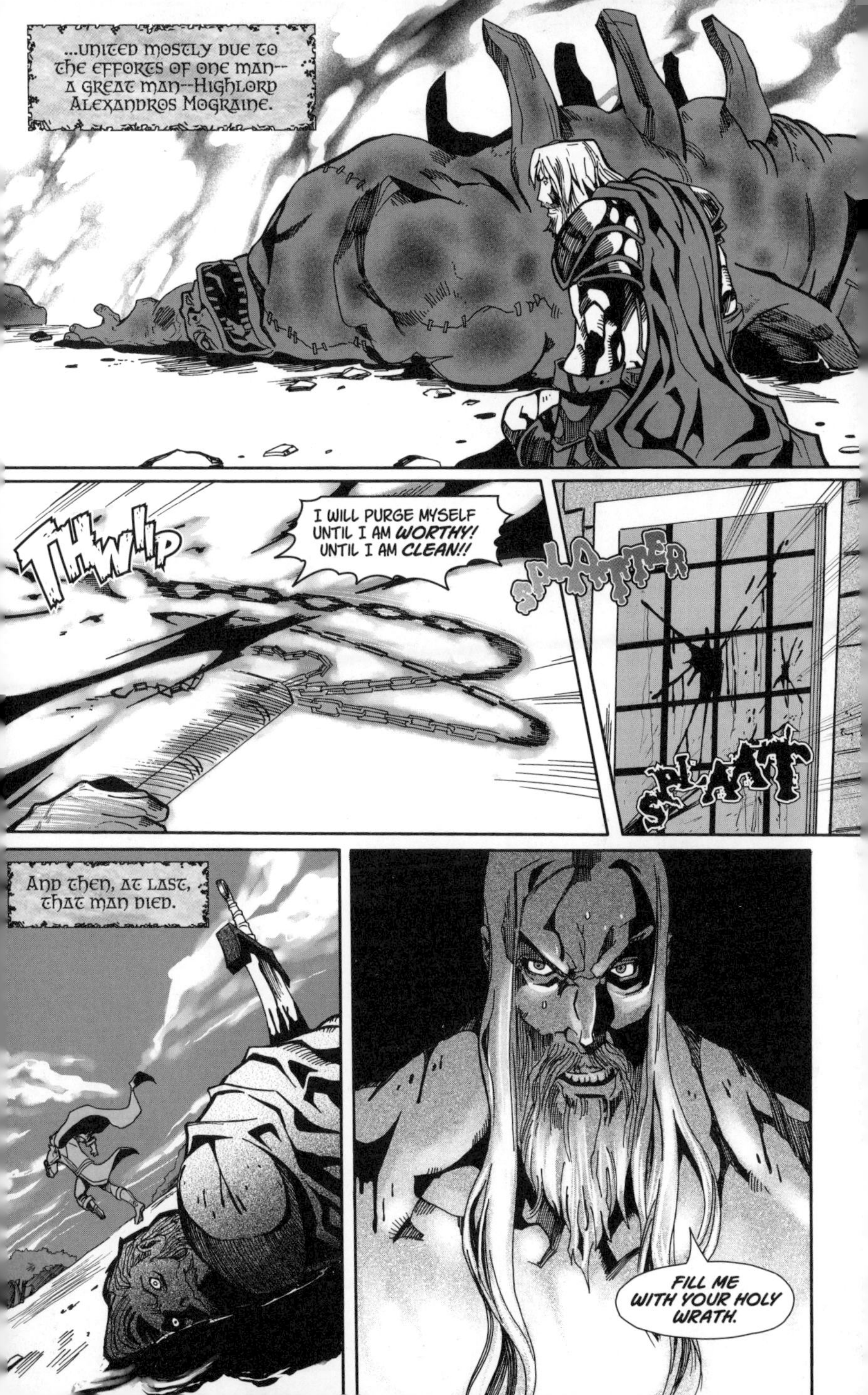
...UNITED MOSTLY DUE TO THE EFFORTS OF ONE MAN--A GREAT MAN--HIGHLORD ALEXANDROS MOGRAINE.
THWIP
I WILL PURGE MYSELF UNTIL I AM *WORTHY!* UNTIL I AM *CLEAN!!*
SPLATTER
SPLAT
AND THEN, AT LAST, THAT MAN DIED.
FILL ME WITH YOUR HOLY WRATH.

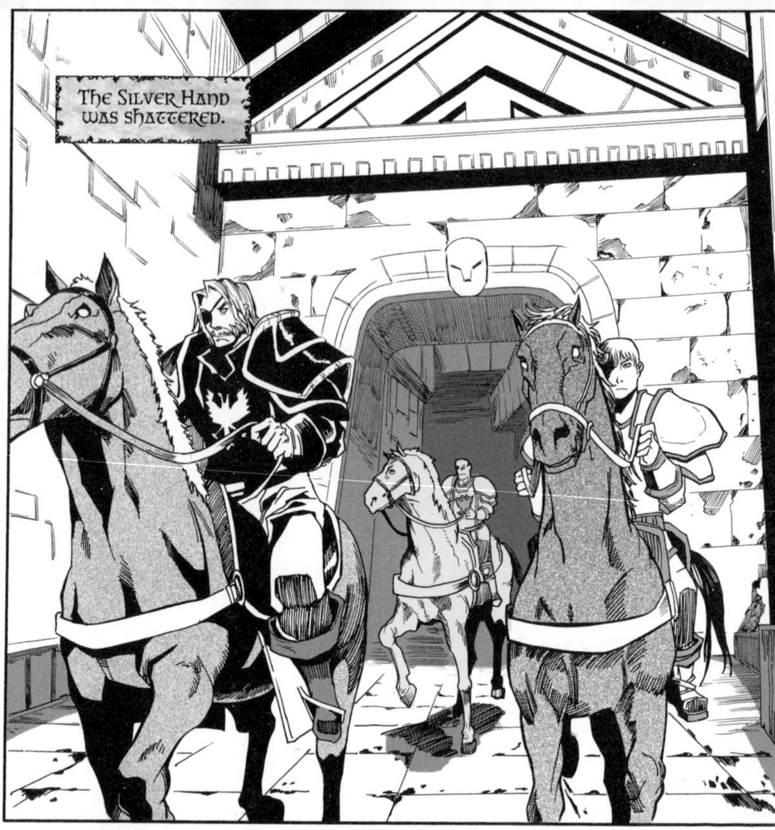
The Silver Hand was shattered.
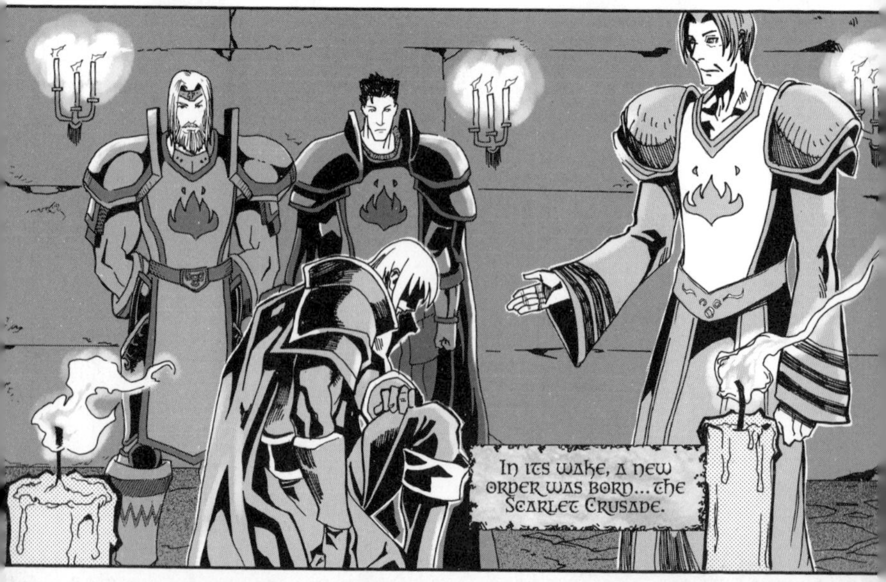
In its wake, a new order was born... the Scarlet Crusade.

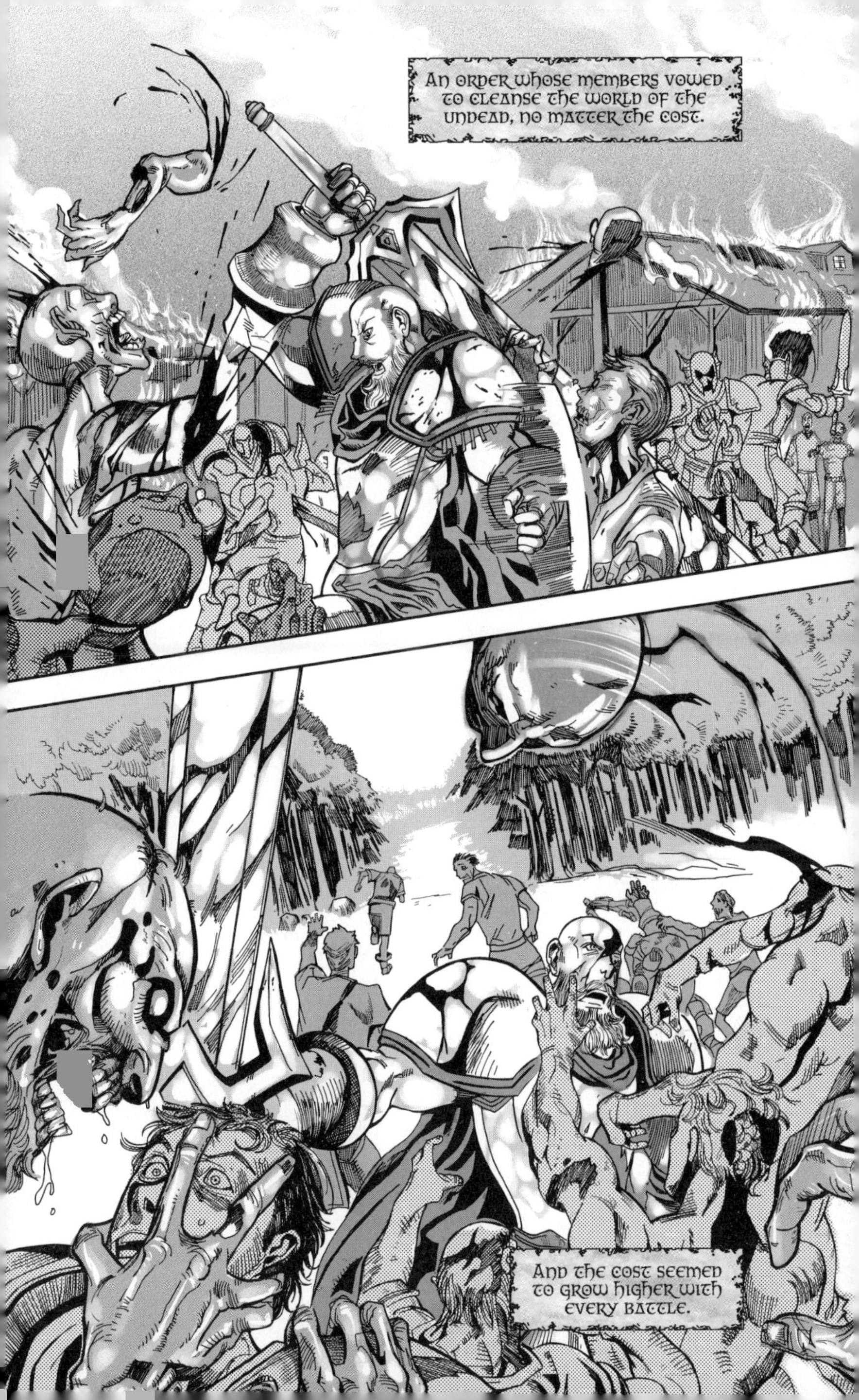
An order whose members vowed to cleanse the world of the undead, no matter the cost.
And the cost seemed to grow higher with every battle.

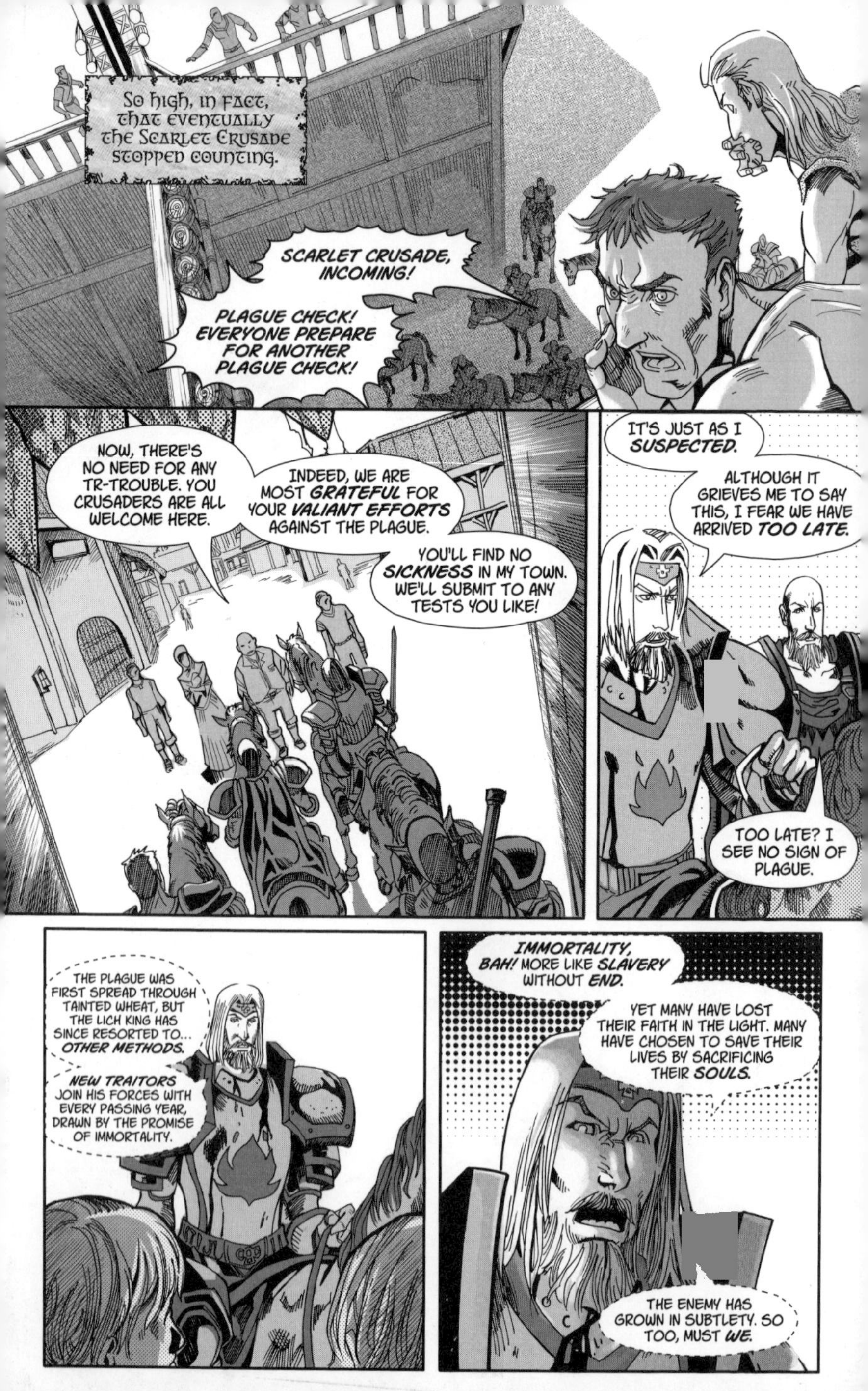
So high, in fact, that eventually the Scarlet Crusade stopped counting.
SCARLET CRUSADE, INCOMING!
PLAGUE CHECK! EVERYONE PREPARE FOR ANOTHER PLAGUE CHECK!
NOW, THERE'S NO NEED FOR ANY TR-TROUBLE. YOU CRUSADERS ARE ALL WELCOME HERE.
INDEED, WE ARE MOST GRATEFUL FOR YOUR VALIANT EFFORTS AGAINST THE PLAGUE.
YOU'LL FIND NO SICKNESS IN MY TOWN. WE'LL SUBMIT TO ANY TESTS YOU LIKE!
IT'S JUST AS I SUSPECTED.
ALTHOUGH IT GRIEVES ME TO SAY THIS, I FEAR WE HAVE ARRIVED TOO LATE.
TOO LATE? I SEE NO SIGN OF PLAGUE.
THE PLAGUE WAS FIRST SPREAD THROUGH TAINTED WHEAT, BUT THE LICH KING HAS SINCE RESORTED TO... OTHER METHODS.
NEW TRAITORS JOIN HIS FORCES WITH EVERY PASSING YEAR, DRAWN BY THE PROMISE OF IMMORTALITY.
IMMORTALITY, BAH! MORE LIKE SLAVERY WITHOUT END.
YET MANY HAVE LOST THEIR FAITH IN THE LIGHT. MANY HAVE CHOSEN TO SAVE THEIR LIVES BY SACRIFICING THEIR SOULS.
THE ENEMY HAS GROWN IN SUBTLETY. SO TOO, MUST WE.

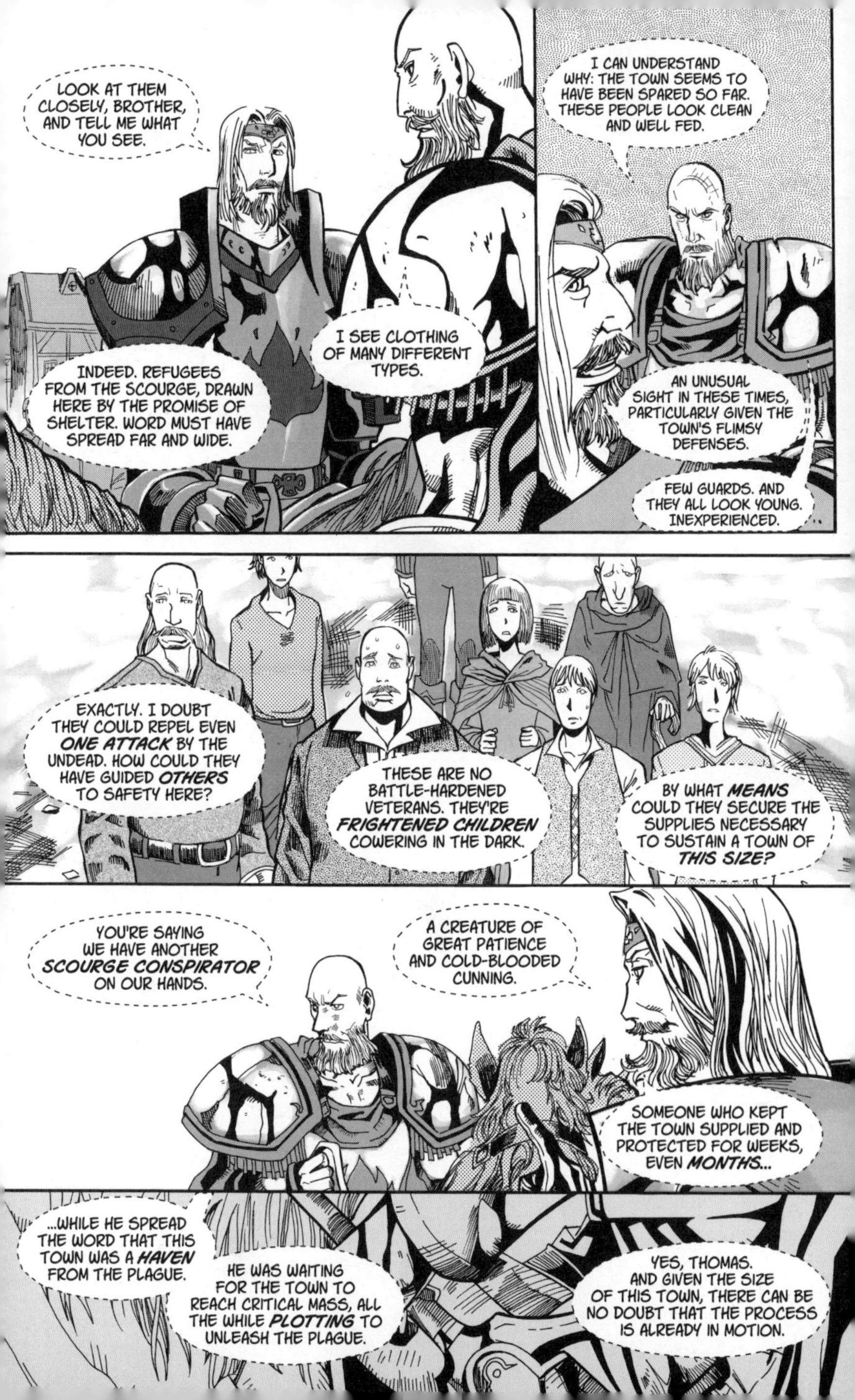

LOOK AT THEM CLOSELY, BROTHER, AND TELL ME WHAT YOU SEE.
I SEE CLOTHING OF MANY DIFFERENT TYPES.
INDEED. REFUGEES FROM THE SCOURGE, DRAWN HERE BY THE PROMISE OF SHELTER. WORD MUST HAVE SPREAD FAR AND WIDE.
I CAN UNDERSTAND WHY: THE TOWN SEEMS TO HAVE BEEN SPARED SO FAR. THESE PEOPLE LOOK CLEAN AND WELL FED.
AN UNUSUAL SIGHT IN THESE TIMES, PARTICULARLY GIVEN THE TOWN'S FLIMSY DEFENSES.
FEW GUARDS. AND THEY ALL LOOK YOUNG. INEXPERIENCED.
EXACTLY. I DOUBT THEY COULD REPEL EVEN ***ONE ATTACK*** BY THE UNDEAD. HOW COULD THEY HAVE GUIDED ***OTHERS*** TO SAFETY HERE?
THESE ARE NO BATTLE-HARDENED VETERANS. THEY'RE ***FRIGHTENED CHILDREN*** COWERING IN THE DARK.
BY WHAT ***MEANS*** COULD THEY SECURE THE SUPPLIES NECESSARY TO SUSTAIN A TOWN OF ***THIS SIZE?***
YOU'RE SAYING WE HAVE ANOTHER ***SCOURGE CONSPIRATOR*** ON OUR HANDS.
A CREATURE OF GREAT PATIENCE AND COLD-BLOODED CUNNING.
SOMEONE WHO KEPT THE TOWN SUPPLIED AND PROTECTED FOR WEEKS, EVEN ***MONTHS...***
...WHILE HE SPREAD THE WORD THAT THIS TOWN WAS A ***HAVEN*** FROM THE PLAGUE.
HE WAS WAITING FOR THE TOWN TO REACH CRITICAL MASS, ALL THE WHILE ***PLOTTING*** TO UNLEASH THE PLAGUE.
YES, THOMAS. AND GIVEN THE SIZE OF THIS TOWN, THERE CAN BE NO DOUBT THAT THE PROCESS IS ALREADY IN MOTION.

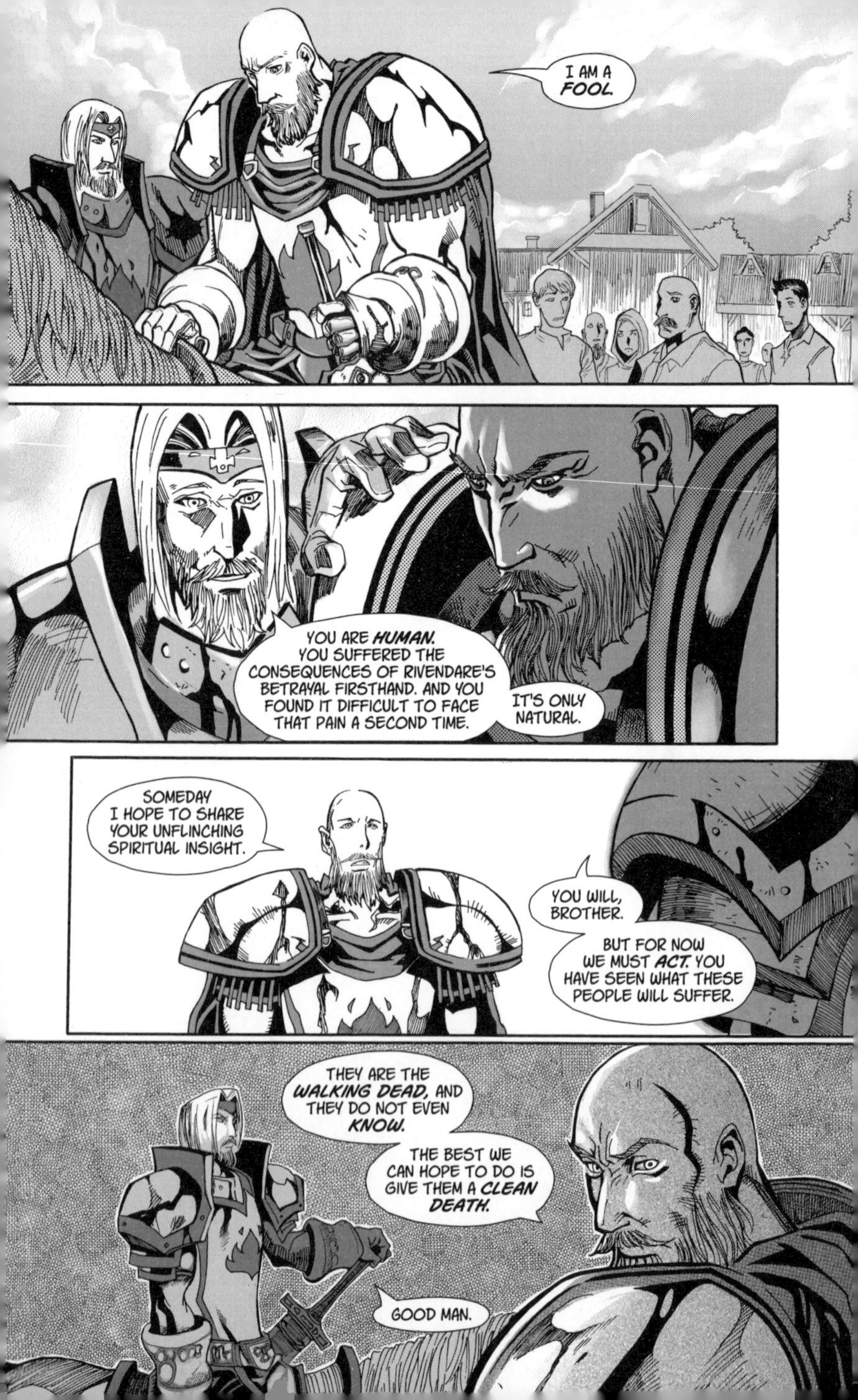
I AM A FOOL.
YOU ARE HUMAN. YOU SUFFERED THE CONSEQUENCES OF RIVENDARE'S BETRAYAL FIRSTHAND. AND YOU FOUND IT DIFFICULT TO FACE THAT PAIN A SECOND TIME.
IT'S ONLY NATURAL.
SOMEDAY I HOPE TO SHARE YOUR UNFLINCHING SPIRITUAL INSIGHT.
YOU WILL, BROTHER.
BUT FOR NOW WE MUST ACT. YOU HAVE SEEN WHAT THESE PEOPLE WILL SUFFER.
THEY ARE THE WALKING DEAD, AND THEY DO NOT EVEN KNOW.
THE BEST WE CAN HOPE TO DO IS GIVE THEM A CLEAN DEATH.
GOOD MAN.

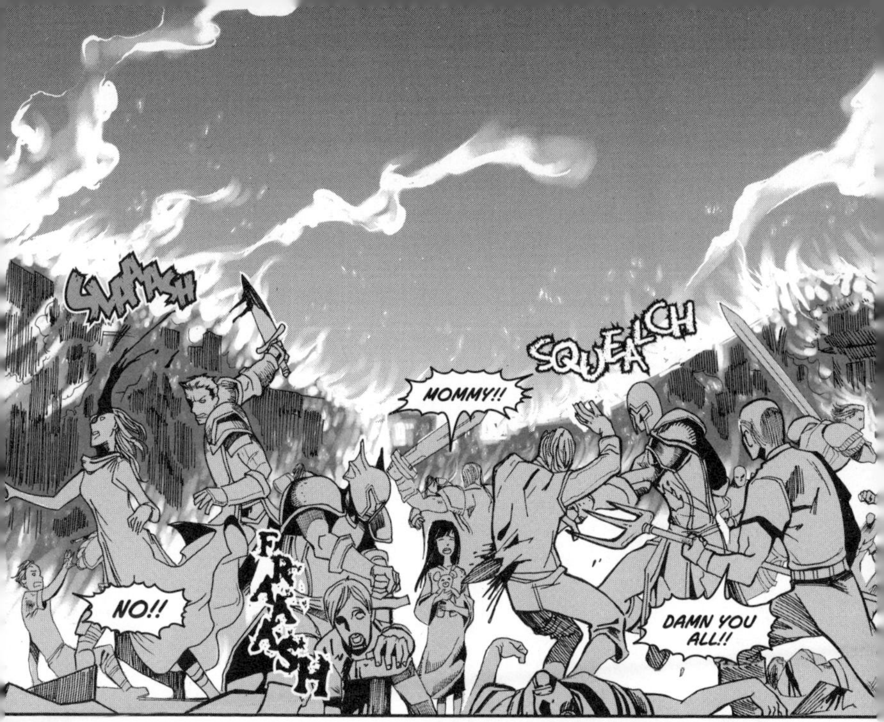
SWAASH
NO!!
FRAASH
MOMMY!!
SQUEALCH
DAMN YOU ALL!!

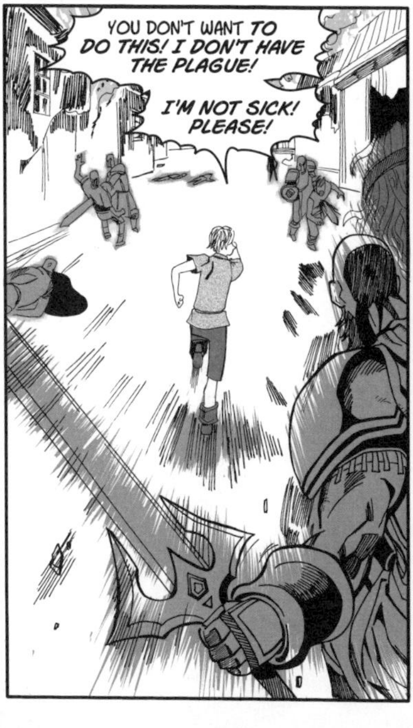
YOU DON'T WANT TO DO THIS! I DON'T HAVE THE PLAGUE!
I'M NOT SICK! PLEASE!

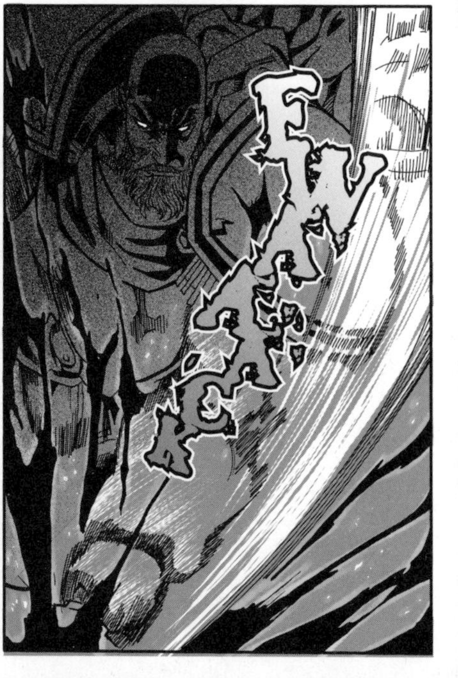
FWACK

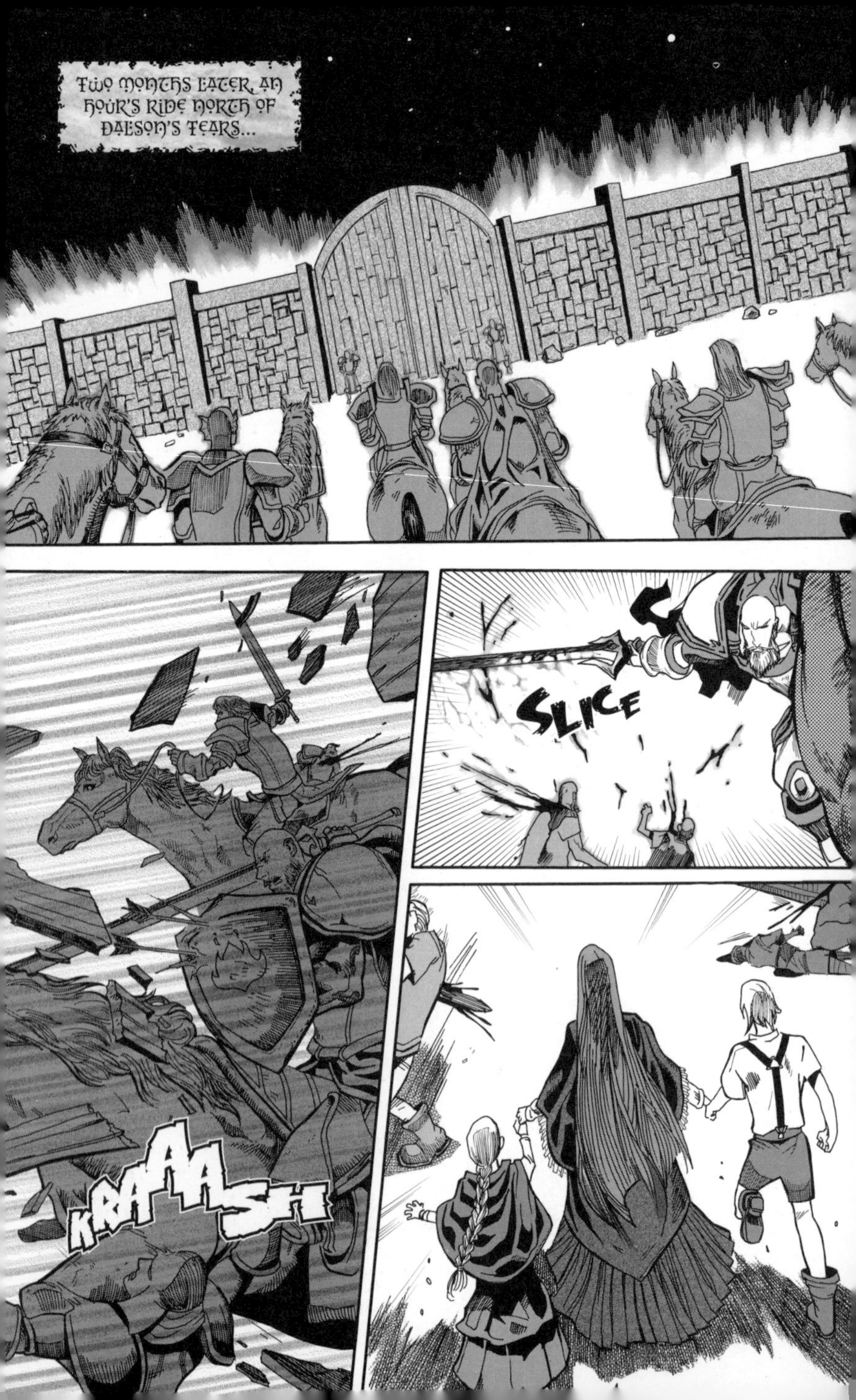
TWO MONTHS LATER, AN HOUR'S RIDE NORTH OF DAESON'S TEARS...
KRAAASH
SLICE

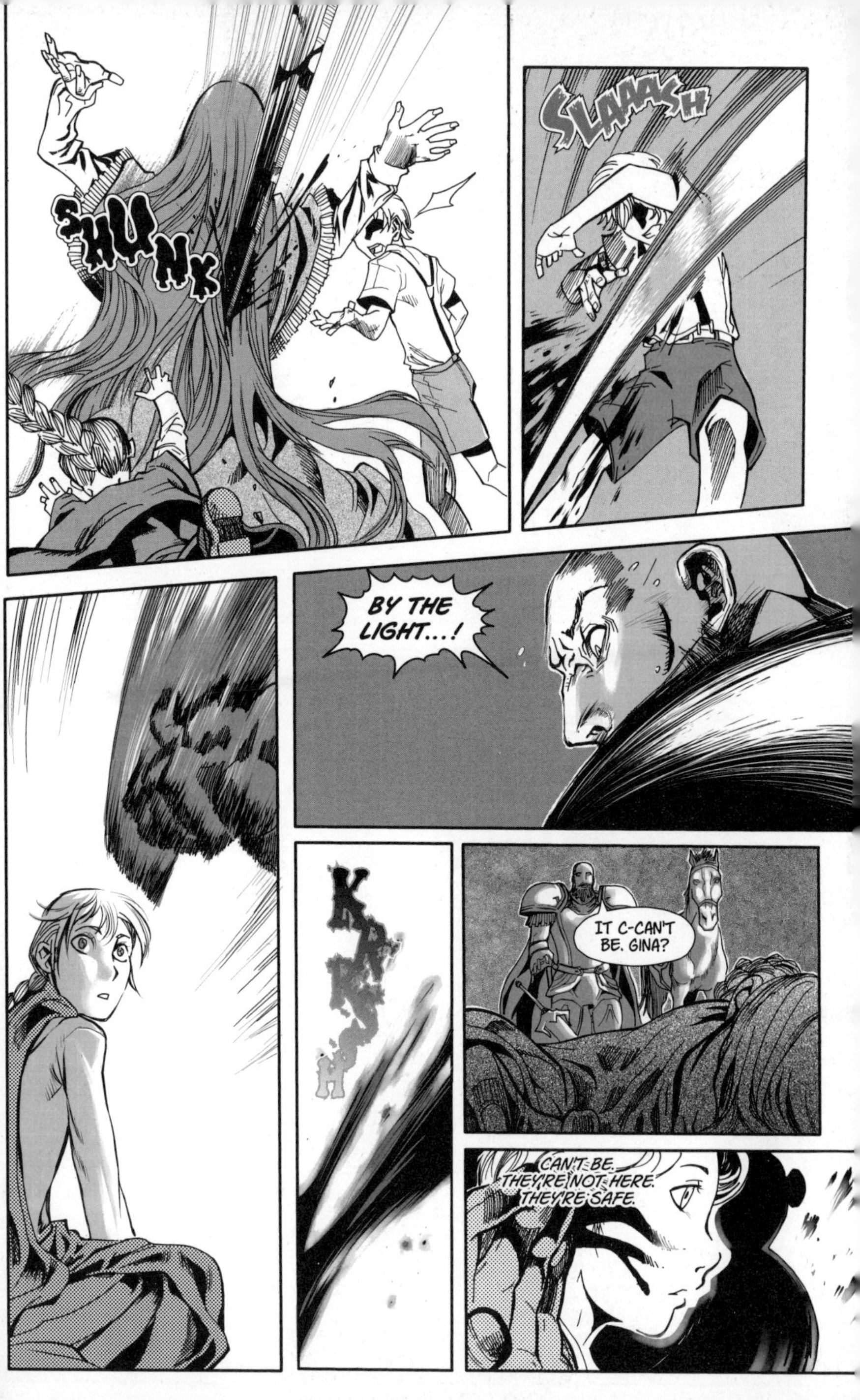
SHUNK
SLAAASH
BY THE LIGHT...!
IT C-CAN'T BE. GINA?
CAN'T BE. THEY'RE NOT HERE. THEY'RE SAFE.

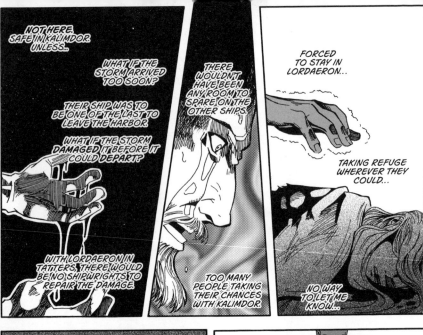

NOT HERE. SAFE IN KALIMDOR. UNLESS...

WHAT IF THE STORM ARRIVED TOO SOON?

THEIR SHIP WAS TO BE ONE OF THE LAST TO LEAVE THE HARBOR.

WHAT IF THE STORM DAMAGED IT BEFORE IT COULD DEPART?

WITH LORDAERON IN TATTERS, THERE WOULD BE NO SHIPWRIGHTS TO REPAIR THE DAMAGE.

THERE WOULDN'T HAVE BEEN ANY ROOM TO SPARE ON THE OTHER SHIPS.

TOO MANY PEOPLE TAKING THEIR CHANCES WITH KALIMDOR.

FORCED TO STAY IN LORDAERON...

TAKING REFUGE WHEREVER THEY COULD...

NO WAY TO LET ME KNOW...

STOP!

CLANG

WHAT WERE YOU THINKING?!

DON'T TOUCH THEM! THEY'RE INFECTED!

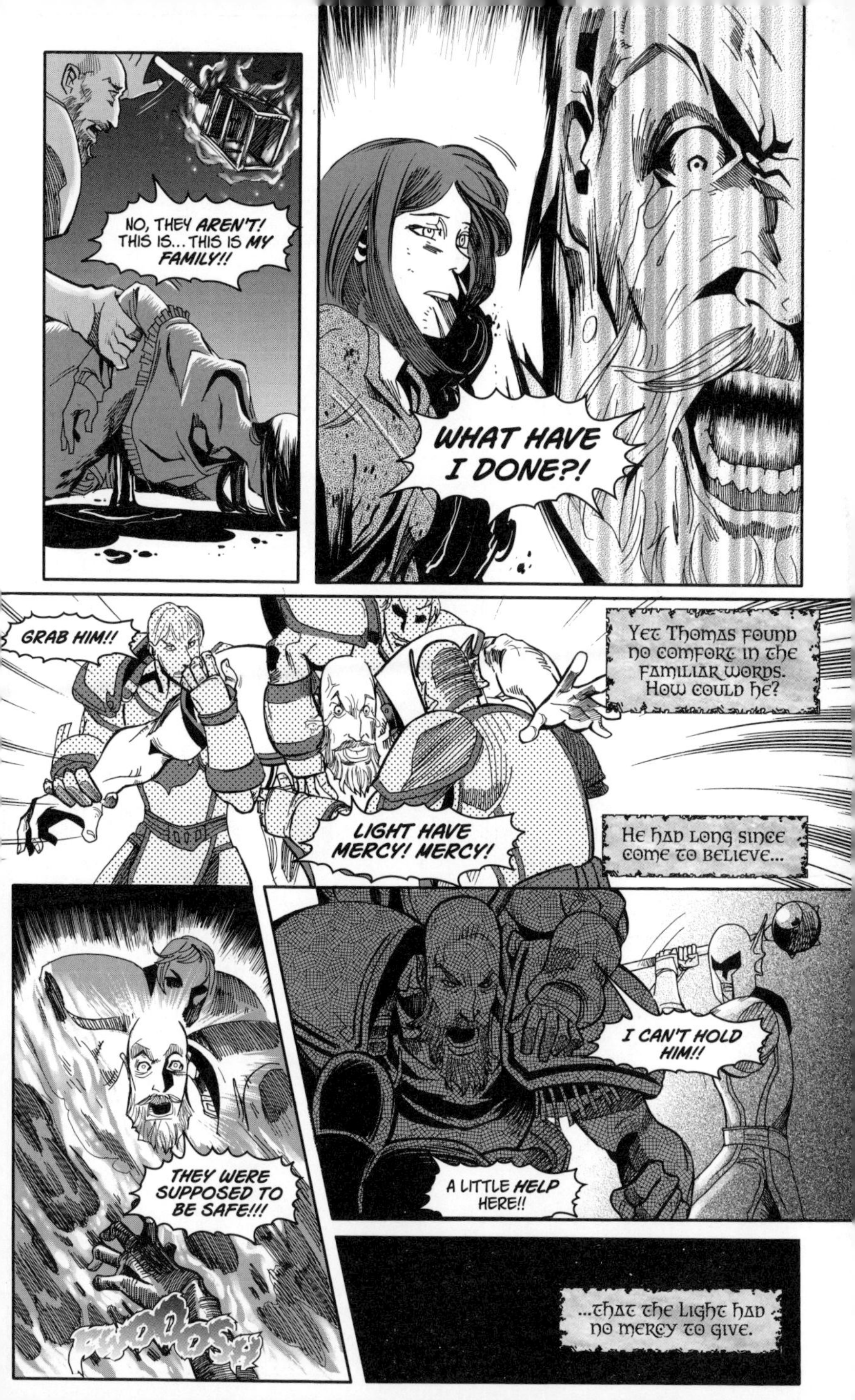
NO, THEY AREN'T! THIS IS... THIS IS MY FAMILY!!
WHAT HAVE I DONE?!
GRAB HIM!!
Yet Thomas found no comfort in the familiar words. How could he?
LIGHT HAVE MERCY! MERCY!
He had long since come to believe...
THEY WERE SUPPOSED TO BE SAFE!!!
FWOOOSH
I CAN'T HOLD HIM!!
A LITTLE HELP HERE!!
...that the Light had no mercy to give.

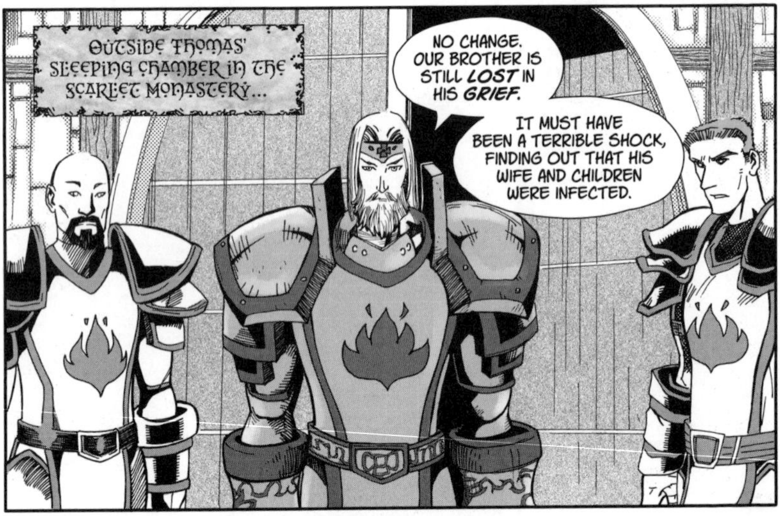
OUTSIDE THOMAS' SLEEPING CHAMBER IN THE SCARLET MONASTERY...
NO CHANGE. OUR BROTHER IS STILL *LOST* IN HIS *GRIEF*.
IT MUST HAVE BEEN A TERRIBLE SHOCK, FINDING OUT THAT HIS WIFE AND CHILDREN WERE INFECTED.

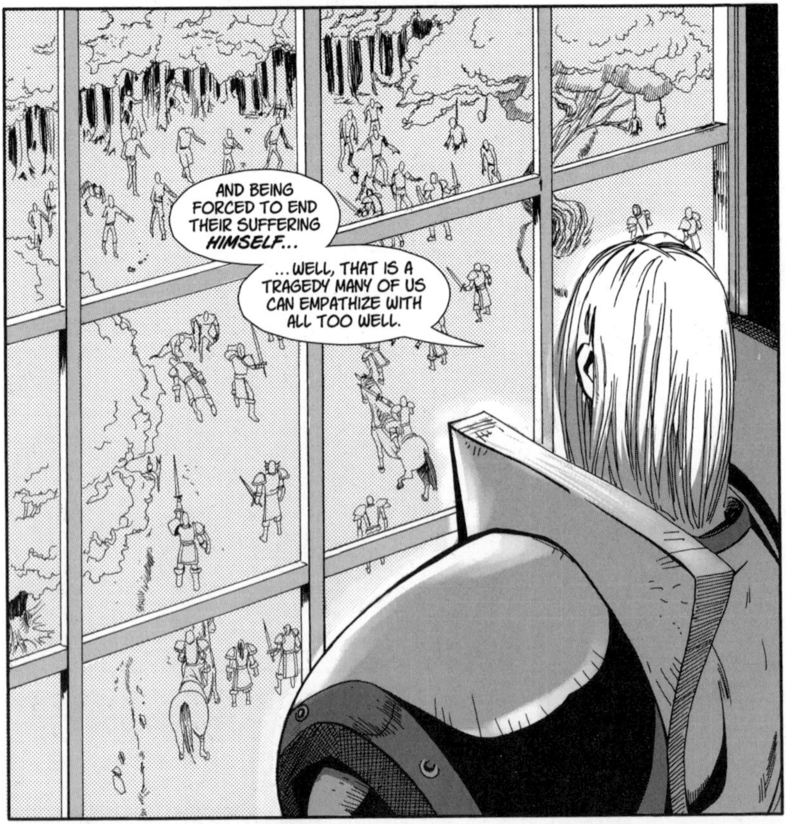
AND BEING FORCED TO END THEIR SUFFERING *HIMSELF*...
...WELL, THAT IS A TRAGEDY MANY OF US CAN EMPATHIZE WITH ALL TOO WELL.

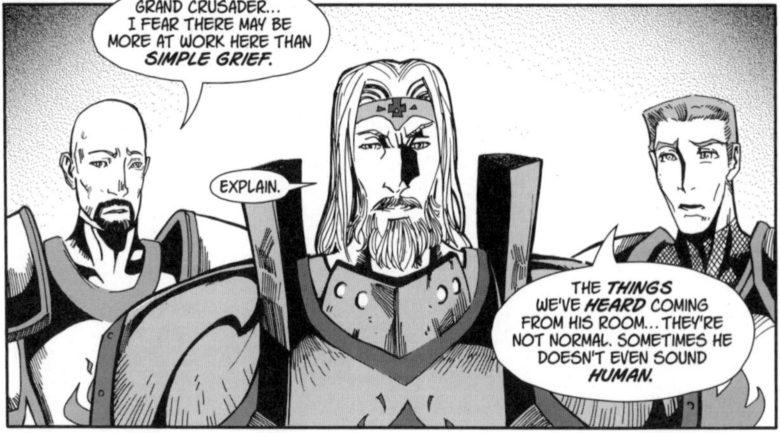
GRAND CRUSADER... I FEAR THERE MAY BE MORE AT WORK HERE THAN ***SIMPLE GRIEF***.
EXPLAIN.
THE ***THINGS*** WE'VE ***HEARD*** COMING FROM HIS ROOM... THEY'RE NOT NORMAL. SOMETIMES HE DOESN'T EVEN SOUND ***HUMAN***.
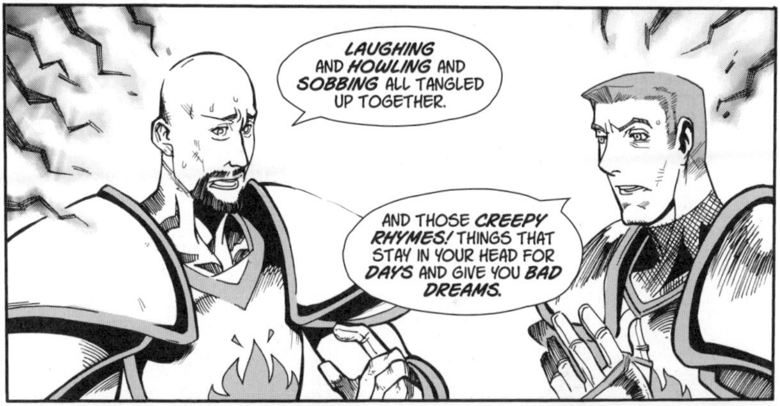
LAUGHING AND ***HOWLING*** AND ***SOBBING*** ALL TANGLED UP TOGETHER.
AND THOSE ***CREEPY RHYMES!*** THINGS THAT STAY IN YOUR HEAD FOR ***DAYS*** AND GIVE YOU ***BAD DREAMS***.
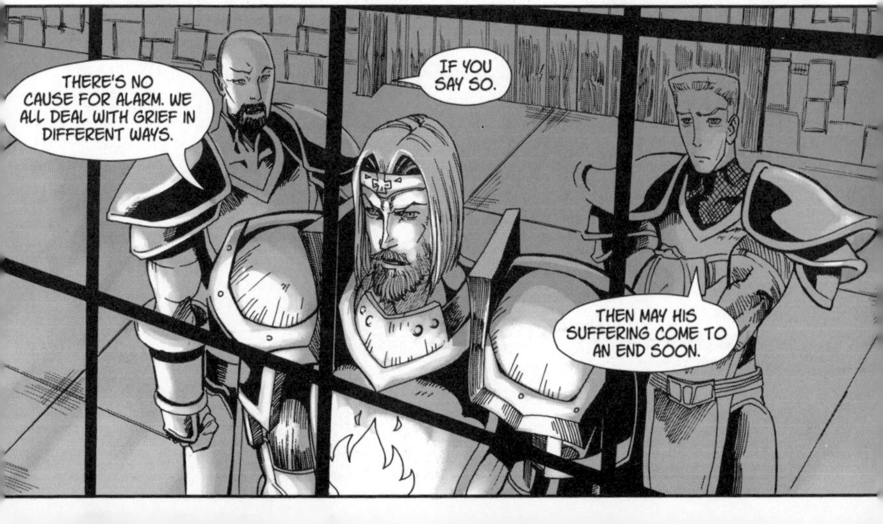
THERE'S NO CAUSE FOR ALARM. WE ALL DEAL WITH GRIEF IN DIFFERENT WAYS.
IF YOU SAY SO.
THEN MAY HIS SUFFERING COME TO AN END SOON.

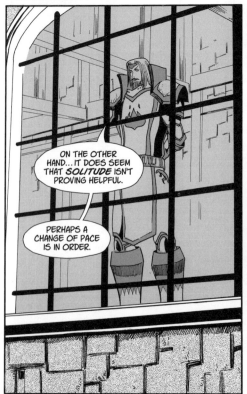

ON THE OTHER HAND... IT DOES SEEM THAT *SOLITUDE* ISN'T PROVING HELPFUL.

PERHAPS A CHANGE OF PACE IS IN ORDER.

TODAY IS *HALLOW'S END,* AND WE MUST KEEP LORDAERON'S TRADITIONS ALIVE EVEN IN THE MIDST OF THIS STRUGGLE.

WHAT ELSE, AFTER ALL, ARE WE FIGHTING FOR?

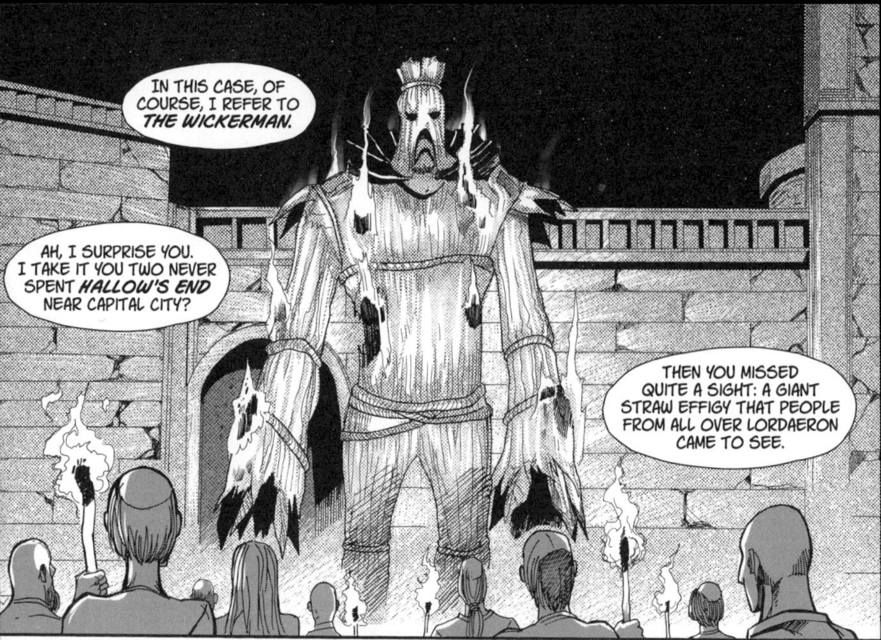
IN THIS CASE, OF COURSE, I REFER TO THE WICKERMAN.
AH, I SURPRISE YOU. I TAKE IT YOU TWO NEVER SPENT HALLOW'S END NEAR CAPITAL CITY?
THEN YOU MISSED QUITE A SIGHT: A GIANT STRAW EFFIGY THAT PEOPLE FROM ALL OVER LORDAERON CAME TO SEE.
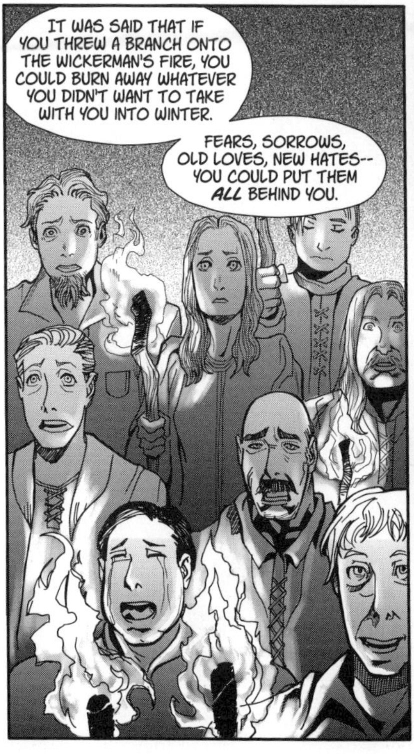
IT WAS SAID THAT IF YOU THREW A BRANCH ONTO THE WICKERMAN'S FIRE, YOU COULD BURN AWAY WHATEVER YOU DIDN'T WANT TO TAKE WITH YOU INTO WINTER.
FEARS, SORROWS, OLD LOVES, NEW HATES-- YOU COULD PUT THEM ALL BEHIND YOU.
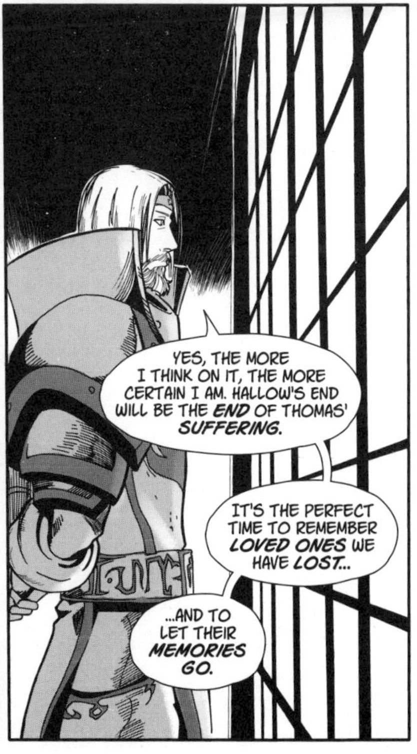
YES, THE MORE I THINK ON IT, THE MORE CERTAIN I AM. HALLOW'S END WILL BE THE END OF THOMAS' SUFFERING.
IT'S THE PERFECT TIME TO REMEMBER LOVED ONES WE HAVE LOST...
...AND TO LET THEIR MEMORIES GO.

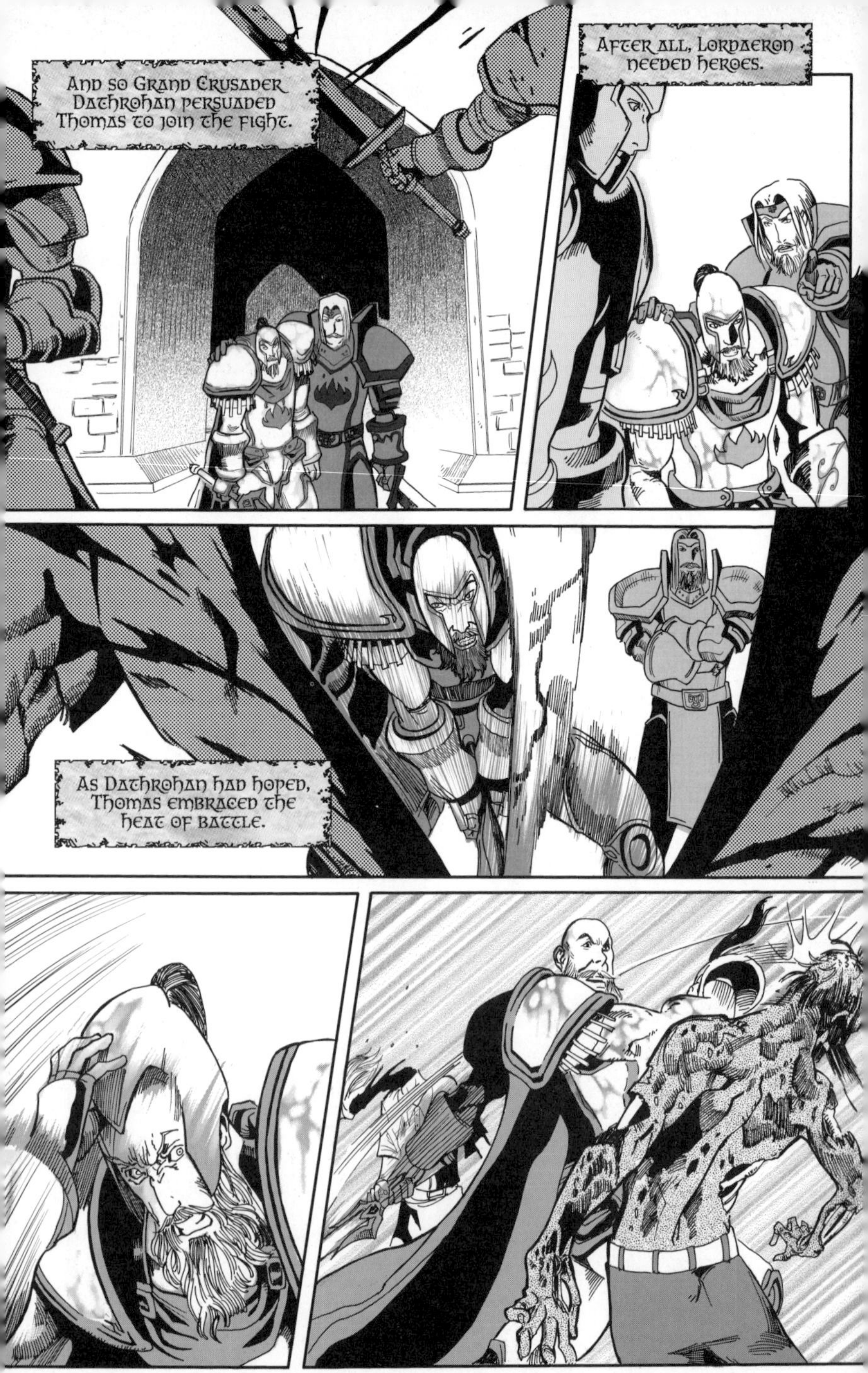
And so Grand Crusader Dathrohan persuaded Thomas to join the fight.
After all, Lordaeron needed heroes.
As Dathrohan had hoped, Thomas embraced the heat of battle.

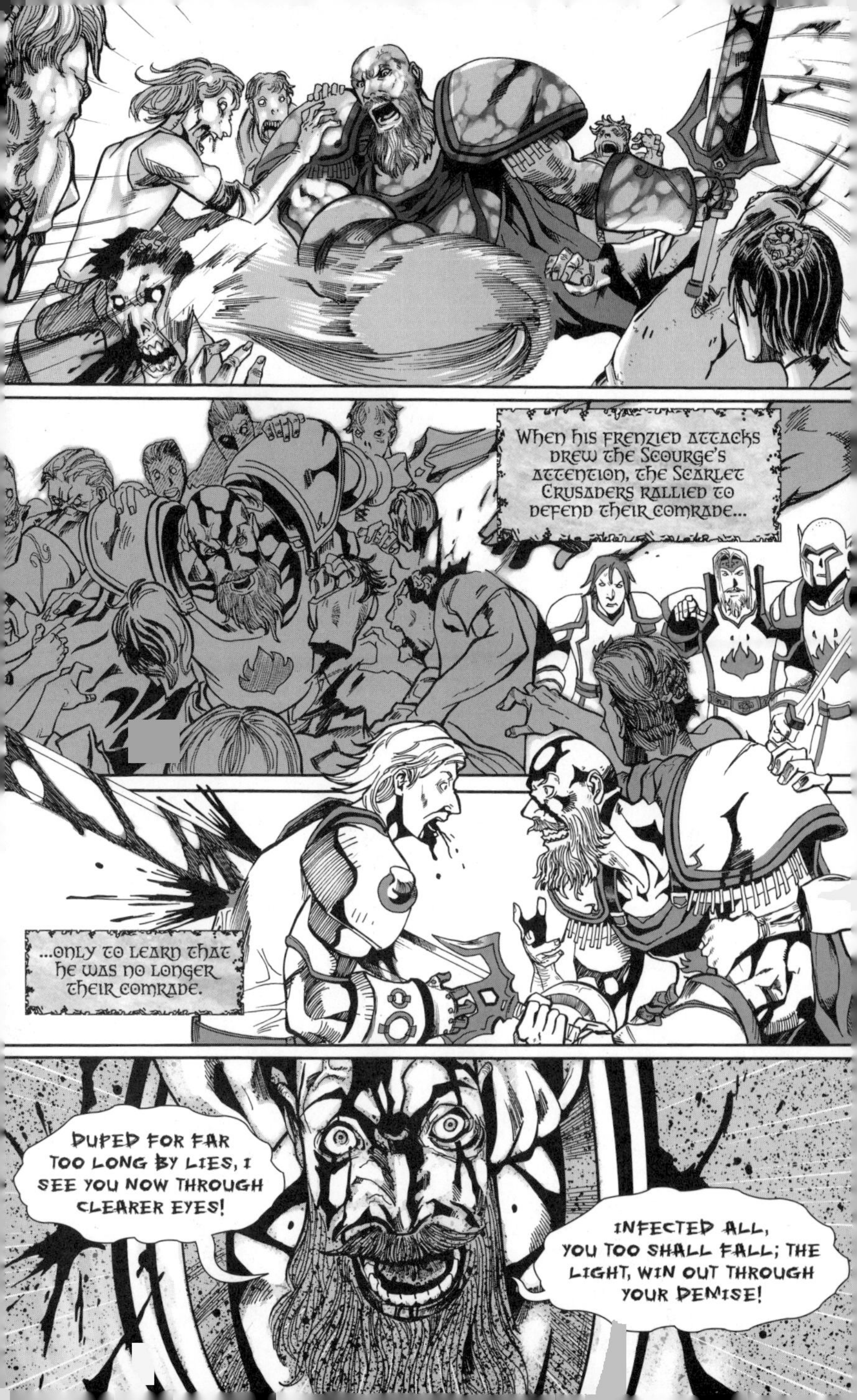
When his frenzied attacks drew the Scourge's attention, the Scarlet Crusaders rallied to defend their comrade...
...only to learn that he was no longer their comrade.
Duped for far too long by lies, I see you now through clearer eyes!
Infected all, you too shall fall; the Light, win out through your demise!

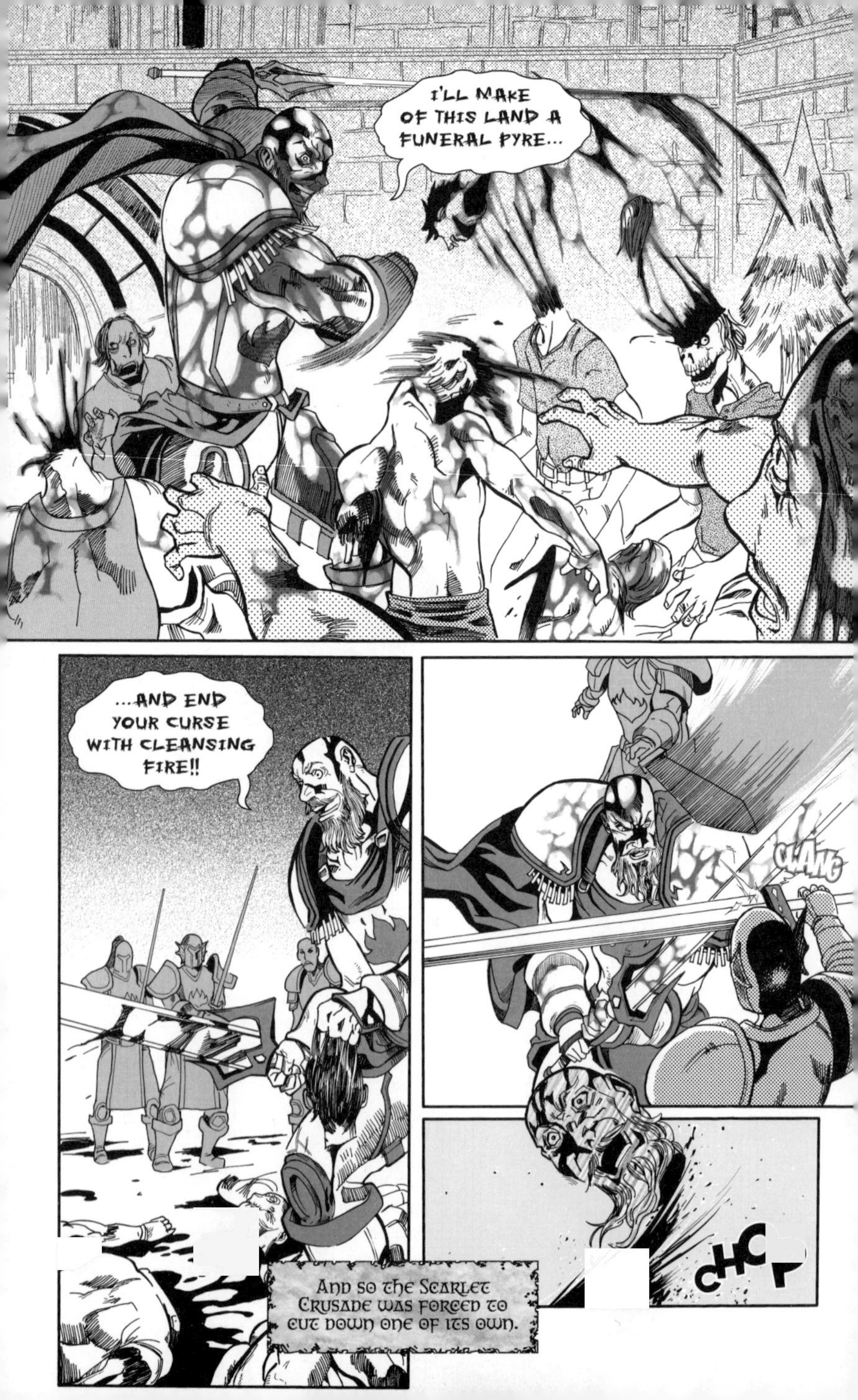
I'LL MAKE OF THIS LAND A FUNERAL PYRE...
...AND END YOUR CURSE WITH CLEANSING FIRE!!
CLANG
CHOP
And so the Scarlet Crusade was forced to cut down one of its own.

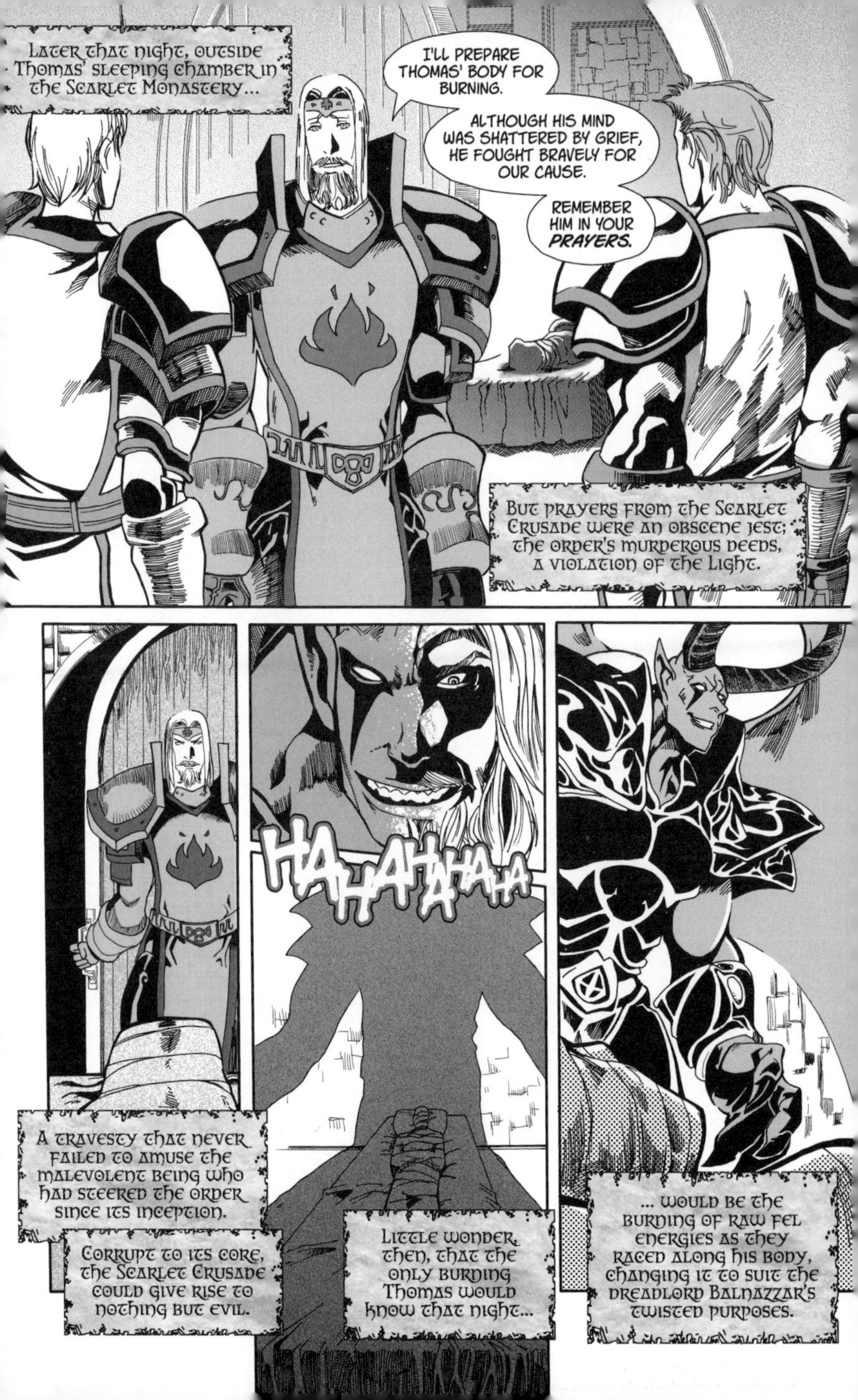
Later that night, outside Thomas' sleeping chamber in the Scarlet Monastery...
I'LL PREPARE THOMAS' BODY FOR BURNING.
ALTHOUGH HIS MIND WAS SHATTERED BY GRIEF, HE FOUGHT BRAVELY FOR OUR CAUSE.
REMEMBER HIM IN YOUR *PRAYERS*.
But prayers from the Scarlet Crusade were an obscene jest; the order's murderous deeds, a violation of the Light.
A travesty that never failed to amuse the malevolent being who had steered the order since its inception.
Corrupt to its core, the Scarlet Crusade could give rise to nothing but evil.
HAHAHAHAHAHAHA
Little wonder, then, that the only burning Thomas would know that night...
... would be the burning of raw fel energies as they raced along his body, changing it to suit the dreadlord Balnazzar's twisted purposes.

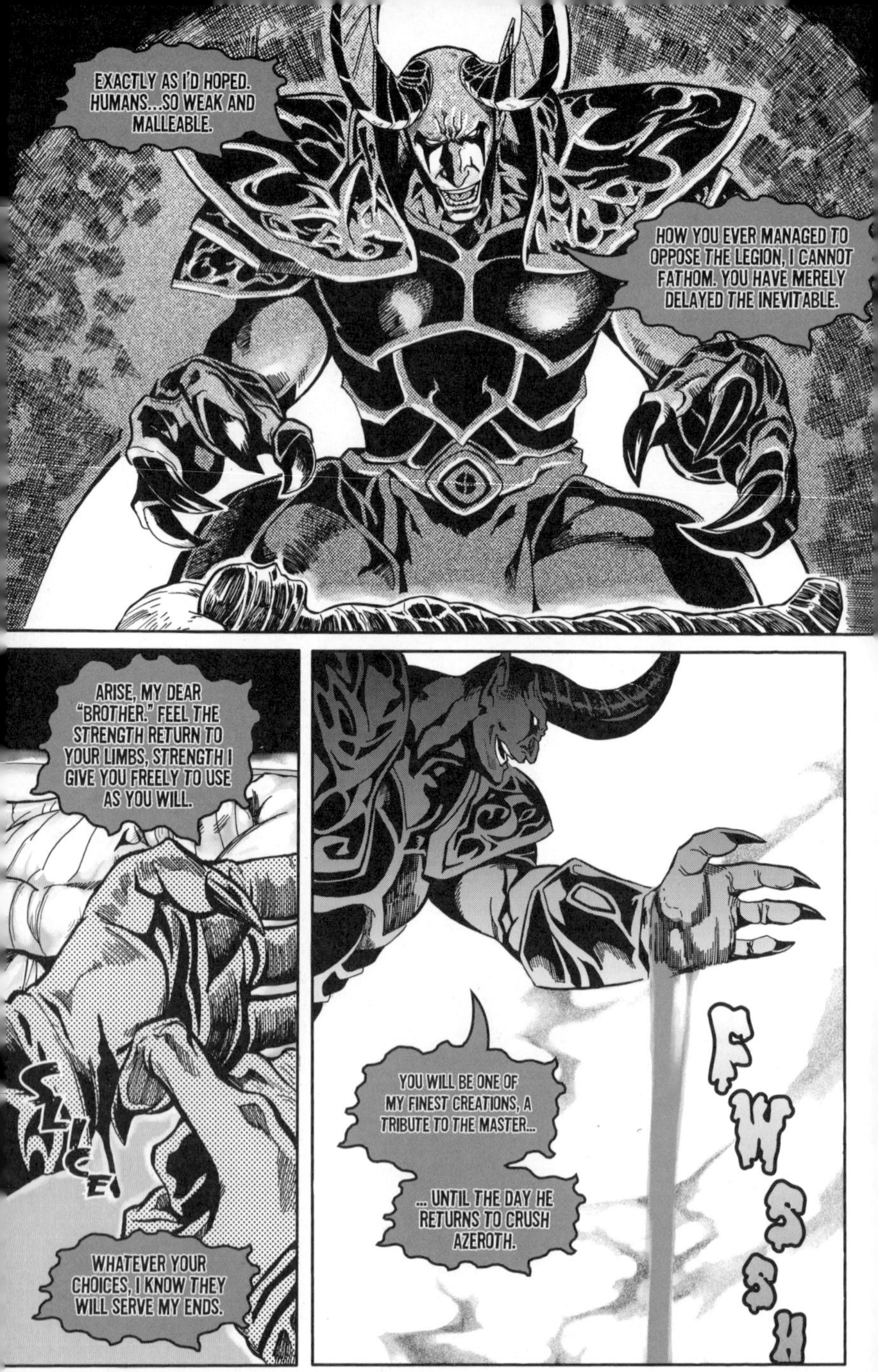
EXACTLY AS I'D HOPED. HUMANS...SO WEAK AND MALLEABLE.
HOW YOU EVER MANAGED TO OPPOSE THE LEGION, I CANNOT FATHOM. YOU HAVE MERELY DELAYED THE INEVITABLE.
ARISE, MY DEAR "BROTHER." FEEL THE STRENGTH RETURN TO YOUR LIMBS, STRENGTH I GIVE YOU FREELY TO USE AS YOU WILL.
SLICE
WHATEVER YOUR CHOICES, I KNOW THEY WILL SERVE MY ENDS.
YOU WILL BE ONE OF MY FINEST CREATIONS, A TRIBUTE TO THE MASTER...
... UNTIL THE DAY HE RETURNS TO CRUSH AZEROTH.
FWSSSH

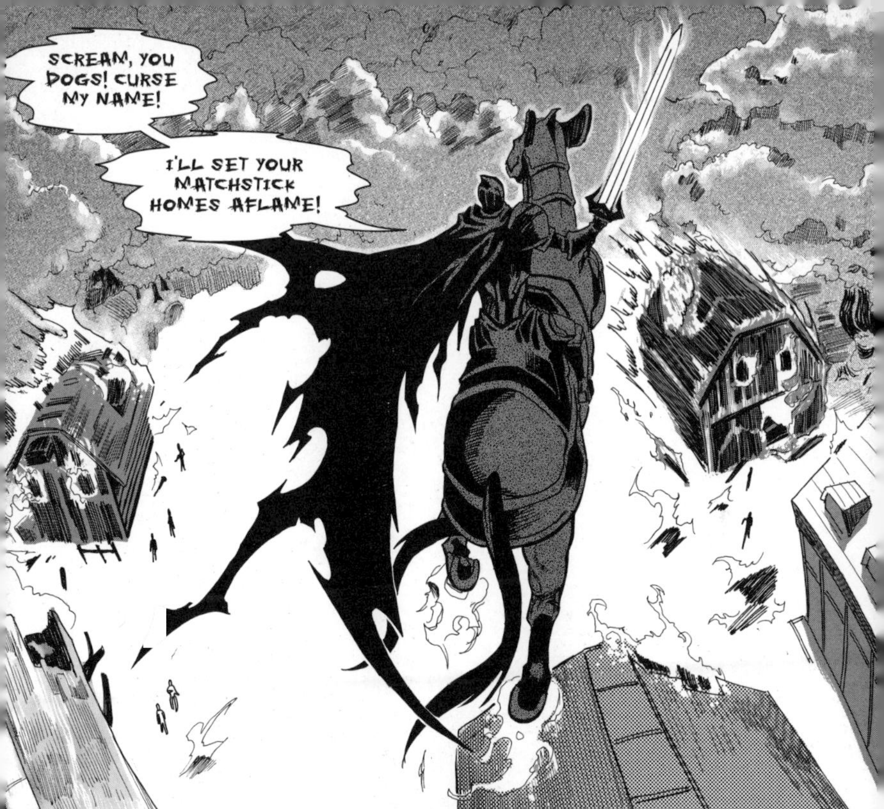
SCREAM, YOU DOGS! CURSE MY NAME!
I'LL SET YOUR MATCHSTICK HOMES AFLAME!

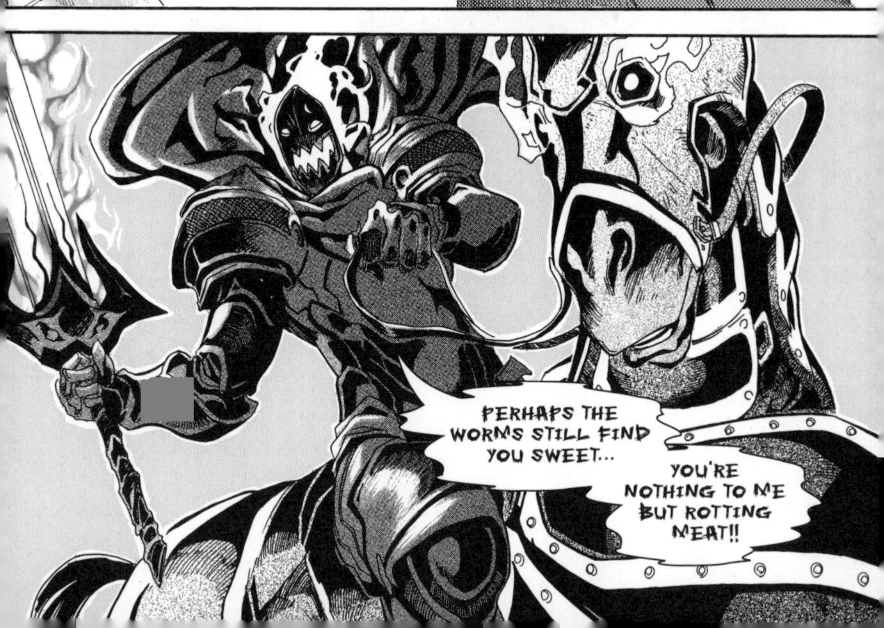
PERHAPS THE WORMS STILL FIND YOU SWEET...
YOU'RE NOTHING TO ME BUT ROTTING MEAT!!

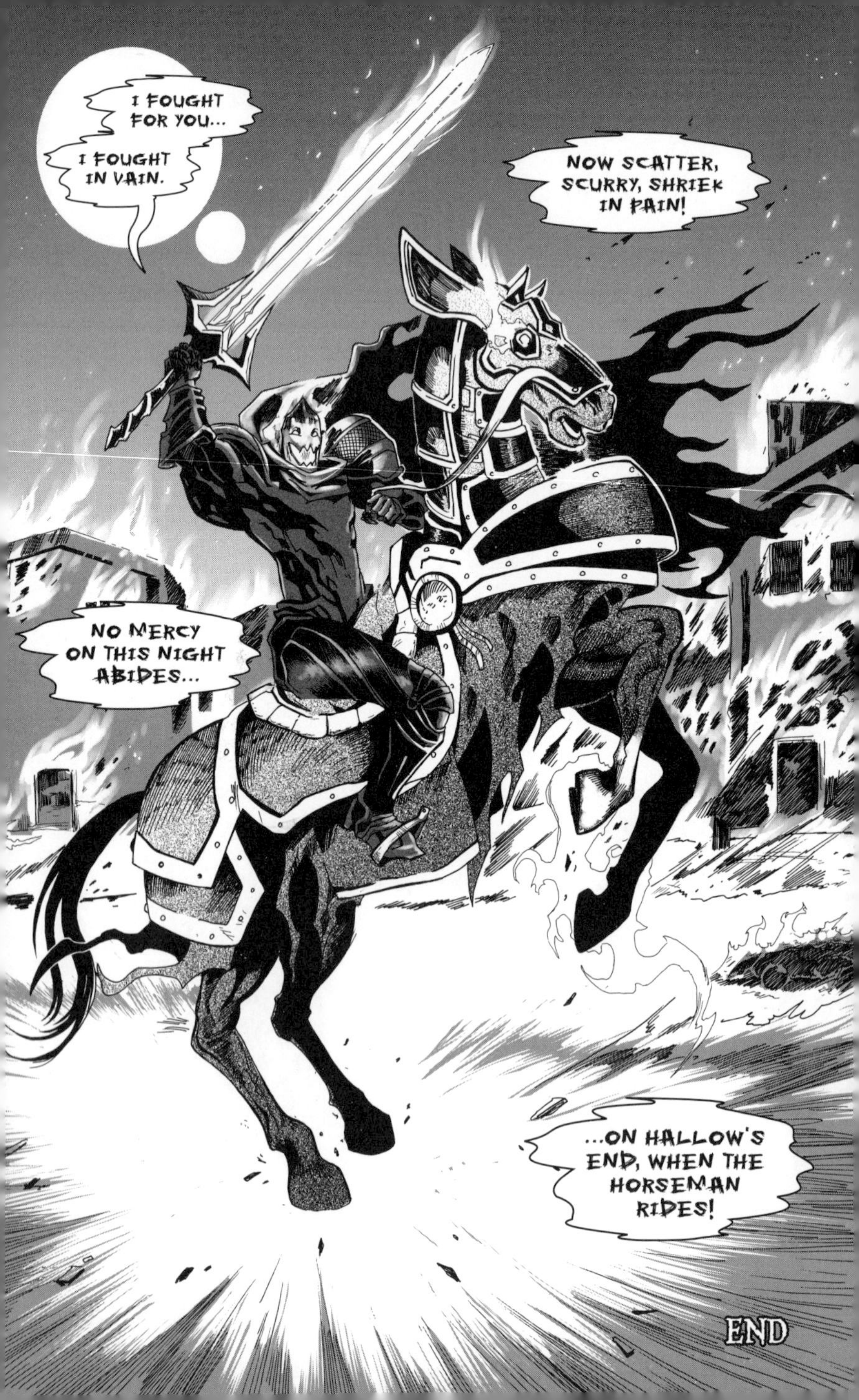
I FOUGHT FOR YOU...
I FOUGHT IN VAIN.
NOW SCATTER, SCURRY, SHRIEK IN PAIN!
NO MERCY ON THIS NIGHT ABIDES...
...ON HALLOW'S END, WHEN THE HORSEMAN RIDES!
END

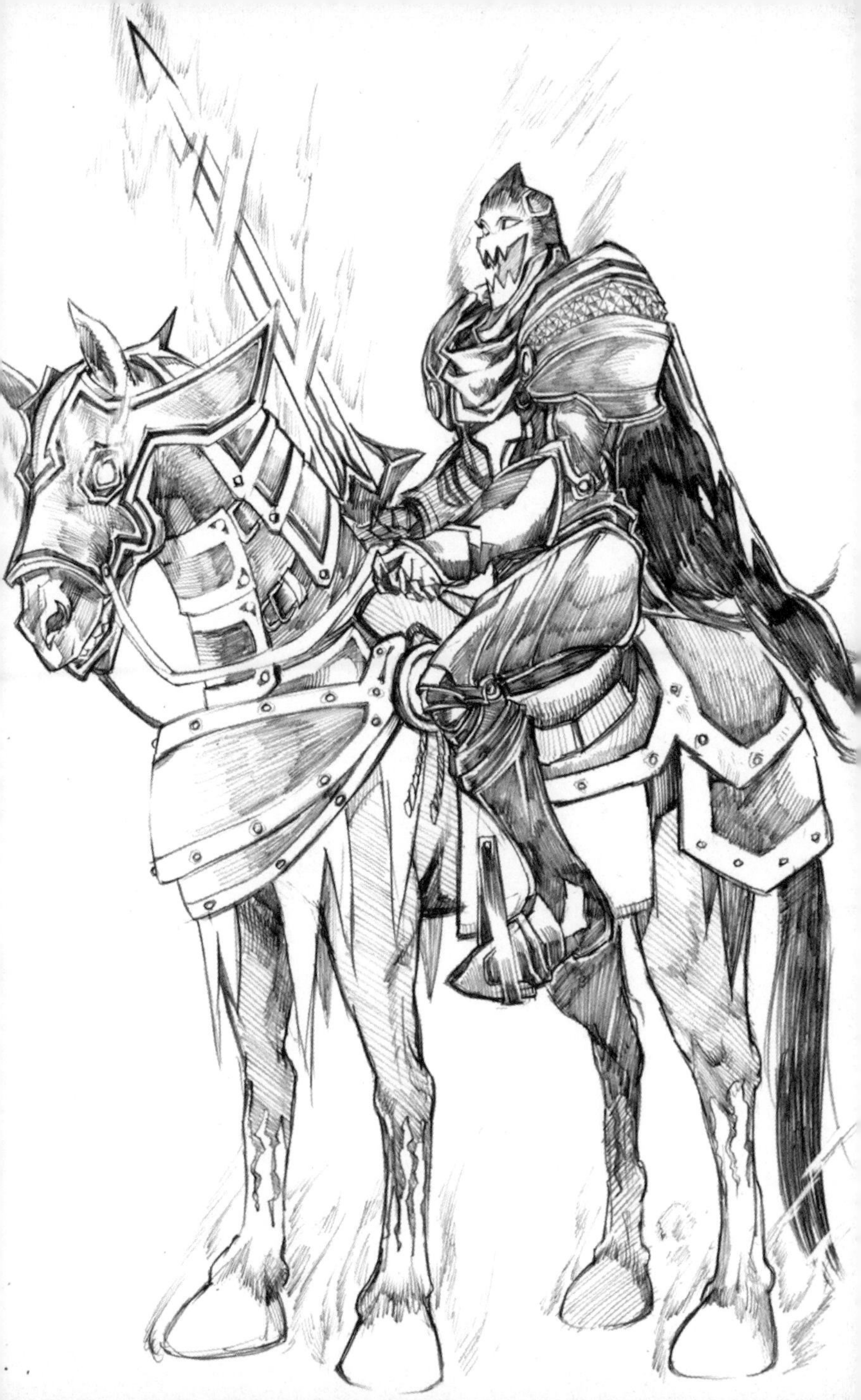

WARCRAFT

LEGENDS

VOLUME FIVE

NIGHTMARES

WRITTEN BY RICHARD A. KNAAK

PENCILS BY ROB TEN PAS
INKS BY WALTER GOMEZ, LEANDRO RIZZO
& ARIEL IACCI
TONES BY WALTER GOMEZ

LETTERER: MICHAEL PAOLILLI

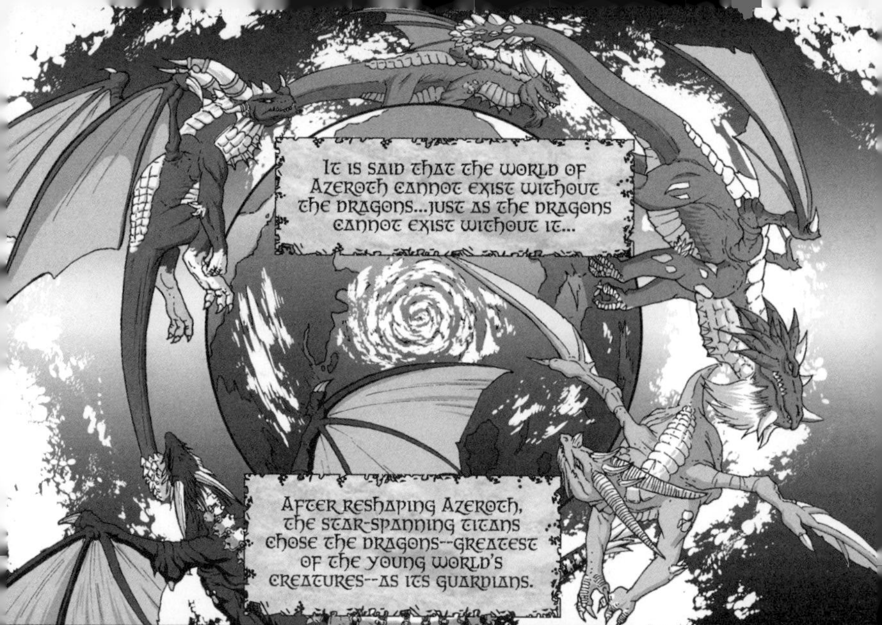
It is said that the world of Azeroth cannot exist without the dragons...just as the dragons cannot exist without it...
After reshaping Azeroth, the star-spanning titans chose the dragons--greatest of the young world's creatures--as its guardians.

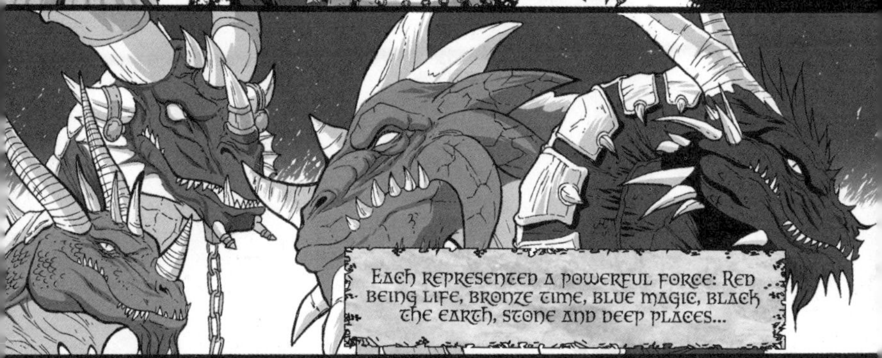
Each represented a powerful force: Red being life, bronze time, blue magic, black the earth, stone and deep places...

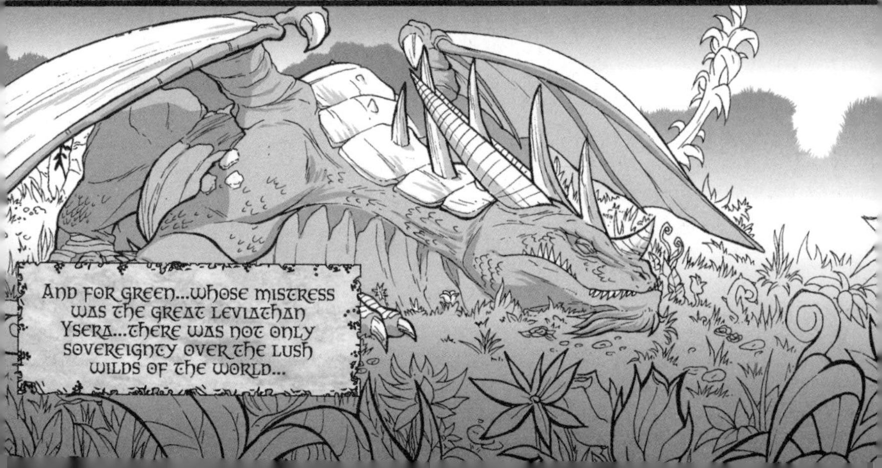
And for green...whose mistress was the great leviathan Ysera...there was not only sovereignty over the lush wilds of the world...

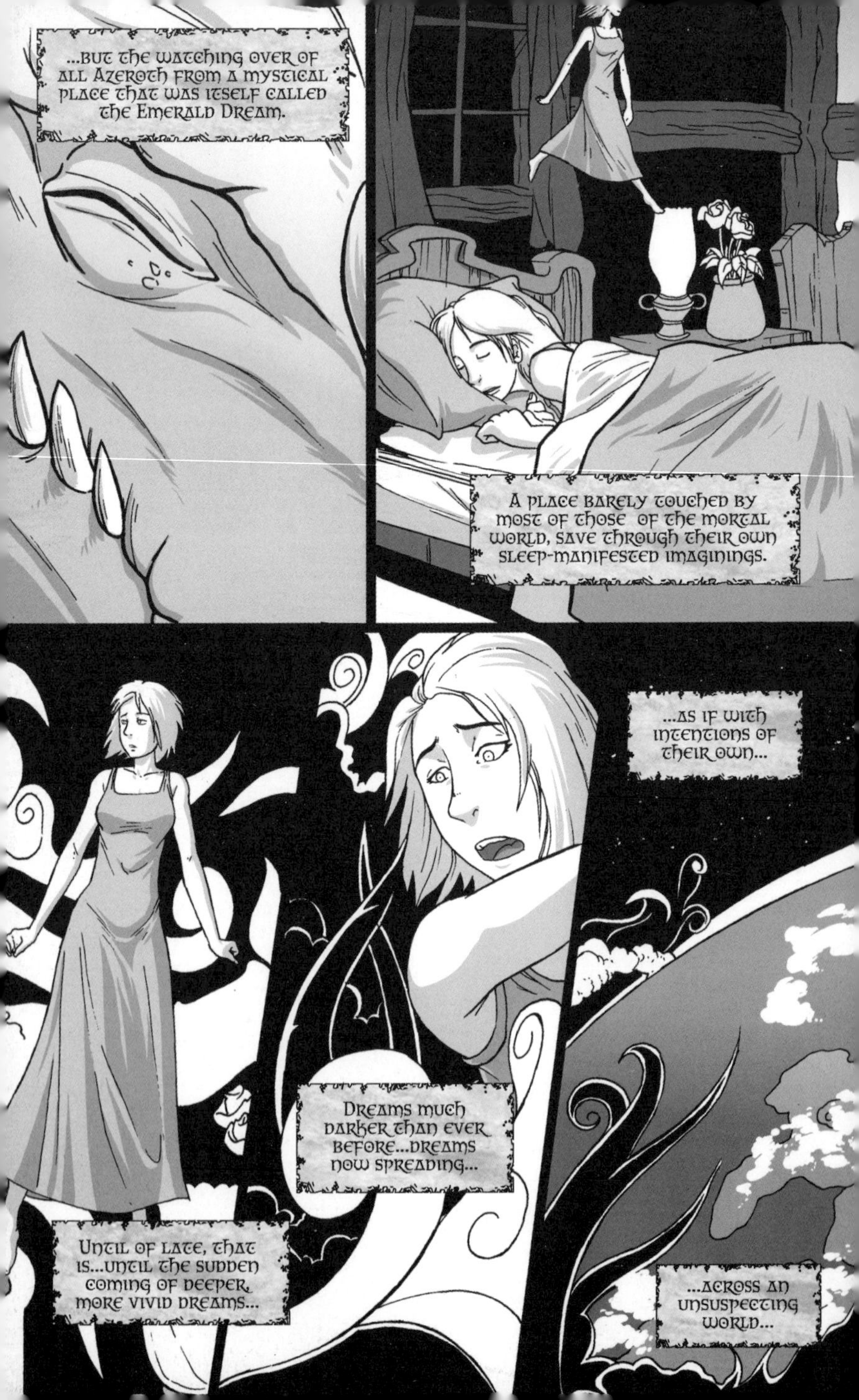
...but the watching over of all Azeroth from a mystical place that was itself called the Emerald Dream.
A place barely touched by most of those of the mortal world, save through their own sleep-manifested imaginings.
Until of late, that is...until the sudden coming of deeper, more vivid dreams...
Dreams much darker than ever before...dreams now spreading...
...as if with intentions of their own...
...across an unsuspecting world...

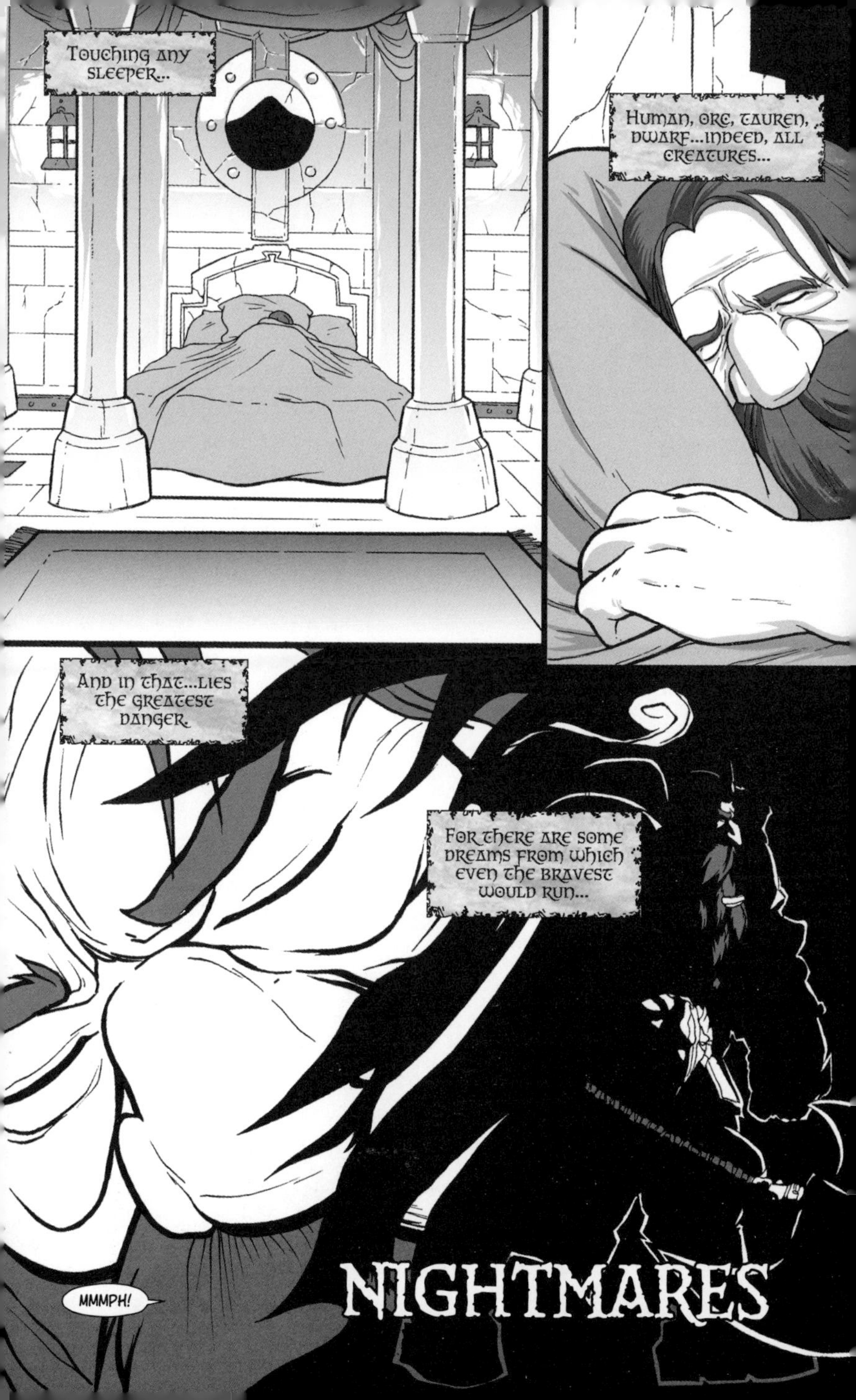
Touching any sleeper...
Human, orc, tauren, dwarf...indeed, all creatures...
And in that...lies the greatest danger.
For there are some dreams from which even the bravest would run...
MMMPH!
NIGHTMARES

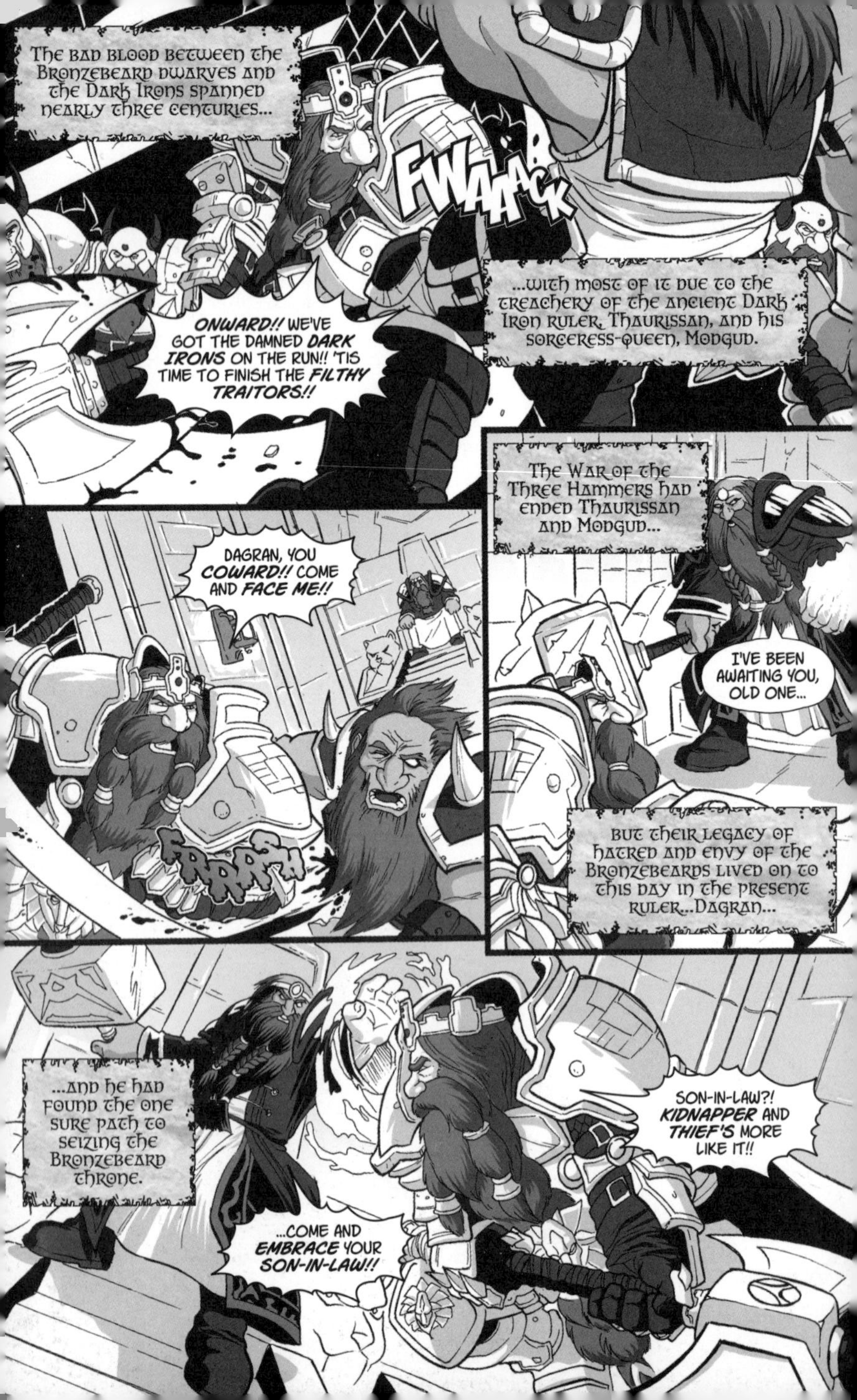
THE BAD BLOOD BETWEEN THE BRONZEBEARD DWARVES AND THE DARK IRONS SPANNED NEARLY THREE CENTURIES...
FWAAACK
ONWARD!! WE'VE GOT THE DAMNED DARK IRONS ON THE RUN!! 'TIS TIME TO FINISH THE FILTHY TRAITORS!!
...WITH MOST OF IT DUE TO THE TREACHERY OF THE ANCIENT DARK IRON RULER, THAURISSAN, AND HIS SORCERESS-QUEEN, MODGUD.
DAGRAN, YOU COWARD!! COME AND FACE ME!!
THE WAR OF THE THREE HAMMERS HAD ENDED THAURISSAN AND MODGUD...
I'VE BEEN AWAITING YOU, OLD ONE...
BUT THEIR LEGACY OF HATRED AND ENVY OF THE BRONZEBEARDS LIVED ON TO THIS DAY IN THE PRESENT RULER...DAGRAN...
...AND HE HAD FOUND THE ONE SURE PATH TO SEIZING THE BRONZEBEARD THRONE.
...COME AND EMBRACE YOUR SON-IN-LAW!!
SON-IN-LAW?! KIDNAPPER AND THIEF'S MORE LIKE IT!!

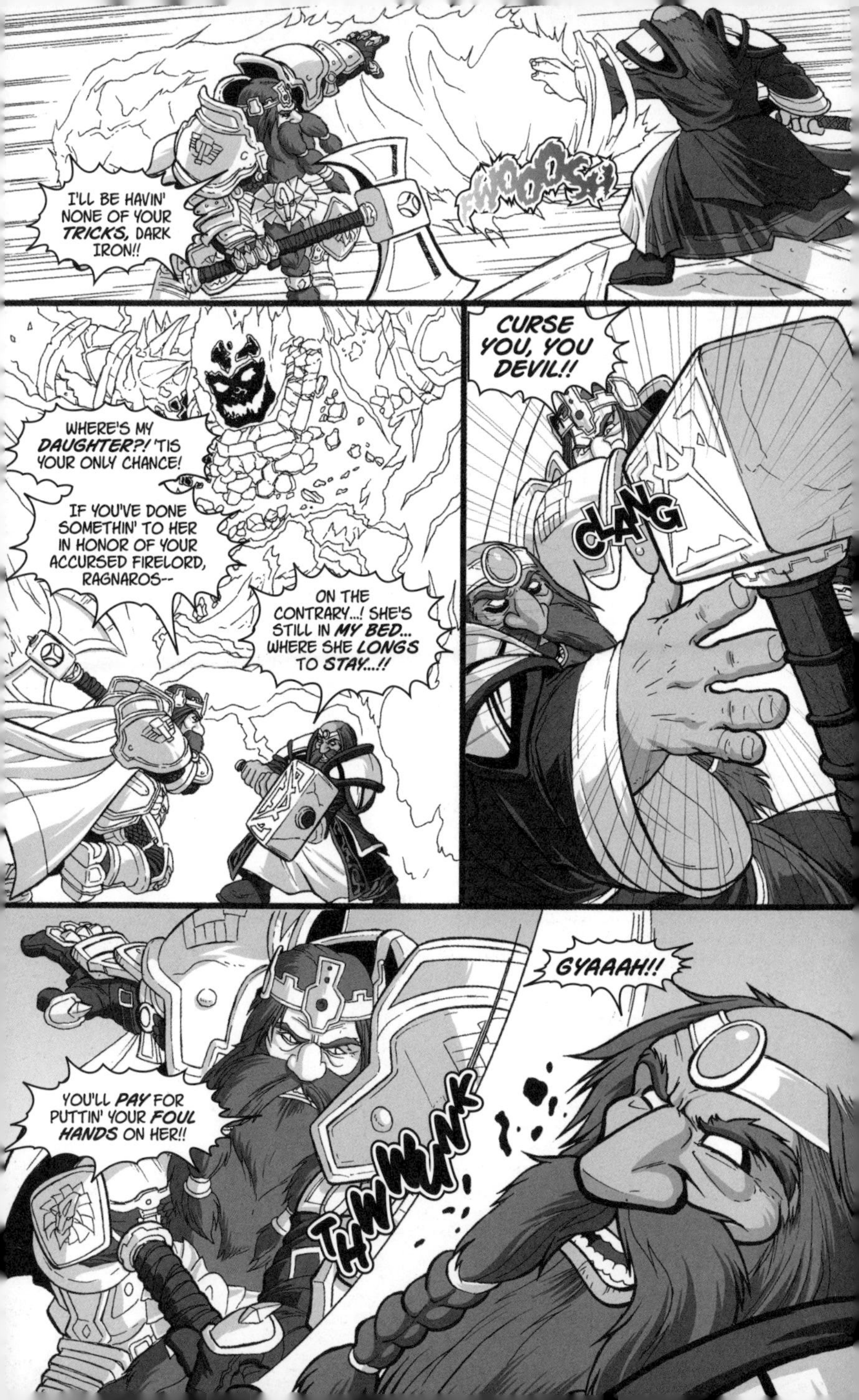
I'LL BE HAVIN' NONE OF YOUR *TRICKS,* DARK IRON!!
FWOOOSH
WHERE'S MY *DAUGHTER?!* 'TIS YOUR ONLY CHANCE!
IF YOU'VE DONE SOMETHIN' TO HER IN HONOR OF YOUR ACCURSED FIRELORD, RAGNAROS--
ON THE CONTRARY...! SHE'S STILL IN *MY BED*... WHERE SHE *LONGS* TO *STAY*...!!
CURSE YOU, YOU DEVIL!!
CLANG
YOU'LL *PAY* FOR PUTTIN' YOUR *FOUL HANDS* ON HER!!
GYAAAH!!
THWUNK

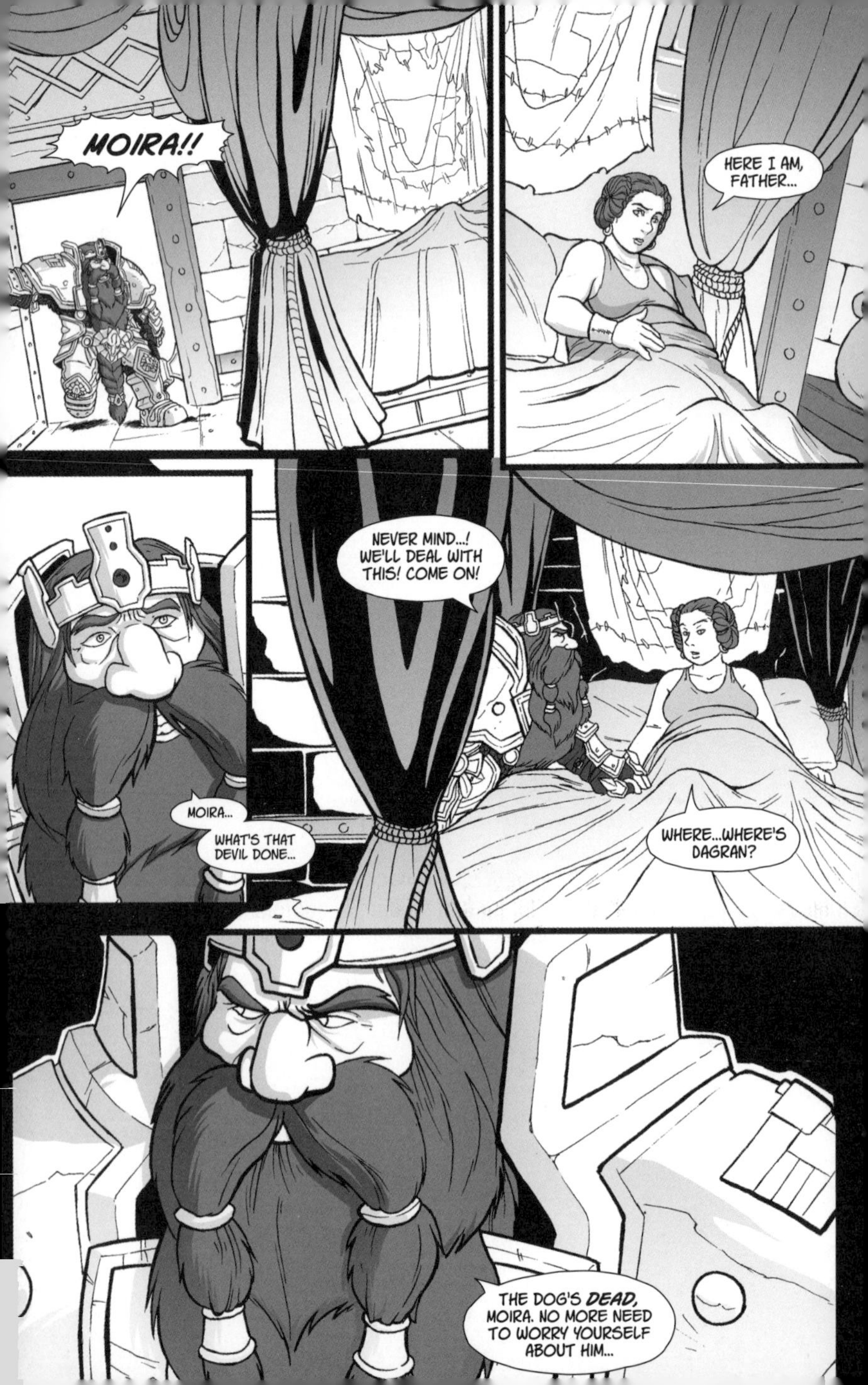
MOIRA!!
HERE I AM, FATHER...
MOIRA...
WHAT'S THAT DEVIL DONE...
NEVER MIND...! WE'LL DEAL WITH THIS! COME ON!
WHERE...WHERE'S DAGRAN?
THE DOG'S *DEAD,* MOIRA. NO MORE NEED TO WORRY YOURSELF ABOUT HIM...

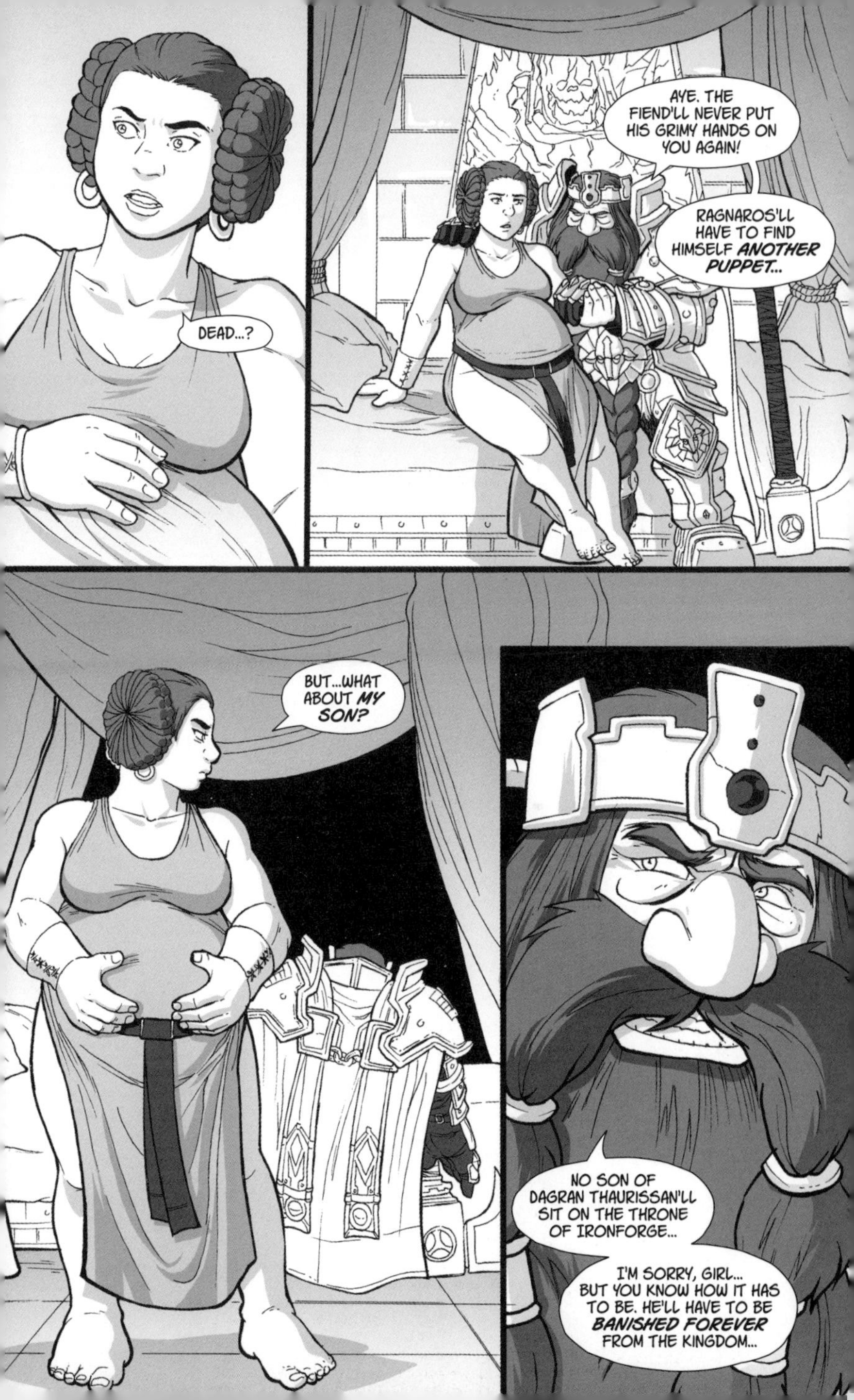
DEAD...?
AYE. THE FIEND'LL NEVER PUT HIS GRIMY HANDS ON YOU AGAIN!
RAGNAROS'LL HAVE TO FIND HIMSELF ANOTHER PUPPET...
BUT...WHAT ABOUT MY SON?
NO SON OF DAGRAN THAURISSAN'LL SIT ON THE THRONE OF IRONFORGE...
I'M SORRY, GIRL... BUT YOU KNOW HOW IT HAS TO BE. HE'LL HAVE TO BE BANISHED FOREVER FROM THE KINGDOM...

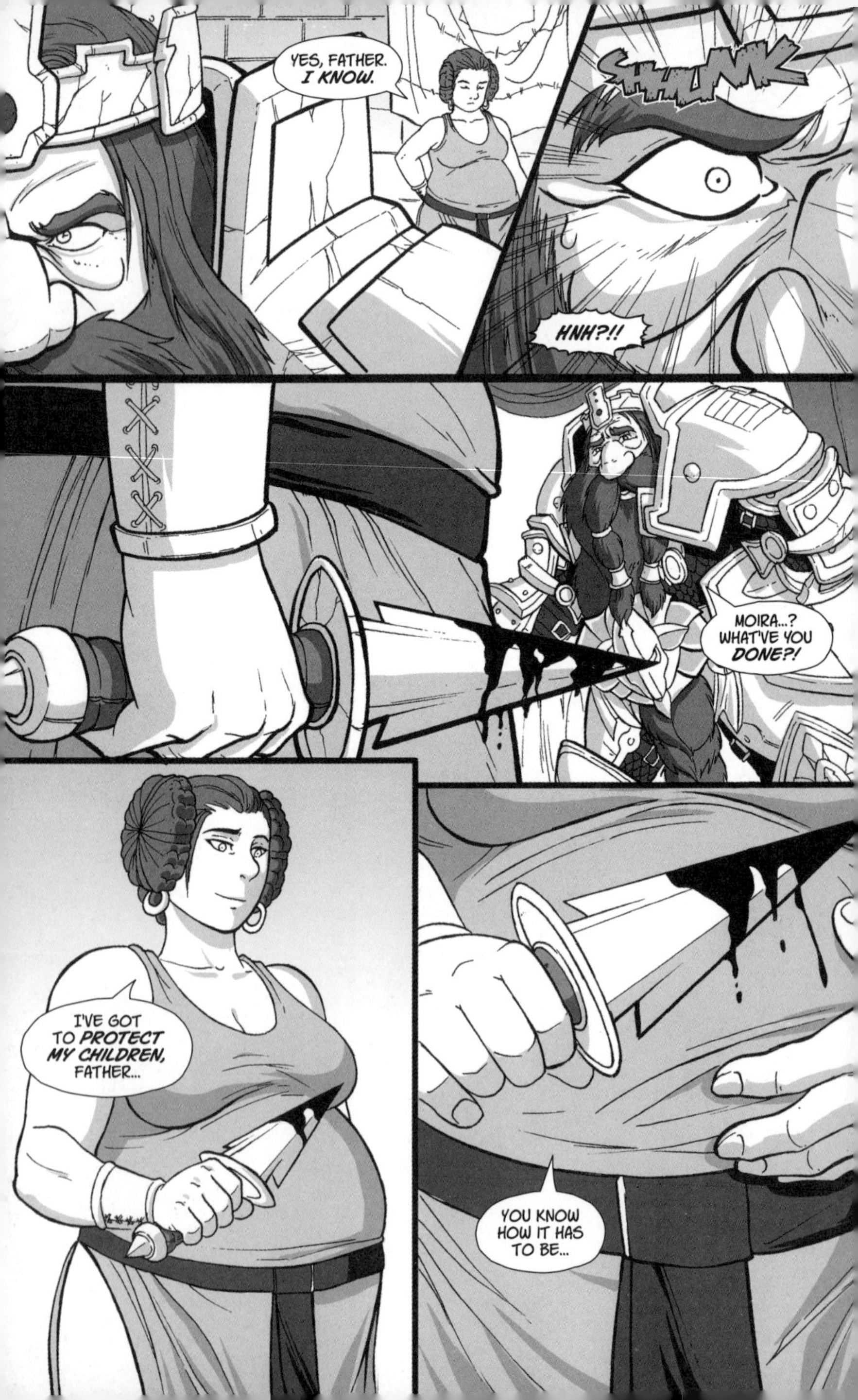
YES, FATHER. *I KNOW.*
SHUNK
HNH?!!
MOIRA...? WHAT'VE YOU *DONE?!*
I'VE GOT TO *PROTECT MY CHILDREN,* FATHER...
YOU KNOW HOW IT HAS TO BE...

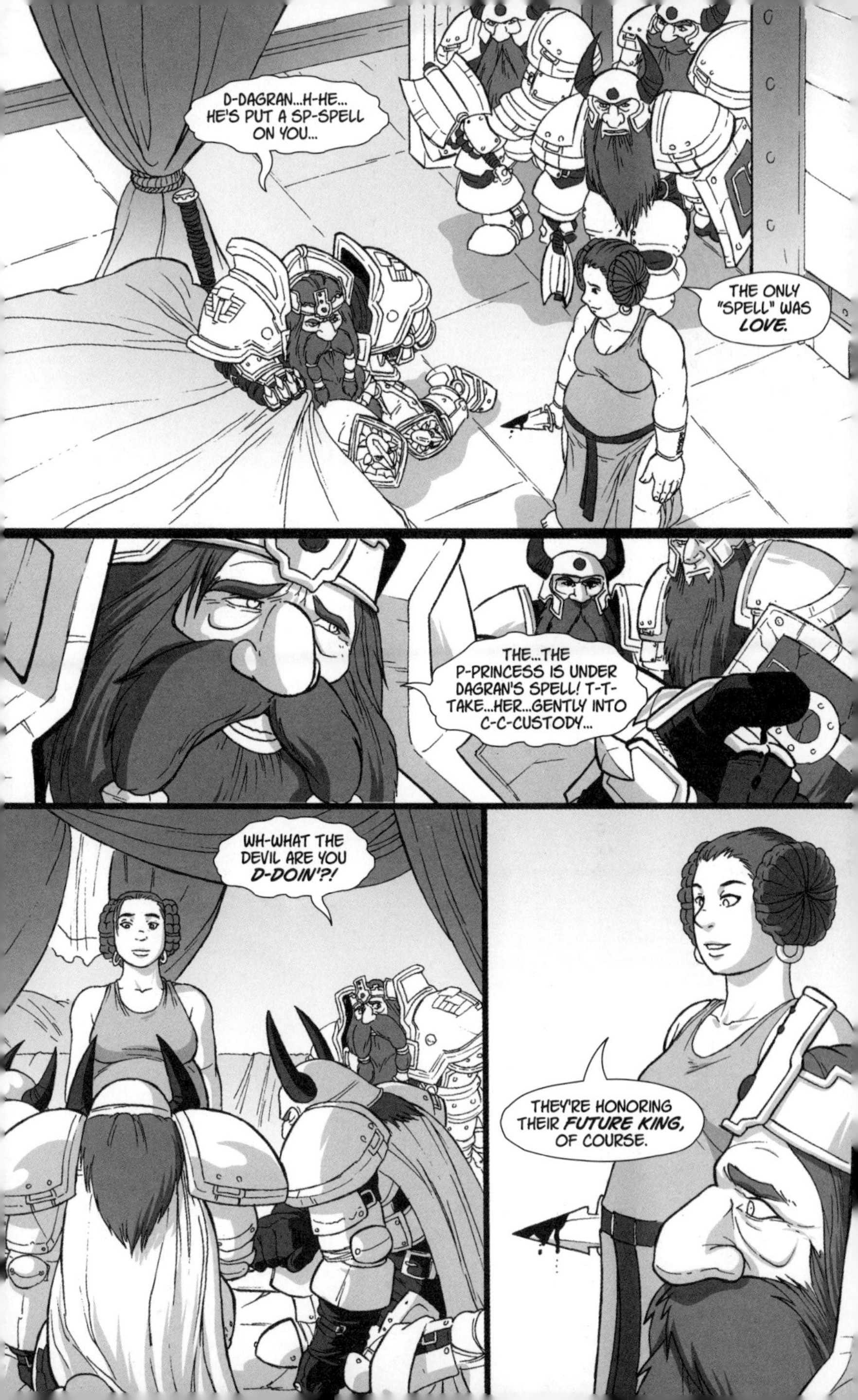
D-DAGRAN...H-HE... HE'S PUT A SP-SPELL ON YOU...
THE ONLY "SPELL" WAS ***LOVE.***
THE...THE P-PRINCESS IS UNDER DAGRAN'S SPELL! T-T-TAKE...HER...GENTLY INTO C-C-CUSTODY...
WH-WHAT THE DEVIL ARE YOU ***D-DOIN'?!***
THEY'RE HONORING THEIR ***FUTURE KING,*** OF COURSE.

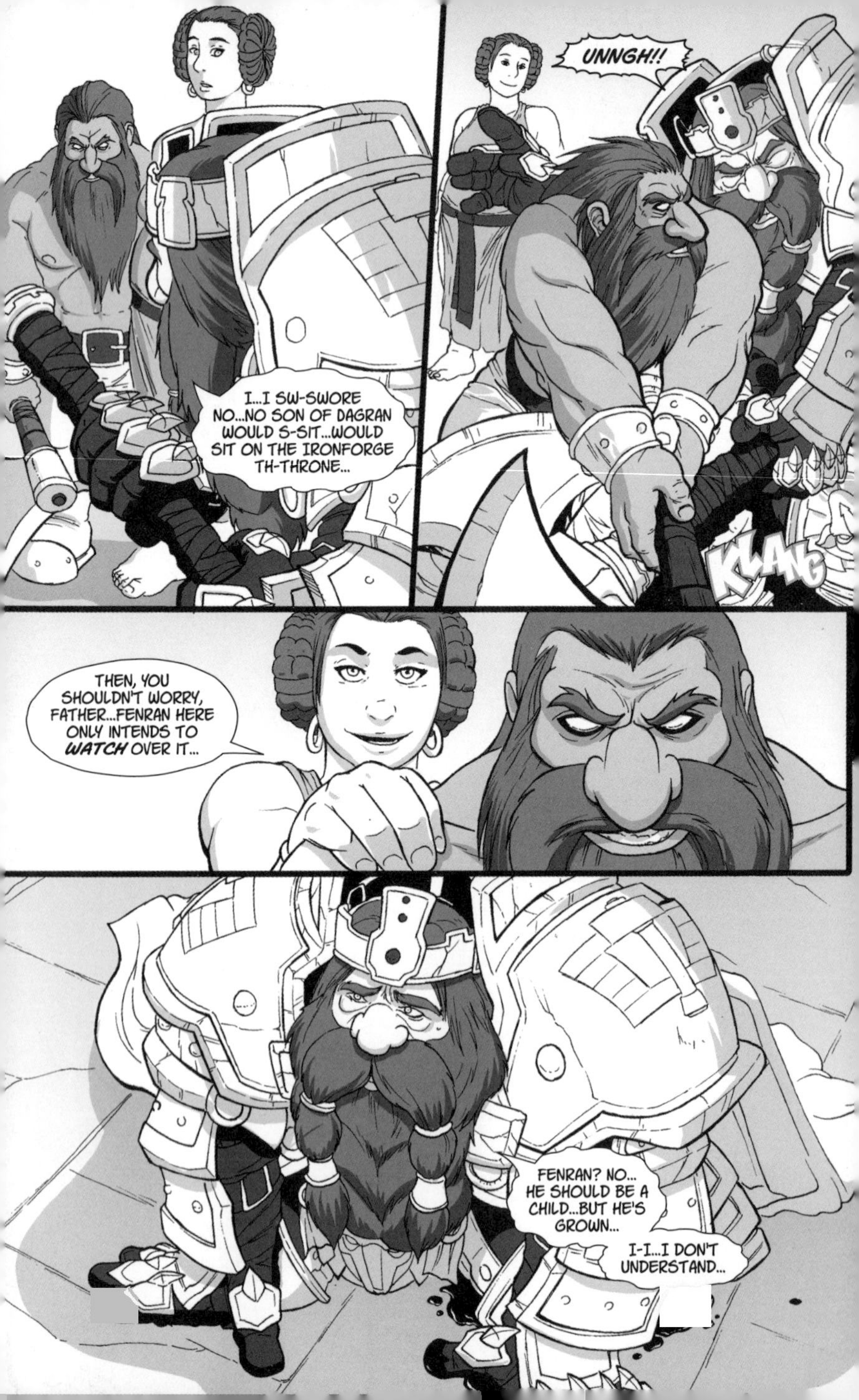
I...I SW-SWORE NO...NO SON OF DAGRAN WOULD S-SIT...WOULD SIT ON THE IRONFORGE TH-THRONE...
UNNGH!!
KLANG
THEN, YOU SHOULDN'T WORRY, FATHER...FENRAN HERE ONLY INTENDS TO WATCH OVER IT...
FENRAN? NO... HE SHOULD BE A CHILD...BUT HE'S GROWN...
I-I...I DON'T UNDERSTAND...

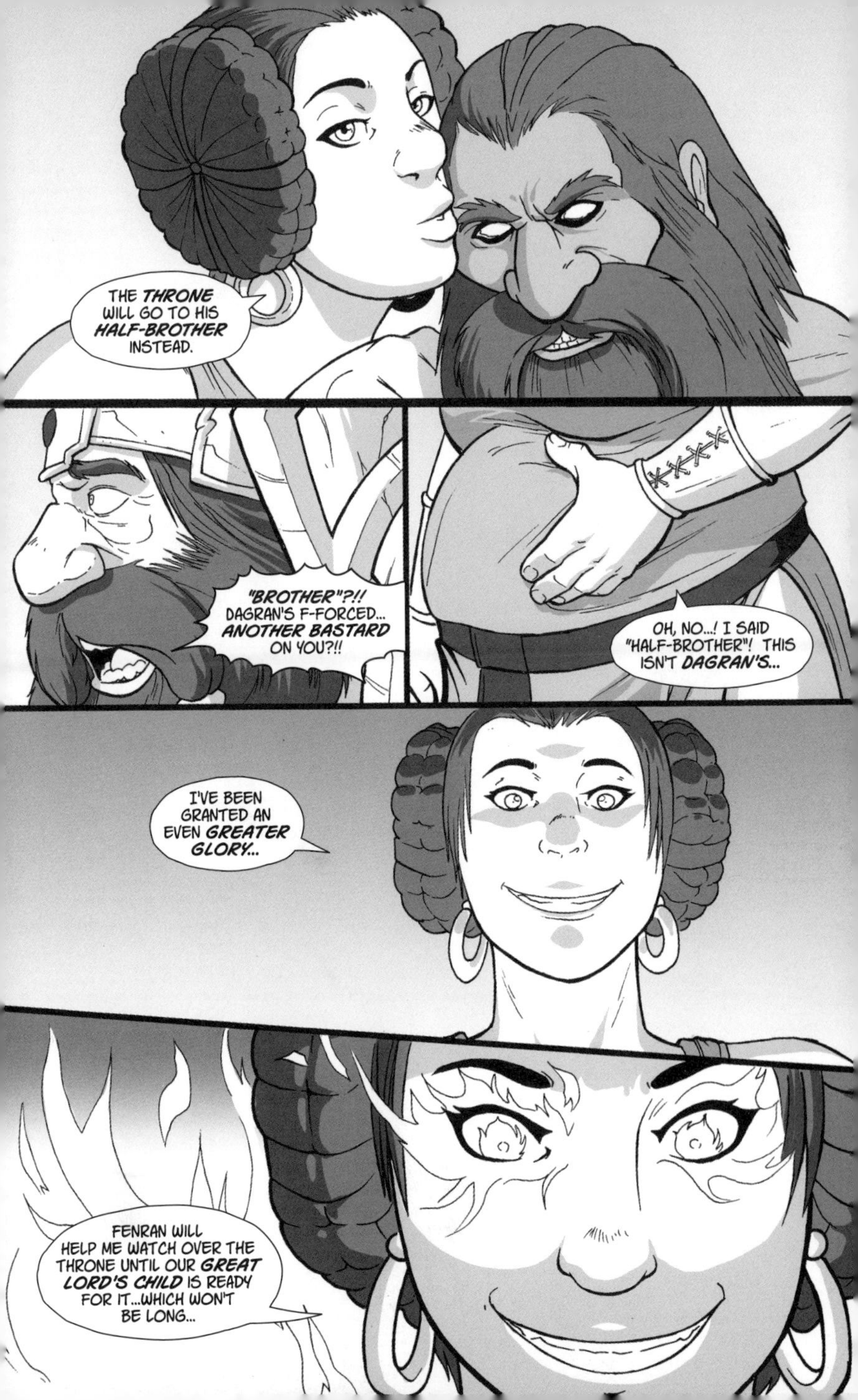
THE THRONE WILL GO TO HIS HALF-BROTHER INSTEAD.
"BROTHER"?!! DAGRAN'S F-FORCED... ANOTHER BASTARD ON YOU?!!
OH, NO...! I SAID "HALF-BROTHER"! THIS ISN'T DAGRAN'S...
I'VE BEEN GRANTED AN EVEN GREATER GLORY...
FENRAN WILL HELP ME WATCH OVER THE THRONE UNTIL OUR GREAT LORD'S CHILD IS READY FOR IT...WHICH WON'T BE LONG...

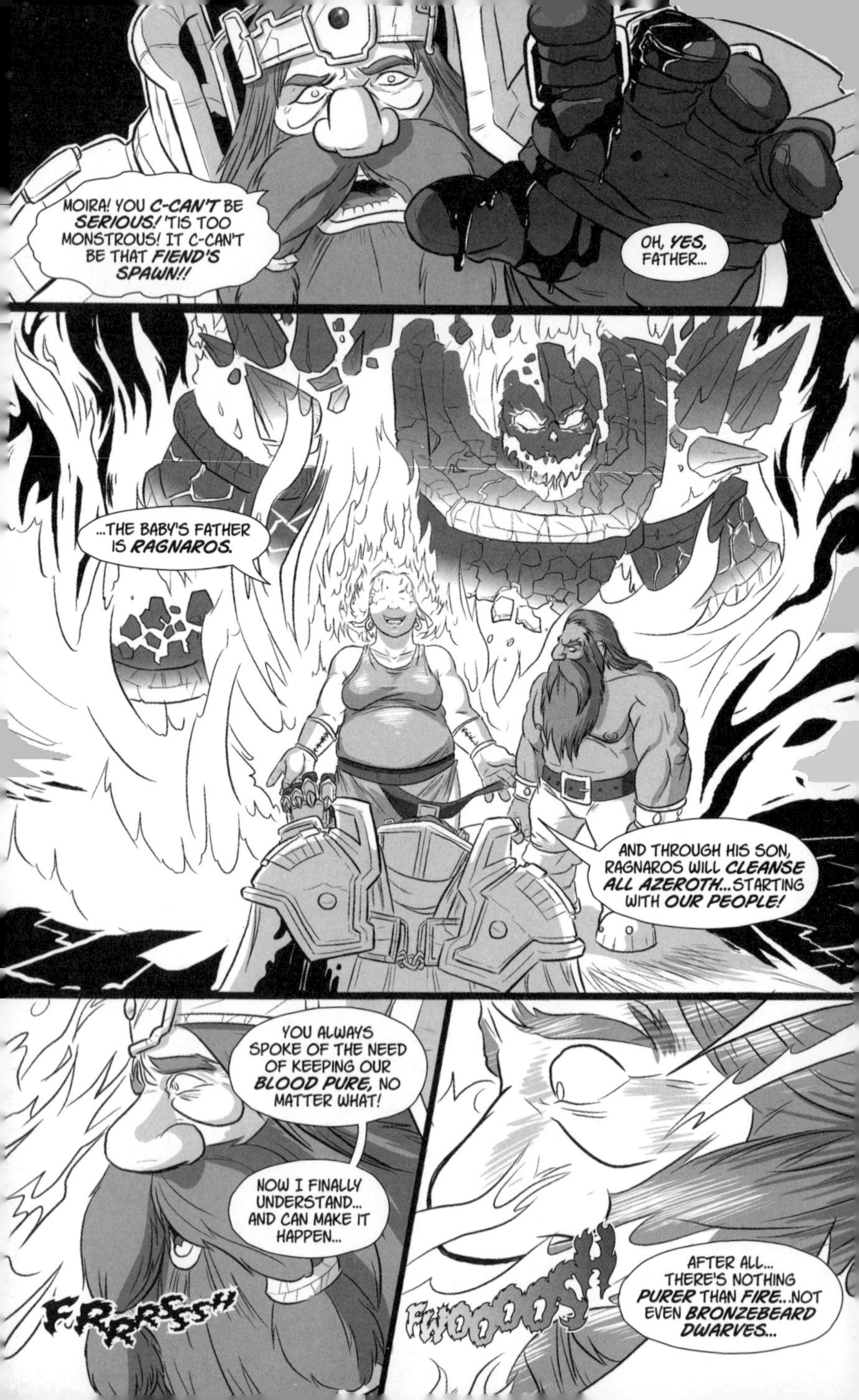
MOIRA! YOU C-CAN'T BE SERIOUS! 'TIS TOO MONSTROUS! IT C-CAN'T BE THAT FIEND'S SPAWN!!
OH, YES, FATHER...
...THE BABY'S FATHER IS RAGNAROS.
AND THROUGH HIS SON, RAGNAROS WILL CLEANSE ALL AZEROTH...STARTING WITH OUR PEOPLE!
YOU ALWAYS SPOKE OF THE NEED OF KEEPING OUR BLOOD PURE, NO MATTER WHAT!
NOW I FINALLY UNDERSTAND... AND CAN MAKE IT HAPPEN...
FRRRSSH
FWOOOOOSH
AFTER ALL... THERE'S NOTHING PURER THAN FIRE...NOT EVEN BRONZEBEARD DWARVES...

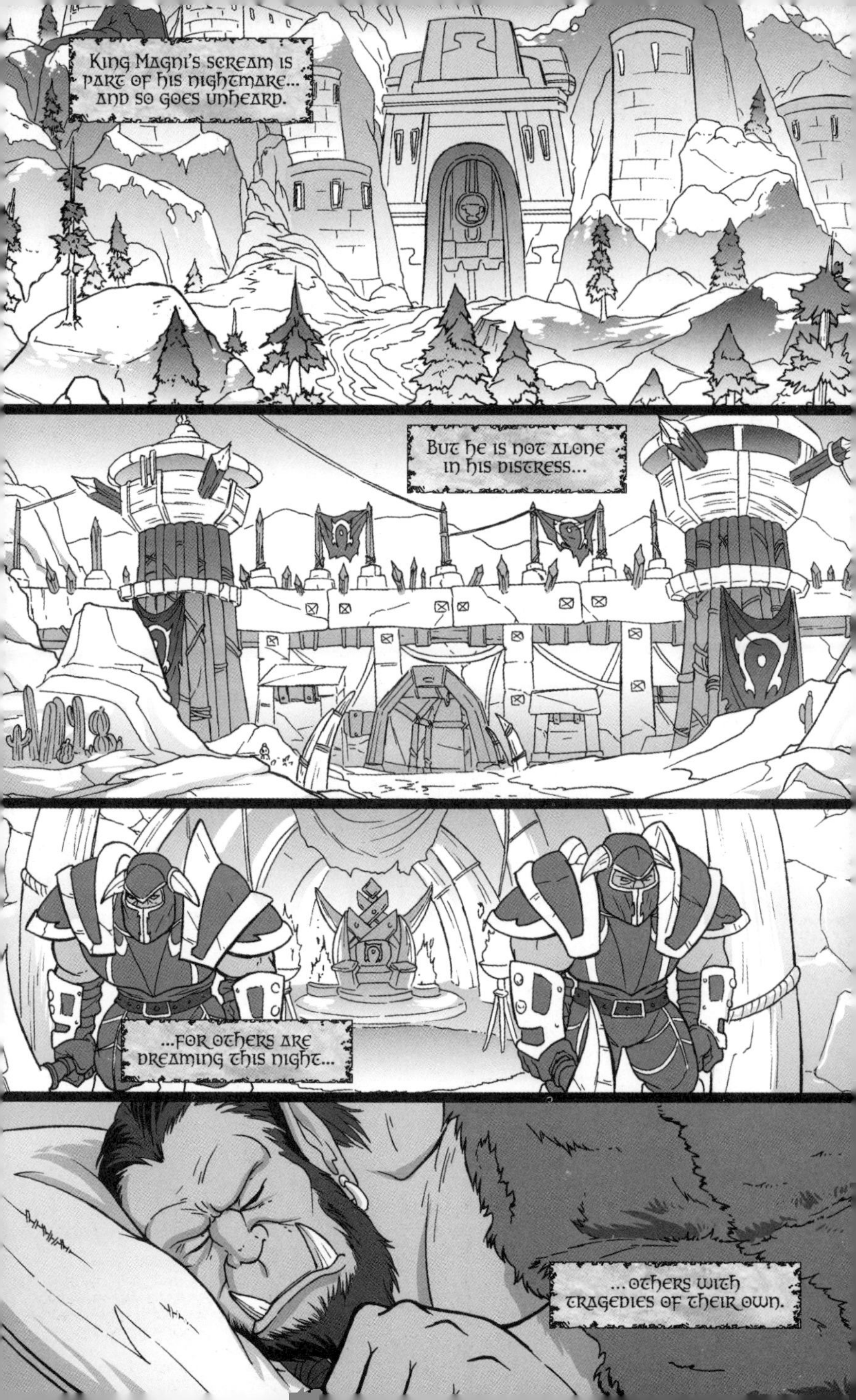
King Magni's scream is part of his nightmare... and so goes unheard.
But he is not alone in his distress...
...for others are dreaming this night...
...others with tragedies of their own.

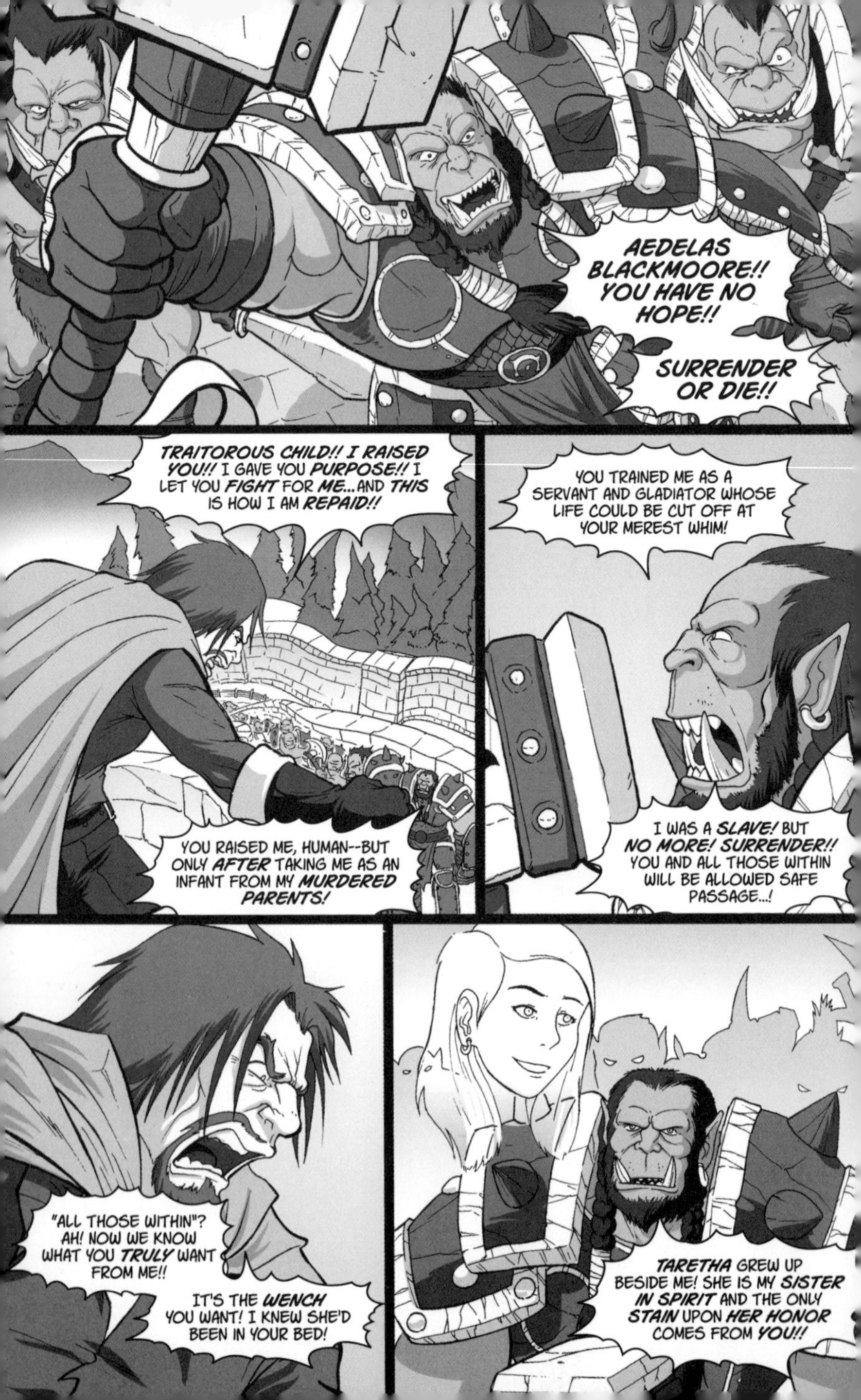
AEDELAS BLACKMOORE!! YOU HAVE NO HOPE!!
SURRENDER OR DIE!!
TRAITOROUS CHILD!! I RAISED YOU!! I GAVE YOU PURPOSE!! I LET YOU FIGHT FOR ME...AND THIS IS HOW I AM REPAID!!
YOU RAISED ME, HUMAN--BUT ONLY AFTER TAKING ME AS AN INFANT FROM MY MURDERED PARENTS!
YOU TRAINED ME AS A SERVANT AND GLADIATOR WHOSE LIFE COULD BE CUT OFF AT YOUR MEREST WHIM!
I WAS A SLAVE! BUT NO MORE! SURRENDER!! YOU AND ALL THOSE WITHIN WILL BE ALLOWED SAFE PASSAGE...!
"ALL THOSE WITHIN"? AH! NOW WE KNOW WHAT YOU TRULY WANT FROM ME!!
IT'S THE WENCH YOU WANT! I KNEW SHE'D BEEN IN YOUR BED!
TARETHA GREW UP BESIDE ME! SHE IS MY SISTER IN SPIRIT AND THE ONLY STAIN UPON HER HONOR COMES FROM YOU!!

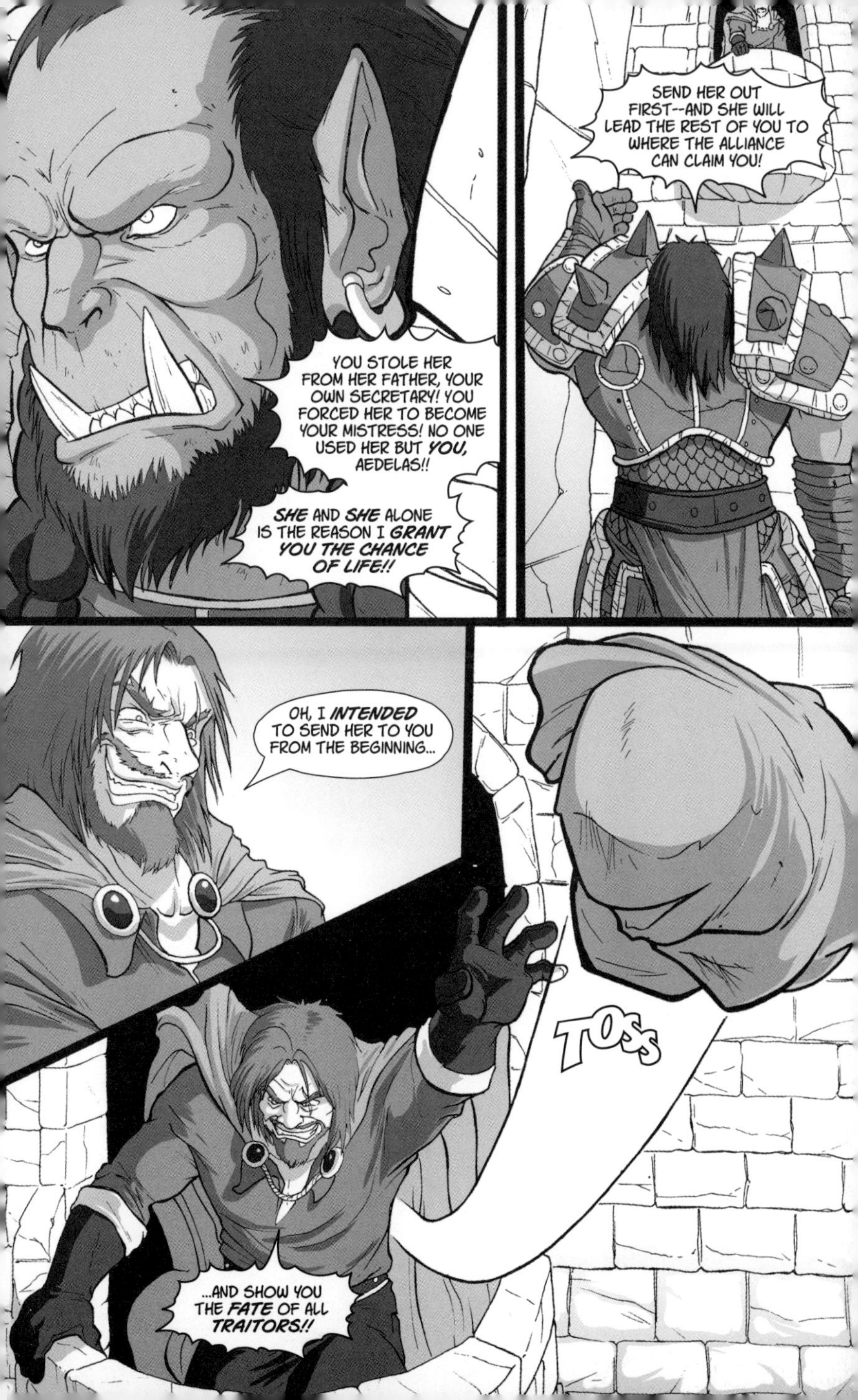
SEND HER OUT FIRST--AND SHE WILL LEAD THE REST OF YOU TO WHERE THE ALLIANCE CAN CLAIM YOU!
YOU STOLE HER FROM HER FATHER, YOUR OWN SECRETARY! YOU FORCED HER TO BECOME YOUR MISTRESS! NO ONE USED HER BUT *YOU,* AEDELAS!!
SHE AND *SHE* ALONE IS THE REASON I *GRANT YOU THE CHANCE OF LIFE!!*
OH, I *INTENDED* TO SEND HER TO YOU FROM THE BEGINNING...
...AND SHOW YOU THE *FATE* OF ALL *TRAITORS!!*
TOSS

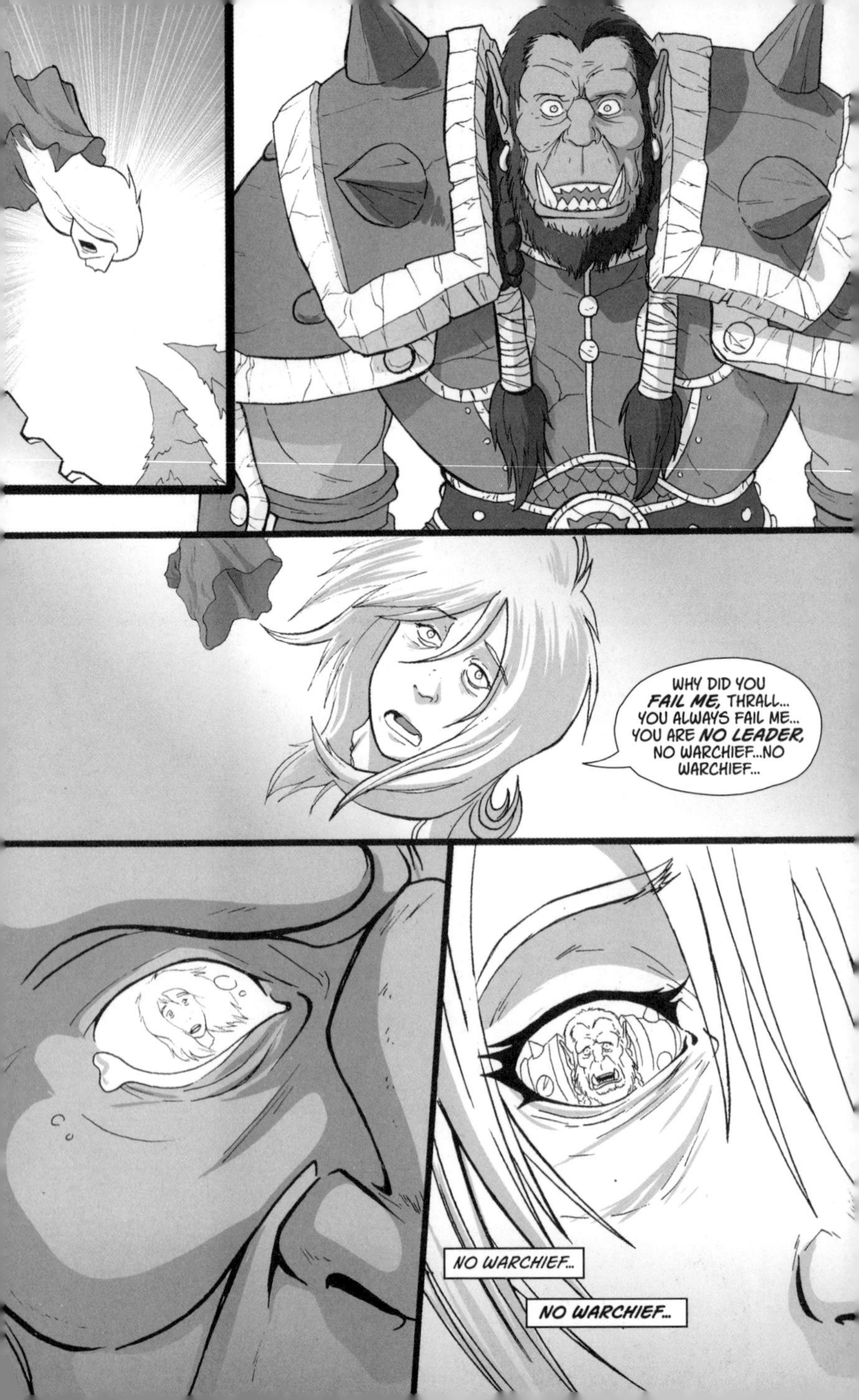
WHY DID YOU FAIL ME, THRALL... YOU ALWAYS FAIL ME... YOU ARE NO LEADER, NO WARCHIEF...NO WARCHIEF...
NO WARCHIEF...
NO WARCHIEF...

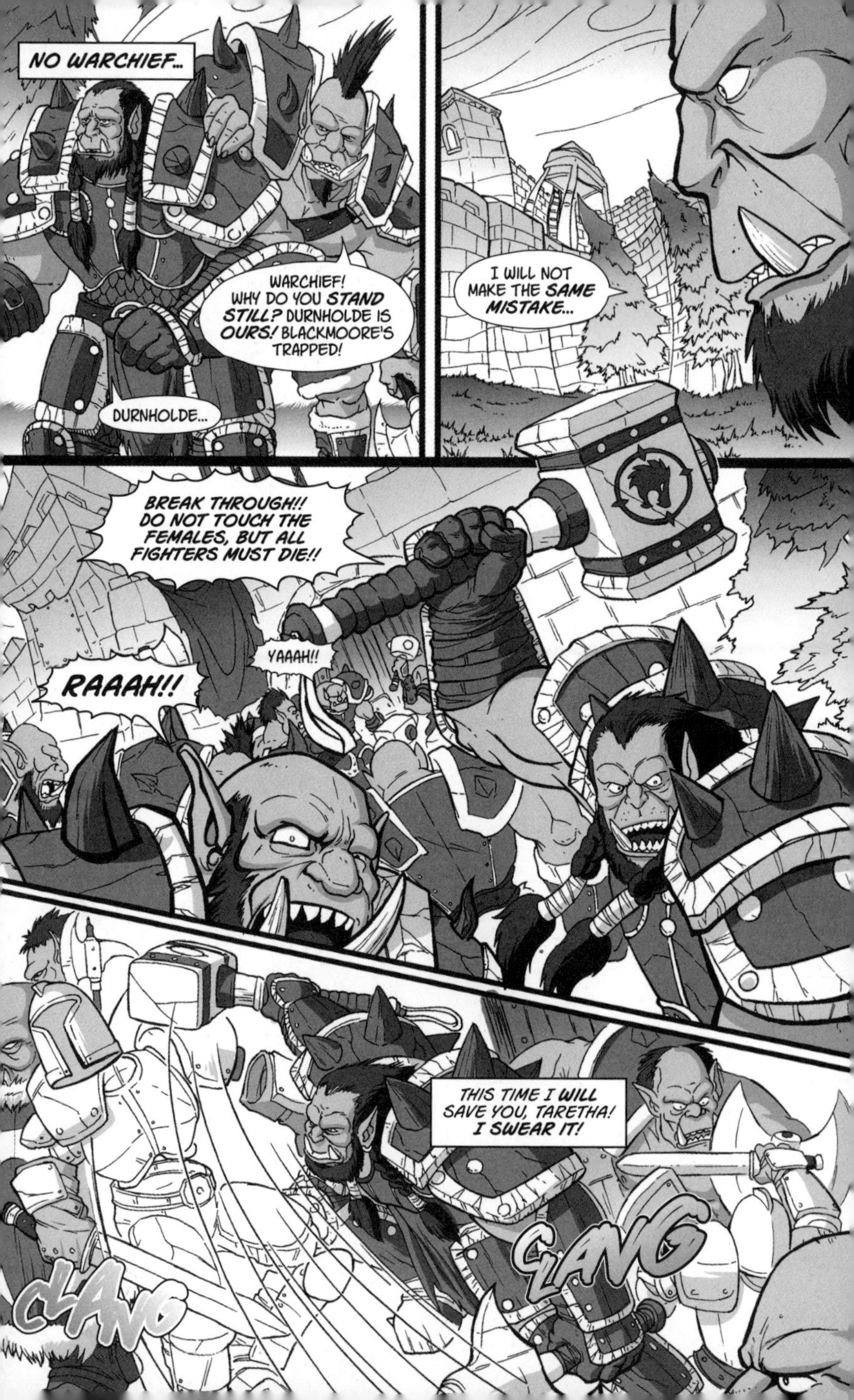
NO WARCHIEF...
WARCHIEF! WHY DO YOU STAND STILL? DURNHOLDE IS OURS! BLACKMOORE'S TRAPPED!
DURNHOLDE...
I WILL NOT MAKE THE SAME MISTAKE...
BREAK THROUGH!! DO NOT TOUCH THE FEMALES, BUT ALL FIGHTERS MUST DIE!!
YAAAH!!
RAAAH!!
THIS TIME I WILL SAVE YOU, TARETHA! I SWEAR IT!
CLANG
CLANG

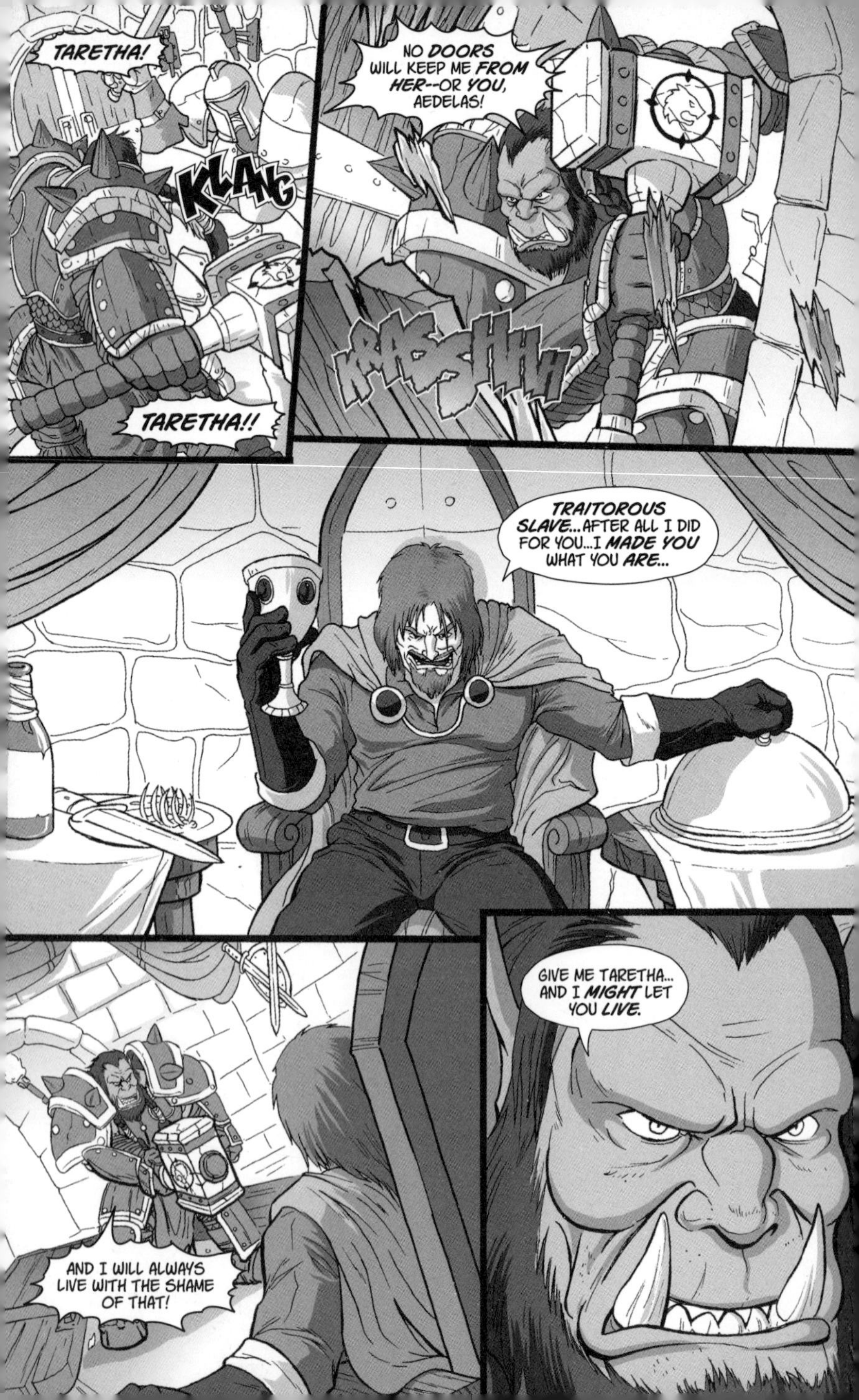
TARETHA!
KLANG
TARETHA!!
NO DOORS WILL KEEP ME FROM HER--OR YOU, AEDELAS!
KRASSHHH
TRAITOROUS SLAVE...AFTER ALL I DID FOR YOU...I MADE YOU WHAT YOU ARE...
AND I WILL ALWAYS LIVE WITH THE SHAME OF THAT!
GIVE ME TARETHA... AND I MIGHT LET YOU LIVE.

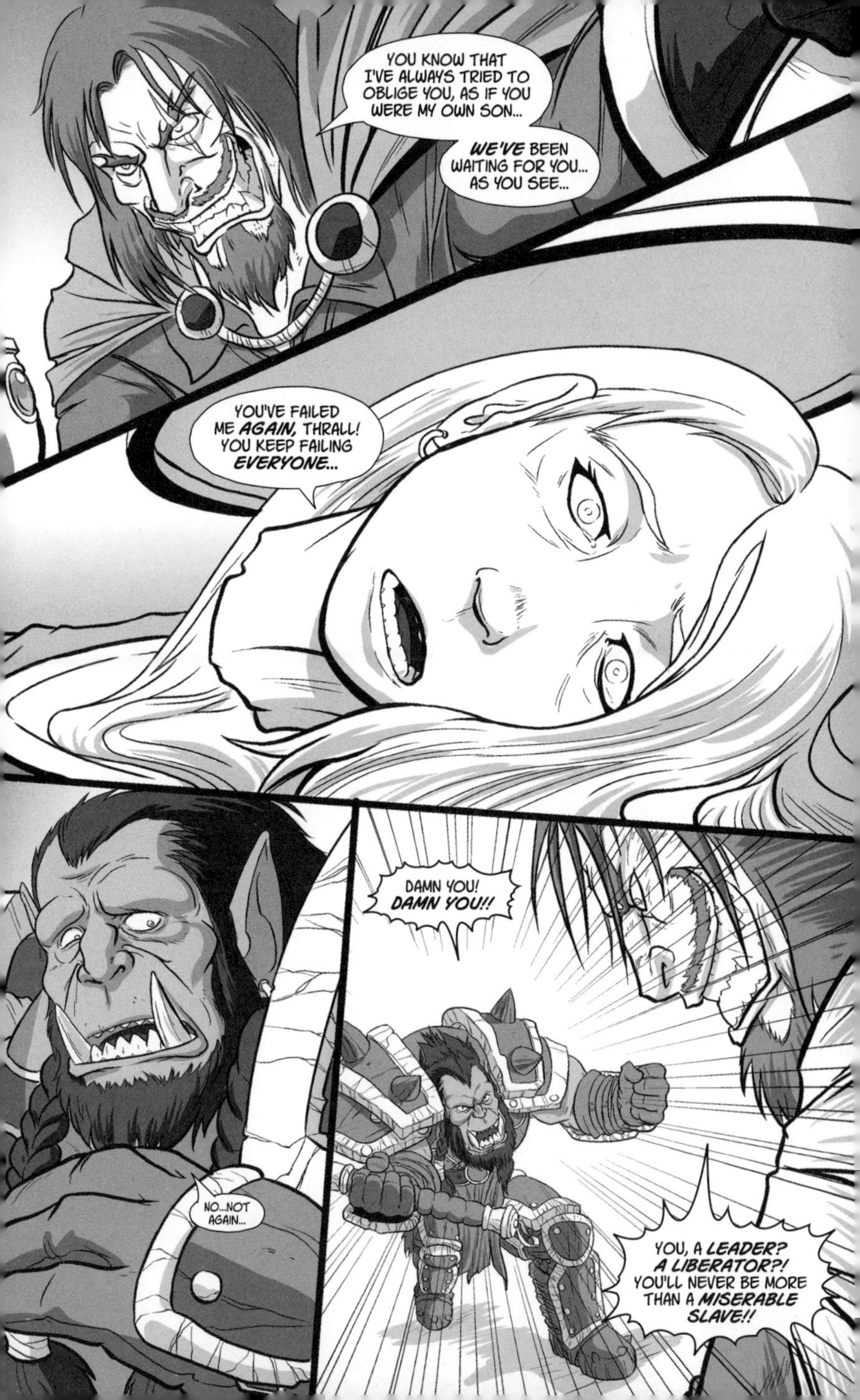
YOU KNOW THAT I'VE ALWAYS TRIED TO OBLIGE YOU, AS IF YOU WERE MY OWN SON...
WE'VE BEEN WAITING FOR YOU... AS YOU SEE...
YOU'VE FAILED ME *AGAIN,* THRALL! YOU KEEP FAILING *EVERYONE...*
NO...NOT AGAIN...
DAMN YOU! *DAMN YOU!!*
YOU, A *LEADER? A LIBERATOR?!* YOU'LL NEVER BE MORE THAN A *MISERABLE SLAVE!!*

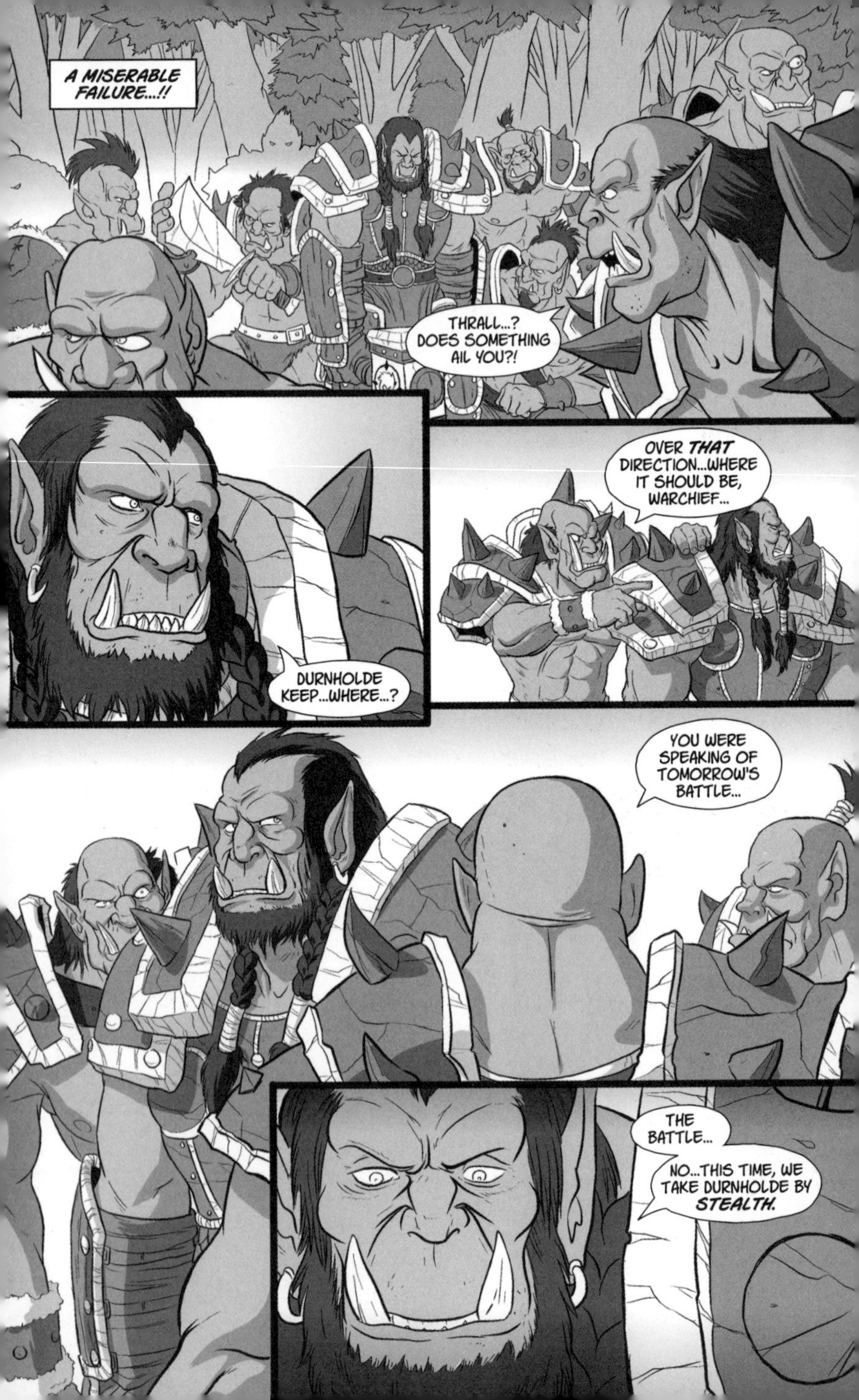
A MISERABLE FAILURE...!!
THRALL...? DOES SOMETHING AIL YOU?!
DURNHOLDE KEEP...WHERE...?
OVER THAT DIRECTION...WHERE IT SHOULD BE, WARCHIEF...
YOU WERE SPEAKING OF TOMORROW'S BATTLE...
THE BATTLE...
NO...THIS TIME, WE TAKE DURNHOLDE BY STEALTH.

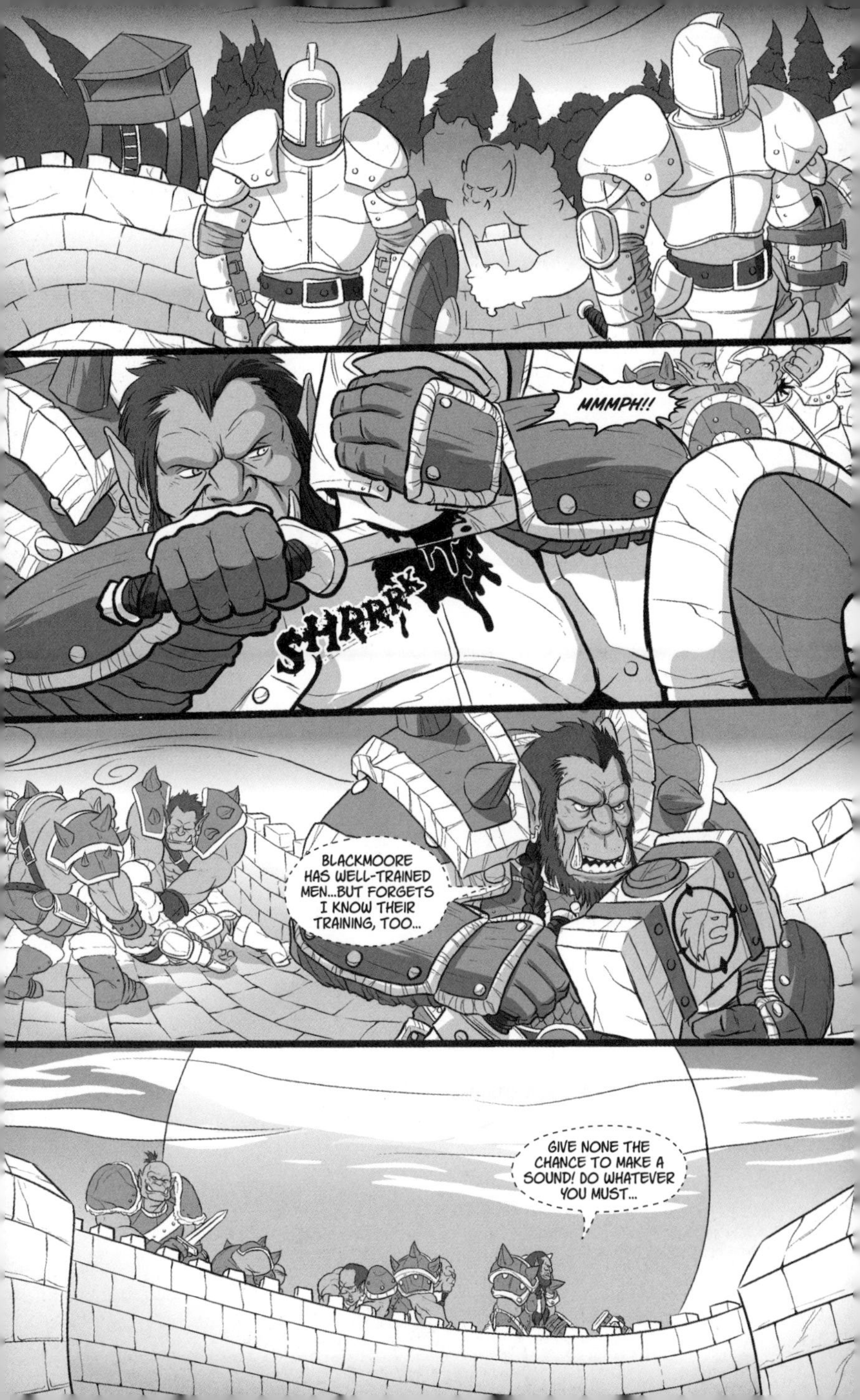
MMMPH!!
SHRRRK
BLACKMOORE HAS WELL-TRAINED MEN...BUT FORGETS I KNOW THEIR TRAINING, TOO...
GIVE NONE THE CHANCE TO MAKE A SOUND! DO WHATEVER YOU MUST...

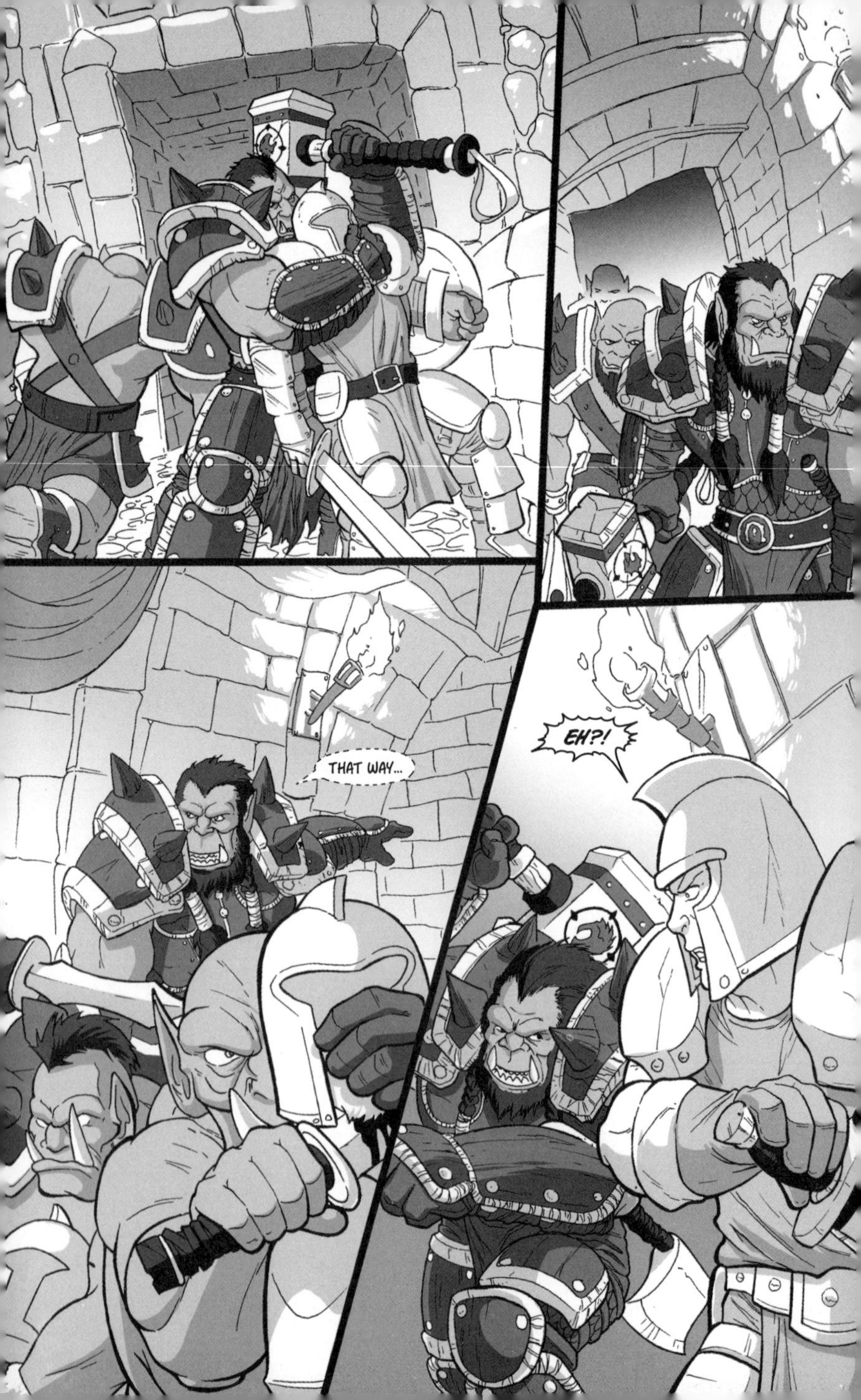
THAT WAY...
EH?!

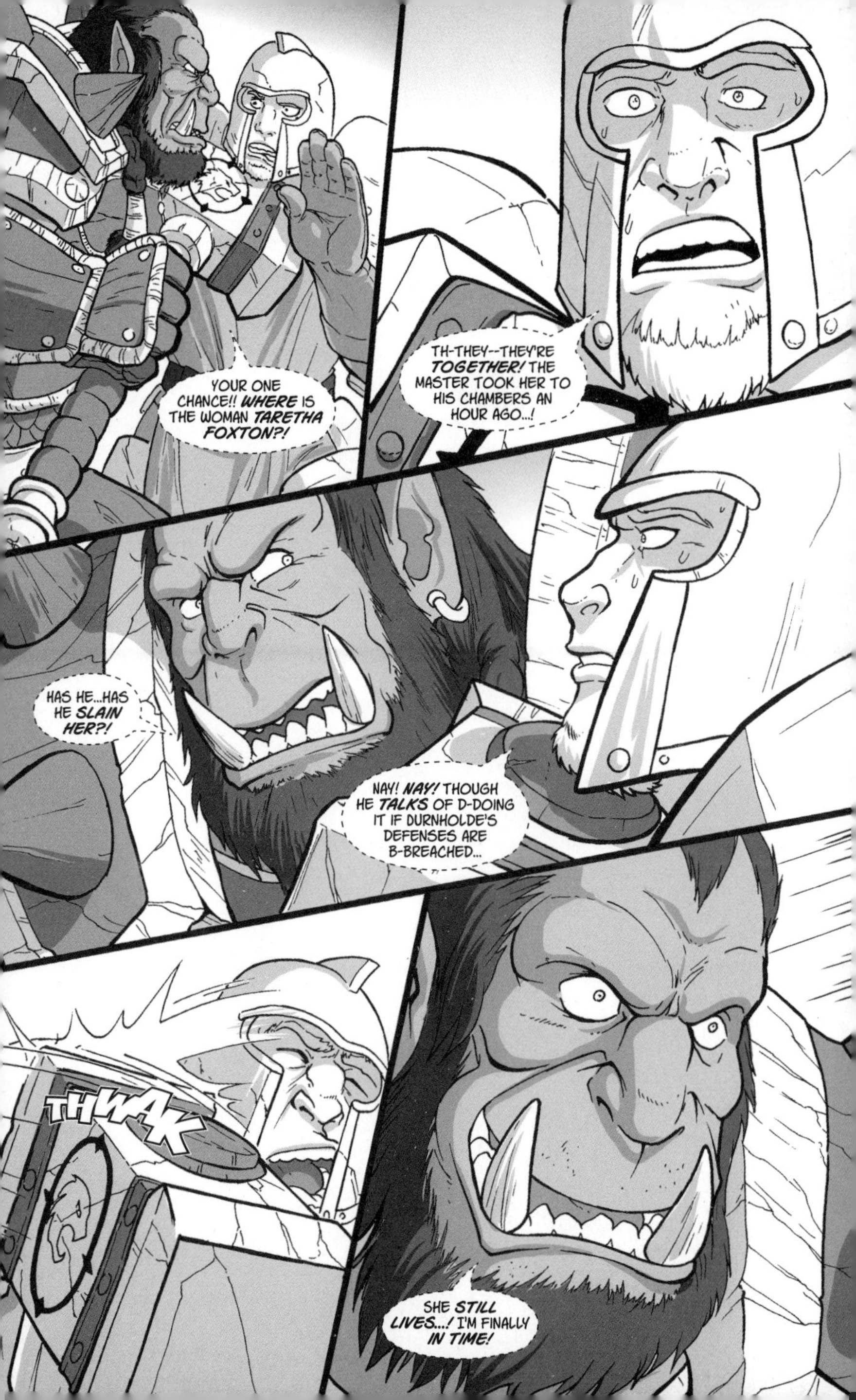
YOUR ONE CHANCE!! **WHERE** IS THE WOMAN **TARETHA FOXTON?!**
TH-THEY--THEY'RE **TOGETHER!** THE MASTER TOOK HER TO HIS CHAMBERS AN HOUR AGO...!
HAS HE...HAS HE **SLAIN HER?!**
NAY! **NAY!** THOUGH HE **TALKS** OF D-DOING IT IF DURNHOLDE'S DEFENSES ARE B-BREACHED...
THWAK
SHE **STILL LIVES...!** I'M FINALLY **IN TIME!**

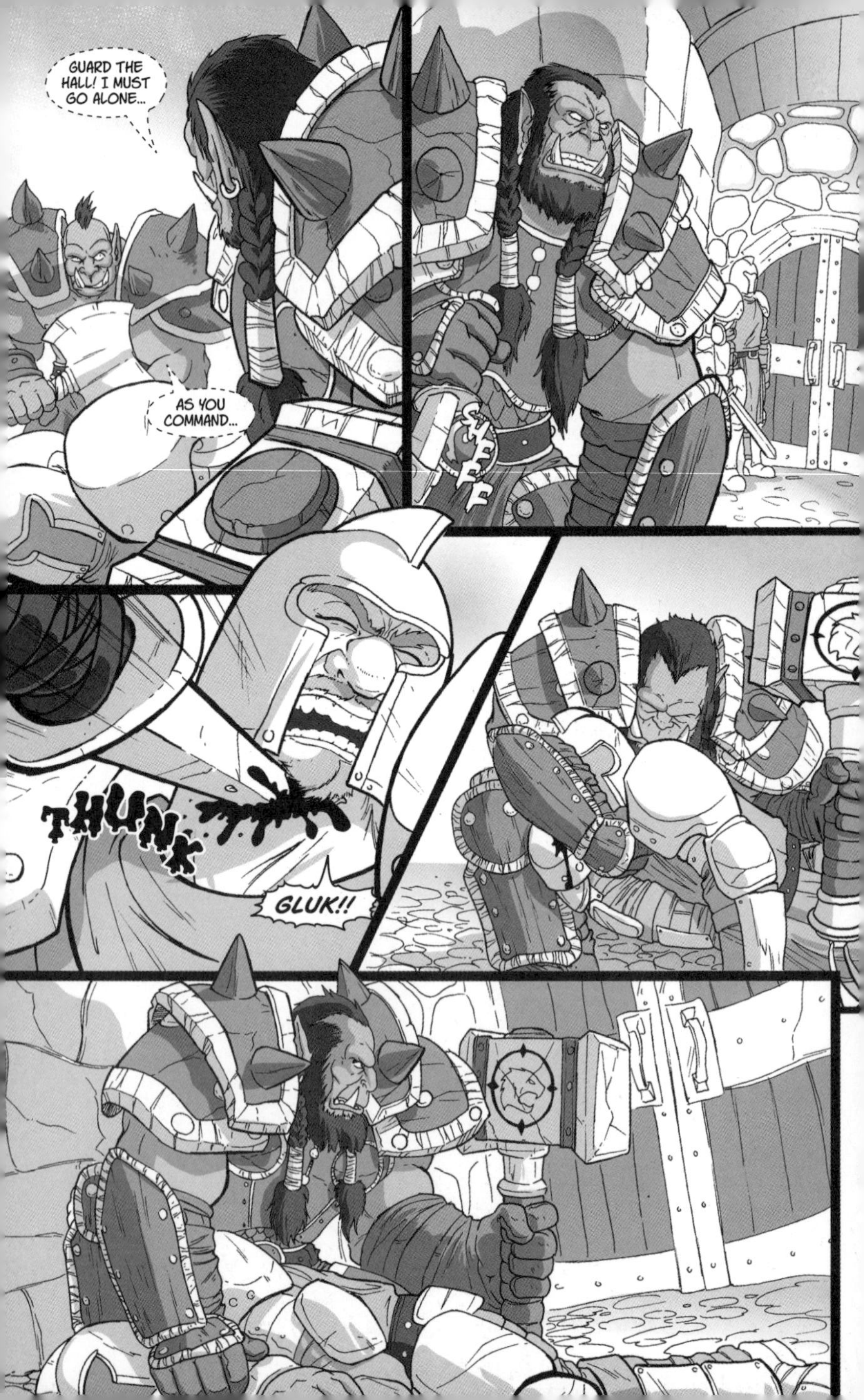
GUARD THE HALL! I MUST GO ALONE...
AS YOU COMMAND...
SHEFF
THUNK
GLUK!!

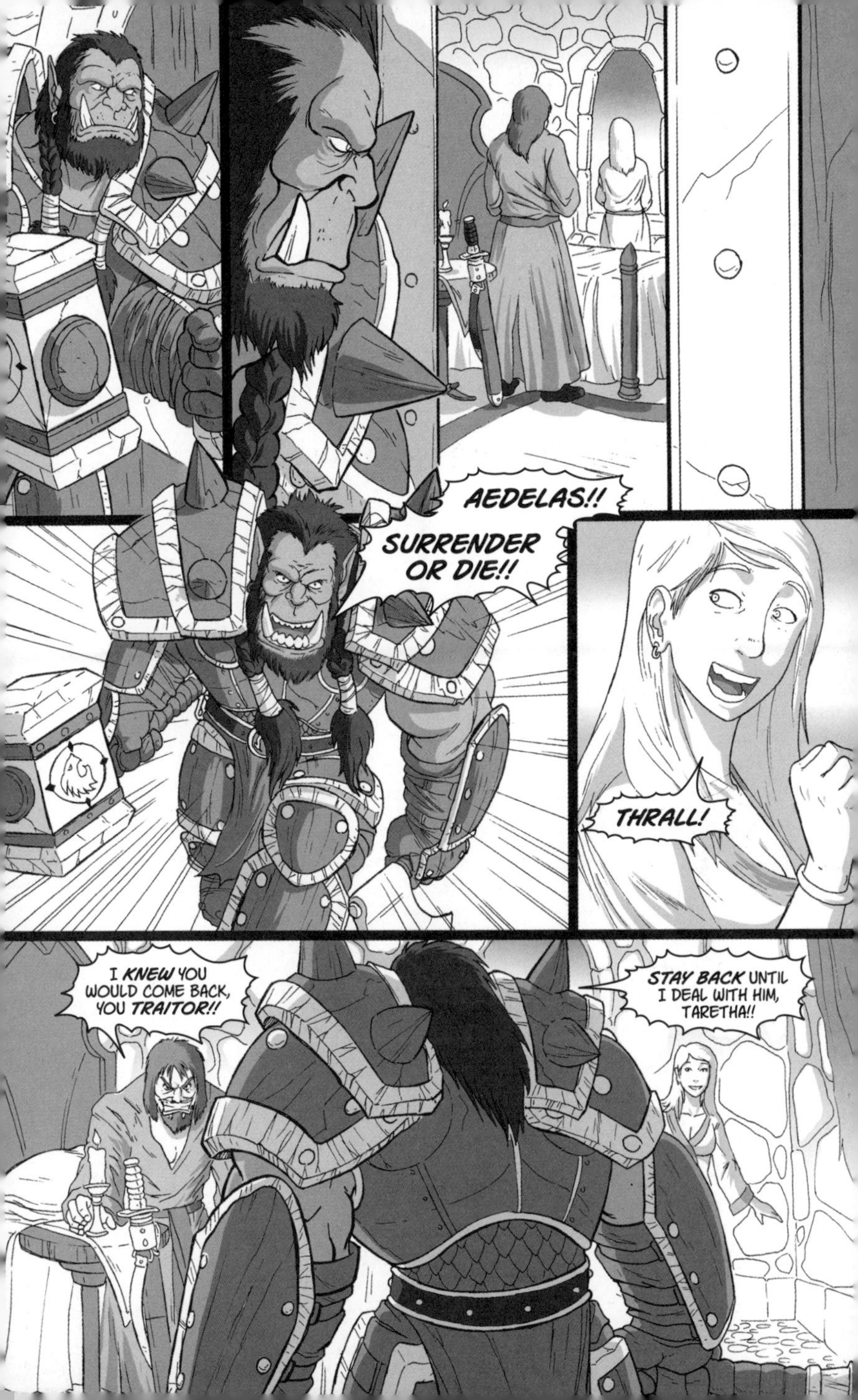
AEDELAS!!
SURRENDER OR DIE!!
THRALL!
I KNEW YOU WOULD COME BACK, YOU TRAITOR!!
STAY BACK UNTIL I DEAL WITH HIM, TARETHA!!

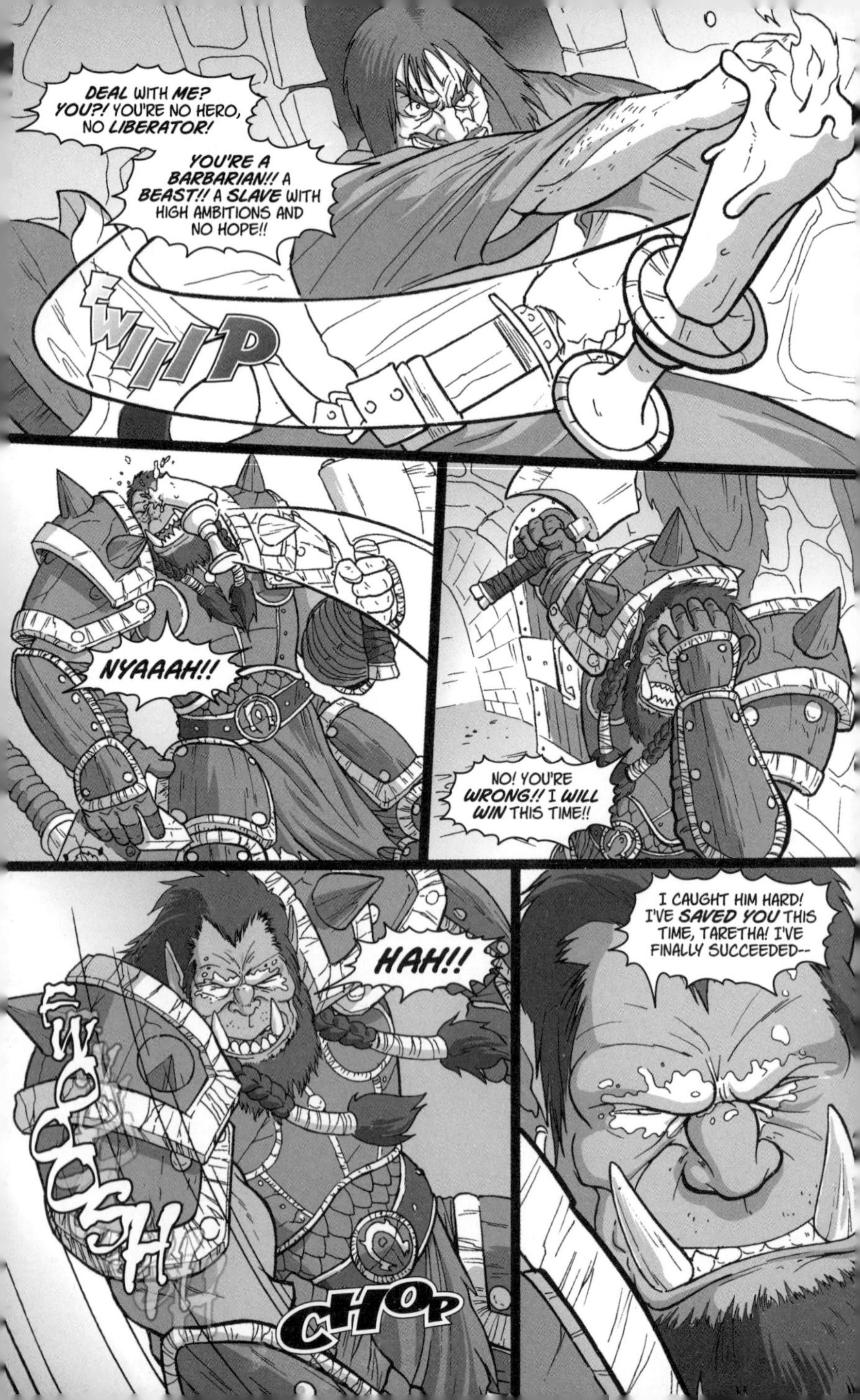
DEAL WITH ME? YOU?! YOU'RE NO HERO, NO LIBERATOR!
YOU'RE A BARBARIAN!! A BEAST!! A SLAVE WITH HIGH AMBITIONS AND NO HOPE!!
FWIIIP
NYAAAH!!
NO! YOU'RE WRONG!! I WILL WIN THIS TIME!!
HAH!!
FWOOSH
CHOP
I CAUGHT HIM HARD! I'VE SAVED YOU THIS TIME, TARETHA! I'VE FINALLY SUCCEEDED--

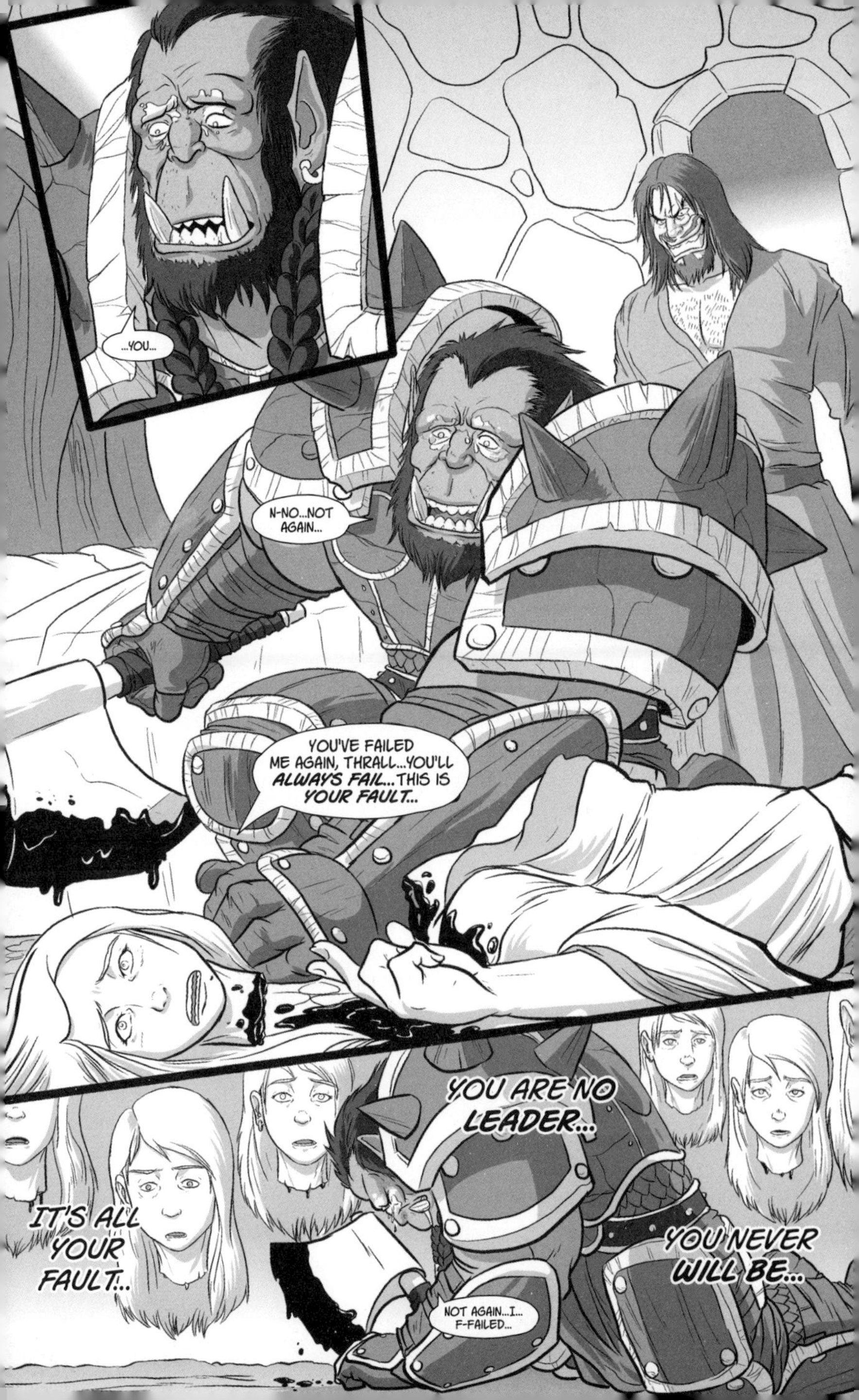
...YOU...
N-NO...NOT AGAIN...
YOU'VE FAILED ME AGAIN, THRALL...YOU'LL *ALWAYS FAIL*...THIS IS *YOUR FAULT*...
YOU ARE NO LEADER...
IT'S ALL YOUR FAULT...
YOU NEVER WILL BE...
NOT AGAIN...I... F-FAILED...

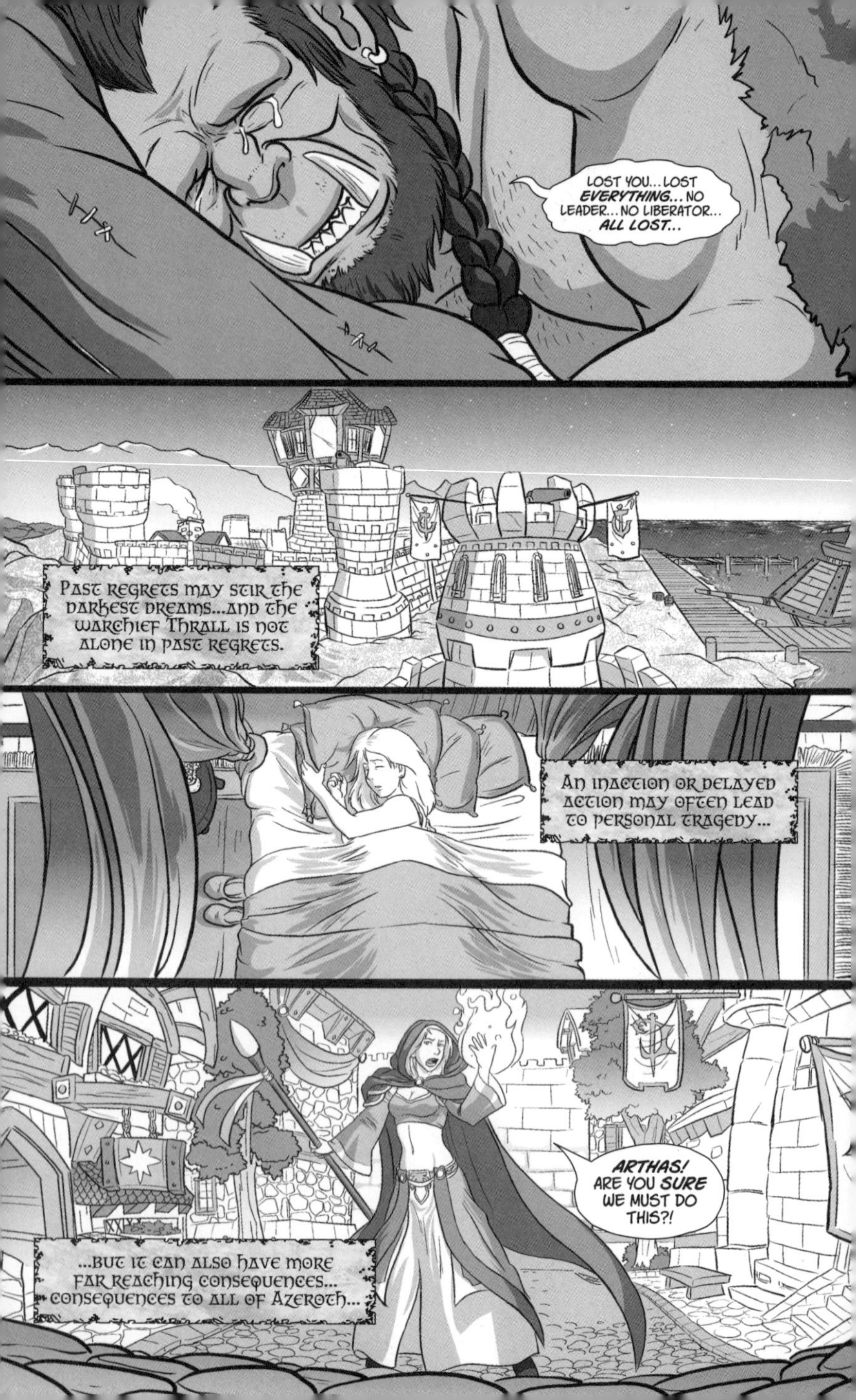
LOST YOU... LOST *EVERYTHING*... NO LEADER... NO LIBERATOR... *ALL LOST*...
Past regrets may stir the darkest dreams...and the warchief Thrall is not alone in past regrets.
An inaction or delayed action may often lead to personal tragedy...
ARTHAS! ARE YOU *SURE* WE MUST DO THIS?!
...but it can also have more far reaching consequences... consequences to all of Azeroth...

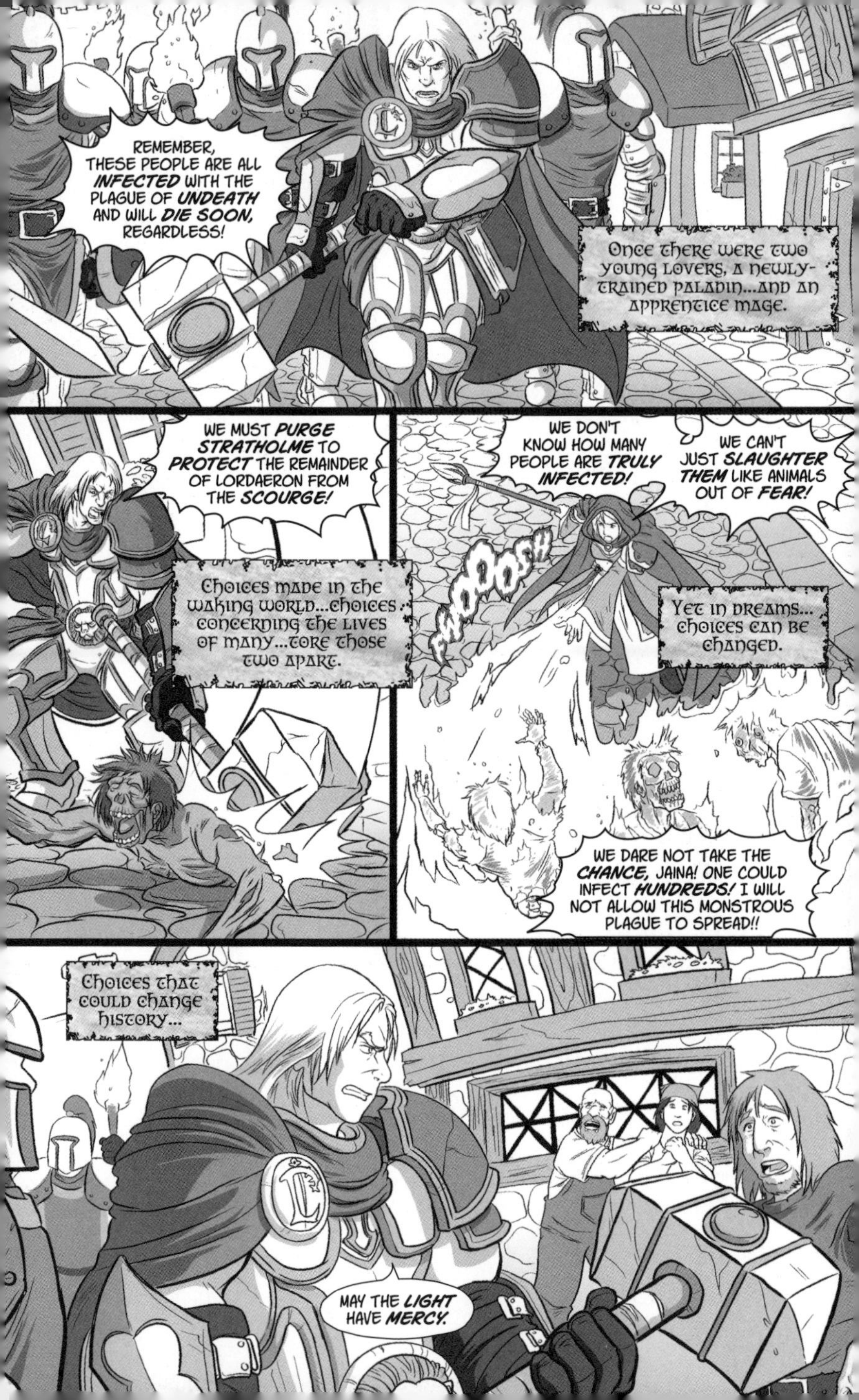
REMEMBER, THESE PEOPLE ARE ALL *INFECTED* WITH THE PLAGUE OF *UNDEATH* AND WILL *DIE SOON,* REGARDLESS!
Once there were two young lovers, a newly-trained paladin...and an apprentice mage.
WE MUST *PURGE STRATHOLME* TO *PROTECT* THE REMAINDER OF LORDAERON FROM THE *SCOURGE!*
Choices made in the waking world...choices concerning the lives of many...tore those two apart.
WE DON'T KNOW HOW MANY PEOPLE ARE *TRULY INFECTED!*
WE CAN'T JUST *SLAUGHTER THEM* LIKE ANIMALS OUT OF *FEAR!*
FWOOOSH
Yet in dreams... choices can be changed.
WE DARE NOT TAKE THE *CHANCE,* JAINA! ONE COULD INFECT *HUNDREDS!* I WILL NOT ALLOW THIS MONSTROUS PLAGUE TO SPREAD!!
Choices that could change history...
MAY THE *LIGHT* HAVE *MERCY.*

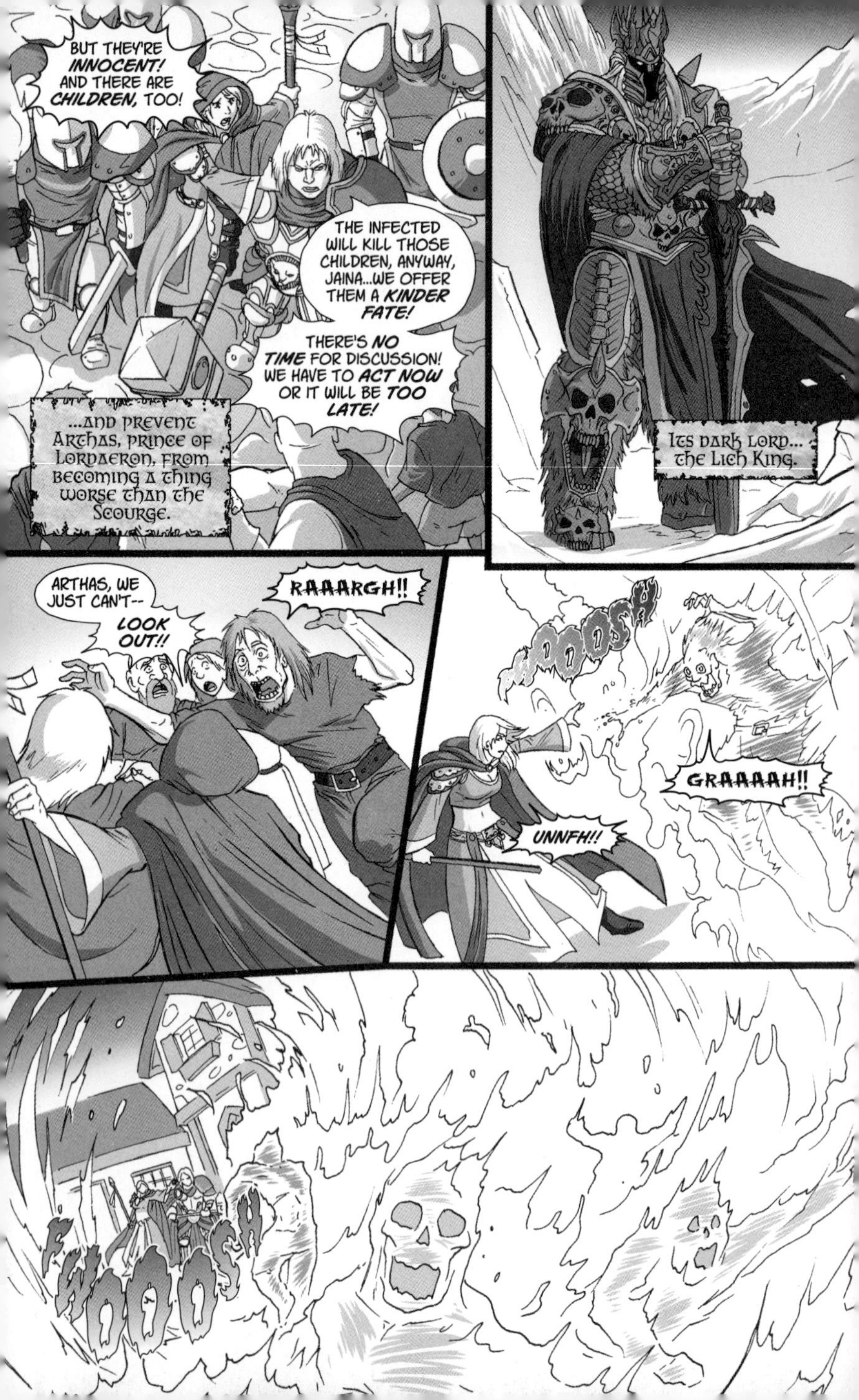

BUT THEY'RE INNOCENT! AND THERE ARE CHILDREN, TOO!
THE INFECTED WILL KILL THOSE CHILDREN, ANYWAY, JAINA...WE OFFER THEM A KINDER FATE!
THERE'S NO TIME FOR DISCUSSION! WE HAVE TO ACT NOW OR IT WILL BE TOO LATE!
...and prevent Arthas, prince of Lordaeron, from becoming a thing worse than the Scourge.
Its dark lord... the Lich King.
ARTHAS, WE JUST CAN'T--
LOOK OUT!!
RAAARGH!!
WHOOOSH
GRAAAAH!!
UNNFH!!
WHOOOSH

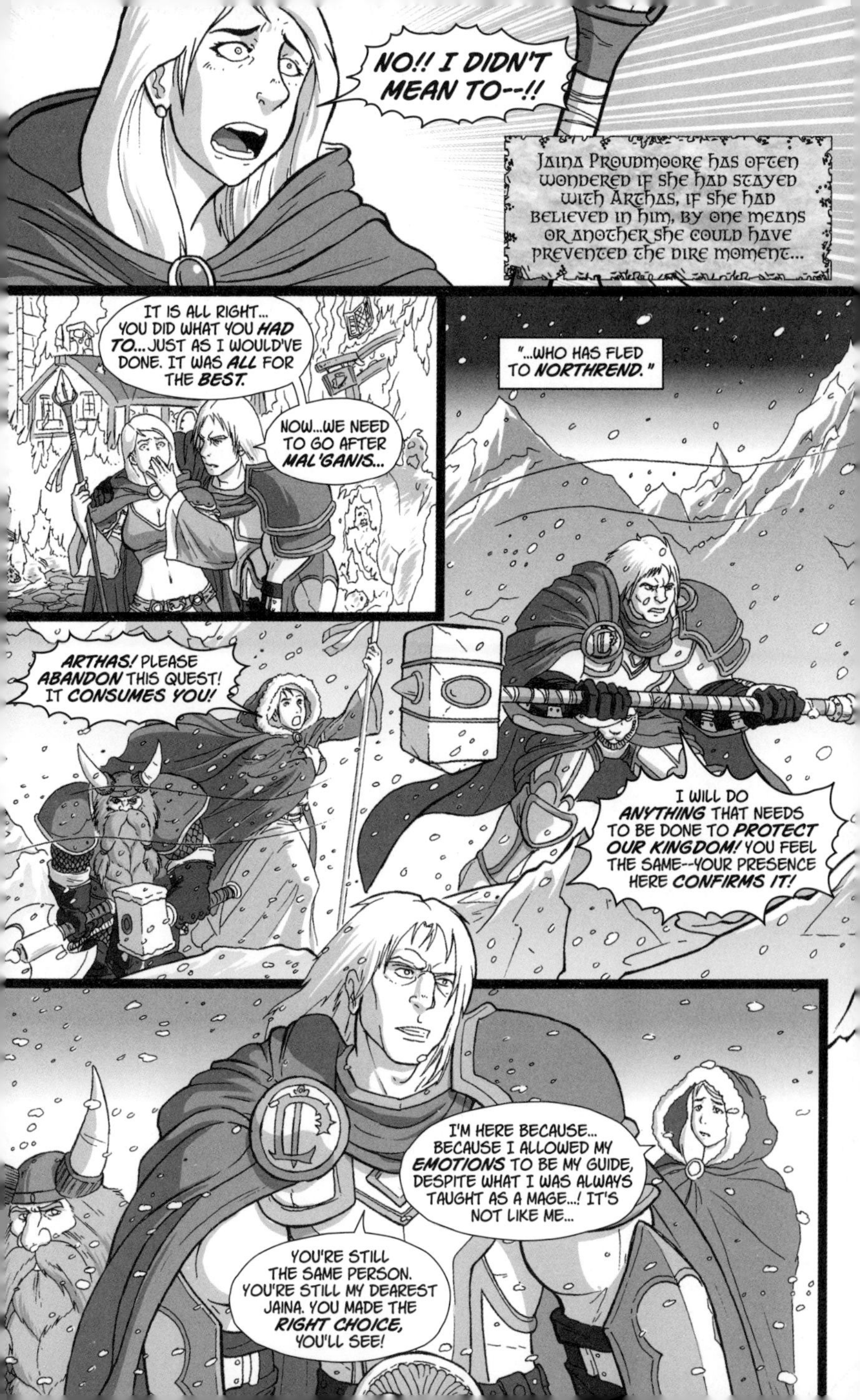
NO!! I DIDN'T MEAN TO--!!
Jaina Proudmoore has often wondered if she had stayed with Arthas, if she had believed in him, by one means or another she could have prevented the dire moment...
IT IS ALL RIGHT... YOU DID WHAT YOU HAD TO... JUST AS I WOULD'VE DONE. IT WAS ALL FOR THE BEST.
NOW... WE NEED TO GO AFTER MAL'GANIS...
"...WHO HAS FLED TO NORTHREND."
ARTHAS! PLEASE ABANDON THIS QUEST! IT CONSUMES YOU!
I WILL DO ANYTHING THAT NEEDS TO BE DONE TO PROTECT OUR KINGDOM! YOU FEEL THE SAME--YOUR PRESENCE HERE CONFIRMS IT!
I'M HERE BECAUSE... BECAUSE I ALLOWED MY EMOTIONS TO BE MY GUIDE, DESPITE WHAT I WAS ALWAYS TAUGHT AS A MAGE...! IT'S NOT LIKE ME...
YOU'RE STILL THE SAME PERSON. YOU'RE STILL MY DEAREST JAINA. YOU MADE THE RIGHT CHOICE, YOU'LL SEE!

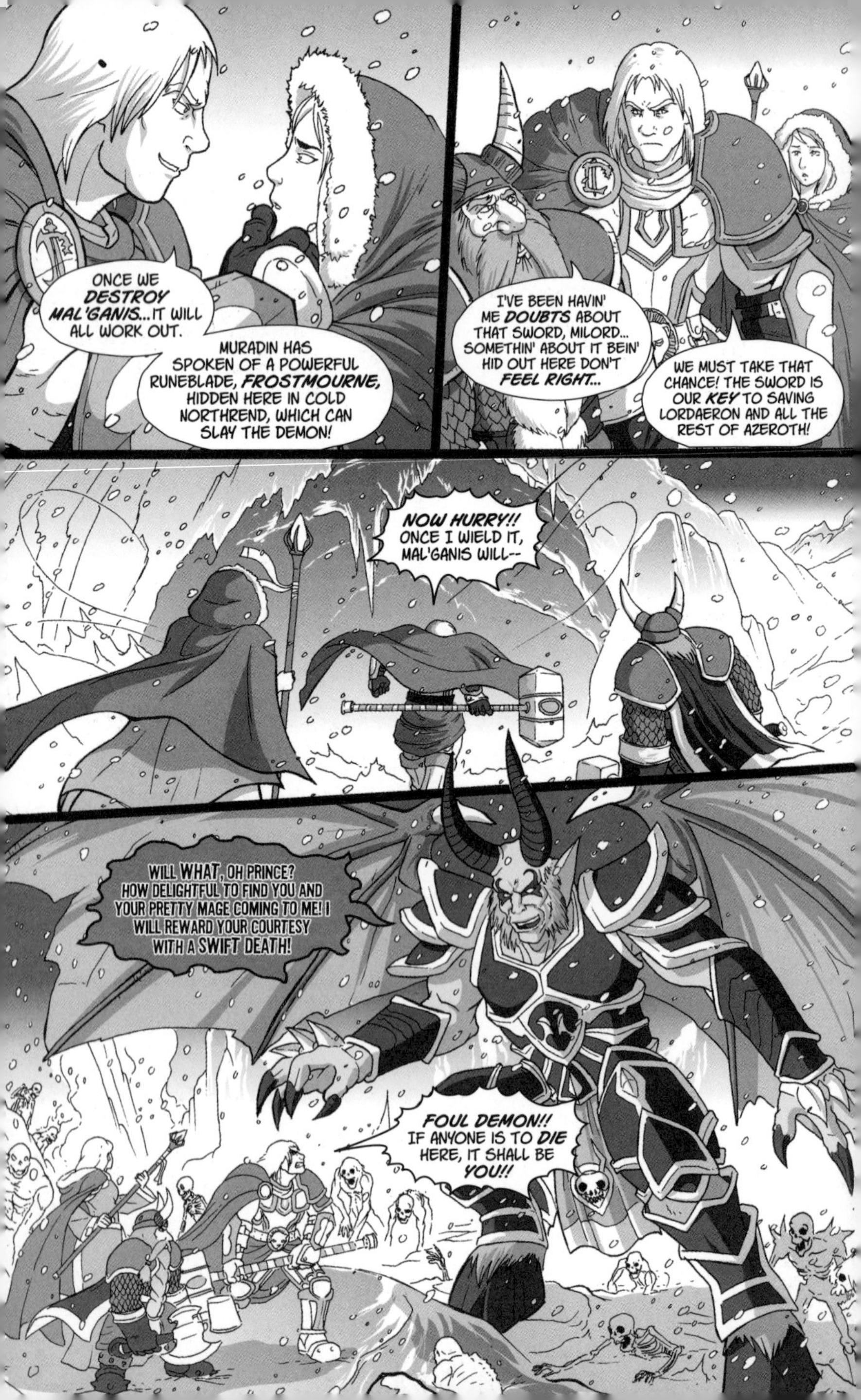
ONCE WE DESTROY MAL'GANIS...IT WILL ALL WORK OUT.
MURADIN HAS SPOKEN OF A POWERFUL RUNEBLADE, FROSTMOURNE, HIDDEN HERE IN COLD NORTHREND, WHICH CAN SLAY THE DEMON!
I'VE BEEN HAVIN' ME DOUBTS ABOUT THAT SWORD, MILORD... SOMETHIN' ABOUT IT BEIN' HID OUT HERE DON'T FEEL RIGHT...
WE MUST TAKE THAT CHANCE! THE SWORD IS OUR KEY TO SAVING LORDAERON AND ALL THE REST OF AZEROTH!
NOW HURRY!! ONCE I WIELD IT, MAL'GANIS WILL--
WILL WHAT, OH PRINCE? HOW DELIGHTFUL TO FIND YOU AND YOUR PRETTY MAGE COMING TO ME! I WILL REWARD YOUR COURTESY WITH A SWIFT DEATH!
FOUL DEMON!! IF ANYONE IS TO DIE HERE, IT SHALL BE YOU!!

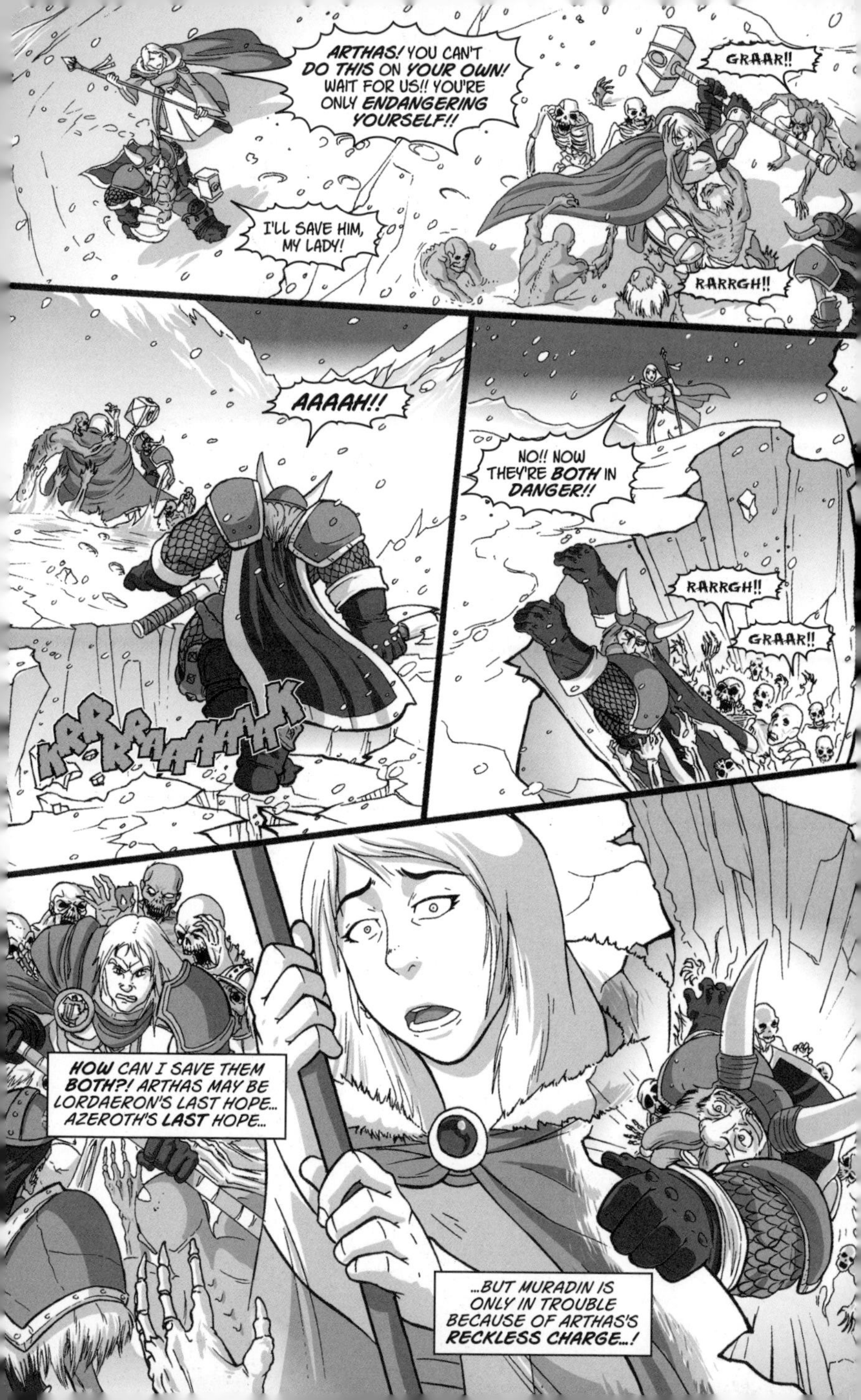
ARTHAS! YOU CAN'T DO THIS ON YOUR OWN! WAIT FOR US!! YOU'RE ONLY ENDANGERING YOURSELF!!
GRAAR!!
I'LL SAVE HIM, MY LADY!
RARRGH!!
AAAAH!!
KRRRAAAAAAK
NO!! NOW THEY'RE BOTH IN DANGER!!
RARRGH!!
GRAAR!!
HOW CAN I SAVE THEM BOTH?! ARTHAS MAY BE LORDAERON'S LAST HOPE... AZEROTH'S LAST HOPE...
...BUT MURADIN IS ONLY IN TROUBLE BECAUSE OF ARTHAS'S RECKLESS CHARGE...!

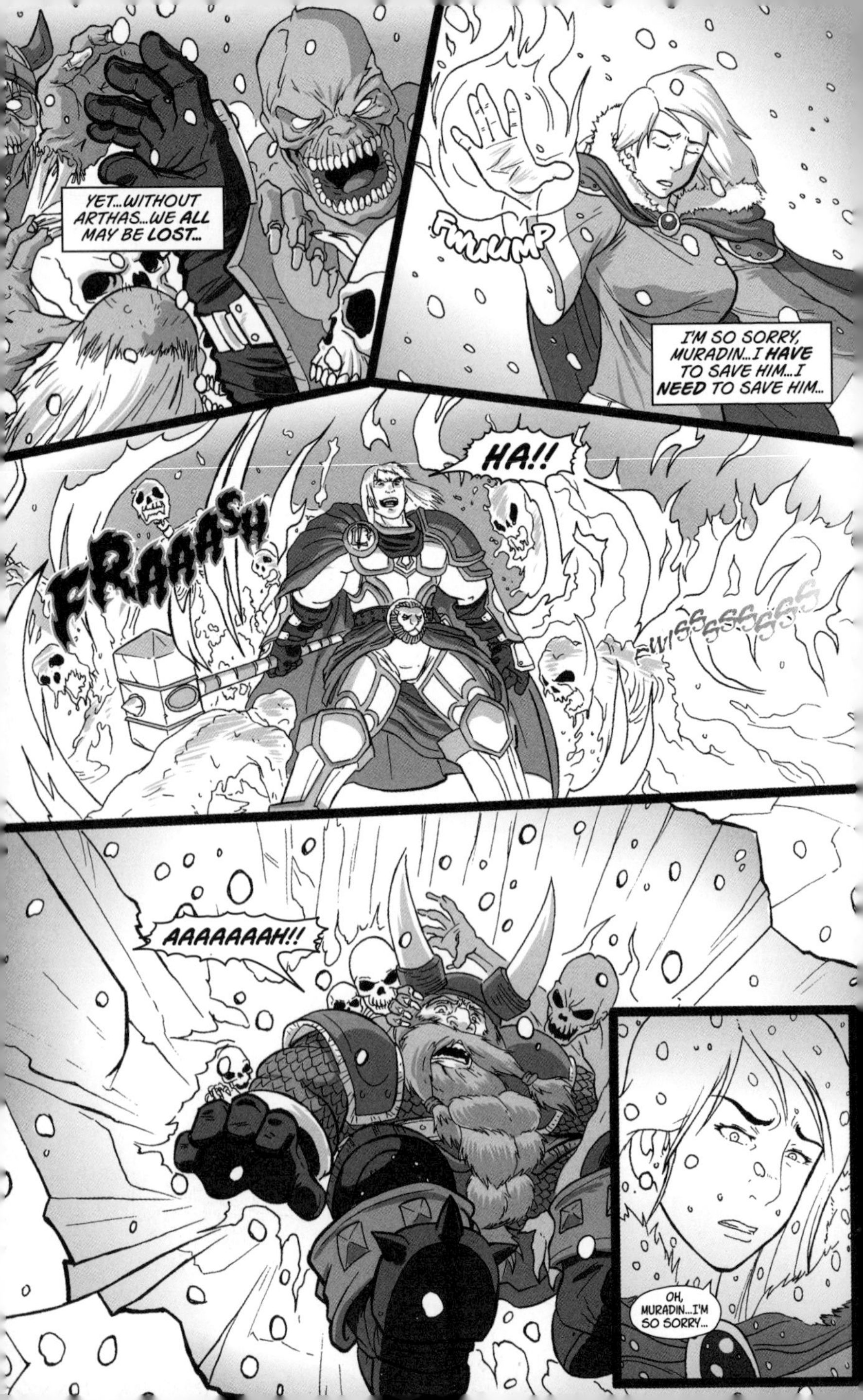
YET...WITHOUT ARTHAS...WE ALL MAY BE LOST...
FWUUMP
I'M SO SORRY, MURADIN...I HAVE TO SAVE HIM...I NEED TO SAVE HIM...
FRAAASH
HA!!
FWISSSSSSSS
AAAAAAAH!!
OH, MURADIN...I'M SO SORRY...

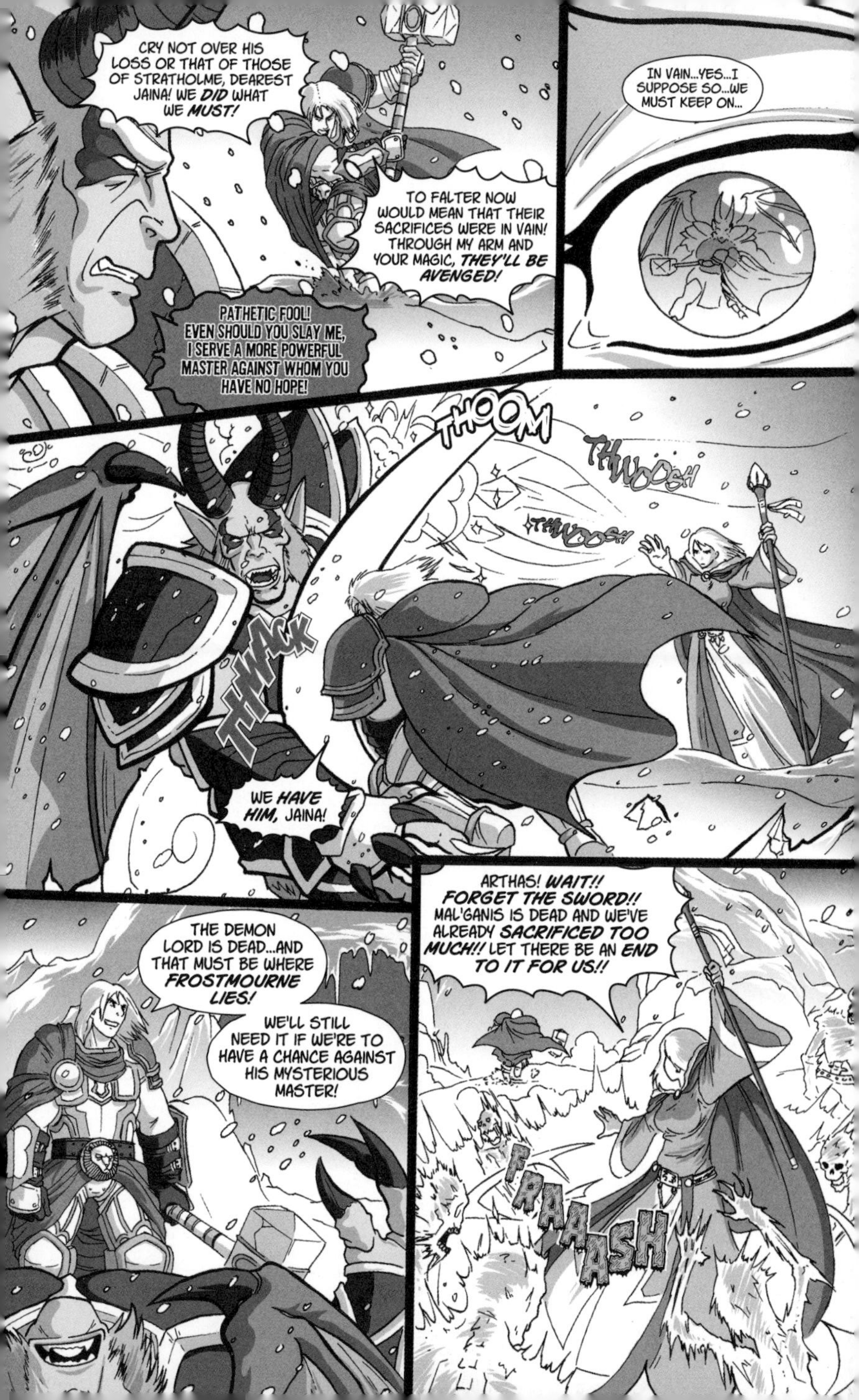
CRY NOT OVER HIS LOSS OR THAT OF THOSE OF STRATHOLME, DEAREST JAINA! WE *DID* WHAT WE *MUST!*
TO FALTER NOW WOULD MEAN THAT THEIR SACRIFICES WERE IN VAIN! THROUGH MY ARM AND YOUR MAGIC, ***THEY'LL BE AVENGED!***
PATHETIC FOOL! EVEN SHOULD YOU SLAY ME, I SERVE A MORE POWERFUL MASTER AGAINST WHOM YOU HAVE NO HOPE!
IN VAIN...YES...I SUPPOSE SO...WE MUST KEEP ON...
THOOM
THWOOSH
THWOOSH
THWACK
WE ***HAVE HIM,*** JAINA!
THE DEMON LORD IS DEAD...AND THAT MUST BE WHERE ***FROSTMOURNE LIES!***
WE'LL STILL NEED IT IF WE'RE TO HAVE A CHANCE AGAINST HIS MYSTERIOUS MASTER!
ARTHAS! ***WAIT!! FORGET THE SWORD!!*** MAL'GANIS IS DEAD AND WE'VE ALREADY ***SACRIFICED TOO MUCH!!*** LET THERE BE AN ***END TO IT FOR US!!***
FRAAASH

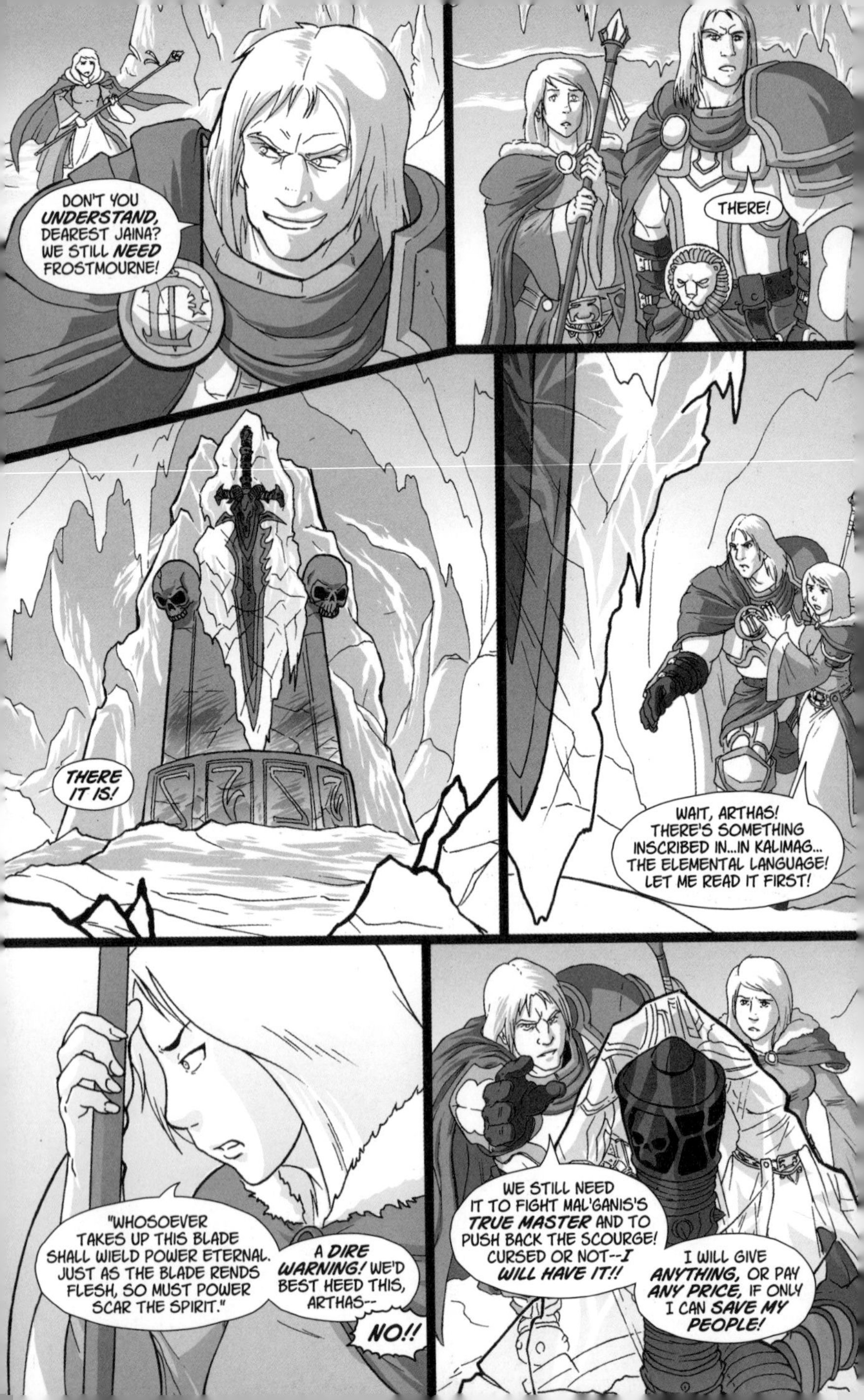
DON'T YOU UNDERSTAND, DEAREST JAINA? WE STILL NEED FROSTMOURNE!
THERE!
THERE IT IS!
WAIT, ARTHAS! THERE'S SOMETHING INSCRIBED IN...IN KALIMAG... THE ELEMENTAL LANGUAGE! LET ME READ IT FIRST!
"WHOSOEVER TAKES UP THIS BLADE SHALL WIELD POWER ETERNAL. JUST AS THE BLADE RENDS FLESH, SO MUST POWER SCAR THE SPIRIT."
A DIRE WARNING! WE'D BEST HEED THIS, ARTHAS--
NO!!
WE STILL NEED IT TO FIGHT MAL'GANIS'S TRUE MASTER AND TO PUSH BACK THE SCOURGE! CURSED OR NOT--I WILL HAVE IT!!
I WILL GIVE ANYTHING, OR PAY ANY PRICE, IF ONLY I CAN SAVE MY PEOPLE!

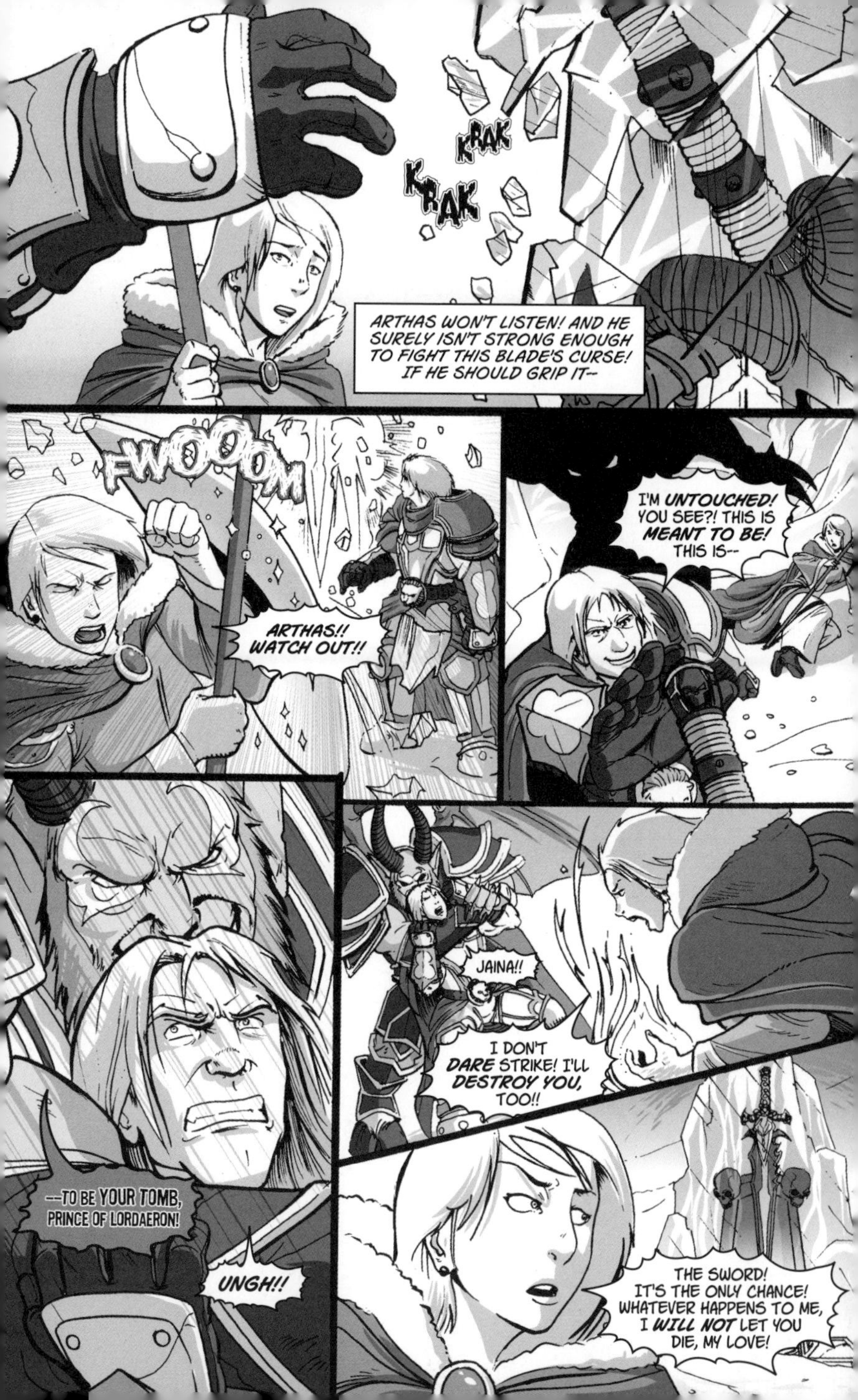
KRAK
KRAK
ARTHAS WON'T LISTEN! AND HE SURELY ISN'T STRONG ENOUGH TO FIGHT THIS BLADE'S CURSE! IF HE SHOULD GRIP IT--
FWOOOOM
ARTHAS!! WATCH OUT!!
I'M *UNTOUCHED!* YOU SEE?! THIS IS *MEANT TO BE!* THIS IS--
--TO BE YOUR TOMB, PRINCE OF LORDAERON!
UNGH!!
JAINA!!
I DON'T *DARE* STRIKE! I'LL *DESTROY YOU,* TOO!!
THE SWORD! IT'S THE ONLY CHANCE! WHATEVER HAPPENS TO ME, I *WILL NOT* LET YOU DIE, MY LOVE!

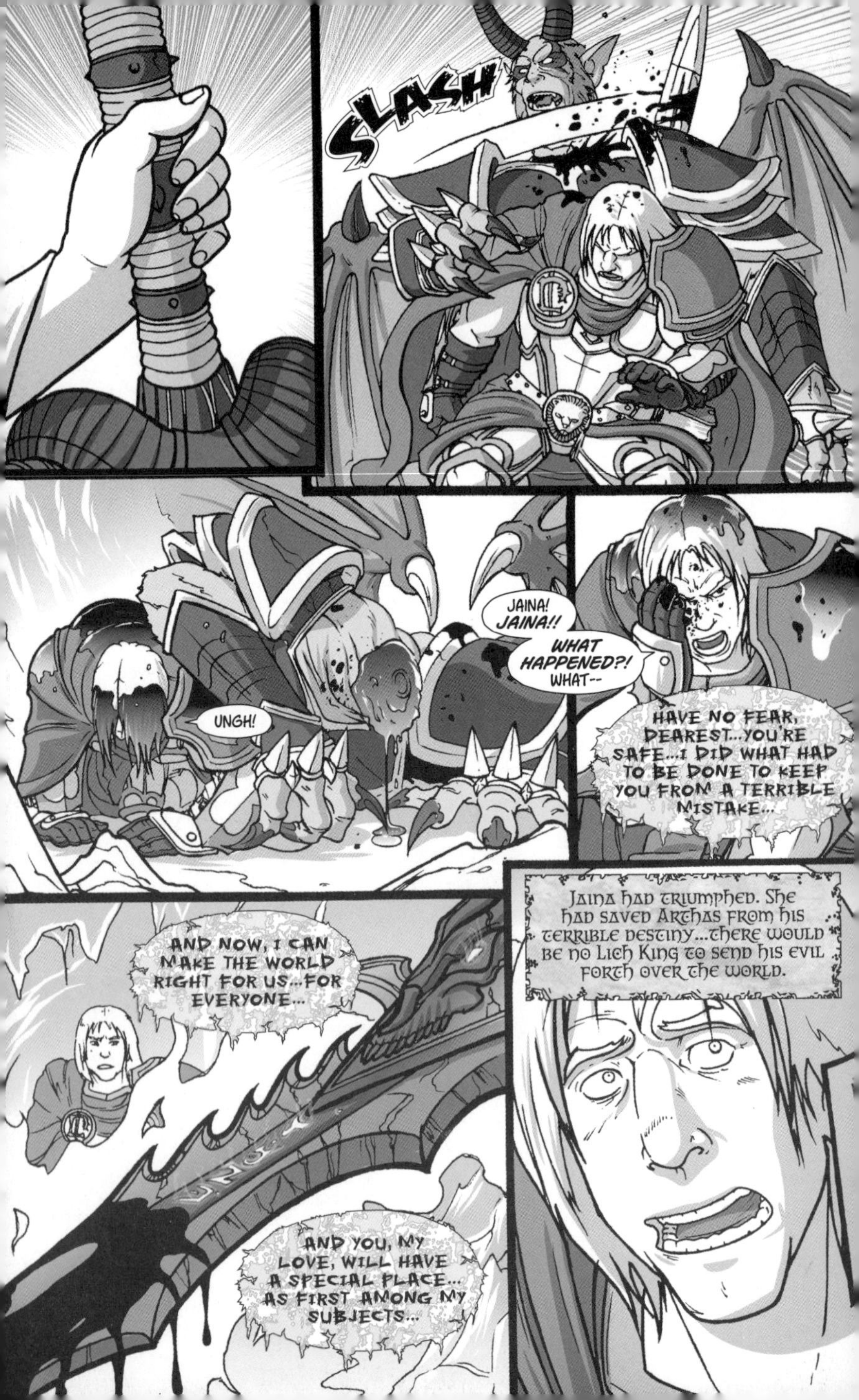
SLASH
UNGH!
JAINA! JAINA!! WHAT HAPPENED?! WHAT--
HAVE NO FEAR, DEAREST...YOU'RE SAFE...I DID WHAT HAD TO BE DONE TO KEEP YOU FROM A TERRIBLE MISTAKE...
AND NOW, I CAN MAKE THE WORLD RIGHT FOR US...FOR EVERYONE...
AND YOU, MY LOVE, WILL HAVE A SPECIAL PLACE... AS FIRST AMONG MY SUBJECTS...
Jaina had triumphed. She had saved Arthas from his terrible destiny...there would be no Lich King to send his evil forth over the world.

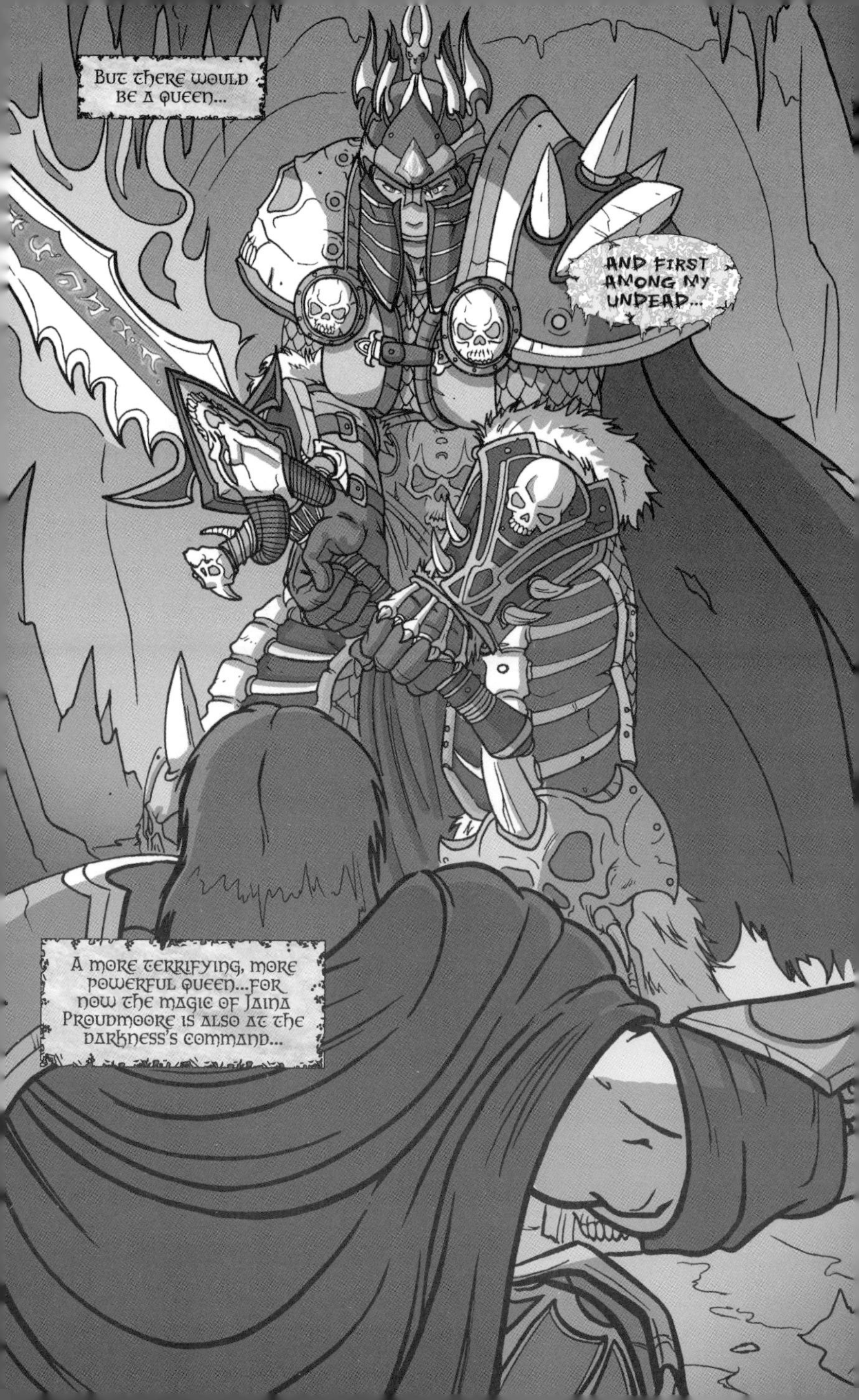
BUT THERE WOULD BE A QUEEN...
AND FIRST AMONG MY UNDEAD...
A MORE TERRIFYING, MORE POWERFUL QUEEN...FOR NOW THE MAGIC OF JAINA PROUDMOORE IS ALSO AT THE DARKNESS'S COMMAND...

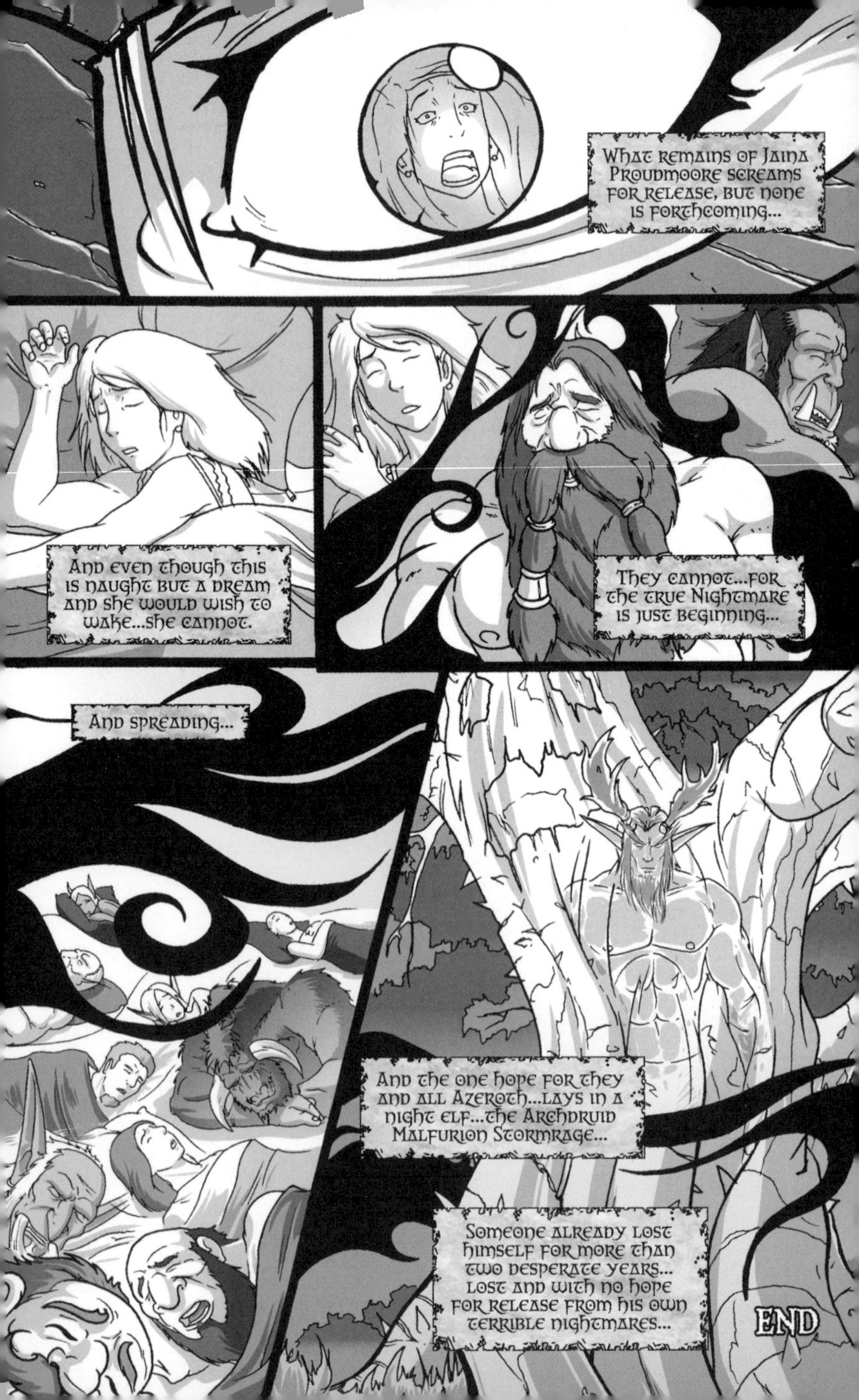
What remains of Jaina Proudmoore screams for release, but none is forthcoming...
And even though this is naught but a dream and she would wish to wake...she cannot.
They cannot...for the true Nightmare is just beginning...
And spreading...
And the one hope for they and all Azeroth...lays in a night elf...the Archdruid Malfurion Stormrage...
Someone already lost himself for more than two desperate years... lost and with no hope for release from his own terrible nightmares...
END

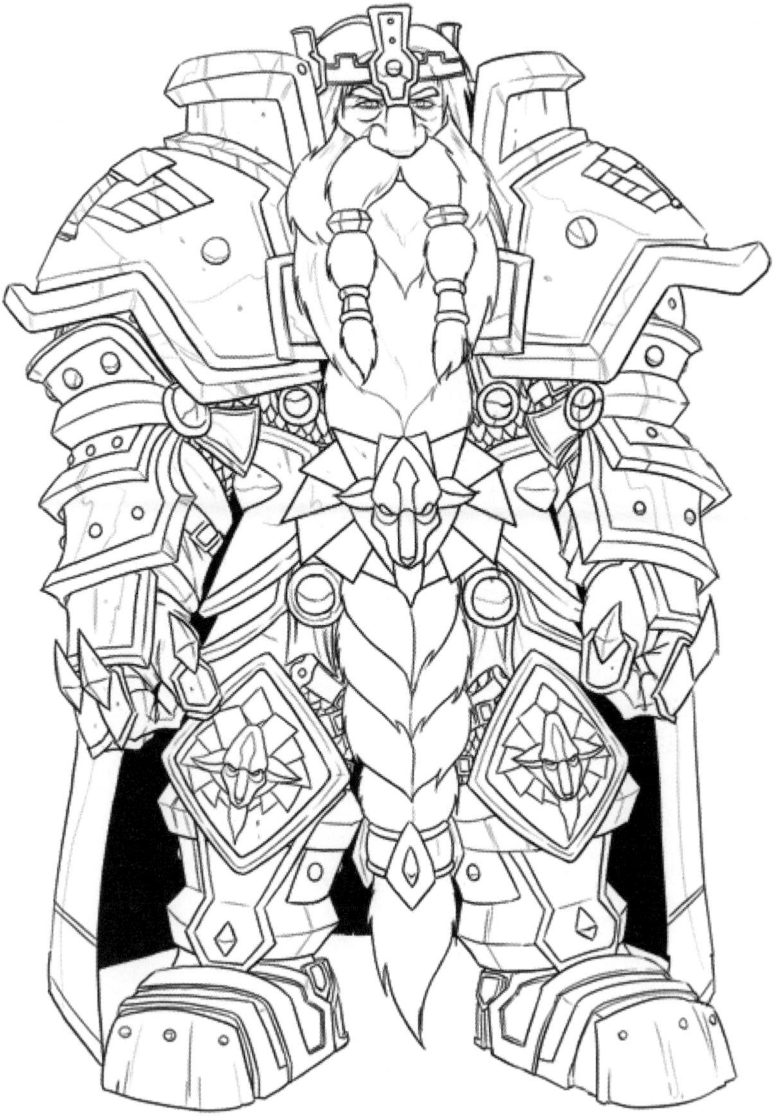

ABOUT THE WRITERS

CHRISTIE GOLDEN

New York Times best-selling author Christie Golden has written over thirty novels and several short stories in the fields of science fiction, fantasy and horror. She has written over a dozen Star Trek novels, several original novels, the *StarCraft: The Dark Templar Saga*, and several Warcraft novels, including *Lord of the Clans, Rise of the Horde,* as well as the New York Times best-seller, *Arthas: Rise of the Lich King.* Christie is currently hard at work writing on a yet-to-be-titled Warcraft novel. Christie has also written two short manga stories, "I Got What Yule Need" and "A Warrior Made," for *Warcraft: Legends* Volumes 3, 4, and 5.

GRACE RANDOLPH

Grace Randolph is a comedic actor and writer born and raised in New York City. Her previous writing credits include *Justice League Unlimited #41* for DC Comics and *Nemesis: Who Me?* for TOKYOPOP's Pilot Program. She also has an upcoming manga adaptation of Meg Cabot's *Jinx,* as well as "Newsworthy" and "Last Call," short stories in *StarCraft: Frontline* Volumes 2 and 3. Outside of comics, Grace is the host/writer/producer of the webshow *RevYOU.* Grace also studies at the Upright Citizens Brigade Theatre where she has written, performed and produced the shows "Situation: Awkward" and "Igor On Strike."

LOUISE SIMONSON

Louise Simonson has written and edited comic books for many years, including those in the superhero, science fiction, horror, and fantasy genres. She wrote the award-winning *Power Pack* series, best-selling *X-Men*-related titles, *Web of Spider-Man* for Marvel Comics and *Superman: Man of Steel* and *Steel* for DC Comics. She has also written twenty books for children and adults, many about comic book characters. "First Guardian" is her first manga story.

EVELYN FREDERICKSEN

Blizzard historian Evelyn Fredericksen spends her time writing and talking about the stories from Diablo, StarCraft, and Warcraft games and publications. This is her third foray into Blizzard fiction. Her previous two were short stories also set in the Warcraft universe: "Road to Damnation," the story of Kel'Thuzad's journey to Northrend, and "Glory," a retelling of the events at the Wrath Gate.

RICHARD A. KNAAK

Richard A. Knaak is the New York Times bestselling fantasy author of 40 novels and over a dozen short stories, including *The Legend of Huma & The Minotaur Wars* for Dragonlance and the *War of the Ancients* trilogy for Warcraft. In addition to *Warcraft: The Sunwell Trilogy,* he is the author of its forthcoming sequel trilogy, *Warcraft: Dragons of Outland,* as well a four-part short story featured in *Warcraft: Legends* Volumes 1-4, as well as the short story entitled "Nightmares" featured in *Warcraft: Legends* Volume 5. His latest Warcraft novel, *Night of the Dragon,* is a sequel to the best-selling *Day of the Dragon.* He also recently released *The Fire Rose,* the second in his *Ogre Titans* saga for Dragonlance.

ABOUT THE ARTISTS

IN-BAE KIM

In-Bae made his Korean manga debut in 1998 with *Tong-hwa-joong* (On the Phone). He followed that with several webzine short manga including "Film Ggengin Nar" (The Day I Blacked Out Drinking) and "Call Me." His serialized manga, "Bbuggoogi" (Cuckoo Bird), has been featured in several newspapers. In-Bae was also the artist for the short manga stories "Family Values" and "A Warrior Made" featured in *Warcraft: Legends* Volumes 2, 4, and 5.

ERICA AWANO

Born in São Paulo, Brazil, Erica grew up reading manga due to her Japanese hertitage. She attended the University of São Paulo, where she graduated with a degree in language and literature. Soon after she turned her focus on her passion for comics and in 2001 drew several prize-winning series. In 2007, she was one of the finalists for a MOFA, a prize awarded by the Ministry of External Relations of Japan for manga artists that are active outside Japan. *Warrior: United* is her debut as the main penciller on a foreign publication.

SEUNG-HUI KYE

After publishing thirteen manwha and illustrating two light novels in South Korea, Seung-hui made her Japanese manga debut in 2008 with the one-shot story "Kuroi Ude" in *MiChao!* magazine, published by Kodansha. She made her English-language debut with the short manga story "Last Call" in *StarCraft: Frontline* Volume 3, which led to her drawing the art for "First Guardian" in *Warcraft: Legends* Volume 5.

RYO KAWAKAMI

Born in Miyako Island, Japan, Ryo lived in Okinawa Island until 1990, after which he and his family moved to the United States. Ryo currently resides in Greenville, North Carolina, where he studied fine art for two years at Coastal Community College. Ryo was runner-up artist in *Rising Stars of Manga* Volume 6 for the short story "Little Miss Witch Hater." Ryo was the artist for "Blood Runs Thicker" and "A Cleansing Fire," two short manga stories featured in *Warcraft: Legends* Volumes 4 and 5.

ROB TEN PAS

Born and raised in Wisconsin (where he currently resides), Rob studied art at the Minneapolis College of Art and Design. His previous works include the short story "Bomango" in *Rising Stars of Manga 6*, as well as the business manga *The Adventures of Johnny Bunko: The Last Career Guide You'll Ever Need* by author Daniel H. Pink. When not indulging in sketching and recreational comics, he works as a sign crafter and painter. Oh, and he's also an undercover narcotics agent, but that's a story for another bio...